State Assessment Policy and Practice for English Language Learners: A National Perspective

State Assessment Policy and Practice
for English Language Learners:
A National Perspective

Edited by

Charlene Rivera
Eric Collum

The George Washington University
Center for Equity and Excellence in Education

LAWRENCE ERLBAUM ASSOCIATES, PUBLISHERS
2006   Mahwah, New Jersey   London

List of Tables

STUDY 3

List of Figures

STUDY 2

STUDY 3

Preface

For some time, educators have recognized the importance of including the growing population of English language learners (ELLs) in state assessment and accounting for the progress of these students. With the recent reauthorizations of the Elementary and Secondary Education Act (ESEA), the No Child Left Behind Act (NCLB) in particular, accounting for the academic progress of ELLs through large-scale assessment has been set as a national priority. Although the recent focus on ELLs affects educators at all levels, NCLB has placed particular emphasis on the role of states in ensuring that ELLs will be assessed appropriately and that ELL achievement data will be reported in appropriate ways. Unfortunately, little information is available regarding states' strategies for including and accounting for the academic achievement of this student group. Furthermore, the limited data and research available are scattered across the internet and throughout various reports and professional journals, offering policymakers, educators, and researchers a frustratingly limited and fragmented perspective on states' policies and practices regarding their strategies for addressing the assessment needs of ELLs.

The three studies in this volume were conducted to address this gap in our understanding and to contribute to the development of a more coherent and accessible knowledge base around ELL assessment. Because the primary strategy used by states to include ELLs in large-scale assessments is to provide accommodations, the research team determined that a national examination of states' policies regarding accommodations should be conducted to enable state policymakers to look across state boundaries and learn about strategies other state education agencies are using to address the needs of ELLs.

A second study was undertaken to examine in detail one particular accommodation. Test translation was selected for particular attention, not because it is the only form of accommodation appropriate to ELLs, but because it is used across a wide number of states. It is also mentioned specifically in NCLB as a means of assessing ELLs.

Appropriate testing of ELLs is important, but unless ELL achievement data are reported, testing alone remains ineffective as a lever for change. Therefore, a third study was conducted to examine states' score reporting practices.

The studies were originally conceived as stand-alone examinations of state assessment policies and practices for ELLs. Each study would help inform researchers and policymakers regarding an important aspect of inclusion or accountability. As we began looking at the studies side by side, we realized that together they would provide a perspective that, although by no means comprehensive, would offer the most complete examination of state assessment policy to date. The resulting volume is a sourcebook that can be used to inform the work of educators and policymakers as they attempt to develop strategies to ensure that English language learners have access to the same education as that provided to their more fully English-proficient peers.

The introduction to this volume provides a context for understanding the findings of the three studies. The difficulties facing educators attempting to include and account for ELLs are discussed, including factors that, historically, have motivated states to exclude ELLs from state assessment and score reports, and the challenges to score validity presented by the inclusion of ELLs in these tests. Inclusion and accountability requirements of ESEA are outlined, and studies examining state assessment policy related to ELLs are reviewed.

Study 1, "An Analysis of State Assessment Policies Regarding the Accommodation of English Language Learners," describes and analyzes states' policies regarding the use of accommodations for ELLs during the 2000–2001 school year. The study provides an overview of key issues related to accommodations for ELLs, including current research regarding the effectiveness of such accommodations. The body of the study considers the kinds of accommodations addressed in states' policies and the degree to which these policies offer guidance in the selection of accommodations appropriate for individual ELLs. First, the extent to which states' policies were successful in identifying the needs of ELLs eligible for accommodations is examined. Next, the authors focus on the types of accommodations supported by states' policies. This part of the study describes the various accommodations states' policies indicated were available to ELLs. For many states this included accommodations relevant only to students with disabilities. Accommodations are analyzed using a taxonomy developed specifically for this study to examine those accommodations relevant to ELLs.

After careful consideration of the accommodations cited in states' policies as available to ELLs, the authors examine the extent to which states' policies supported a decision-making process whereby accommodations were appropriately matched to the needs of individual ELLs. The study then examines policies regarding accommodations of two subgroups of states: those 19 states requiring high school exit exams and the 10 states with the highest populations of ELLs. Finally, a discussion of findings and recommendations are provided.

Whereas Study 1 focuses solely on states' assessment policies, Study 2, "Test Translation and State Assessment Policies for English Language Learners," bridges the policy–practice gap by examining in depth one accommodation—test translation—and analyzing in detail policies supporting the use of this accommodation and practices regarding its development and implementation at the state and district level. This study begins with an overview of the key issues affecting the development and implementation of translated tests. These issues involve psychometric concerns regarding the validity of translated tests as well as more practical considerations influencing states' decisions to translate tests and the processes states use to develop test translations.

Findings for Study 2 are presented in two parts. The first examines the state policy context governing the use of translated versions of state assessments. This part of the study provides data on states' allowing or prohibiting sight translation, the spontaneous oral rendering of test content in the student's native language, and written translation. With regard to sight translation, special attention is paid to the qualifications of sight translators cited in states' assessment policies. For written translation, the languages into which tests are translated for each state as well as policy regarding eligibility of ELLs to take translated tests are discussed. The second part of the findings consists of a collection of case studies of the 12 states allowing test translation in the 2000–2001 school year. Data presented in this part are based primarily on interviews conducted with state assessment officials. Information gathered covers seven major categories: background of testing program, test translation process, other forms of communication in the non-English language, use of technology, research and analysis of translated tests, test translation at the district level, and the future of test translation in the state. A discussion of the findings and recommendations conclude the study.

Study 3, "State Practices for Reporting Participation and Performance of English Language Learners in State Assessments," examines state practice regarding the participation and performance of ELLs in state assessments and legislative requirements under the Improving America's Schools Act and NCLB to include this student subgroup in standards-based reform and assessments. Data for the study were drawn from the 1999–2000 school year because, during the timeframe of the study, a majority of states were not prepared to provide reports disaggregating data for ELLs for the 2000–2001 school year. The study has two primary goals: (a) to develop an understanding of the level of participation of ELLs in state assessment systems, and (b) to establish baseline reporting practices for ELLs on statewide assessments across the United States.

The authors examine state score reports from a number of perspectives. A key focus is the extent to which comprehensive reports of participation and performance data for ELLs were made publicly available. The authors also examine the categories used to report ELL assessment data, such as format of test taken (norm- or criterion-referenced), type of test (e.g., accommodated tests, alternate assessments), and content area tested. Reporting practices are also examined from the perspective of population. Data for the 10 states with the highest ELL populations are compared to data for the 10 states with the lowest ELL populations. Another major focus of the study is the examination of the best practices for presenting useful and comprehensive data on ELLs.

Building on recommendations offered at the end of each study, the conclusion to the volume encourages educators and policymakers to view the identification and inclusion of ELLs, as well as the reporting of ELL assessment data, as a cohesive and self-reinforcing process. Only by tracking ELL data systematically can we hope to bridge the achievement gap that separates ELLs from other student groups.

ACKNOWLEDGMENTS

It is our pleasure to acknowledge those who contributed their time and effort to this project. Without their support, from inception to completion, this volume would not have been possible. In particular we are grateful to the Office of English Language Acquisition (OELA) for recognizing the need to fund this research. Kathleen Leos, OELA Associate Deputy Secretary, provided support and feedback on the project, and OELA program officers Dr.

Socorro Lara and Tim D'Emilio provided unflagging encouragement throughout the project.

Those involved in the early stages of the project deserve recognition and thanks for ensuring the quality and accuracy of the data used in the studies. Assessment directors and Title III directors for the 50 states and the District of Columbia graciously supplied the state assessment policy documents and ensured the accuracy of our data by clarifying questions and verifying coding of the data. Without their assistance, Studies 1 and 2 simply would not have been possible. Members of a panel convened by The George Washington University Center for Equity and Excellence in Education (CEEE) generously lent their time and considerable expertise to review the analytic framework used to organize data from the policies and provide suggestions for improvement. Panel members included Tim Boals, Wisconsin Department of Public Instruction; Pasquale DeVito, President, Assessment and Evaluation Concepts; Richard Duran, University of California, Santa Barbara; William Shaefer, University of Maryland; and Carolyn Vincent, RMC Research Corporation. Once the analytic framework was finalized, Lloyd Cundiff customized a database to facilitate storage and retrieval of data used in the study. Laura Golden, Rita Maximilian, and Katherine Calvert worked for long hours with unerring consistency to code the data. Rita deserves special recognition for her commitment to the project and for working with the writers to clarify the nuances of states' policies. Diane Staehr served as an intern on the project.

We also are grateful for the work of colleagues contributing to the writing and editing of Study 1. Kristina Anstrom, Lisa Bushey, and Janet Voight-Miró made significant contributions to the review of literature. Lynne Sacks contributed to early drafts of the study findings. The project benefited from the input of Charles Stansfield and Melissa Bowles of Second Language Testing, Inc., whose insight into sight translation enriched our understanding of the use of native language accommodations.

For their contributions to Study 2, we would like to acknowledge all of the state assessment directors, Title III directors, testing contractors, and other state education agency officials who took time out of their demanding schedules to be interviewed for the study. Without their insights into the intersection of state policy and daily practice in terms of test translation and adaptation, Study 2 would not have been possible.

Study 3 benefited from review by CEEE staff, most notably from the careful eye of Lisa Bushey, who provided substantive editing and coordinated the efforts of CEEE staff in producing the final manuscript.

education and coauthored "Brokering External Policies to Raise Student Achievement: The Case of Plainfield, New Jersey School District," a study of the implementation of comprehensive school reform in New Jersey. Dr. Collum is currently managing the collection and analysis of data for the NCES study of the inclusion and accommodation of ELLs in the NAEP Trial Urban District Assessment program.

Kristin K. Liu is a Research Fellow at the National Center on Educational Outcomes. She has a variety of experiences working on state and federally funded projects relating to large-scale assessment and standards-based instruction for ELLs and ELLs with disabilities. She has over 7 years of experience teaching ESL at the secondary, postsecondary, and adult levels in the United States. She has written and presented extensively on the assessment of ELLs and ELLs with disabilities.

Charlene Rivera is a Research Professor at The George Washington University's Department of Teacher Preparation and Special Education and Executive Director of The George Washington University Center for Equity and Excellence in Education (CEEE). For the CEEE, she oversees the work of a number of state and national projects. Dr. Rivera's research has focused on the education and assessment of ELLs. Among her publications are several articles and reports on state assessment policies for ELLs including a national study of state policies guiding the inclusion and accommodation of ELLs in state assessment programs during the 1998–1999 school year. Currently, she is leading a study for the NCES examining the relationship between (a) practices for including and accommodating ELLs participating in the National Assessment of Educational Progress (NAEP) in urban districts and (b) policies guiding the participation of ELLs in NAEP as well as in state and district assessments.

Lynn Shafer Willner worked as a Senior Research Consultant and assisted Charlene Rivera and Eric Collum with the research design and analysis for this volume. As part of that work, she has presented at national education conferences on the issue of providing accommodations to ELLs during large-scale tests. Having completed her doctorate in Education at George Mason University, Dr. Shafer Willner now works as a Senior Research Scientist at The George Washington University Center for Equity and Excellence in Education. She is a former ESOL teacher at Bailey's Elementary School for the Arts and Sciences in the Fairfax County (Virginia) Public Schools, selected by the parents and her colleagues at Bailey's for the Agnes Meyer/Washington Post Teacher of the Year Award in Fall 1996.

Jose Ku Sia, Jr. During his tenure at The George Washington Center for Equity and Excellence in Education, Mr. Sia was the information technology manager, a quantitative analyst, and the internal graphic designer and Web site maintenance provider. He holds a Bachelor of Science degree from the Massachusetts Institute of Technology and a Master's of Science in Systems Engineering from The George Washington University. He currently resides in Chicago, Illinois, where he is a candidate for a Master's of Industrial Design degree at the Illinois Institute of Technology.

Charles W. Stansfield is President of Second Language Testing, Inc. His company translates and adapts standardized tests into other languages. It also makes translation exams for federal agencies and the Written Examination section of the Federal Court Interpreter Certification Exam. Dr. Stansfield served as Director of the ERIC Clearinghouse for Languages and Linguistics and the Division of Foreign Language Education and Testing at the Center for Applied Linguistics in Washington, DC. Prior to that, he was director of TOEFL research, the Test of Spoken English, and the Test of Written English at Educational Testing Service. He was also a professor of Spanish and applied linguistics at the University of Colorado. He has edited or authored a dozen books and 60 articles on language testing, and was the founding president of the International Language Testing Association.

Martha L. Thurlow is Director of the National Center on Educational Outcomes. In this position, she addresses the implications of contemporary U.S. policy and practice for students with disabilities and ELLs, including national and statewide assessment policies and practices, standards-setting efforts, and graduation requirements. Dr. Thurlow has conducted research for the past 35 years in a variety of areas, including assessment and decision making, learning disabilities, early childhood education, dropout prevention, effective classroom instruction, and integration of students with disabilities in general education settings. During the past decade, Dr. Thurlow's research has focused on participation of students with special needs in large-scale assessments. Her work has been widely published and has covered a range of topics, including participation decision making, accommodations, computer-based testing, graduation exams, and alternate assessments.

Introduction

Including and Accounting for English Language Learners in State Assessment Systems

Charlene Rivera and Eric Collum

Over the past 10 years, accounting for the academic achievement of English language learners (ELLs) through standards-based state assessment has become a major national priority. Educators and policymakers have come to acknowledge that ELLs must be enabled to participate meaningfully in statewide assessments and that their performance on these tests must be made publicly available so that their academic progress can be compared to that of other student groups. Including ELLs in state assessments and holding states, districts, and schools accountable for the academic progress of these students, it is believed, will ensure that the needs of these students will be made evident and that educators can respond more appropriately to the instructional needs of this growing population of students.

Despite widespread recognition of the importance of including and accounting for all students in state assessment systems, ELLs have continued to be systematically excluded from state tests until very recently (Lachat, 1999b, pp. 57–60; Rivera, Stansfield, Scialdone, & Sharkey, 2000, p. x). Two major concerns have motivated the exclusion of ELLs from state assessment. First, some educators feared that, because of linguistic and cultural barriers, state assessment would not provide an accurate measure of ELLs' academic knowledge. Second, because ELLs have generally not been provided with the same curricula as that offered to their more English-proficient peers, it has often been observed that testing ELLs on the same standards would be inappropriate.

These two factors have led to a third concern regarding accountability—that ELLs will perform less well on state assessment than will their native English-speaking peers and that, consequently, these students' participation in assessment will lower overall school, district, and state scores. The concern over accountability has affected ELLs by providing a motivation for excluding these students from state tests or for excluding the scores of these students from state and district assessment reports.

With regard to the first concern, as ELLs' performance on large-scale tests can be affected by their level of English language proficiency and knowledge of U.S. culture, many educators have questioned the wisdom of including ELLs in state assessment (AERA, APA, & NCME, 1999, p. 91; Lachat, 1999b, pp. 51–56). In a discussion of "traditional testing policies and practices," Lachat (1999b) argued that "testing programs ... have been particularly limiting for English language learners because tests written in English cannot adequately assess ... the content knowledge of these students" (p. 55). Hence, one of the most obvious limitations of large-scale testing involves ELLs' unfamiliarity with English vocabulary and American schooling culture.

A second concern among educators has been that ELLs might not have knowledge of test topics because they have not participated in the same curriculum as their more English-proficient peers. Some researchers have claimed that ELLs' schooling during their initial years in the United States often focuses more on the development of surface language proficiency than on the integration of English language development with deeper, cognitive academic development (Butler, 1999; Cummins, 2000; O'Malley & Pierce, 1996).

A study by Berman and his colleagues (1992) of ELLs in eight schools highlights the extent to which these students have been denied full access to the standard curricula. In this study, it was found that ELLs received different curricula than did their monolingual peers. Also, ELLs were required to demonstrate proficiency in English before gaining access to curricula being taught in grade-level mathematics and science courses. Moreover, ELLs often were excluded from core courses taught in English or placed into remedial or compensatory classes in which the curricula were different from that offered to monolingual English-speaking students and where instruction took place at a slower pace. The recent work of Rumberger and Gandara (2004) reinforces Berman's findings. In a report prepared for the lawsuit *Williams v. State of California,* the authors documented a number of factors that inhibit ELLs' ability to succeed academically, including lack of access to appropriate curricula and instructional materials.

In short, it is generally acknowledged that ELLs have had "less access [than their native English-speaking peers] to a challenging curriculum that would prepare them for success on today's standards" (Herman & Abedi,

2004, p. 2). Without comparable instruction, it is "unlikely that [ELLs] will achieve at high levels or be fairly assessed by programs designed to measure high level learning" (Lachat 1999a, p. 18).

These two factors affect the willingness of states to be held accountable for ELLs' academic performance for the simple reason that the participation of these students in state assessment might lower overall test scores. Two studies in particular raised awareness of the political dimension of ELL participation in state assessment: Cannell's (1988) study, *Nationally Normed Elementary Achievement Testing in America's Public Schools: How All Fifty States Are Above Average,* and Zlatos's (1994a) article "Don't Test, Don't Tell." Both studies showed that states and school districts commonly excluded ELLs from assessments and that this exclusion was most likely linked to the fear that these students' test scores would lower overall state and district scores. The mandates of the Improving America's Schools Act (IASA) and, more recently, No Child Left Behind (NCLB) to include all students in state assessment have increased the stakes for states and intensified these concerns.

Cannell's (1988) controversial study documented above average performance of elementary students across all states. According to Cannell's findings, "all states showed steady achievement gains, regardless of school quality, if they used a commercial test without rotating test questions in some manner." The outcome of this study became known as "the Lake Wobegon effect," based on Garrison Keillor's mythical town, Lake Wobegon, where "all the children are above average." Gary Phillips (1990), acting Commissioner of the National Center for Education Statistics (NCES) at the time, identified five potential reasons for the above average phenomenon. Of relevance in this discussion is the common practice of excluding from testing "difficult" to assess subgroups, among these ELLs. He noted that, "While local educators were preaching rigorous standards for accountability, they were practicing procedures that led to positive self evaluations" (pp. 3, 14).

Zlatos (1994a) studied test inclusion practices in 14 big-city school districts across the country and found large gaps in how many students were tested. His findings indicated that the proportion of students tested in the districts studied ranged from 93% in Memphis to 66% in Boston. Students assigned to special education and bilingual and English as a second language (ESL) programs often were among the student subpopulations not accounted for in test data or excluded from district tests. These findings led Zlatos to conclude that exclusion of any student subgroup created a twofold accountability problem: First, schools might have lower expectations for exempted students and therefore reduce the likelihood that they will be taught or learn as much as students not exempted from testing. Second, the performance of exempted students cannot be tracked (Zlatos, 1995b). As Zlatos noted, a lack of inclusion of all students in district assessments creates an accountability void at all levels: national, district, and school.

State officials perceive the stakes of inclusion to be high. However, the discomfort at including ELLs can be made more acute for educators, as well as for students, when these tests are used for high-stakes purposes—that is, when test scores are used to determine such key issues as high school graduation, grade promotion, and placement.

The consequences of interpreting high-stakes test scores are so great that educators are particularly concerned that these scores accurately reflect ELLs' academic achievement. For instance, in 2000 the American Educational Research Association (AERA) issued a statement listing 12 conditions "essential to sound implementation of high-stakes educational testing programs" (AERA, 2000). Among the cautions offered by the policy statement is that ELLs' lack of proficiency in English could compromise test validity.

Despite the impact high-stakes tests have on students and educators, little is known regarding the extent to which ELLs have been included equitably in these tests. In a study of states' policies for including ELLs in high-stakes high school graduation tests, Rivera and Vincent (1997) examined state assessment policies for ELLs during the 1993–1994 school year. Of the 51 states—the District of Columbia was counted as a state—included in the study, 17 required students to pass one or more content-area tests to receive a standard high school diploma. The researchers found that states approached the inclusion of ELLs in high-school graduation tests in a number of ways: States (a) deferred students from the first administration of the test, (b) allowed test accommodations (e.g., provided extra time), (c) provided the test in students' native languages, and (d) used alternate assessment procedures. The researchers noted that accommodations alone would not provide ELLs with equitable access to the test if they did not receive instruction pertinent to the content assessed. In states where high school graduation tests were in place, the researchers indicated that the combination of high-quality instruction and technically sound assessment practices could facilitate equitable assessment.

Spicuzza, Liu, Swierzbin, Bielinski, and Thurlow (2000) conducted a study of ELL participation in a high-stakes state test, the Basic Standards Test (BST). Passage of the BST is required to fulfill high school graduation standards in the state of Minnesota; students can retake the BST until they pass. The researchers documented student performance in Grades 8 through 12, examining how ELLs performed over time on the reading and mathematics components of the BST. Among students who failed the BST in 1997 and then subsequently passed in 1998, the pass rate varied widely in both reading and mathematics between ELLs and English-only speakers (reading: ELLs, 17%; English-only, 52%; mathematics: ELLs, 20%; English-only, 35%). Although the findings were based on only 2 years of test data, the researchers identified instruction in the content area being assessed as a probable determinant factor in passing the BST.

More recently, the Center for Education Policy (CEP) documented the increased use by states of high school exit exams. CEP found that "20 states had mandatory exit exams in 2004" and that an additional five states "plan to phase in these tests by 2009" (CEP, 2004, p. 5). The implications of this trend can have a significant impact on ELLs, as "there continue to be serious concerns about gaps [up to 40%] in pass rates by race and ethnicity, income, home language, and disability status" (p. 22). Although CEP did not examine ELL performance in detail, available data for states using exit exams show ELL pass rates consistently below overall pass rates for the state (p. 38).

As this review suggests, level of English language proficiency and lack of exposure to the same curriculum as that provided to native English speakers, as well as lack of familiarity with American culture, make ELLs' inclusion in state assessment problematic. Moreover, it is difficult to ensure that ELLs will be provided with tests that produce valid data on their achievement, a concern that is especially urgent in a high-stakes context. Nonetheless, to exclude these students from testing and state assessment reporting is to diminish our understanding, however limited, of a growing part of the U.S. student population. Inclusion and accountability for ELLs are two of the centerpieces of the Elementary and Secondary Education Act (ESEA), which currently requires virtually all ELLs to be included in state assessments and for the scores of these students to be a part of state assessment reports.

THE LEGISLATIVE DRIVE TO ACCOUNT FOR ELLS

The 1965 ESEA, which established federal requirements for the education of language minority students, did not require state education agencies (SEAs) to account for the academic performance of ELLs. However, since the 1994 and 2002 reauthorizations of ESEA (IASA and NCLB, respectively) states have been required to include ELLs in state assessment for purposes of accountability. The current initiative for the inclusion of all students in state assessments and the reporting of student performance data is based on two premises: First, only by measuring the performance of all students can achievement gaps be identified and addressed appropriately in instruction; second, only by including all students in state assessments is it possible to develop a complete picture of the academic progress of states' student populations.

The studies in this volume use data from the 1999–2000 and 2000–2001 school years, during which time states' policies and practices were governed by IASA. However, as NCLB has set new targets for SEAs, it is important to see states' policies and practices from the perspective of the requirements of both laws. This dual perspective is possible because NCLB represents less a shift in policy away from the goals of IASA than an intensification of these goals. Focusing on both laws allows us to understand the extent to which states were in compliance with IASA and to gauge their progress toward reaching inclusion targets set by NCLB. This focus is especially important given that schools not reaching benchmarks set by NCLB can be designated as schools "in need of improvement" and, subsequently, be categorized as schools "under corrective action."

Legislative requirements governing the assessment of ELLs are found primarily in two sections of the 1994 and 2002 reauthorizations of ESEA: that pertaining to the education of disadvantaged children—Title I—and that relating to the education of language minority children—Title VII (under IASA) and Title III (under NCLB). Most of the requirements for IASA and NCLB touching on the assessment of ELLs, and thus relevant to the three studies in this volume, can be found in Title I, Section 1111. Section 1111 of each law sets out requirements for state assessment and accountability plans. Failure to meet ESEA benchmarks can result in states' loss of Title I funds.

In this section we briefly review the legislative requirements that address ELLs' inclusion in state assessment systems for purposes of accountability. The requirements are examined from two perspectives. *Inclusion requirements*, or requirements designed to ensure that ELLs participate fully and appropriately in state assessments, cover the use of English language proficiency measures, as well as accommodations (including test translation) on state assessments and alternate assessments. *Accountability requirements,* address requirements regarding how ELLs' scores should be reported and to whom these scores should be made available.

Inclusion Requirements

IASA stipulated that states must "provide for … the inclusion of *limited English proficient students* who shall be assessed, to the extent practicable, in the language and form most likely to yield accurate and reliable information on what such students know and can do, to determine such students' mastery of skills in subjects other than English" (Sec. 1111 [b][3][F][iii]). NCLB supports the same schema, adding the clarification that ELLs should be eligible for other assessments only "until such students have achieved English language proficiency" (Sec. 1111 ([b][3][C][ix][III]).

In terms of frequency of testing, IASA required states to adopt "a set of high-quality, yearly student assessments ... in at least mathematics and reading or language arts." These assessments were to be administered "at some time" during grade spans 3 to 5, 6 to 9, and 10 to 12 (Sec. 1111[b][3][D][i–iii]). States were to begin testing students annually no more than 2 years from the year the legislation was enacted; that is, by school year 1996.

NCLB strengthens IASA requirements by putting in place stricter timelines and more specific requirements for demonstrating progress (Koenig & Bachman, 2004). The law specifies that the academic proficiency of all students, including ELLs, be assessed in reading or language arts and mathematics "not less than once" during grade spans 3 to 5, 6 to 9, and 10 to 12, and, by 2007–2008, in science "not less than once" during the same grade spans (Sec. 1111, [3][C][v][I–II]). By school year 2005–2006, states are to test students yearly in reading or language arts and mathematics in Grades 3 through 8.

Under NCLB, exemptions of ELLs from participating in state assessment are not permitted after the first year of a student's enrollment in a U.S. school. The law allows some leeway on the requirement of 100% participation, but is designed to prevent the systematic exemption of students from particular subgroups. Hence, under NCLB, it is required that "not less than 95 percent of each group of students ... enrolled in the school are required to take the [state] assessments" (Sec. 1111 [b][3][I][ii]).

Finally, although reference was made in IASA (7123[c][1]) to the measurement of English language proficiency, the 2002 law provides a greater focus on this component. NCLB requires that the English language proficiency of ELLs be measured annually: SEAs are to "provide for an annual assessment of English proficiency (measuring students' oral language, reading, and writing skills in English) of all students with limited English proficiency in the schools served by the State educational agency" (Sec. 1111 [b][7]).

Accountability Requirements

IASA "created an obligation and an opportunity for states, local educational agencies, and schools to disaggregate and analyze data resulting from assessments of their students' achievement in ways that would be useful and illuminating" (Jaeger & Tucker, 1998, p. 1). NCLB continues the emphasis on reporting, requiring SEAs to provide aggregated and disaggregated data as well as individual student reports.

Under IASA, states were required to report performance data for all students, including ELLs. In the language of the policy, states were to report on "how students are achieving the State student performance standards ... including data comparing children and youth of limited English proficiency with nonlimited English proficient children and youth with regard to school retention, academic achievement, and gains in English (and, where applicable, native language) proficiency" (Sec. 7123 [c][1]). States were required to disaggregate student performance data "within each State, local education agency, and school" by the following categories: gender, racial and ethnic group, English proficiency status, migrant status, students with disabilities (as compared to nondisabled students), and economically disadvantaged students (as compared to students not economically disadvantaged) (Sec. 1111 [b][3][H] and [I]).

Performance data were to be used to determine adequate yearly progress of students who had attended the same school for a full academic year. Furthermore, IASA stipulated that SEAs were to provide for individual student "interpretive and descriptive reports." These reports were to "include scores, or other information on the attainment of student performance standards" (Sec. 1111 [b][3][H]).

Currently, under NCLB, states must report student achievement in the areas of reading/language arts and mathematics for accountability purposes. SEAs are required to provide evidence that English language learners are making adequate yearly progress (AYP) in academic content by providing "statistically valid and reliable" data regarding student test scores (Sec. 1111 [b][2][C][ii]).[1] States must also demonstrate that these students are making improvements in English language proficiency (Sec. 3121 [a][3]).

Each state must provide this and other information to the public in a "report card" that includes information on student achievement disaggregated by the entire student population and by student subgroup, including ELLs (Sec. 1111 [h][1][C][i]). It is further stipulated that this information be "presented in an understandable and uniform format and, to the extent practicable, provided in a language that the parents can understand" (Sec. 1111 [h][1][B][ii]). In addition to providing data about student groups, states are also instructed to produce individual student reports to "allow parents,

---

[1]Federal requirements for AYP can be found in NCLB, Sec. 1111 (b)(2)(B–C).

teachers, and principals to understand and address the specific academic needs of students" (Sec. 1111 [B][3][C][ix][III]).

Overall, NCLB represents an intensification of the goals of IASA, instituting more specific requirements regarding the inclusion of ELLs in assessment and the reporting of ELL performance data in state accountability systems. With regard to participation, NCLB requires the inclusion of virtually all ELLs enrolled in a U.S. school for more than one school year. Furthermore, the 2002 law mandates the annual assessment of the English language proficiency of ELLs. Reporting requirements for NCLB are similar but more stringent. States must (a) report the percentage of each group of students not tested; (b) provide disaggregated state assessment data for ELLs; (c) include ELL performance data in states' calculations of AYP; (d) ensure that the results of state assessments administered in one school year are available to school districts before the beginning of the next school year; and (e) report assessment results in a manner that is clear and easy to understand and that can be used by school districts, schools, and teachers to improve the educational achievement of individual students.

THE CHALLENGE OF INCLUDING ELLS AND ACCOUNTING FOR ELLS' ACADEMIC PERFORMANCE

One of the mandates of ESEA is to gather and report meaningful information on the academic progress of all students. Currently, this information is collected via two kinds of large-scale assessments: the National Assessment of Educational Progress (NAEP) and state assessments. NAEP is administered to a sample of students from each state; results are used to "inform national and state policy makers about student performance, assisting them in evaluating the conditions and progress of the nation's education system" (Koenig & Bachman, 2004, p. 30).[2] By contrast, virtually every student is required to participate in state assessments; data from these tests are used to track the academic progress of students (and student subgroups) in each state. Whereas NAEP data are used to provide a national perspective on student achievement across several academic content areas, state assessment data are used for accountability purposes.

Although NAEP and state officials have responded to the need to include and account for ELLs, state assessments have been the primary tar-

---

[2]The National Research Council's *Keeping Score for All* (Koenig & Bachman, 2004) offers a thorough and highly accessible account of issues involved in the inclusion of ELLs in NAEP and other large-scale assessments.

get of ESEA and are a key mechanism for tracking student achievement. To include ELLs appropriately in state assessment systems, states face a major challenge: Tests must be valid—in other words, be administered to ELLs in such a way as to give these students appropriate access to test content (most commonly, through accommodations) so that test results will be comparable to those of native English-speaking students.

Validity is acknowledged as a central concern in the assessment of ELLs in the *Standards for Educational and Psychological Testing* (AERA et al., 1999). As defined by the *Standards*, *validity* refers to "the degree to which evidence and theory support the interpretations of test scores entailed in the uses of tests" (p. 9). Validity has important implications for the inclusion of ELLs in large-scale assessment.

The *Standards* recognize that knowledge and degree of English language development is a factor that has the potential of affecting anyone taking a test because "any test that employs language is, in part, a measure of … language skills." If, for example, a mathematics test with difficult vocabulary is given to a student while in the early stages of learning English, then such a test is likely to be a measure of the student's skills in English rather than a measure of his or her knowledge of mathematics. In short, variations in students' scores might not be a consequence of differences among students' knowledge of mathematics, but a reflection of differences in their knowledge of English. Such distortion is known as *construct-irrelevant variance*. When construct-irrelevant variance occurs, "test results may not reflect accurately the qualities and competencies intended to be measured" (AERA et al., 1999, p. 91; see also Abedi, 2004). Further variance can be introduced by the fact that "language differences are almost always associated with concomitant cultural differences that need to be taken into account when tests are used" (p. 91). When student performance data are affected by construct-irrelevant variance, scores cannot with confidence be compared across student groups.

States pursue two basic strategies to mitigate construct-irrelevant variance, or to overcome the linguistic barriers that inhibit ELLs' access to test content: offering testing accommodations and allowing alternate assessment.

In general, accommodations involve changes to a test or testing situation and are used widely for the assessment of students who, because of limited proficiency in English or physical or cognitive disabilities, are deemed unable to participate meaningfully in state assessments without adjustments to the language or administration of a test. Although accommodations are meant to address construct-irrelevant variance by allowing

ELLs greater access to test content, there is a risk that an accommodation may over- or undercorrect in a way that distorts a student's performance and undermines validity. In such cases the interpretation of scores from accommodated tests can be problematic.

Nevertheless, *accommodations* can be effective if they are designed and implemented in such a way as to address the unique needs of the students for whom they are provided without invalidating the test construct. In the case of ELLs, this means providing the test taker with assistance in overcoming the linguistic and sociocultural barriers that prevent them from accessing the content of the test. Without this support, ELLs' test scores will likely reflect their English language proficiency rather than their knowledge of the academic content being tested (see Study 1 in this volume).

In the broadest sense, *alternate assessments* provide ELLs the opportunity to take an assessment in place of the regular state assessment. To fulfill NCLB accountability requirements, alternate assessments for ELLs also must measure the same constructs measured by regular state assessment and yield scores comparable to those produced by regular state assessment. Unfortunately, the nature of alternate assessment makes this requirement problematic. Alternate assessment for ELLs comprises a variety of measures including statewide portfolios and matrices as well as classroom measures. In some cases, these measures are aligned to standards different from those to which regular state assessments are aligned; in most cases, the lack of uniformity of these measures inhibits comparisons between alternate assessment scores and scores from regular state assessment. Therefore, current alternate assessments for ELLs may raise concerns for validity and score comparability.

REVIEW OF STATE ASSESSMENT POLICY STUDIES

State officials' struggles to include ELLs meaningfully in large-scale assessment and to account for the academic progress of these students are reflected in state assessment policies. These policies can be a key mechanism for promoting compliance with legislation and offering guidance to districts as educators in each state attempt to include and account for ELLs. A limited number of studies have examined how these policies respond to the needs of ELLs. On the whole, the literature suggests that policies and practices vary across states, as does the extent to which states address the needs of ELLs. This variability contributes to the difficulty of collecting comprehensive data regarding the inclusion of ELLs in state assessment.

In a study designed to examine the extent to which standards-based reforms for ELLs were being implemented by states following the 1994 enactment of IASA, Lara and August (1996) surveyed SEAs. Data were collected from states on a variety of key components of standards reform, including, for example, the development of state content and performance standards and state assessments. Findings from the study indicated that states were struggling to align content and performance standards. Indeed, most states had not specifically addressed how ELLs were to be incorporated into state assessments. The majority of states providing state assessment performance data for the study (35 of 43) reported exempting ELLs from district and state tests.

Rivera, Vincent, Hafner, and LaCelle-Peterson (1997) examined the extent to which ELLs participated in state assessment during the 1993–1994 school year. The research team developed a survey that incorporated data from the 1994 *CCSSO Annual Survey of State Student Assessment Programs*, which summarizes the activities of state assessment programs and provides information on trends. The researchers incorporated into the study aspects of the Council of Chief State School Officers (CCSSO) survey data for 1993–1994 relevant to the participation of ELLs in state assessment. The intent was to expand the data to include information specific to ELLs' participation in state assessment. The researchers also collected and reviewed state assessment policy documents to examine states' policies for ELLs. Collected responses provided data on state practice and policy information regarding ELLs' participation on key components of state assessment programs. The authors found that survey responses were difficult to interpret, particularly when more than one respondent (i.e., state assessment directors and bilingual and ESL directors) offered conflicting or incomplete data related to ELL inclusion and accountability. The findings from the study indicated that 45 states included some or all ELLs in at least one state assessment; however, the actual number of ELLs taking at least one state assessment was reported by only 15 states (Rivera et al., 1997).

In a study of school year 1998–1999 data, Rivera et al. (2000) examined state assessment policies for ELLs. The researchers requested state policy documents from the 50 states and the District of Columbia. The states provided hundreds of written state assessment policies, relevant letters, and other forms of memoranda. For each state, data were placed into a researcher-developed framework from which individual state reports were produced. State assessment and bilingual and ESL directors verified completed state reports. Analysis of the data indicated that 48 states had policies regarding the inclusion of ELLs in statewide assessment. Forty-six states allowed ELLs to be exempted and 2 prohibited exemptions. Of the 46 states allowing exemptions, 11 states specified a 2-year exemption time limit; 21 states allowed a 3-year exemption time limit; 2 states allowed more than a 3-year exemption time limit; and 12 states did not specify time limits. Forty-five states provided criteria for determining which ELLs were to be included in or exempted from state assessment; 39 states designated individuals or teams to make these determinations.

Goertz and Duffy (2001) surveyed the 50 states for a study of state assessment and accountability systems for the 1999–2000 school year. The common elements of accountability systems studied included assessments, standards, performance reporting, and consequences for performance. Findings from the study demonstrated that the variations in accountability systems across states reflect differences in demographics, political culture, educational governance structures and policies, and educational performance. States' capacities to develop inclusive accountability systems varied widely. Regarding ELLs, the researchers found that a large number of states continued to exempt these students from state tests, a practice in conflict with the requirements of the 1994 ESEA.

Because the practice of exempting ELLs from testing or excluding achievement data for these students has been fairly commonplace in recent decades, the majority of states must now expedite the development or improvement of inclusive accountability systems. These systems must be capable of tracking the extent to which ELLs are achieving to state standards at rates proportionate to their monolingual peers (Goertz & Duffy, 2001). By studying state assessment policies and practices we can promote a better understanding of the inclusion strategies adopted by states and inform policymakers and educators at the national and state levels.

CONCLUSION

Accounting for the academic progress of ELLs continues to be a major challenge to educators at all levels: state, district, and school. ELLs have been regularly excluded from state tests and ELLs' test scores have been excluded from state assessment reports because of fears that inclusion of these students will lower overall test scores for states and districts. These fears have not been unfounded: ELLs' lack of access to the curriculum to which state tests are aligned put them at a disadvantage when participating in state assessment. Language and cultural barriers also can limit the ability of ELLs to demonstrate their knowledge of academic subject areas on state assessments. The use of tests for high-stakes purposes amplifies these concerns for educators, students, and parents.

Nonetheless, accounting for the academic performance of these students is crucial. Achievement gaps can be identified and addressed in instruction and policy only by measuring the performance of all students. If ELLs are to benefit from the state assessment systems they must be included meaningfully in state tests. To this end, SEAs have begun to embrace the systematic use of accommodations to allow ELLs access to test content and mitigate the validity concerns that have, in the past, made state and NAEP officials hesitant to include ELLs in large-scale assessments.

States' policies are a key mechanism for promoting compliance with legislation and offering guidance to districts as educators in each state attempt to include ELLs appropriately in their state assessment system. Unfortunately, despite the centrality of states' policies to statewide and national inclusion efforts, there is no comprehensive description of states' policies or analysis of how the implementation of these policies might support or inhibit the inclusion of ELLs in state assessment and of ELLs' scores in state assessment reports. We know that states have developed a number of inclusion and accountability strategies, including the use of accommodated assessments (e.g., translated tests, use of dictionaries and glossaries) and alternate assessments. However, the limited data and research available regarding states' strategies for including ELLs in large-scale assessment is scattered across the Internet and throughout various reports and professional journals, offering a partial and fragmented perspective on states' policies and practices regarding the inclusion of ELLs in state assessment. A more integrated perspective of what has been learned is needed if we are to understand how policymakers and practitioners can improve policies and practices for including ELLs in state assessment and reporting on the progress of these students.

This volume presents three studies that each examine a crucial aspect of states' strategies to account for the academic performance of ELLs. Study 1, "An Analysis of State Assessment Policies Regarding the Accommodation of English Language Learners," describes and analyzes states' policies regarding the use of accommodations for ELLs during the 2000–2001 school year. Study 2, "Test Translation and State Assessment Policies for English Language Learners," builds on the data provided in Study 1, focusing on the development and use of a single accommodation—test translation. In addition to discussing states' policies pertaining to test translation, this study examines how test translations are developed and implemented in those 12 states that allowed test translation during the 2000–2001 school year. Study 3, "State Practices for Reporting Participation and Performance of English Language Learners in State Assessments," examines score reporting practices. Based on data from school year 1999–2000 (the latest data available from states during the time frame of the study) this study examines state assessment reports to address the kinds of data reported for ELLs taking state assessments.

REFERENCES

Abedi, J. (2004). The No Child Left Behind Act and English language learners: Assessment and accountability issues. *Educational Researcher, 33,* 4–14

American Educational Research Association. (2000). Position statement concerning high-stakes testing in pre-k–12 education. Washington, DC: Author. Retrieved September 29, 2004 from http://www.aera.net/about/policy/stakes.htm

American Educational Research Association, American Psychological Association, & National Council on Measurement in Education. (1999). *Standards for educational and psychological tests.* Washington, DC: American Psychological Association.

Berman, P., Chambers, J., Gandara, P., McLaughlin, B., Minicucci, C., Nelson, B., et al. (1992). *Meeting the challenge of language diversity: An evaluation of programs for pupils with limited proficiency in English* (5 vols.) Berkeley, CA: BW Associates.

Butler, F. (1999, February). *Issues in aligning standards, instruction, and assessment for LEP students.* Paper delivered at the American Association of School Administrators National Conference, New Orleans, LA.

Cannell, J. J. (1988). *Nationally normed elementary achievement testing in America's public schools: How all fifty states are above average.* Daniels, WV: Friends for Education.

Center for Education Policy. (2004). *State high school exit exams: A maturing reform.* Washington, DC: Author.

Cummins, J. (2000). *Language, power, and pedagogy: Bilingual children in the crossfire.* Tonawanda, NY: Multilingual Matters.

Goertz, G. E., & Duffy, C. M. (2001). *Assessment and accountability systems in the 50 states: 1999–2000.* Philadelphia: Consortium for Policy Research in Education.

Herman, J. L., & Abedi, J. (2004). *Issues in assessing English language learners' opportunity to learn mathematics* (CSE Rpt. No. 633) Los Angeles: Center for the Study of Evaluation.

Improving America's Schools Act (Public Law 103-383). (1994). Washington, DC: U.S. Government Printing Office.

Jaeger, R. M., & Tucker, C. G. (1998). *Analyzing, disaggregating, reporting, and interpreting students' achievement test results: A guide to practice for Title I and beyond.* Washington, DC: Council of Chief State School Officers.

Koenig, J. A., & Bachman, L. F. (Eds.). (2004). *Keeping score for all: The effects of inclusion and accommodation policies on large-scale educational assessments.* Washington, DC: National Research Council.

Lachat, M. A. (1999a). *Standards, equity, and cultural diversity.* Providence, RI: The Education Alliance, LAB at Brown University.

Lachat, M. A. (1999b). *What policymakers and school administrators need to know about assessment reform for English language learners.* Providence, RI: Brown University.

Lara, J., & August, D. (1996). *Systemic reform and limited English proficient students.* Washington, DC: Council of Chief State School Officers.

O' Malley, J. M., & Pierce, L. V. (1996). *Authentic assessment for English language learners: Practical approaches for teachers.* Reading, MA: Addison-Wesley.

No Child Left Behind Act of 2001 (Public Law 107-110). (2002). Washington, DC: U.S. Government Printing Office.

Phillips, G. (1990). The Lake Wobegon effect. *Educational Measurement: Issues and Practice, 9,* (3), 3, 14.

Rivera, C., Stansfield, C. W., Scialdone, L., & Sharkey, M. (2000). *An analysis of state policies for the inclusion and accommodation of English language learners in state assessment programs.* Arlington, VA: The George Washington University Center for Equity and Excellence in Education.

Rivera, C., & Vincent, C. (1997). *High school graduation testing: Policies and practices in the assessment of English language learners.* Arlington, VA: The George Washington University Center for Equity and Excellence in Education.

Rivera, C., Vincent, C., Hafner, A., & LaCelle-Peterson, M. (1997). *Statewide assessment programs: Policies and practices for the inclusion of limited English proficient students* (ERIC/AE Digest Series EDO-TM-97-02). Washington, DC: U.S. Department of Education.

Rumberger, R. W., & Gandara, P. (2004). Seeking equity in the education of California's English learners. *Teachers College Record, 106,* 2032–2056.

Spicuzza, R., Liu, K., Swierzbin, B., Bielinski, J., & Thurlow, M. (2000, June). Participation and performance of limited English proficient students during second attempts on a graduation exam. (State Assessment Series, Minnesota Rpt. 28). Minneapolis, MN: University of Minnesota, National Center for Education Outcomes.

Zlatos, B. (1994a, November). Don't test, don't tell. "Academic red-shirting." *American School Board Journal,* 24–28.

Zlatos, B. (1994b, November 6). Scores that don't add up. *New York Times,* Section 4A, pp. 28–29.

Study 1

An Analysis of State Assessment Policies Regarding the Accommodation of English Language Learners

Charlene Rivera, Eric Collum, Lynn Shafer Willner,
and Jose Ku Sia, Jr.

One of the primary ways in which states have attempted to respond to the federal mandate to include all students in accountability systems is to allow the use of accommodations on state mandated assessments. In general, accommodations involve changes to a test or testing situation and are used widely for the assessment of students who, because of limited proficiency in English or physical or cognitive disabilities, are deemed unable to participate meaningfully in state assessments without adjustments to the language or administration of the test. To be effective, accommodations must address the unique needs of the students for whom they are provided without invalidating the test construct. In the case of ELLs, this means providing the test takers with assistance in overcoming the linguistic and sociocultural barriers that prevent them from accessing the content of the test. Without this support, ELLs will, to a great extent, be tested on their knowledge of the language of the test rather than its content.

Although states' policies have addressed the use of accommodations as a tool for the inclusion of ELLs in state assessment, typically, these policies have not done so systematically or in a way that has targeted ELLs. Because accommodations represent one of the most powerful tools for including ELLs in state accountability systems, it is imperative that states' approaches to the use of accommodations are fully understood.

The aim of this study is to examine states' policies regarding the use of accommodations on state assessments for school year 2000–2001, the by educators is the selection of accommodations that fulfill these two requirements. Focusing on data from the NAEP and research conducted on accommodations and second language acquisition, the following section reviews current research on accommodations for ELLs.

Research on Accommodations

Two research perspectives have dominated the knowledge base on accommodations for ELLs. The first perspective is inspired by the challenge to include a more representative sample of students in the NAEP.[3] The second perspective is motivated by the need for an empirical understanding of the effects of particular accommodations or groups of accommodations on ELLs. This section provides an overview of research related to each perspective.

To identify research related to these two perspectives, the research team consulted a range of resources. For NAEP data, the team examined studies issued by the National Center for Education Statistics (NCES) and the Educational Testing Service (ETS). To identify studies of accommodations pertaining to ELLs, the research team consulted Psychological Abstracts and Language Testing, along with the online resources of the National Clearinghouse on English Language Acquisition (NCELA), and the Educational Resources Information Center (ERIC). In addition, the relevant studies and syntheses produced by the National Center on Educational Outcomes (NCEO), the National Academy of Sciences (NAS), and the Center for Research on Evaluation, Standards, and Student Testing (CRESST) were reviewed.

NAEP Inclusion Studies

Currently, information regarding the academic progress of students in the United States is collected via two kinds of large-scale assessments: the NAEP and state assessments. The NAEP is administered to a sample of students from each state; results are used to "inform national and state policy makers about student performance, assisting them in evaluating the conditions and progress of the nation's education system" (Koenig & Bachman, 2004, p.30). By contrast, virtually every student is required to

---

[3]The NAEP, also known as "the Nation's report card," is "the nation's only ongoing survey of student achievement in core subject areas" (Lutkus & Mazzeo, 2003, p. vii). Since 1969, assessments have been conducted periodically in reading, mathematics, science, writing, history, civics, geography, and the arts. The NAEP includes students drawn from both public and nonpublic schools and reports results for student achievement at Grades 4, 8, and 12. State-level results for NAEP have been provided since 1990.

participate in state assessments; data from these tests are used to track the academic progress of students (and student subgroups) in each state. Whereas NAEP data are used to provide a national perspective on student achievement across several academic content areas, state assessment data are used for accountability purposes within a state.

Although NAEP and state assessments differ in scope and purpose, administrators of these tests face many of the same challenges in attempting to include ELLs. Because of NAEP's scope and consistency of administration, data collected regarding the use of accommodations for this assessment can provide insight into the impact of accommodations on state assessments.

Prior to 1995, NAEP policy allowed for the exclusion of ELLs judged incapable of participating meaningfully in the assessment. However, in the mid-1990s, NAEP's inclusion policies underwent significant modification to broaden participation among special needs students, which NAEP defined as ELLs and students with disabilities (NCES, 2003). In an effort to make the NAEP more inclusive, researchers began to experiment with test accommodations for ELLs and students with disabilities.

In 1995, six accommodations for ELLs and students with disabilities were field tested in NAEP science and mathematics assessments. The 1995 field test was designed to evaluate not the effect of individual accommodations on student performance, but rather how accommodated field test scores would affect data comparability over time (Lutkus & Mazzeo, 2003, p. vii). Although analysis verified that inclusion of accommodated data would have an impact on NAEP trend data, to meet the goal of increasing ELLs' participation in NAEP, all accommodations used in the field test, with the exception of the Spanish-only assessment, were permitted in the 1996 operational NAEP science and mathematics assessments (Olson & Goldstein, 1997). Thus, accommodations have been permitted for the NAEP since 1996. Currently, NAEP offers a total of 21 accommodations for ELLs and students with disabilities (NCES, 2004).

Primarily, the body of research produced by NAEP focuses on the impact that the use of accommodations has on inclusion rates of ELLs in NAEP. However, NAEP research offers no guidance on which specific accommodations are most appropriate for ELLs and which have the potential to raise ELLs' scores without invalidating the construct of the test.

Studies Examining the Effect of Accommodations on ELLs

The second body of research has been produced by a variety of researchers and examines the effects of particular accommodations or groups of accommodations on ELLs and non-ELLs.[4] Within the limited pool of available research on accommodations, few studies focus on accommodations intended to address the linguistic needs of ELLs or on how accommodations, separately or in combination, affect ELLs' performance (Sireci, Li, & Scarpati, 2002, p. 49). Of the 150 articles reviewed by Sireci et al. (2002), only 38 were studies that examined the effects of test accommodations on the performance of students with disabilities or ELLs; of these, 13, or just under 9% of all studies examined, focused on ELLs (Sireci, 2003).

The current review is informed by the work of Sireci et al. (2002) but conducted separately with a focus on studies examining the effect of accommodations for ELLs (as opposed to ELLs and students with disabilities). In conducting research for this review, the research team examined studies conducted between 1990 and 2003. Only those studies meeting the following criteria were included in the final review: (a) examined effects of specific accommodations or groups of accommodations on performance, and (b) used experimental and quasi-experimental research designs that allowed examination of the effect of the accommodation(s) on ELLs and non-ELLs.[5] Studies using ex post facto designs, such as that carried out by Shepard, Taylor, and Betebenner (1998), are not reviewed here because the design does not permit a direct examination of the effect of individual accommodations on test scores. A total of 15 studies were identified for inclusion in this review.

Each of the 15 studies examined one or more of the following types of accommodations: (a) linguistic simplification, (b) customized English dictionaries and glossaries (e.g., English-to-Spanish glossary, Spanish–English glossaries, simplified English glossaries, computer test with pop-up glossary), (c) use of the native language (e.g., dual-language tests), (d) reading items or directions or both aloud, and (e) providing extra time in combination with other accommodations. Eight of the studies focused on individual accommodations; seven examined more than one accommodation.

Findings from the studies must be viewed cautiously for several reasons. First, 15 studies constitute a very small pool of research from which to generalize regarding the effectiveness of specific accommodations.

---

[4]Tindal and Fuchs (1999) first summarized the literature related to test changes for students with disabilities. A discussion of studies of accommodations relevant to students with disabilities can also be found in Sireci et al. (2002, pp. 16–48).

[5]Studies using an experimental design include those that involved (a) manipulation of test administration and (b) random assignment of test conditions. Studies using quasi-experimental designs included those that involved (a) manipulation of test administration but not (b) random assignment of test conditions (Sireci et al., 2002, p. 11).

The difficulty of generalizing from this limited pool is compounded by the fact that these studies often differed both methodologically and in the clarity with which methodology was explained. Hence, there is no common measure for what constitutes an effective accommodation.

Another significant challenge for the interpretation of findings from the studies was the use of combinations of accommodations without tracking the use of particular accommodations. For instance, one study examining "oral presentation" allowed oral delivery of directions in English or native language. The researchers did not record which of these options was adopted by the test administrators even though these accommodations are significantly different.

Student sample sizes vary significantly across the studies: ELL samples ranged from 82 to 864, and non-ELL sample sizes ranged from 69 to 11,306. In one study, a student sample that included only ELLs was used. The student samples of 14 of the studies, however, included ELLs and non-ELLs. In these studies, students' status as ELLs, the use of an accommodation (or group of accommodations), and the interaction of these two factors could be examined.[6] In some of these studies, student samples were divided further to take into account factors differentiating ELLs, such as amount of time a student received instruction in English, reading ability, and level of English language proficiency.

Finally, criteria for classifying students as English language learners or limited English proficient (LEP) students were not always transparent.[7] For example, the California ESL designation was used in one study to classify the group of LEP students provided with accommodations. In this case, ESL categories included students designated initially fluent in English (IFE), fully English proficient (FEP), as well as LEP students. In other studies, ELL or LEP student samples were designated using such methods as student self-reports and teacher reports from background questionnaires.

Despite these limitations, the studies reviewed can offer insight into the affect of accommodations on ELL performance. These studies are presented next and are organized according to accommodation examined: (a) linguistic simplification, (b) dictionaries and glossaries, (c) native language, (d) reading test items or directions aloud, and (e) extra time. In cases where a single study examined more than one accommodation, that study is listed under each type of accommodation. More complete de-

---

[6]For a discussion of the significance of this research design, see the Thurlow et al. (2000) discussion of "Group Research Designs" (pp. 12–13).

[7]It is important to recognize that researchers sometimes used the terms ELL and LEP interchangeably. LEP is used in federal legislation as well as in some states' legislation, whereas the term ELL is favored by many educators and researchers.

scriptions of the studies are provided in Appendix 1.A. Table 1A.1 (in Appendix 1.A) lists the 15 studies and provides information regarding the content for which accommodations were used along with the size and characteristics of the samples for the studies.

Linguistic Simplification. As a test accommodation, *linguistic simplification* refers to the process of decreasing the linguistic complexity of test items or directions or both to make the meaning more accessible to the test taker without changing the meaning conveyed by the text. Simplified, plain English, or plain language text incorporates vocabulary that avoids ambiguity, colloquialisms, or synonyms and uses uncomplicated linguistic structure. The goal of linguistic simplification is to ensure understanding of the test items and, in some cases, directions without compromising the construct being tested. Properly applied, linguistic simplification does not compromise the validity and comparability of test scores by "dumbing down" the test, but affords ELLs and non-ELLs equal access to the content-based complexities of test items.

As shown in Table 1.1, eight studies examined linguistic simplification. Six of the studies used fourth- and eighth-grade NAEP math and science items. These studies used California's designations for student subgroups, and the samples were classified into two categories: LEP and non-LEP. A seventh study used NAEP mathematics items to simulate the Colorado State Assessment Program. For this study, students confirmed the student designation of ELL by responding to a background questionnaire. The eighth study, using the state's designation of LEP students, examined the effects of linguistic simplification on fourth- and sixth-grade science items in the Delaware Student Testing Program.

A number of studies found that the use of linguistic simplification had positive results for ELLs. Abedi, Courtney, Mirocha, et al. (2003) indicated that linguistic simplification was among those accommodation strategies studied that were "effective in increasing the performance of ELLs students and reducing the performance gap between ELLs and non-ELL students" (p. xiii). Rivera and Stansfield (2004) found evidence that linguistic simplification did not impose a threat to score comparability for monolingual English students. Unfortunately, the sample sizes for ELLs ($n = 109$) were too small to compare their performance on the simplified and nonsimplified versions of the items. The results of other studies were more equivocal. For instance, Abedi and Lord (2001) found that the linguistically modified versions of test items were only slightly easier for students to comprehend than the original items and the difference in difficulty was not statistically significant. Furthermore, the accommodation was found to be no more beneficial to ELLs than to non-ELLs. Similarly, Abedi, Lord, and Plummer (1997) found that, irrespective of LEP status, students in low- and average-level math classes performed best on linguistically modified versions of the test items. However, it should be noted that Abedi and his colleagues were unable to determine the LEP status of 70% of the students.

Although no definitive conclusions can be drawn from the studies, it is possible to make three major observations based on these studies. First, and perhaps most important, the use of linguistic simplification as a type of

TABLE 1.1

Studies Examining the Effectiveness of Linguistic Simplification as an Accommodation for ELLs

| Study | Content | | | | Sample | | | |
	Reading	Math	Science	Social Studies	ELLs	Non-ELLs	Total	Grade(s)
Rivera & Stansfield (2004)			✓		109	11,306	11,415	4, 6
Abedi, Courtney, Mirocha, et al. (2003)			✓		317	294	611	4, 8
Hofstetter (2003)		✓			676	173	849	8
Abedi, Hofstetter, Baker, & Lord (2001)[a]		✓			501	445	946	8
Abedi & Lord (2001)		✓			372	802	1,174	8
Kiplinger, Haug, & Abedi (2000) [a]								
Abedi, Lord, & Hofstetter, (1998)[a]		✓			864	530	1,394	8
Abedi, Lord, & Plummer (1997)		✓			320	711	1,031	8

Note. In describing student samples some researchers used the terms LEP and non-LEP rather than ELL and non-ELL.

[a]In the study, the ELL and non-ELL populations were reported as percentages of the total study sample; the *n*s provided here were calculated based on the percentages of the total sample reported for each group.

accommodation for mathematics and science appears promising. Second, ELLs' level of language proficiency must first be considered to gauge whether the use of linguistic simplification is merited. That is, for students at lower levels of English language proficiency, linguistic simplification appears useful; conversely, for students at higher levels of English language proficiency, the effects of linguistic simplification need to be examined more closely (Abedi & Lord, 2001; Abedi et al., 1997). Third, researchers should explain the process used to simplify test items including the safeguards employed to ensure that the linguistic simplification in no way compromises the content of individual items.

Dictionaries or Glossaries.   Bilingual dictionaries and native language glossaries are provided to ELLs to help them understand the meaning of words that might be less familiar due to their limited English language proficiency. Glossaries and bilingual dictionaries are designed to help students comprehend the language of English-language test items (e.g., mathematics or science) and not to provide explanations or clues regarding the construct being tested.

Although the function of dictionaries and glossaries is similar, there is an important difference between these two accommodations. Broadly speaking, a dictionary provides a general definition of a word, whereas a glossary provides an explanation of a word customized for a particular context and audience.

The types of dictionaries used in studies of accommodations for ELLs include standard English dictionaries, learners' dictionaries, and customized dictionaries. A *learner's dictionary* is designed specifically for ELLs and defines words in simplified English. Like some standard English dictionaries, learners' dictionaries also give examples of usage and might provide synonyms. The term *customized dictionary* is used by researchers to refer to a dictionary that has been altered or specially compiled for a given context. It can refer to a learner's dictionary where language has been simplified specifically for ELLs. A customized dictionary also can contain a specialized list of standard dictionary definitions compiled for a particular assessment and containing words relevant to that assessment.

In accommodation studies, *glossaries* appear as specialized lists of key words in English with definitions or explanations customized to fit the perceived needs of the test taker. Glossaries can use simplified language and can also be provided in the student's native language, but glossaries can take other forms as well. For example, in one study (Abedi, Courtney, & Leon, 2003), instead of a combined list of words, students were provided with a *pop-up glossary*. In this case, computer testing was employed, and the explanation (or *gloss*) of a key term appeared when the student passed a cursor over that term on his or her computer screen. In another study (Abedi, Lord, Boscardin, & Miyoshi, 2001), marginal glosses printed on the test booklet were used. The gloss on one margin included a definition or explanation in English, and the gloss on the other provided a Spanish translation of the English gloss.

However, the distinctions made here are not applied consistently in accommodations research. Abedi, Courtney, and Leon (2003) described the customized English dictionary used in their study as "a glossary of non-content words in the math test ... composed of exact excerpts from an ELL dictionary" (p. 5). Abedi, Courtney, Mirocha, et al. (2003) referred to commercial bilingual dictionaries as glossaries on the basis that, unlike English dictionaries, these texts provide translations of terms rather than definitions (p. 18, footnote 2). On the whole, in the research examined there is little agreement on what constitutes a dictionary as opposed to a glossary. Consequently, no identifiable standard is offered in the research on accommodations to govern the use of a dictionary versus a glossary as an accommodation.

Although glossaries also appear to have the promise of being useful, only three studies were found that examined the use of glossaries. When English dictionaries and glossaries were used as accommodations, dictionaries generally were found to be more useful (Abedi, Courtney, & Leon, 2003; Abedi, Courtney, Mirocha, et al., 2003; Abedi, Lord, et al., 2001).

The six studies listed in Table 1.2 examined dictionaries and glossaries as accommodations. Four studies examined the use of dictionaries; two of these also examined the use of a glossary. Two studies examined the effect of glossaries only.

The available research suggests that, with regard to using dictionaries in a testing situation, the effect of the accommodation on test validity is a key concern. For example, test validity can be compromised by the use of a dictionary that defines key vocabulary or illustrates content tested (Laufer & Hadar, 1997; Rivera & Stansfield, 2004). In light of this concern, Abedi, Lord, et al. (2001) suggested that dictionaries should be customized to control vocabulary and other types of information provided to test takers. Some researchers have noted that a positive aspect of using dictionaries as a test accommodation is that they are widely used as part of instruction and should therefore be familiar to students (e.g., Abedi, Courtney, Mirocha, et al., 2003; Albus, Bielinski, Thurlow, & Liu, 2001). Researchers at the NCEO (Albus et al., 2001) contended that customized dictionaries in particular do not burden administrators and students with the bulk of pub-

TABLE 1.2

Studies Examining the Effectiveness of Dictionaries and Glossaries as an Accommodation for ELLs

Study	Content				Sample			
	Reading	Math	Science	Social Studies	ELLs	Non-ELLs	Total	Grade
Abedi, Courtney, Mirocha et al. (2003)[b,c]			✓		317	294	611	4, 8
Abedi, Courtney, & Leon (2003)[b]		✓			535	614	1,149	4, 8
Abedi, Hofstetter, Baker, & Lord, (2001)[a,c]		✓			501	445	946	8
Abedi, Lord, Boscardin, & Miyoshi (2001)[b,c]			✓		183	236	419	8
Albus, Bielinski, Thurlow, & Liu (2001)[b]	✓				133	69	202	Middle school
Kiplinger, Haug, & Abedi (2000)[a,c]		✓			152	1,046	1,198	4

Note. In describing student samples some researchers used the terms LEP and non-LEP rather than ELL and non-ELL.

[a]In the study, the ELL and non-ELL populations were reported as percentages of the total study sample; the ns provided here were calculated based on the percentages of the total sample reported for each group. [b]Study examined use of dictionary. [c]Study examined use of glossary.

lished dictionaries, nor do they contain words that assist students with test content. In cases where concerns arise that providing ELLs with a traditional dictionary might provide an unfair advantage, customized dictionaries offer a potentially viable alternative (Abedi, 2001).

In a study using Spanish language glosses, Abedi, Courtney, Mirocha, et al. (2003) found that it was difficult to understand the effect of the accommodation in the absence of data on students' level of Spanish language proficiency. Overall, English language glossaries seemed to be more useful than Spanish language glossaries. For those students not literate in Spanish who are being instructed in English, it stands to reason that a Spanish language glossary might not be helpful. However, for students with basic literacy in Spanish or students participating in a dual-language program, it is possible that Spanish language glosses could prove useful. These observations support the need to consider student background variables carefully prior to selecting an accommodation. Overall, however, more research needs to be conducted to examine the effects of English and native language glossaries.

Given the limited number of studies and the often blurred definitions between dictionary and glossary conditions, it is imperative that future researchers make clear distinctions between these two conditions. This classification is necessary if researchers are to understand clearly the separate effects on test validity of the two approaches. It is also important to examine these linguistic accommodations in conjunction with the provision of extra time.

Native Language. Accommodations in the native language are wide-ranging and might include written translation of test directions or items, or both, bilingual or dual-language versions of the test, oral repetition of test directions or items, or both in the native language via audiotape, or sight translation (i.e., a spontaneous, oral rendition of the test content in the student's native language).

The effects of native language accommodations were examined in five studies (see Table 1.3). Three of the five studies—Garcia (2000), Abedi, Lord,

TABLE 1.3

Studies Examining the Effectiveness of the Use of Native Language as an Accommodation for ELLs

	Content				Sample			
Study	Reading	Math	Science	Social Science	ELLs	Non-ELLs	Total	Grade
Hofstetter (2003)		✓			676	173	849	8
Anderson, Liu, Swierzbin, Thurlow, & Bielinski (2000)	✓				105	101	206	8
Garcia (2000)		✓			320	82	402	8
Hafner (2000)		✓			82	288	370	4, 7
Abedi, Lord, & Hofstetter (1998)[a]		✓			864	530	1,394	8

Note. In describing student samples some researchers used the terms LEP and non-LEP rather than ELL and non-ELL.

[a]In the study, the ELL and non-ELL populations were reported as percentages of the total study sample; the *n*s provided here were calculated based on the percentages of the total sample reported for each group.

and Hofstetter (1998), and Hofstetter (2003)—examined the use of written translation of test directions, test items, or both or bilingual versions of the test. In the Anderson, Liu, Swierzbin, Thurlow, and Bielinski (2000) study, examinees were provided with both written and audiotaped test directions and questions in Spanish. No data were collected on the effect of oral versus written delivery of directions and questions in Spanish. Hafner (2000) examined the oral delivery of native language accommodations in the context of "extended oral presentation," an accommodation that included the option of reading directions in the student's native language (as well as other options unrelated to native language accommodation). As extended oral presentation was examined as a single accommodation, no data were collected on the effectiveness of the native language component of this accommodation.

With regard to written translation, Abedi et al. (1998) examined the use of math items translated into Spanish. The researchers found that ELLs performed less well on a Spanish version of the test than on the standard version but noted that most students in the study were receiving mathematics instruction in English, not in Spanish. Anderson et al. (2000) found that, overall, Spanish-speaking students did not benefit from the provision of instructions and test questions in Spanish. However, like Abedi et al. (1998), Anderson et al. (2000) conceded that students in the study had not received academic instruction in Spanish. Garcia (2000) examined the use of bilingual and standard (English) versions of test items. In general, students less proficient in English performed better on the dual-language test booklet than on the English-only version. Hofstetter (2003) found that students taking a Spanish version of NAEP math items scored slightly lower than students taking the English version. However, students taking the Spanish version who also received math instruction in Spanish performed better than students who received math instruction in Spanish but took the standard version of the test. She concluded that this provides "strong evidence that students perform better when the language of the mathematics test matches the students' language of instruction" (p. 183).

These studies highlight the need to make decisions about the use of native language accommodations based on whether students are being instructed in whole or in part in the native language. In cases in which a student is instructed in the native language or when a student literate in the native language is recently enrolled in a U.S. school, this limited pool of research suggests that testing in the student's native language can facilitate access to the content of the test. By contrast, when students are being instructed only in English, a native language test has the potential to affect student performance adversely (Hofstetter, 2003).

Reading Test Items or Directions Aloud.   As a test accommodation, reading aloud is used primarily for dyslexic and blind students. It requires the student to listen to the text, comprehend, and process it based on short-term memory. No written text is provided. By contrast, when reading aloud is used for ELLs, the student typically is allowed to hear and read text at the same time.

In the two available research studies using this accommodation for ELLs, two approaches were taken. In one study, an exact oral rendition of the items was provided; in a second study, an interpretation of test directions was allowed. Both studies allowed extra time and utilized a quasi-experimental design. Table 1.4 profiles these studies.

The two studies provide a contrast in offering a read-aloud accommodation to ELLs. Castellon-Wellington (2000) allowed test items to be read aloud, whereas Hafner (2000) allowed test directions to be provided to students as an extended oral presentation. A perhaps more significant difference, however, is that whereas Castellon-Wellington allowed an exact reading of the test items, Hafner allowed a great deal of latitude on the part of the test administrator to choose what form the oral presentation of directions would take, including simplification, rereading test directions, providing additional examples, or reading directions in a student's native language. Furthermore, for the Hafner study, no record was kept of the form of oral presentation provided.

Because the two studies examining reading aloud differed widely in terms of approach, it is difficult to assess the rationale, processes, and purposes for providing a read-aloud accommodation to ELLs. One study focused on test items, whereas the other study centered only on test directions; one provided

TABLE 1.4

**Studies Examining the Effectiveness of Reading Aloud
as an Accommodation for ELLs**

Study	Reading	Math	Science	Social Science	ELLs	Non-ELLs	Total	Grade
	Content				*Sample*			
Castellon-Wellington (2000)				✓	106	0	106	7
Hafner (2000)	✓				82	288	370	4, 7

Note. In describing student samples some researchers used the terms LEP and non-LEP rather than ELLs and non-ELL.

a literal rendering of the test items orally, whereas the second study allowed the tester latitude in administering the accommodation. In sum, from the limited number of studies available, many questions remain unanswered regarding whether reading aloud is an accommodation appropriate for and of benefit to ELLs.

Extra Time. The use of extra time on an assessment is "based on the premise that if language poses a problem for ELLs, students under normal testing conditions may not be able to carefully consider all of the items on the test" (Castellon-Wellington, 2000, p. 3). Although extra time can be provided as a single accommodation, it is more commonly provided in conjunction with other accommodations. For example, students might be permitted both to use a customized dictionary and to receive extra time. The only type of test for which the provision of extra time violates the construct measure is speeded assessment, or testing that assesses students' rates of item completion as part of the construct being measured.

Six studies made use of extra time. Of these, four examined the use of extra time as an accommodation, whereas two studies simply permitted all students to use extra time in combination with other accommodations; these studies did not examine the effect of extra time separately (Abedi, Courtney, Mirocha et al., 2003; Albus et al., 2001). The four studies directly examining the use of extra time are presented in Table 1.5.

Abedi, Courtney, and Leon (2003) compared use of extra time on math asessment with three other separate accommodations: a customized English dictionary, a computer test with pop-up glosses, and test administration in small groups. ELLs performed better with extra time than they did under most other conditions, but less well than they did on a computer version provided with pop-up glosses. Abedi, Hofstetter, Baker, and Lord (2001) used NAEP mathematics items to examine the effect of extra time, either as a single accommodation or paired with the use of a glossary. Overall, ELLs and non-ELLs performed best when given extra time and the use of a glossary and next best when given extra time only. However, the effect of these accommodations specifically on ELLs was inconclusive. Castellon-Wellington (2000) examined the use of extra time for seventh-grade ELLs who were offered a choice between receiving extra time to complete a test or having the items read aloud. Data indicated that neither accommodation improved the performance of ELLs, even when the accommodation was preferred by the examinee. Hafner (2000) studied the provision of extra time only and the provision of extra time along with extended oral presentation for ELLs and non-ELLs; approximately one third of the participants were students with dis-

TABLE 1.5

**Studies Examining the Effectiveness of Extra Time
as an Accommodation for ELLs**

	Content				Sample			
Study	*Reading*	*Math*	*Science*	*Social Studies*	*ELLs*	*Non-ELLs*	*Total*	*Grade*
Abedi, Courtney, & Leon (2003)[a]		✓			535	614	1,149	4, 8
Abedi, Hofstetter, Baker, & Lord, (2001)		✓			501	445	946	8
Castellon-Wellington (2000)				✓	106	0	106	7
Hafner (2000)	✓				82	288	370	4, 7

Note. In describing student samples some researchers used the terms LEP and non-LEP rather than ELL and non-ELL.

[a]In the study, the ELL and non-ELL populations were reported as percentages of the total study sample; the *n*s provided here were calculated based on the percentages of the total sample reported for each group.

abilities. Students who received extra time had significantly higher scores than those who had been provided with extended oral presentation of directions only. As Sireci et al. (2002) observed, however, Hafner (2000) did not consider whether the accommodations were more beneficial to ELLs in particular.

With the single exception of the speeded test, in which time is integral to the construct being measured, there appears to be no harm, and, in some cases, potential advantage, from the provision of extra time as a form of accommodation. The majority of studies reviewed demonstrate that extra time generally is helpful—ELLs might not have performed to advanced levels, but often performed better when afforded extra time. However, these studies also appear to indicate that extra time offered in isolation is not necessarily helpful for ELLs. At least one study (Abedi et al., 2001) has demonstrated positive effects for ELLs in cases where extra time was coupled with glossaries, dictionaries, or both.

Summary of Research on Accommodations. In its review of accommodations, the National Research Council (NRC, 1999) reached the conclusion that "research on the effects of test accommodations for English-language learners is inconclusive" (p. 62). Five years later, this seems still to be the case. Although some accommodations, such as linguistic simplification, appear to be promising, the body of available research is far too limited and inconsistent to provide conclusive evidence regarding the utility of specific accommodations. Additional studies designed to examine promising types of accommodations with appropriate, sizable student populations need to be carried out. Native English speakers also must be included in the studies, along with control groups (i.e., students who do not receive accommodations) to examine the full effects of the accommodation (Thurlow et al., 2000). In designing studies, researchers also must take into account other factors that could affect outcomes, such as the diversity within samples of ELLs (e.g., differing cultural backgrounds, level of English language proficiency, education in the native language), as well as the methods used to create and implement accommodations (Thurlow et al., 2000).

A complementary perspective from which to study strategies that support ELLs' use of accommodations is research on second language acquisition. By understanding how ELLs process language, researchers will be better able to judge the effectiveness of individual accommodations in allowing ELLs access to the content of the test. This research is examined in the following section.

How Second Language Acquisition Research Informs the Use of Accommodations

The tendency of ELLs to process the language of a test in English by focusing on linguistic structures, lexical items, and phonological features leaves fewer cognitive resources available for accessing the test content. Compared to native English speaking peers, who have automatized processing in English, ELLs are at a distinct disadvantage when taking a test in English.

Research from second language acquisition provides insight into how second language learners process language and how specific linguistic strategies influence their comprehension of the second language. Three strategies that can be used to help second language learners negotiate a second language were identified in the second language acquisition literature: linguistic simplification, repetition, and clarification. These same strategies are implicit in many of the accommodations used for ELLs in state assessment. This section reviews the research on these strategies and relates this research to the accommodation of ELLs.

Linguistic Simplification

The process of linguistic simplification is intended to reduce the semantic and syntactic complexity of the English used in the text of a test including directions, items, and response options. Second language researchers have identified a number of syntactical features as difficult for both ELLs and native English speakers to process: passive voice constructions (Forster & Olbrei, 1973), long noun phrases (Halliday & Martin, 1993), long question phrases (Adams, 1990), comparative structures (Jones, 1982), propositional phrases, conditional clauses (Celce-Murcia & Larsen-Freeman, 1983), and relative clauses (Schachter, 1983). In addition, low-frequency, long, or morphologically complex words and long sentences are especially difficult for ELLs to process (Abedi, Lord, & Plummer, 1995).

In the process of simplification, late-acquired or complex linguistic structures are minimized, replaced by simpler ones (Abedi, Hofstetter, et al., 2001). Simplification of this type makes the language more accessible to ELLs, thereby allowing them to more easily access the core messages of a test item (Chaudron, 1988).

Even those ELLs with more than a beginning knowledge of English might encounter difficulties in effectively marshaling their knowledge in a testing situation. Despite their increased proficiency in English, research shows that second language learners in the earlier stages of language acquisition carry out encoding and decoding in the weaker language at slower processing speeds (Blair & Harris, 1981; Dornic, 1979; Mack, 1986; Soares & Grosjean, 1984). In addition, during second language processing, both short-term and working memory can be significantly taxed (Ellis, 1996; Ellis & Schmidt, 1997; Ellis & Sinclair, 1996; Hoosain & Salili, 1987; Miyake & Friedman, 1998; Naveh-Benjamin & Ayres, 1986; Robinson, 1995, 2001; Skehan, 1998).

These findings suggest that linguistic simplification of test language can facilitate ELLs' comprehension and reduce the linguistic load placed on them during an assessment.

Repetition

In second language acquisition research *repetition* most frequently refers to the restatement or rephrasing of an utterance to keep a conversation flowing. This type of repetition contrasts with exact repetition, which occurs when test directions or items, or both are read more than once. In the context of accommodations, however, repetition usually refers to exact repetition. The small body of second language acquisition research focusing on exact repetition has found that this form of repetition has a positive effect on comprehension of a particular utterance (Cervantes, 1983; Jensen & Vinther, 2003; Van Patton, 1990). This research is based on the premise that second language learners will try to extract the meaning of an utterance on a first listening, but, if comprehension fails, will use the repetition to notice linguistic details they missed the first time to make a more accurate hypothesis about meaning (Cervantes, 1983; Van Patton, 1990).

In a testing context, repetition of test directions or items, or both might afford ELLs an additional opportunity to process the language of the test by reducing the impact of processing speed and memory capacity on comprehension.

Clarification

Clarification can be provided either as an input strategy (through explanation provided in anticipation of a language learner's needs) or as an output strategy (as a response to an individual's request for clarification). The latter form of clarification has been studied by a number of second language acquisition researchers. Clarification requests occur when negotiating meaning by native and nonnative speakers of a language when something in the linguistic input is unclear. When ELLs negotiate meaning through clarification requests, they receive support for just the specific portions of the linguistic input not understood, and the reformulated input is more manageable and within their processing capacities (Long, 1980, 1983, 1996). ELLs at an intermediate stage of acquiring English are thought to be more successful at negotiating meaning and making clarification requests because they have access to a larger number of linguistic resources in English than do ELLs at the beginning stages of learning English (Pica, Lincoln-Porter, Paninos, & Linnell, 1996).

Some second language acquisition research has also suggested that situations requiring a second language learner to produce language might serve an even more important function—having to produce language could force learners to notice the gap between what they know and what they want to be able to say (Swain, 1985, 1995). Opportunities for language output in a testing situation, such as having the student verify his or her understanding of test directions, might be limited. However, Ellis (1999) argued that such opportunities could allow ELLs to notice specific linguistic features that are particularly problematic and, therefore, compel them to engage in a deeper level of language processing.

In a testing situation, clarification can be used to help ELLs gain access to the language of a test. Clarification can be provided to students from a prepared script or spontaneously at the time of test administration.

Conclusion

This literature review highlights the key issues educators and policymakers must face when considering the use of accommodations for ELLs taking state assessment. Accommodations might provide a viable tool for including

ELLs in state assessment, but, as this review shows, the effect accommodations have on the validity of test scores must be taken into consideration. As the federal legislation makes clear, only accommodations that yield "reliable information" (1994 ESEA) or "reliable data" (2001 ESEA) will enable states to include ELLs meaningfully in state assessment systems. Appropriately accommodated tests for ELLs must have the explicit purpose of allowing the student access to the content of the test without compromising the validity, score comparability, or other technical aspects of a test.

Although legislation dictates that ELLs be assessed "in the language and form most likely to yield accurate and reliable information on what such students know and can do," more research clearly is needed to determine the most appropriate test accommodations for ELLs. Our review highlights the fact that, although the evidence on the effectiveness of different accommodations for ELLs is somewhat mixed, several types of accommodations, including simplified language and customized dictionaries, appear to hold promise. In the absence of additional empirical data, however, the extent to which a particular test accommodation affects validity remains unknown. As a result, Stansfield (2002) argued that it is critical for research to be conducted to determine whether accommodations pose a threat to a test's reliability and validity or to score comparability between ELL and non-ELL test takers. Ideally, only after score comparability has been established can an accommodation reasonably be endorsed.

A promising direction for accommodations research is the research on second language acquisition. As this review shows, second language acquisition research sheds light on the utility of accommodations that provide direct linguistic support to ELLs. The research identifies the various forms of direct linguistic support identified in the literature (i.e., simplification, repetition, and clarification). Such support can reduce the cognitive resources needed to process the language of the test and leave more resources available to ELLs for processing the test content. By implication accommodations that reduce the cognitive resources needed to process the language of the test can help ELLs better attend to test content.

In the following pages, findings are presented from the analysis of state assessment policy documents provided by 51 states for the 2000–2001 school year. The data presented provide a profile of states' approaches to the accommodation of ELLs, including the accommodations designated for ELLs and the components of the decision-making process states used to support the selection of appropriate accommodations for eligible students. The final section provides a discussion and offers recommendations for the accommodation of ELLs on statewide assessments.

ACCOMMODATIONS FOR ELLS IN STATE ASSESSMENT POLICIES

The data presented in this study provide a comprehensive view of policies regarding the use of accommodations on state assessments for school year 2000–2001, the year in which states' assessment systems were to have been fully implemented under IASA. By examining the status of states' reporting efforts under IASA, it is possible to gauge the extent to which states are adequately positioned to comply with the more stringent accountability requirements of NCLB. The data presented here can serve as baseline for future studies of states' efforts to report ELL-specific data as required by state accountability provisions of NCLB.

This section is divided into five subsections. The first addresses the general characteristics of states' assessment policies and provides data relevant to (a) the number of states addressing accommodations specifically for ELLs, (b) the approaches these states' policies took in addressing the needs of ELLs, and (c) the extent to which states' policies addressed the appropriateness of particular accommodations for specific content areas. The next subsection reviews the individual accommodations listed in states' policies and, using a taxonomy developed to classify ELL-responsive accommodations, analyzes states' presentations of accommodations. Data regarding the criteria and decision makers designated in states' policies to facilitate the selection of suitable accommodations for appropriate ELLs are examined in the third subsection. The fourth subsection provides an analysis of the accommodations policies from the perspective of two state subgroups: those states requiring high school exit exams and those states having the greatest populations of ELLs. The final subsection summarizes and concludes the analysis of findings from states' policies for the 2000–2001 school year.

General Characteristics of States' Assessment Policies Addressing the Accommodation of ELLs

A large majority of states' policies for school year 2000–2001 addressed the accommodation of ELLs. As illustrated in the map in Fig. 1.1, of the 51 states,[8] only 4 (Alaska, Georgia, Idaho, and Illinois) had no policies addressing the accommodation of ELLs. Nearly all the policies of the remaining 47 states named particular accommodations districts might use for the assessment of ELLs. Iowa's policy was the only exception. This state's pol-

---

[8]For the purposes of this study, the District of Columbia is referred to as a state, bringing the total number of states included in the study to 51.

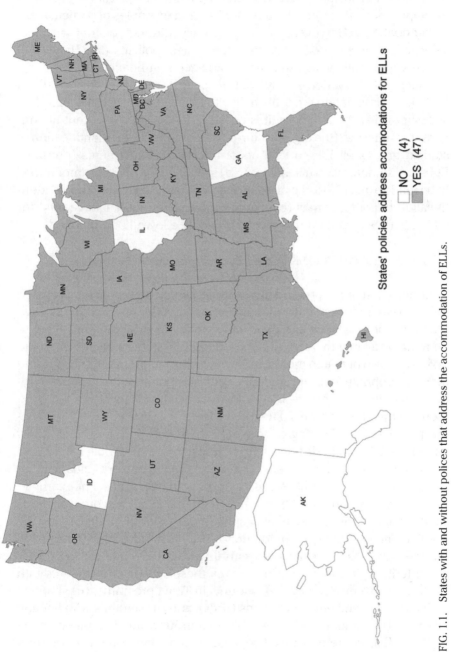

States' policies address accomodations for ELLs

☐ NO (4)
■ YES (47)

FIG. 1.1.   States with and without polices that address the accommodation of ELLs.

icy provided inclusion guidelines, which provided suggestions for selecting appropriate accommodations for ELLs and examples of particular accommodations. However, the Iowa policy did not delimit districts'
selection of accommodations as other states' policies did. Hence, 46
states were identified as listing or naming accommodations.

States' policies varied greatly in addressing the use of accommodations
for ELLs. This variation limits the ability to make generalizations regarding
states' policies. Nonetheless, it is possible to identify three central concerns that informed the organization of states' policies: (a) identification of
student groups eligible to take accommodated assessments (primarily
ELLs and students with disabilities), (b) identification of accommodations
to be made available to eligible students within these groups, and (c) identification of content areas (e.g., mathematics, English language arts) for
which particular accommodations should be allowed or prohibited.

How States' Policies Designated ELLs Eligible for Accommodation

In designating accommodations, state assessment policies provided
guidance to help local education agencies (LEAs) identify students eligible for accommodation and determine which accommodations were to
be made available to these students. However, states' policies often did
not distinguish between those accommodations appropriate for ELLs and
those appropriate for other students, such as students with disabilities. Indeed, in policy documents, ELLs and student with disabilities often were
grouped together as "special needs students," "at-risk students," or "special populations." The degree to which the needs of ELLs and students
with disabilities were distinguished varied across states' policies.

On the one hand, some states' policies provided cursory guidance that
combined the needs of ELLs and students with disabilities. For example,
Vermont policy addressed both student groups in an "Accommodations
Grid" designed for "students with special needs" without discussing the
specific needs of ELLs. Colorado policy also lacked focus with regard to
the needs of ELLs. The state's assessment policy was organized to address
all students eligible for accommodations, these included (a) students with
limited English proficiency, (b) students in Title I programs, (c) students
with individualized education plans (IEPs), and (d) students with Section
504 plans (i.e., students addressed by Section 504 of the Rehabilitation Act
of 1973). ELLs were addressed separately in a short appendix, where it
was indicated simply that ELLs were "entitled to the same assessment accommodations ... as their English-speaking peers."

On the other hand, some states' policies provided guidance on accommodations organized more clearly around the needs of ELLs. For instance, North Carolina's assessment policy grouped ELLs and students with disabilities in a document entitled *Testing Accommodations for Students With Disabilities and Students Identified as Limited English Proficient*. This document featured a section offering guidance regarding accommodations specifically for ELLs that offered descriptions of individual accommodations along with administrative procedures. In addition, the state provided a separate policy document focusing exclusively on the assessment of ELLs: *Guidelines for Testing Students With Limited English Proficiency*. Similarly, Maryland's assessment policy, as expressed in the policy document *Requirements for Accommodating, Excusing, and Exempting Students in Maryland Assessment Programs*, referenced ELLs and students with disabilities eligible to be accommodated. Like North Carolina policy, Maryland policy treated ELLs and students with disabilities separately.

As these examples indicate, state assessment policies for the 2000–2001 school year embodied a number of approaches to the accommodation of ELLs. The inconsistencies among states' policies made it difficult to assess the overall extent to which states' policies addressed the accommodation needs of ELLs specifically; however, it should be noted that this variation in itself suggests a lack of consistent focus on the needs of ELLs.

How States' Policies Organized Individual Accommodations Available for ELLs

Approaches taken in states' policies to organizing individual accommodations were characterized by a blurring of distinction between accommodations appropriate for ELLs and those appropriate for students with disabilities. This lack of distinction was evidenced in policy documents in two ways. First, many states' policies presented accommodations for ELLs according to a taxonomy developed to classify accommodations for students with disabilities. Second, lists of accommodations found in states' policies intended for ELLs were often not organized to address their specific needs; rather, accommodations were directed to eligible students requiring accommodation, including ELLs and students with disabilities. Such lists of accommodations often contained a preponderance of accommodations designed for students with disabilities and irrelevant to ELLs (e.g., use of Braille, use of assistive devices).

As Table 1.6 shows, the majority of states' policies (27) adopted a taxonomy used to classify accommodations for students with disabilities. The

TABLE 1.6

**States' Use of the Traditional Taxonomy
for Classifying Accommodations for ELLs**

State	Addressed Use of Accommodations for ELLs	Used Traditional Taxonomy to Classify Accommodations
AK	—	—
AL	✓	✓
AR	✓	—
AZ	✓	—
CA	✓	✓
CO	✓	✓
CT	✓	—
DC	✓	✓
DE	✓	✓
FL	✓	—
GA	—	—
HI	✓	—
IA	✓	—
ID	—	—
IL	—	—
IN	✓	—
KS	✓	✓
KY	✓	—
LA	✓	✓
MA	✓	—
MD	✓	✓
ME	✓	✓
MI	✓	—
MN	✓	✓
MO	✓	—
MS	✓	✓
MT	✓	✓

NC	✓	—
ND	✓	✓
NE	✓	✓
NH	✓	✓
NJ	✓	—
NM	✓	—
NV	✓	✓
NY	✓	—
OH	✓	—
OK	✓	✓
OR	✓	✓
PA	✓	✓
RI	✓	✓
SC	✓	—
SD	✓	✓
TN	✓	—
TX	✓	—
UT	✓	✓
VA	✓	✓
VT	✓	✓
WA	✓	✓
WI	✓	—
WV	✓	✓
WY	✓	✓
Total	47	27

traditional taxonomy includes four categories of accommodations: (a) timing and scheduling, (b) setting, (c) presentation, and (d) response. These categories of accommodations are described as follows.

Timing and scheduling accommodations affect the amount of time allowed for the test; the number, frequency, or duration of breaks; or the scheduling of tests or test components (e.g., test time increased). *Setting accommodations* affect the environment in which the test is given (e.g., test administered in a small group). *Presentation accommodations* affect the written and oral format of test directions and test items (e.g., directions repeated, directions clarified or explained in English, audiotaped directions in native language, language reference materials, or a simplified or sheltered English version of the test). *Response accommodations* affect how the test taker is allowed to respond to test questions or items (e.g., marking answers in test booklet, verifying that he or she understands the directions, responding in his or her native language and having that response translated into English, or being provided with spelling assistance.

Because it was developed without an explicit focus on ELLs' needs, this taxonomy provides no clear guidance to districts regarding which accommodations might be appropriate specifically for ELLs and which are appropriate only for students with disabilities. With the exception of Iowa, all 47 states' policies addressing accommodations for ELLs listed individual accommodations. A number of states' policies provided single lists of accommodations meant to address all students with special needs, including ELLs and students with disabilities. Table 1.7 shows which states' policies listed accommodations for ELLs together with those for other students, and which provided a list of accommodations selected specifically for ELLs.

The policies of 18 states listed accommodations for all students eligible to take accommodated assessments. The policies of 28 states provided separate lists of accommodations for ELLs. Many of these policies provided extensive lists of accommodations for ELLs; a few supplemented a general list of accommodations for all students with a shorter list of accommodations intended only for ELLs. A comparison of data from Tables 1.6 and 1.7 reveals that, of the 28 states' policies providing a separate list of accommodations for ELLs, 14 listed accommodations within the taxonomy traditionally used to respond to the needs of students with disabilities.

Content Areas for Which Accommodations Were Addressed in States' Policies

States' assessment policies often, although not always, specified which accommodations were allowed or prohibited for use with designated content area tests. Content areas addressed in states' policies included English language arts (ELA)—often divided into reading and writing—mathematics, science, social studies, and other subjects. As Table 1.8 shows, 38 states addressed the use of accommodations for particular content areas. It must

TABLE 1.7

States' Policies Listing Accommodations for ELLs Separately or in Combination With Those for Students With Disabilities

State	Named Accommodations	Combined List of Accommodations	Listed ELL Accommodations Separately
AK	—	—	—
AL	✓	—	✓
AR	✓	✓	—
AZ	✓	—	✓
CA	✓	✓	—
CO	✓	✓	—
CT	✓	—	✓
DC	✓	—	✓
DE	✓	—	✓
FL	✓	—	✓
GA	—	—	—
HI	✓	—	✓
IA	—	—	—
ID	—	—	—
IL	—	—	—
IN	✓	—	✓
KS	✓	—	✓
KY	✓	—	✓
LA	✓	—	✓
MA	✓	—	✓
MD	✓	✓	—
ME	✓	✓	—
MI	✓	✓	—
MN	✓	—	✓
MO	✓	—	✓
MS	✓	✓	—

(continued)

TABLE 1.7 *(continued)*

State	Named Accommodations	Combined List of Accommodations	Listed ELL Accommodations Separately
MT	✓	✓	—
NC	✓	—	✓
ND	✓	✓	—
NE	✓	✓	—
NH	✓	✓	—
NJ	✓	—	✓
NM	✓	—	✓
NV	✓	—	✓
NY	✓	—	✓
OH	✓	✓	—
OK	✓	✓	—
OR	✓	✓	—
PA	✓	✓	—
RI	✓	✓	—
SC	✓	—	✓
SD	✓	—	✓
TN	✓	—	✓
TX	✓	✓	—
UT	✓	—	✓
VA	✓	—	✓
VT	✓	✓	—
WA	✓	—	✓
WI	✓	—	✓
WV	✓	—	✓
WY	✓	—	✓
Total	46	18	28

TABLE 1.8

**Content Areas for Which Accommodations
Were Designated in States' Policies**

State	Policy Explicitly Addressed Content	ELA/Literature		Math	Science	Social Studies	Other
		Reading	Writing				
AK	—	—	—	—	—	—	—
AL	✓	✓	✓	✓	✓	✓	—
AR	✓	✓	✓	✓	—	—	—
AZ	✓	✓	✓	✓	—	—	—
CA	✓	✓	✓	✓	✓	✓	—
CO	✓	✓	✓	✓	✓	—	—
CT	—	—	—	—	—	—	—
DC	—	—	—	—	—	—	—
DE	✓	✓	✓	✓	✓	✓	—
FL	✓	✓	✓	✓	—	—	—
GA	—	—	—	—	—	—	—
HI	✓	✓	✓	✓	—	—	—
IA	—	—	—	—	—	—	—
ID	—	—	—	—	—	—	—
IL	—	—	—	—	—	—	—
IN	✓	✓	✓	✓	—	—	✓
KS	✓	✓	—	—	—	—	—
KY	—	—	—	—	—	—	—
LA	✓	✓	✓	✓	✓	✓	—
MA	✓	—	✓	✓	✓	✓	—
MD	✓	✓	✓	✓	✓	✓	—
ME	✓	✓	✓	✓	✓	✓	✓
MI	✓	✓	✓	✓	✓	—	—
MN	✓	✓	✓	✓	—	—	—
MO	✓	✓	—	✓	—	✓	—

TABLE 1.8 *(continued)*

State	Policy Explicitly Addressed Content	ELA/Literature		Math	Science	Social Studies	Other
		Reading	Writing				
MS	✓	✓	✓	✓	✓	✓	—
MT	✓	✓	✓	✓	✓	✓	—
NC	✓	✓	✓	✓	✓	✓	✓
ND	✓	✓	✓	✓	✓	✓	—
NE	✓	—	✓	—	—	—	—
NH	✓	✓	✓	✓	✓	✓	—
NJ	—	—	—	—	—	—	—
NM	—	—	—	—	—	—	—
NV	✓	✓	✓	✓	✓	—	—
NY	✓	✓	✓	✓	✓	✓	—
OH	✓	✓	✓	✓	✓	✓	—
OK	✓	✓	✓	✓	—	—	—
OR	✓	✓	—	✓	✓	—	—
PA	✓	✓	✓	✓	—	—	—
RI	✓	✓	✓	✓	—	—	✓
SC	✓	—	—	✓	—	—	—
SD	—	—	—	—	—	—	—
TN	✓	✓	✓	✓	✓	✓	—
TX	✓	✓	✓	✓	✓	✓	—
UT	✓	✓	✓	✓	✓	✓	—
VA	—	—	—	—	—	—	—
VT	✓	✓	—	—	—	—	—
WA	✓	✓	✓	✓	✓	—	—
WI	✓	✓	—	—	—	—	—
WV	—	—	—	—	—	—	—
WY	✓	✓	✓	✓	—	—	—
Total	38	35	32	34	22	18	4

be emphasized that the policies of these 38 states were inconsistent in indicating the content areas for which particular accommodations were allowed or prohibited.

The policies of 37 states addressed at least one component of ELA—35 addressing reading and 32 addressing writing. Of these states, the policies of seven (Kansas, Massachusetts, Missouri, Nebraska, Oregon, Vermont, and Wisconsin) did not explicitly address both ELA components. Of these policies, those of five states (Kansas, Missouri, Oregon, Vermont, and Wisconsin) addressed only the reading component of ELA; the policies of Massachusetts and Nebraska addressed only the writing component.

Mathematics was addressed by a similarly high number of states (34). Often accommodations deemed appropriate for math were also considered appropriate for science; science was explicitly addressed in the policies of 22 states. Social studies was addressed by 18 states. Four states (Indiana, Maine, North Carolina, and Rhode Island) addressed the use of accommodations for other content areas. In addition to ELA and math, Indiana policy treated a test of cognitive skills as a content area. Maine policy addressed ELA, mathematics, science, and social studies as well as health and visual and performing arts. The policy of North Carolina addressed computer skills in addition to the four content areas. Rhode Island policy listed Rhode Island Health Education Assessment as a content area as well as ELA and math.

Because states' policies were not consistent in indicating the subject matter for which specific accommodations were allowed, the research team was unable to show directly which accommodations were allowed or prohibited for particular content areas. Instead, data on accommodations were coded according to whether accommodations were:

- Allowed for at least one content area (A).
- Prohibited for some content areas (PS).
- Prohibited for all content areas (PA).

This coding is used throughout this study when individual accommodations are analyzed in detail.

The coding does not transparently identify the content areas for which accommodations were available. First, the present coding does not allow for a distinction between states allowing a particular accommodation for all content areas and those states that allowed a particular accommodation for only one content area. Second, some overlap between those accommodations allowed for at least one content area (A) and prohibited for some content areas (PS) is inevitable. It can be assumed that a state's policy that prohibited an accommodation for some content areas (PS), allowed that accommodation on at least one content area (A). However, such determinations often required information beyond that provided by the policies themselves. As the goal of this study was to present only that information explicitly represented in the states' policies, the research team chose not to code implied references to the allowance or prohibition of accommodations for particular content areas.

Despite the limitations of this approach, the coding used throughout this study provides the clearest possible picture of the extent to which states' policies took content area into consideration when listing accommodations. It should be noted that, in general, it was found that accommodations prohibited in some content areas (PS) were prohibited for ELA but allowed for mathematics (and often for science).

Analysis of Individual Accommodations Found in States' Assessment Policies

As described in the previous section, state policy documents for school year 2000–2001 had as a primary point of reference students with disabilities, not ELLs. That over half (27) of the 47 states with policies addressing accommodations chose to use or adapt a classification system designed for students with disabilities is evidence of this tendency. Although the use of the traditional taxonomy has the potential to obscure differences between ELLs and students with disabilities, it was the only framework to have been adopted consistently in states' assessment policies. Therefore, analysis of state assessment policies must begin with an examination of data within this frame.

This section examines individual accommodations designated in states' policies. First, within the context of the traditional taxonomy responsive to students with disabilities, accommodations are examined regarding the extent to which they address the linguistic and sociocultural needs of ELLs. Second, an accommodations taxonomy developed by the research team as a tool to examine the accommodations cited in states' policies is presented. This taxonomy was designed to help focus on the unique needs of ELLs. Finally, the ELL-responsive accommodations framework is used to analyze accommodations found in states' assessment policies.

Accommodations Classified by Traditional Categories

A total of 75 individual accommodations intended to address ELLs were named in states' assessment policies. As indicated in Table 1.6, of the 47 states with assessment policies that addressed the accommodation of

ELLs, 27 (over half) organized the accommodations within the taxonomy traditionally used to classify accommodations for students with disabilities. Although not all states' policies used this schema for accommodations, because of its prevalence in states' policies—and in the absence of an alternative framework—the research team classified all accommodations within this framework. Table 1.9 presents the 75 accommodations according to the traditional, disabilities-based classification scheme: (a) timing and scheduling, (b) setting, (c) presentation, and (d) response. Two accommodations found in state policies could not be classified meaningfully within this taxonomy: "out of level testing" and "special test preparation."

Table 1.10 shows the distribution of the 75 accommodations, organized by the traditional taxonomy, across all states. As Table 1.10 illustrates, presentation accommodations were listed in the assessment policies of the greatest number of states—46. The two accommodation types adopted with the next highest frequency (by 42 states' policies) involved setting and timing or scheduling. Response accommodations were found in the policies of 34 states. The policies of 6 states supported the use of "other" accommodations (accommodations that did not fit into the traditional categories). The policies of 5 states (those of California, Delaware, Hawaii, North Carolina, and Vermont) addressed the use of out-of-level testing as an accommodation, and Utah policy addressed the use of special test preparation as an accommodation.

To determine the relevance to ELLs of each of the 75 accommodations identified in states' policies, accommodations were examined using the following general rule: Accommodations directly relevant to ELLs are those that provide the test taker with assistance in overcoming the linguistic and sociocultural barriers that prevent them from fully accessing the content of the test, whereas accommodations relevant to students with disabilities support physical or cognitive access to the content of the test. Hence, for instance, directions translated into a student's native language or the simplification of test items or test directions are considered to be directly relevant to ELLs, whereas the use of assistive listening devices or out-of-level testing is considered to address either physical or cognitive needs of students with disabilities. In some instances it was clear that certain accommodations commonly used for students with disabilities—such as increased test time or special test preparation—also could support ELLs' access of test content. These accommodations are discussed in greater detail in the next section.

Examination of the 75 accommodations identified in states' assessment policies revealed that 31 were designed explicitly to meet the needs of students with physical or cognitive disabilities and not the linguistic needs of ELLs. These accommodations were distributed across three traditional ac-

TABLE 1.9

Accommodations Designated for ELLs in States' Policies, Classified by Traditional Accommodation Categories

I. Timing/scheduling (n = 5)

1. Test time increased
2. Breaks provided during test sessions
3. Test schedule extended
4. Subtests flexibly scheduled
5. Test administered at time of day most beneficial to test taker

II. Setting (n = 17)

1. Test individually administered
2. Test administered in small group
3. Test administered in location with minimal distraction
4. Test administered in familiar room
5. Test taker tested in separate location (or carrel)
6. Test administered in ESL/bilingual classroom
7. Individual administration provided outside school (home, hospital, institution, etc.)
8. Test taker provided preferential seating
9. Increased or decreased opportunity for movement provided
10. Teacher faces test taker
11. Special/appropriate lighting provided
12. Adaptive or special furniture provided
13. Adaptive pencils provided
14. Adapted keyboards provided
15. Person familiar with test taker administers test
16. ESL/bilingual teacher administers test
17. Additional one-to-one support provided during test administration in general education classroom (e.g. instructional assistant, special test administrator, LEP staff, etc.)

III. Presentation (n = 35)

1. Directions repeated in English
2. Directions read aloud in English
3. Audiotaped directions provided in English

4. Key words or phrases in directions highlighted
5. Directions simplified
6. Audiotaped directions provided in native language
7. Directions translated into native language
8. Cues provided to help test taker remain on task
9. Directions explained/clarified in English
10. Directions explained/clarified in native language
11. Both oral and written directions in English provided
12. Written directions provided in native language
13. Oral directions provided in native language
14. Test items read aloud in English
15. Test items read aloud in simplified or sheltered English
16. Audiotaped test items provided in English
17. Audiotaped test items provided in native language
18. Test items read aloud in native language
19. Audiotaped test items provided in native language
20. Assistive listening devices, amplification, noise buffers, appropriate acoustics provided
21. Key words and phrases in test highlighted
22. Words on test clarified (e.g., words defined, explained)
23. Language reference materials (mono- or dual-language dictionaries or glossaries) provided
24. Enlarged print, magnifying equipment, Braille provided
25. Memory aids, fact charts, list of formulas, or research sheets provided
26. Templates, masks, or markers provided
27. Cues (e.g., arrows and stop signs) provided on answer form
28. Acetate shield for page provided
29. Colored stickers or highlighters for visual cues provided
30. Augmentative communication systems or strategies provided (e.g., letter boards, picture communication systems, voice output systems, electronic devices)
31. Simplified or sheltered English version of test provided
32. Side-by-side bilingual versions of test provided
33. Translated version of test provided

(continued)

TABLE 1.9 *(continued)*

34. Test interpreted for the deaf or hearing impaired or use of sign language provided

35. Electronic translator provided

IV. Response (n = 16)

1. Test taker marks answers in test booklet

2. Test administrator transfers test taker's answers

3. Test taker 's transferred responses checked for accurate marking

4. Copying assistance provided between drafts

5. Test taker types or uses a machine to respond (e.g.. typewriter, word processor, or computer)

6. Test taker indicates answers by pointing or other method

7. Papers secured to work area with tape or magnets

8. Mounting systems, slant boards, or easels provided to change position of paper, alter test taker 's position

9. Physical assistance provided

10. Enlarged answer sheets provided

11. Alternative writing systems provided (including portable writing devices, computers, and voice-activated technology)

12. Test taker verifies understanding of directions

13. Test taker dictates or uses a scribe to respond in English

14. Test taker responds on audiotape in English

15. Test taker responds in native language

16. Spelling assistance, spelling dictionaries, spell and grammar checker provided

V. Other (n = 2)

1. Out-of-level testing provided

2. Special test preparation provided

Note. $N = 75$ accommodations.

TABLE 1.10

**States with Policies Addressing Accommodations, Organized
by Traditional Categories**

State	Timing or Scheduling	Setting	Presentation	Response	Other
AK	—	—	—		—
AL	✓	✓	✓	✓	—
AR	✓	✓	✓	—	—
AZ	✓	✓	✓	✓	—
CA	✓	✓	✓	✓	✓
CO	✓	✓	✓	✓	—
CT	✓	✓	✓	—	—
DC	✓	✓	✓	—	—
DE	✓	✓	✓	✓	✓
FL	✓	✓	✓	✓	—
GA	—	—	—	—	—
HI	✓	✓	✓	✓	✓
IA	—	—	—	—	—
ID	—	—	—	—	—
IL	—	—	—	—	—
IN	✓	✓	✓	✓	—
KS	✓	✓	✓	—	—
KY	—	✓	✓	✓	—
LA	✓	✓	✓	—	—
MA	—	—	✓	✓	—
MD	✓	✓	✓	✓	—
ME	✓	✓	✓	✓	—
MI	✓	—	✓	—	—
MN	✓	✓	✓	✓	—
MO	✓	✓	✓	✓	—
MS	✓	✓	✓	✓	—

(*continued*)

43

TABLE 1.10 *(continued)*

State	Timing or Scheduling	Setting	Presentation	Response	Other
MT	✓	✓	✓	✓	—
NC	✓	✓	✓	✓	✓
ND	✓	✓	✓	✓	—
NE	✓	✓	✓	✓	—
NH	✓	✓	✓	✓	—
NJ	✓	✓	✓	—	—
NM	—	—	✓	—	—
NV	✓	✓	✓	✓	—
NY	✓	✓	✓	✓	—
OH	✓	—	✓	—	—
OK	✓	✓	✓	✓	—
OR	✓	✓	✓	✓	—
PA	✓	✓	✓	✓	—
RI	✓	✓	✓	✓	—
SC	✓	✓	✓	—	—
SD	✓	✓	✓	✓	—
TN	✓	✓	✓	✓	—
TX	—	✓	✓	✓	—
UT	✓	✓	✓	✓	✓
VA	✓	✓	✓	✓	—
VT	✓	✓	✓	✓	✓
WA	✓	✓	✓	✓	—
WI	✓	✓	✓	—	—
WV	✓	✓	✓	—	—
WY	✓	✓	✓	✓	—
Total	42	42	46	34	6

commodation categories. The remaining 44 accommodations were relevant either exclusively to ELLs or to both ELLs and students with disabilities. As shown in Fig. 1.2, 6 of 17 setting accommodations, 11 of 35 presentation accommodations, and 13 of 16 response accommodations addressed the needs of students with disabilities exclusively. However, it should be noted that the research team found all timing and scheduling accommodations to be potentially appropriate for use with ELLs (five of five accommodations).

Among the other types of accommodations there was a range in the number of accommodations that could address the needs of ELLs: 11 of 17 setting, 24 of 35 presentation, and 3 of 16 response accommodations. Two accommodations—listed in Fig. 1.2 as "other"—did not fit into the traditional taxonomy. These were out-of-level testing and special test preparation. Out-of-level testing is relevant only to students with disabilities, whereas special test preparation relevant to ELLs.

In summary, as these data show, although a large majority of states' assessment policies listed setting, presentation, and response accommodations for ELLs, 44 of the 75 accommodations, or 59%, were responsive to ELLs or to both ELLs and students with disabilities. The remaining 31, or 41%, were found to address the assessment needs of students with disabilities exclusively. Table 1.11 lists the accommodations judged to be appropriate only for students with disabilities.

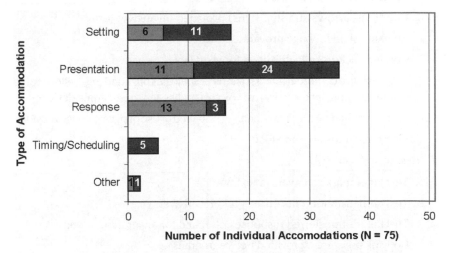

FIG. 1.2. Number of accommodations addressing the needs of students with disabilities (SDs) exclusively versus number of accommodations addressing the needs of ELLs and SDs.

TABLE 1.11

Accommodations Responsive Exclusively to Students With Disabilities in States' Policies

I. Timing or Scheduling (0 of 5)

II. Setting (6 of 17)

1. Individual administration provided outside school (home, hospital, institution, etc.)
2. Increased or decreased opportunity for movement provided
3. Special or appropriate lighting provided
4. Adaptive or special furniture provided
5. Adaptive pencils provided
6. Adapted keyboards provided

III. Presentation (11 of 35)

1. Cues provided to help test taker remain on task
2. Assistive listening devices, amplification, noise buffers, appropriate acoustics provided
3. Enlarged print, magnifying equipment, Braille provided
4. Memory aids, fact charts, list of formulas, or research sheets provided
5. Templates, masks, or markers provided
6. Cues (e.g., arrows and stop signs) provided on answer form
7. Acetate shield for page provided
8. Colored stickers or highlighters for visual cues provided
9. Augmentative communication systems or strategies provided (e.g., letter boards, picture communication systems, voice output systems, electronic devices)
10. Test interpreted for the deaf or hearing impaired or use of sign language provided
11. Electronic translator provided

IV. Response (13 of 16)

1. Test taker marks answers in test booklet
2. Test administrator transfers test taker's answers
3. Test taker's transferred responses checked for accurate marking
4. Copying assistance provided between drafts
5. Test taker types or uses a machine to respond (e.g., typewriter, word processor, or computer)
6. Test taker indicates answers by pointing or other method

7. Papers secured to work area with tape or magnets

8. Mounting systems, slant boards, or easels provided to change position of paper, alter test taker's position

9. Physical assistance provided

10. Enlarged answer sheets provided

11. Alternative writing systems provided (including portable writing devices, computers and voice-activated technology)

12. Test taker dictates or uses a scribe to respond in English

13. Test taker responds on audiotape in English

V. Other (1 of 2)

1. Out-of-level testing provided

Note. $n = 31$ of 75 total accommodations.

Because the traditional taxonomy does not focus attention on accommodations appropriate for ELLs, the research team created a new, ELL-responsive taxonomy that takes into account ELLs' linguistic and sociocultural needs. This new taxonomy was used to classify the accommodations judged to be potentially ELL responsive.

New Taxonomy for Classifying Accommodations for ELLs

As an initial step in building a taxonomy for classifying accommodations for ELLs, the research team reviewed the classification of accommodations used for the 1998–1999 study of state assessment policies for ELLs (Rivera et al., 2000). In this study, Rivera et al. (2000) identified accommodations appropriate for ELLs and classified these as linguistic accommodations in both English and ELLs' native languages. All other accommodations, including those designed for students with disabilities, were classified as nonlinguistic. For the 1998–1999 study, 16 of 37 accommodations found in state policies were classified as linguistic. The remaining accommodations were classified as nonlinguistic.

In addition, the research team examined second language acquisition research for insight into additional approaches that might offer ELLs access to the language of the assessment. This research provided additional support to the strategies used for linguistic support accommodations. It also revealed that many accommodations classified as nonlinguistic for the 1998–1999 study, even those commonly used for students with disabilities, could also potentially provide indirect linguistic support to ELLs during assessment.

These perspectives enabled the development of a new accommodations taxonomy that accounts for both direct linguistic support accommodations and indirect linguistic support accommodations. Accommodations providing *direct linguistic support* involve adjustments to the language of the test. Such accommodations can be provided in the student's native language or in English. These accommodations include, for example, providing a version of the test translated into the student's native language or clarifying the (English) language of the test items, directions, or both. These types of accommodations are intended to allow testing of the test construct rather than testing of the student's knowledge of English.

Because students in the process of learning English as a second language might have greater linguistic demands placed on them in the testing situation than do their native English-speaking peers, ELLs might need additional forms of support to allow them to demonstrate their true knowledge of the content being assessed. *Indirect linguistic support accommodations* provide this support to ELLs by adjusting the conditions under which they take an assessment. Such accommodations are designed to help ELLs process language more easily, but they are not direct modifications of the language of the test. Hence, indirect linguistic support accommodations include such considerations as increasing the time during which a student is allowed to take an assessment or allowing an ELL to take a test in a familiar room. Table 1.12 provides a complete list of direct and indirect linguistic support accommodations specified in states' policies. Of the 75 accommodations found in states' assessment policies, 44 were deemed to address the needs of ELLs exclusively or to support both ELLs and students with disabilities. The remaining 31 accommodations addressed solely the needs of students with disabilities. Of the 44 ELL-responsive accommodations, the research team identified 27 direct linguistic support accommodations and 17 indirect linguistic support accommodations.

Figure 1.3 illustrates the number of accommodations designated for ELLs in states' assessment policies according to their relevance to ELLs. The analysis of states' assessment policies from the perspective of the ELL-responsive taxonomy provides insight into the extent to which states' policies provide guidance in the use of test accommodations for ELLs.

In the remainder of this section the 44 accommodations identified in states' assessment policies for school year 2000–2001—27 direct linguistic support accommodations and 17 indirect linguistic support accommodations—are examined in the context of the ELL-responsive taxonomy. Data are summarized according to frequency with which states addressed particular accommodations for specific content areas.

TABLE 1.12

ELL-Responsive Accommodations Found in States' Policies

Direct Linguistic Support[a]

1. Directions translated into native language
2. Audiotaped directions provided in native language
3. Written directions provided in native language
4. Oral directions provided in native language
5. Directions explained or clarified in native language
6. Test items read aloud in native language
7. Audiotaped test items provided in native language
8. Language reference materials (mono- or dual-language dictionaries or glossaries) provided
9. Side-by-side bilingual versions of the test provided
10. Translated version of test directions and/or items provided
11. Oral response in native language translated into English
12. Written response in native language translated into English
13. Directions simplified
14. Key words or phrases in directions highlighted
15. Test items read aloud in simplified or sheltered English
16. Key words and phrases in test highlighted
17. Simplified or sheltered English version of test provided
18. Directions read aloud in English
19. Directions repeated in English
20. Audiotaped directions provided in English
21. Both oral and written directions in English provided
22. Test items read aloud in English
23. Audiotaped test items provided in English
24. Directions explained or clarified in English
25. Test taker verifies understanding of directions
26. Words on test clarified (e.g., words defined, explained)
27. Spelling assistance, spelling dictionaries, spell or grammar checker

(continued)

TABLE 1.12 *(continued)*

Indirect Linguistic Support[b]

1. Test time increased

2. Test schedule extended

3. Subtests flexibly scheduled

4. Test administered at time of day most beneficial to test taker

5. Breaks during test sessions

6. Test individually administered

7. Test administered in small group

8. Teacher faces test taker

9. Test administered in location with minimal distraction

10. Test taker provided preferential seating

11. Test taker tested in separate location (or carrel)

12. Special test preparation provided

13. Person familiar to test taker administers test

14. ESL or bilingual teacher administers the test

15. Additional one-to-one support during test administration in general education classroom (e.g., instructional assistant, special test administrator, LEP staff, etc.)

16. Test administered in familiar room

17. Test administered in ESL or bilingual classroom

Note. $N = 44$ of 75 accommodations.
[a]$n = 27$ accommodations. [b]$n = 17$ accommodations.

Accommodations Providing Direct Linguistic Support. As discussed in the review of literature, second language acquisition research shows that during an assessment, ELLs are sometimes overwhelmed with linguistic input in a nonnative language, which they may receive faster than they are able to process effectively. Direct linguistic support accommodations are intended to provide ELLs linguistic support that mitigates the language demands placed on them during assessment. At the same time, these accommodations must preserve the validity of the test by ensuring that the construct being tested remains unaltered. In other words, linguistic accommodations are not intended to give ELLs support on how to respond to test items correctly.

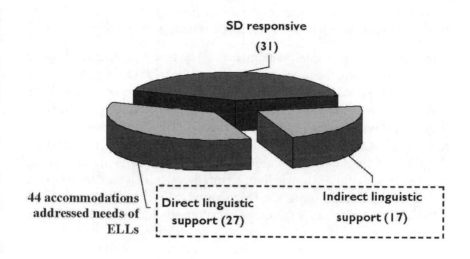

FIG. 1.3.   Accommodations found in states' policies addressing the unique needs of ELLs versus those of students with disabilities (SDs).

Direct linguistic support accommodations support ELLs by providing modified input in the native language or in English. Native language accommodations involve (a) written translation of parts or all of the test, (b) oral translation from a prepared script, (c) sight translation (i.e., oral translation by an on-site translator), or (d) allowing the student to respond in his or her native language. English language accommodations involve (a) the simplification of some or all aspects of the test language, (b) repetition of the test language, or (c) clarification of parts of the test language.

It is important to keep in mind that states' policies provided different levels of detail in addressing accommodations. Therefore, accommodations organized under the ELL-responsive taxonomy (see Table 1.10) might overlap in purpose. This means that some accommodations listed separately might in practice be identical. Three accommodations involving test directions are a case in point: (a) reading aloud of test directions, (b) repeating test directions, and (c) providing both oral and written directions. In most cases states' policies did not make clear whether or not directions read aloud were also intended to be presented in written form, making it difficult to distinguish these three options. If directions read aloud were also presented in writing, then all three would be identical. Unfortunately, because there is no information on practice it is not always possible to identify which accommodations listed in states' policies serve the same purpose. In the interest of accuracy, the wording of the states' policies in which these accommodations appeared has been preserved where possible.

Native Language Accommodations.   The fewer English language resources an ELL has, the more difficulty he or she might have comprehending the language of the test. With test directions, test items, or both in the student's native language, ELLs who have limited linguistic resources in English and who have been taught in their native language are given linguistic access to the tasks on which they are being assessed. Native language accommodations are intended to provide direct linguistic support to ELLs through written translation, scripted oral translation, sight translation, and by permitting the student to respond in his or her native language. Table 1.13 classifies native language accommodations specified in states' policies.

Some form of native language accommodation was addressed in the policies of 35 states. Figure 1.4 provides an overview of how these states' policies addressed the four different kinds of native language accommodation from the perspective of content area (i.e., subject matter tested.) As

TABLE 1.13
Native Language Accommodations Found in States' Policies

Written translation

1. Written directions provided
2. Side-by-side dual language versions of the test provided
3. Translated test provided

Scripted oral translation

4. Oral directions in native language
5. Audiotaped directions provided in native language
6. Audiotaped test items provided in native language

Sight translation

7. Directions translated into native language
8. Directions explained or clarified in native language
9. Test items read aloud in native language
10. Interpreter or sight translator provided

Student response

11. Student responds in native language

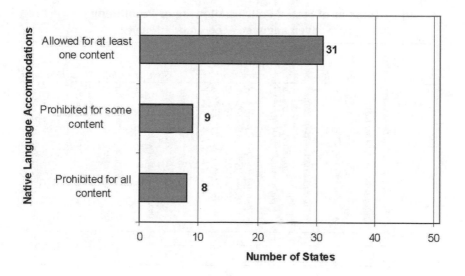

FIG. 1.4. Overview of accommodations in native language allowcd or prohibited by states' policies.

Fig. 1.4 shows, the policies of 31 states allowed at least one native language accommodation for at least one content area; 9 states prohibited at least one of these accommodations for some content areas; and 8 prohibited at least one native language accommodation for all content areas. In most cases, native language accommodations prohibited for some content areas were prohibited for ELA but allowed for mathematics (and often for science). This finding might highlight a concern among state policymakers that native language accommodations are more likely to affect the validity of ELA assessments than they are to affect the validity of mathematics or science assessments.

Table 1.14 provides a breakdown of native language accommodation by state, showing the number of states with policies allowing four different types of native language accommodations: written translation, scripted oral translation, sight translation, and student response in native language. Specific accommodations under each category are identified as allowing written translation accommodations for at least one content area (A), prohibiting written accommodations for some content areas (PS), and prohibiting written language accommodations for all content areas (PA). Content areas for which accommodations were allowed or prohibited were not addressed with consistency in states' policies and therefore are not represented directly in the data.

TABLE 1.14

Number of States' Policies Allowing or Prohibiting Native Language Accommodations

State	Policy Addressed Native Language Accommodation	Written Translation			Scripted Oral Translation			Sight Translation				Response
		Written Directions Provided	Side-by-Side Dual-Language Versions of the Test Provided	Translated Version of the Test Provided	Oral Directions Provided in Native Language	Audiotaped Test Directions Provided in Native Language	Audiotaped Test Items Provided in Native Language	Directions Translated Into Native Language	Directions Explained or Clarified in Native Language	Test Items Read Aloud in Native Language	Interpreter or Sight Translator Provided	Student Responds in Native Language
AK	—	—	—	—	—	—	—	—	—	—	—	—
AL	✓	—	—	—	—	—	—	A	—	PA	A	—
AR	—	—	—	—	—	—	—	—	—	—	—	—
AZ	✓	—	—	A	—	—	—	A	—	A	PS	A
CA	✓	—	—	—	—	A	—	A	A	—	—	—
CO	✓	—	—	A	—	—	—	A	PA	—	—	A
CT	✓	—	—	—	—	—	—	A	A	PS	—	—
DC	✓	—	—	—	—	—	—	—	—	A	—	—
DE	✓	—	A	A	—	A	—	A	A	A	A	A
FL	✓	—	—	—	—	—	—	A	A	—	A	—
GA	—	—	—	—	—	—	—	—	—	—	—	—
HI	—	—	—	—	—	—	—	—	—	—	—	—
IA	—	—	—	—	—	—	—	—	—	—	—	—
ID	—	—	—	—	—	—	—	—	—	—	—	—
IL	—	—	—	—	—	—	—	—	—	—	—	—
IN	✓	—	—	PA	—	—	—	PA	—	PA	PA	PA
KS	✓	—	—	—	—	A	—	A	—	—	A	—
KY	✓	—	—	—	—	—	—	A	A	A	—	—
LA	—	—	—	—	—	—	—	—	—	—	—	—
MA	✓	—	—	A	—	—	—	—	—	—	—	A
MD	—	—	—	—	—	—	—	—	—	—	—	—
ME	✓	—	—	A	—	—	—	A	—	A	A	—
MI	—	—	—	—	—	—	—	—	—	—	—	—

MN	✓	A	A	—	A	A	A	A	—	—	—	—
MO	—	—	—	—	—	—	—	—	—	—	—	—
MS	—	—	—	—	—	—	—	—	—	—	—	—
MT	✓	—	—	—	—	—	—	A	A	PS	A	—
NC	✓	—	—	—	—	A	—	PA	PA	PA	PA	—
ND	—	—	—	—	—	—	—	—	—	—	—	—
NE	✓	—	—	A	—	—	—	A	—	—	—	—
NH	✓	—	—	—	—	—	—	A	—	A	A	—
NJ	✓	—	—	—	—	—	—	PS	—	PA	—	—
NM	✓	—	—	PS	—	—	—	—	—	—	—	—
NV	—	—	—	—	—	—	—	—	—	—	—	—
NY	✓	—	—	A	—	—	—	A	—	A	PS	A
OH	✓	—	—	—	—	—	—	—	A	A	A	—
OK	✓	—	—	—	—	—	—	A	A	PS	—	—
OR	✓	—	A	—	A	—	—	A	—	—	—	A
PA	✓	A	—	—	A	—	—	A	—	—	—	—
RI	✓	—	—	PS	—	PS	—	A	—	A	—	—
SC	✓	—	—	—	—	—	—	A	A	—	—	—
SD	✓	—	—	A	—	A	—	A	—	A	A	A
TN	—	—	—	—	—	—	—	—	—	—	—	—
TX	✓	—	—	A	—	—	—	A	—	PA	—	—
UT	✓	—	—	A	—	A	—	A	A	PS	—	A
VA	—	—	—	—	—	—	—	—	—	—	—	—
VT	✓	—	—	A	—	—	—	—	—	A	—	—
WA	✓	—	—	—	—	A	—	A	—	PA	—	—
WI	✓	—	—	—	—	—	—	A	—	A	A	—
WV	✓	—	—	PA	—	—	—	—	—	—	—	—
WY	✓	—	—	A	—	—	—	A	—	A	—	—
Total A		2	3	12	3	8	1	26	10	13	10	8
Total PS		0	0	2	0	1	0	1	0	4	2	0
Total PA		0	0	2	0	0	0	2	2	6	2	1
Total states	35	2	3	16	3	9	1	29	12	23	14	9

Note. A = allowed; PS = prohibited sometimes; PA = prohibited always.

Written Translation.   Accommodations involving written translation included the provision of the following:

*   Written directions.
*   Side-by-side dual-language versions of the test.
*   A translated version of the test.

Written translation accommodations can be provided for students for part or all of the test. Of particular interest is the provision of complete translations of state assessments, either in the native language only or in an English and native language format.

The policies of 19 states addressed the use of written translation. As shown in Fig. 1.5, of these states' policies, 15 allowed at least one written translation accommodation for at least one content area, 2 prohibited at least one of these accommodations for some content areas, and 2 prohibited at least one written language accommodation for all content areas.

Working from data in Table 1.14, it can be seen that a number of states (18) addressed translation of complete assessments (see columns 2 and 3 under Written Translation). Sixteen addressed the use of single-language test translation, and three addressed the use of side-by-side, dual-language versions of the test. Of the former states' policies, 12 allowed test

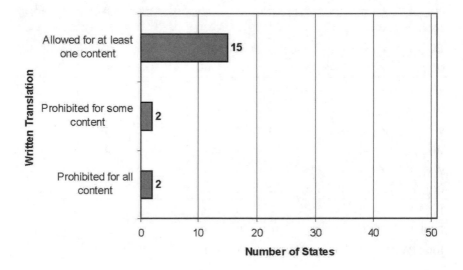

FIG. 1.5.   Overview of accommodations in native language involving written translation allowed or prohibited in states' policies.

translation for at least one content area; 2 (New Mexico's and Rhode Island's) prohibited test translation for some content areas. The use of dual-language tests was allowed for at least one content area by the policies of three states (Delaware, Minnesota, and Oregon). Delaware policy was unique in supporting the use of both types of test translation (mono- and dual-language), which were listed as separate accommodations: ELLs could be administered "two side-by-side written tests at the same time, one version in native language (Spanish version only) and the second in English," or a "written test in Spanish." Delaware policy did not make clear the conditions under which a monolingual as opposed to a dual-language test was to be administered.

Spanish was by far the most common non-English language cited in states' policies. Most states' policies indicated that this was the only language for which translation was available. However, some states offered tests in other languages. For example, New York offered tests in five languages (Chinese, Haitian, Korean, Russian, and Spanish) and Minnesota in four languages (Hmong, Somali, Vietnamese, and Spanish). However, this variety was the exception rather than the rule; most states' policies simply allowed for translation of an assessment into Spanish. Maine's policy was unclear with regard to language of test translation, simply indicating that tests were to be "done by local personnel."

Scripted Oral Translation.   The use of scripted oral translation of test directions, items, or both were addressed in the policies of 11 states. Accommodations found in states' policies involving scripted oral translation included the provision of the following:

- Oral directions in native language.
- Audiotaped test directions in native language.
- Audiotaped test items in native language.

As shown in Fig. 1.6, of these states' policies, 10 allowed scripted oral translation for at least one content area, Rhode Island prohibited at least one native language accommodation for some content areas, and no state policy prohibited scripted oral translation for all content areas.

Table 1.14 shows that the policies of three states allowed the oral delivery of directions. The policies of eight states allowed the use of audiotaped translation of directions for at least one content area. Rhode Island's policy prohibited this accommodation for some content areas. Minnesota's policy allowed the use of scripted oral translation of test items for at least one content area.

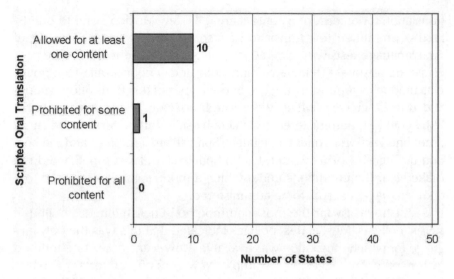

FIG. 1.6.   Overview of accommodations in native language involving scripted oral translation allowed or prohibited by states' policies.

Sight Translation.   A number of native language accommodations listed in states' policies either directly involved or implied the use of sight translation, the oral, on-site rendering of test directions, items, or both from English into a student's native language. Four accommodations are included in the category of sight translation:

- Directions translated into native language.
- Directions explained or clarified in the native language.
- Test items read aloud in native language.
- Interpreter or sight translator provided.

The first three of these accommodations denote an activity: explain or clarify, translate, and read aloud. The fourth accommodation refers to the individual who will perform the task of sight translation. Criteria for selecting an interpreter or sight translator were left unclear in many states' policies, as was the precise role of this individual (see Study 2).

The policies of 32 states addressed the use of sight translation. As shown in Fig. 1.7, of these states' policies, 29 allowed at least one sight translation accommodation for at least one content area, 7 prohibited at least one of these accommodations for some content areas, 7 prohibited at least one sight translation accommodation for all content areas.

Of those accommodations involving sight translation, the translation of directions into the student's native language was cited most frequently in states' policies. The translation of directions was allowed for at least one content area by 26 states' policies. As shown in Table 1.14, translation of directions was prohibited for some content areas by New Jersey policy and prohibited for all content areas by the policies of Indiana and North Carolina. Fourteen states specifically listed the participation of an interpreter or sight translator during assessment as an accommodation: Ten states allowed this individual to participate in assessment for at least one content area. Two states' policies (Arizona's and New York's) prohibited presence of a sight translator for some content areas, and two states' policies (Indiana's and North Carolina's) prohibited the participation of this individual for all content areas.

Student Responds in Native Language. Some states' policies indicated that an eligible ELL would be able to respond to test items in his or her native language. This accommodation involves students' producing written or oral responses in their native language. It should be noted that states' policies were not always clear about how students' responses were to be scored. In some cases, it was indicated that responses were to be translated into English prior to scoring; in other cases it was indicated that the written response was to be scored in the student's native language.

Nine states addressed the use of this accommodation. As Table 1.14 shows, the policies of eight states allowed this accommodation for at least one content area. Indiana's policy prohibited it for all content areas.

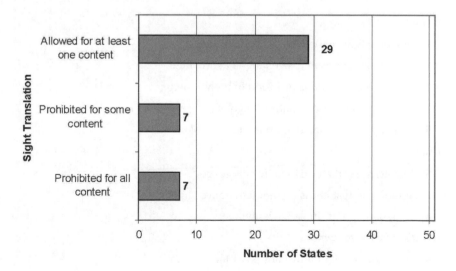

FIG. 1.7.   Overview of accommodations in native language involving sight translation allowed or prohibited by states' policies.

Different Parts of Tests for Which the Use of Native Language Accommodations Were Addressed.   The policies of the 42 states that addressed native language accommodations often specified the parts of the test—test directions, items, or both—for which native language accommodations were to be made available. Table 1.15 lists native language accommodations according to the part of the test to which the accommodation was considered relevant in states' policies.

English Language Accommodations.   Many of the accommodations found in states' policies provided linguistic support to ELLs in English and were classified by the research team as English language accommodations. The classification of these accommodations is based on second language acquisition research. English language accommodations can be understood as employing the following strategies: (a) simplification of some or all aspects of the test language, (b) repetition of the test language, or (c) clarification of parts of the test language. Table 1.16 organizes English language accommodations specified in states' policies according to these strategies.

TABLE 1.15
Parts of Test for Which Native Language Accommodations
Were Addressed

Test directions

1. Oral directions in native language provided

2. Written directions in native language provided

3. Audiotaped directions provided in native language

4. Directions provided in native language

5. Directions explained or clarified in native language

Test items

6. Test items read aloud in native language

7. Audiotaped test items provided in native language

8. Student responds in native language

Test directions and items

9. Interpreter or sight translator provided

10. Side-by-side bilingual versions of the test provided

11. Translated version of test provided

TABLE 1.16

English Language Accommodations Found in States' Policies

Simplification

1. Directions simplified
2. Items read aloud in simplified or sheltered English
3. Simplified or sheltered English version of test provided

Repetition

4. Directions read aloud in English
5. Directions repeated in English
6. Audiotaped directions provided in English
7. Both oral and written directions provided in English
8. Key words or phrases in directions highlighted
9. Items read aloud in English
10. Audiotaped test items provided in English
11. Key words and phrases in test highlighted

Clarification

12. Directions explained or clarified in English
13. Words on test clarified (e.g., words defined, explained)
14. Language reference materials (mono- or dual-language dictionaries or glossaries) provided
15. Spelling assistance, spelling dictionaries, and spell or grammar checker
16. Test taker verifies understanding of directions

Accommodations providing direct linguistic support in English were found in the policies of 44 states. Figure 1.8 provides an overview of how these states' policies addressed the four different kinds of English language accommodations from the perspective of content area. As Fig. 1.8 shows, the policies of 38 states allowed at least one English language accommodation for at least one content area, 28 states prohibited at least one of these accommodations for some content areas, and 7 prohibited at least one English language accommodation for all content areas. As was the case for native language accommodations, in most instances, accommodations prohibited for some content areas were prohibited for ELA but allowed for math (and often for science).

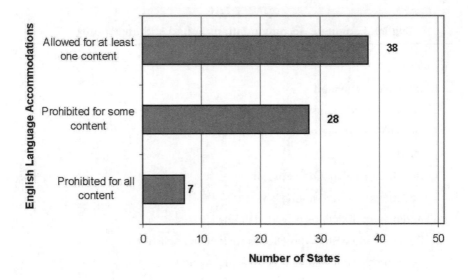

FIG. 1.8.   Overview of accommodations in English allowed or prohibited by states' policies.

Table 1.17 provides a breakdown of the number of states with policies allowing test simplification accommodations for at least one content area (A), prohibiting these accommodations for some content areas (PS), and prohibiting linguistic simplification accommodations for all content areas (PA). Content areas for which accommodations were allowed or prohibited were not addressed with consistency in states' policies and therefore are not represented directly in the table.

Linguistic Simplification.   Simplifying the language of test directions and items can help make the test more accessible to ELLs in the process of developing English language proficiency. Accommodations involving simplification found in states' policies included the following:

- Directions simplified.
- Items read aloud in simplified or sheltered English.
- Simplified or sheltered English version of test provided.

Simplification accommodations identified in states' policies were provided in oral and written formats, although which of these formats were meant to be used was not always made clear. Accommodations were designed to support students' comprehension of directions, items, or both.

TABLE 1.17

Number of States' Policies Allowing or Prohibiting Accommodations Involving Simplification of Text

State	Policy Addressed Simplification	Directions Simplified	Items Read Aloud in Simplified or Sheltered English	Simplified or Sheltered Version of Test Provided
AK	—	—	—	—
AL	—	—	—	—
AR	—	—	—	—
AZ	✓	A	—	—
CA	✓	A	—	—
CO	✓	PA	—	—
CT	—	—	—	—
DC	✓	A	—	—
DE	✓	A	A	—
FL	—	—	—	—
GA	—	—	—	—
HI	—	—	—	—
IA	—	—	—	—
ID	—	—	—	—
IL	—	—	—	—
IN	✓	PA	—	—
KS	✓	—	—	A
KY	—	—	—	—
LA	—	—	—	—
MA	—	—	—	—
MD	—	—	—	—
ME	✓	—	A	—
MI	—	—	—	—
MN	—	—	—	—
MO	—	—	—	—
MS	—	—	—	—
MT	—	—	—	—
NC	✓	PA	—	—

(continued)

TABLE 1.17 *(continued)*

State	Policy Addressed Simplification	Directions Simplified	Items Read Aloud in Simplified or Sheltered English	Simplified or Sheltered Version of Test Provided
ND	—	—	—	—
NE	✓	A	—	A
NH	—	—	—	—
NJ	—	—	—	—
NM	—	—	—	—
NV	—	—	—	—
NY	—	—	—	—
OH	✓	A	—	—
OK	—	—	—	—
OR	✓	A	—	—
PA	✓	A	—	—
RI	✓	A	—	—
SC	✓	A	—	—
SD	✓	A	—	—
TN	—	—	—	—
TX	—	—	—	—
UT	✓	A	—	—
VA	✓	A	—	—
VT	—	—	—	—
WA	—	—	—	—
WI	—	—	—	—
WV	✓	A	—	—
WY	—	—	—	—
Total A		14	2	2
Total PS		0	0	0
Total PA		3	0	0
Total states	19	17	2	2

Note. A = allowed; PS = prohibited sometimes; PA = prohibited always.

The policies of 19 states addressed the use of simplification of test directions and items. As shown in Fig. 1.9, of these states' policies, 16 allowed simplification for at least one content area tested. The policies of three states—Colorado, Indiana, and North Carolina—prohibited at least one simplification accommodation for all content areas. No state's policy prohibited the use of simplification for only some content areas.

The most frequently cited simplification accommodation was "directions simplified." Fourteen states' policies indicated specifically that simplification of test directions would be allowed for at least one content area, whereas the policies of three states (Colorado, Indiana, and North Carolina) prohibited this accommodation for all content areas. Two states, Delaware and Maine, addressed the simplification of test items: Both states allowed test items to be read aloud in simplified or sheltered English for at least one content area. Two states, Kansas and Nebraska, allowed the use of a version of the test in simplified or sheltered English for at least one content area.

Repetition. Many states' policies adopted strategies to support ELLs that involved some form of repetition. The purpose of repetition is to give the student an extra opportunity to process the language of the test. Accommodations involving repetition found in states' policies can be divided

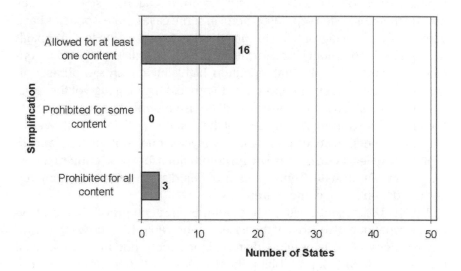

FIG. 1.9. Overview of accommodations involving simplification allowed or prohibited by states' policies.

into three groups: oral, in-person repetition; audiotaped repetition; and highlighting text. These groups include the following accommodations:

Oral, in-person repetition

- Directions read aloud in English.
- Items read aloud in English.
- Directions repeated in English.
- Both oral and written directions provided in English.

Audiotaped repetition

- Audiotaped directions provided in English.
- Audiotaped test items provided in English.

Highlighting text

- Key words or phrases in directions highlighted.
- Key words and phrases in test highlighted.

Most commonly, repetition is delivered orally, in person. Some accommodations listed in this category are very similar. For instance, reading aloud directions in English is, in practice, likely the same as repeating directions in English or providing both oral and written directions. Although distinctions among these accommodations were unclear, these forms of repetition were often listed as separate accommodations in states' policies and are therefore listed separately here. In some cases, states' policies have allowed the use of highlighting to call attention to parts of the test. Although highlighting is commonly used for students with disabilities, it is also potentially useful for ELLs. Like oral repetition, highlighting words or phrases allows the student an extra opportunity to process the language of the test.

The policies of 38 states addressed the use of repetition accommodations for ELLs. As shown in Fig. 1.10, of these states' policies, 32 allowed at least one repetition accommodation for at least one content area, and 23 prohibited at least one of these accommodations for some content areas. The policy of one state, Tennessee, prohibited at least one repetition accommodation for all content areas.

Table 1.18 lists states with policies addressing accommodations involving the repetition of the text of the assessment. Table 1.18 shows the number of states with policies allowing repetition accommodations for at least one content area (A), prohibiting these accommodations for some content areas (PS), and prohibiting repetition for all content areas (PA). Content areas for which accommodations were allowed or prohibited were

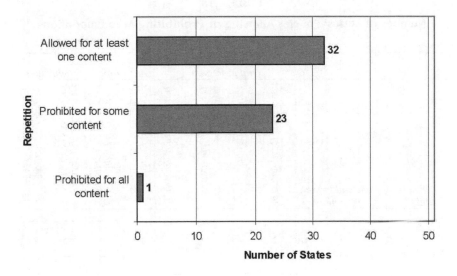

FIG. 1.10. Overview of accommodations involving repetition allowed or prohibited by states' policies.

not addressed with consistency in states' policies and therefore are not represented directly in the data.

As shown in Table 1.18, the oral, in-person delivery of accommodations involving repetition was addressed with the greatest frequency in states' policies. Working from the data in Table 1.18, it can be seen that the policies of 38 states addressed the oral, in-person repetition of test directions, items, or both. The policies of 29 states allowed at least one of these accommodations for one or more content areas, and 22 states' policies prohibited at least one of these accommodations for some content areas. The policy of only one state, Tennessee, prohibited oral, in-person repetition for all content areas.

Of oral, in-person repetition accommodations, the reading aloud of test directions in English was allowed by the policies of the greatest number of states (22). Similarly, the policies of 19 states allowed directions to be repeated in English, and 5 states allowed the use of both oral and written directions. States' policies were much less likely to allow the repetition of test items, however. The policies of 9 states allowed the reading aloud of test items, whereas 22 states' policies explicitly prohibited this accommodation for some content areas.

The policies of 11 states addressed the use of audiotaped directions or items. Nine states' policies allowed the use of audiotaped test directions, and 3 states' policies (those of California, Delaware, and Minnesota) permitted

TABLE 1.18

Number of States' Policies Allowing or Prohibiting Accommodations Involving Repetition of Text

State	Policy addressed repetition	Oral In-Person				Audiotaped		Highlighted	
		Directions Read Aloud in English	Items Read Aloud in English	Directions Repeated in English	Both Oral and Written Directions Provided	Audiotaped Directions Provided in English	Audiotaped Test Items Provided in English	Key Words or Phrases in Directions Highlighted	Key Words and Phrases in Test Highlighted
AK	—	—	—	—	—	—	—	—	—
AL	✓	PS	PS	—	—	—	—	—	—
AR	—	—	—	—	—	—	—	—	—
AZ	✓	—	—	A	—	—	—	—	—
CA	✓	A	A	A	—	A	A	A	A
CO	✓	A	PS	A	—	—	—	PA	PA
CT	✓	A	—	—	—	—	—	—	—
DC	✓	—	A	A	—	—	—	—	—
DE	✓	—	A	—	—	A	A	—	—
FL	✓	—	PS	—	—	—	—	—	—
GA	—	—	—	—	—	—	—	—	—
HI	✓	—	PS	—	—	—	—	—	—
IA	—	—	—	—	—	—	—	—	—
ID	—	—	—	—	—	—	—	—	—
IL	—	—	—	—	—	—	—	—	—
IN	✓	A	PS	—	—	—	—	—	—
KS	✓	—	PS	—	—	A	—	—	—
KY	✓	A	A	—	—	—	—	—	—
LA	✓	PS	PS	A	—	—	—	—	—
MA	—	—	—	—	—	—	—	—	—
MD	✓	PS	PS	A	A	A	PS	—	—
ME	✓	A	A	—	A	—	—	—	—
MI	—	—	—	—	—	—	—	—	—
MN	✓	—	—	A	A	A	A	—	—
MO	✓	—	PS	—	—	—	—	—	—
MS	✓	A	PS	PS	—	—	—	A	—
MT	✓	A	PS	A	—	—	—	—	—
NC	✓	PS	PS	PS	—	A	—	—	—

ND	✓	A	PS	—	—	PS	PS	A	—
NE	✓	A	—	A	—	—	—	A	—
NH	✓	A	PS	A	—	—	—	—	—
NJ	—	—	—	—	—	—	—	—	—
NM	—	—	—	—	—	—	—	—	—
NV	—	—	—	—	—	—	—	—	—
NY	—	—	—	—	—	—	—	—	—
OH	✓	A	A	—	—	—	—	—	—
OK	✓	A	PS	A	—	—	—	A	—
OR	✓	A	PS	A	A	—	—	A	—
PA	✓	A	PS	A	A	—	—	A	—
RI	✓	—	—	A	—	PS	—	A	—
SC	✓	A	A	A	—	—	—	—	—
SD	✓	—	—	A	—	A	—	—	—
TN	✓	PA	PA	—	—	—	—	—	—
TX	✓	—	PS	—	—	—	—	—	—
UT	✓	A	PS	A	—	A	—	A	A
VA	✓	A	A	—	—	—	—	—	—
VT	✓	A	A	—	—	—	—	—	—
WA	✓	A	PS	A	—	A	—	—	—
WI	—	—	—	—	—	—	—	—	—
WV	✓	A	PS	—	—	—	—	—	—
WY	✓	A	PS	A	—	—	—	—	—
Total A		22	9	19	5	9	3	9	2
Total PS		4	22	2	0	2	2	0	0
Total PA		1	1	0	0	0	0	1	1
Total states	38	26	32	21	5	11	5	10	3

Note. A = allowed; PS = prohibited sometimes; PA = prohibited always.

audiotaped test items. The use of audiotaped directions was prohibited for some content areas by the policies of 2 states, North Dakota and Rhode Island.

The highlighting of key words and phrases in test directions was addressed in the policies of 10 states. Nine states' policies allowed this accommodation for test directions in at least one content area, and one state prohibited the highlighting of words and phrases in the directions for at least one content area. The policies of three states addressed the use of highlighting for the entire test: Two states, California and Utah, allowed this accommodation for at least one content area, and one state, Colorado, prohibited it for all content areas.

Clarification.   Test administrators can clarify test directions or test items primarily by defining or explaining words, by providing language reference materials the student can use to clarify words for himself or herself, or by having an ELL verify his or her understanding of test directions. Through clarification of test language, ELLs are offered opportunities to problem-solve language samples that, initially, they do not fully comprehend. Accommodations involving clarification found in states' policies included the following:

* Directions explained/clarified in English.
* Words on test clarified (e.g., words defined, explained).
* Language reference materials (e.g., mono- or dual-language dictionaries or glossaries) provided.
* Spelling assistance, spelling dictionaries, spell or grammar checker provided.
* Test taker verifies understanding of directions.

It should be noted that the wide variety of language reference materials addressed in states' policies made categorization of these materials difficult. Some policies specified using translation dictionaries or glossaries that included only word-to-word translations. Some indicated that the use of general English language or native language dictionaries by ELLs was to be allowed (or, more commonly, prohibited). A number of policies stipulated that dictionaries with definitions could be used for some content areas (e.g., writing) but not for others (e.g., math). Some policies indicated that student-generated dictionaries could not be used. Typically, the intent of providing these materials for ELLs as an accommodation was to allow the students to clarify words on an English language test. For the purposes of this study it was decided that, given the variety of materials addressed and the differing levels of information provided by policy, the most useful way to organize language reference materials was to group them as a single English language accommodation.

It should also be noted that some forms of clarification involve the interaction between test taker and administrator (e.g., when the test taker verifies understanding of test directions). In these cases the act of negotiated interaction assists ELLs by helping them match linguistic support directly to the specific portions of language that lie within their processing capacities. States' policies often underexplained the use of student verification of understanding of directions. For instance, Maine policy simply indicated that the "administrator gave test directions with verification that the student understood them," without specifying the language in which the verification might be made. If the language in which verification took place was not specified, it was assumed to be English and therefore the accommodation was included as an English language accommodation.

Thirty states' policies addressed the use of accommodations to provide clarification of test directions or items. As shown in Fig. 1.11, of these states' policies, 30 allowed at least one clarification accommodation for at least one content area, 14 prohibited at least one of these accommodations for some content areas, and 6 states' policies prohibited at least one clarification accommodation for all content areas.

Table 1.19 lists states with policies addressing accommodations involving the clarification of the text of the assessment. Table 1.19 shows the number of states with policies allowing clarification accommodations for at least one content area (A), prohibiting these accommodations for some content areas (PS), and prohibiting clarification for all content areas (PA). Content areas for which accommodations were allowed or prohibited were not addressed with consistency in states' policies and therefore are not represented directly in the data.

Of those 41 states' policies addressing clarification, a substantial majority (37) explicitly addressed the use of language reference materials. The policies of 24 states allowed this accommodation for at least one content area and the policies of 12 states prohibited this accommodation for at

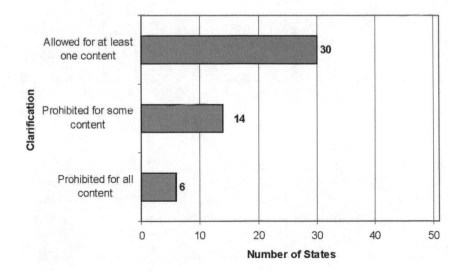

FIG. 1.11.   Overview of accommodations involving clarification allowed or prohibited by states' policies.

TABLE 1.19

Number of States' Policies Allowing or Prohibiting Accommodations Involving Clarification of Text

State	Policy Addressed Clarification	Directions Explained or Clarified in English	Words on Test Clarified (e.g., Words Defined, Explained)	Language Reference Materials (Mono- or Dual-Language Dictionaries or Glossaries) Provided	Spelling Assistance, Spelling Dictionaries, Spell/Grammar Checker Provided	Test Taker Verifies Understanding of Directions
AK	—	—	—	—	—	—
AL	✓	—	—	A	PA	—
AR	—	—	—	—	—	—
AZ	✓	A	—	A	—	—
CA	✓	A	—	A	A	—
CO	✓	PA	PA	—	—	—
CT	✓	A	—	—	—	—
DC	—	—	—	—	—	—
DE	✓	A	—	PS	—	—
FL	✓	A	A	PS	PS	—
GA	—	—	—	—	—	—
HI	✓	A	—	A	—	—
IA	—	—	—	—	—	—
ID	—	—	—	—	—	—
IL	—	—	—	—	—	—
IN	✓	—	—	—	—	—
KS	✓	—	—	A	—	—
KY	✓	A	—	A	A	—
LA	✓	—	—	PS	—	—
MA	—	—	—	PS	—	—
MD	✓	—	—	A	PA	—
ME	✓	—	—	A	—	A
MI	✓	—	—	A	—	—
MN	✓	A	—	—	—	—
MO	✓	—	—	A	—	—
MS	✓	A	—	A	A	—
MT	✓	PS	—	A	—	—
NC	✓	PA	—	PS	—	—

ND	—	—	—	—	—	—
NE	✓	A	—	A	—	—
NH	✓	A	—	A	—	—
NJ	✓	—	—	PS	—	—
NM	—	—	—	—	—	—
NV	✓	PS	PS	PS	—	—
NY	✓	—	—	PS	—	—
OH	✓	—	—	A	—	—
OK	✓	A	A	A	—	—
OR	✓	A	—	PS	—	—
PA	✓	—	—	PS	PS	A
RI	✓	PS	—	PS	PS	—
SC	✓	A	—	A	—	A
SD	✓	—	—	A	—	—
TN	✓	—	—	PA	—	—
TX	✓	—	—	—	PA	—
UT	✓	A	—	A	A	A
VA	✓	—	—	A	—	—
VT	✓	—	—	A	A	—
WA	✓	—	—	PS	—	A
WI	✓	—	—	A	—	—
WV	✓	—	—	A	—	—
WY	✓	PS	A	A	PS	—
Total A		15	3	24	5	5
Total PS		4	1	12	4	0
Total PA		2	1	1	3	0
Total states	41	21	5	37	12	5

least one content area. Only Tennessee policy prohibited the use of language reference materials for all content areas.

Twenty-one states' policies explicitly addressed the clarification or explanation of directions in English. Fifteen of these states' policies allowed this accommodation for at least one content area of the state assessment. Four (those of Montana, Nevada, Rhode Island, and Wyoming) prohibited it for some content areas, and two (Colorado and North Carolina) prohibited clarification or explanation of test directions for all content areas.

Slightly fewer states (18) addressed the remaining three accommodations: words on test clarified, spelling assistance provided, and test taker verifies understanding of directions. Of these states' policies, five allowed some form of spelling assistance on at least one content area. Four states' policies (those of Florida, Pennsylvania, Rhode Island, and Wyoming) prohibited this accommodation for some content areas, and the policies of three states (Alabama, Maryland, and Texas) prohibited this accommodation for all content areas. The policies of three states (Florida, Oklahoma, and Wyoming) allowed the clarification of words on tests for at least one content area, whereas Colorado prohibited this accommodation for all content areas.

Finally, the policies of five states (those of Maine, Pennsylvania, South Carolina, Utah, and Washington) allowed the test taker to verify his or her understanding of test directions.

Different Parts of Tests for Which the Use of English Language Accommodations Was Addressed.   The policies of the 41 states that addressed English language accommodations often specified the parts of the test—test directions or items, or both—for which native language accommodations were to be made available. In Table 1.20, the 15 English language accommodations are organized according to the part of the test for which state policies stipulated that accommodations were to be allowed or prohibited.

Indirect Linguistic Support Accommodations.   The ability of ELLs to process the language of a test can be affected by test conditions as well as by the language of the test. When test conditions hinder ELLs' ability to process language, test performance becomes a reflection of ELLs' English language proficiency rather than their academic capability. Indirect linguistic support accommodations are intended to modify the conditions under which ELLs are assessed so that their full attention can be given to processing the language and content of the test. Indirect linguistic support accommodations include (a) adjustments to test schedule or to the time allowed students to take an assessment, or (b) adjustment of the test environment. A complete list of indirect linguistic support accommodations is provided in Table 1.21.

Adjusting the *test schedule* (providing extra time or allowing the student to take a test at a time of day at which the student is most likely to perform at his or her best) can ease anxiety about the test and, therefore, allow ELLs the opportunity to more fully attend to accessing the language and content of the test. As shown in the review of literature, the provision of extra time can also be helpfully combined with direct linguistic support accommodations, which generally require the student to engage in extra

TABLE 1.20

Parts of Test for Which English Language Accommodations Were Addressed

Test directions

 1. Directions simplified

 2. Directions read aloud in English

 3. Directions repeated in English

 4. Audiotaped directions provided in English

 5. Both oral and written directions provided in English

 6. Key words or phrases in directions highlighted

 7. Directions explained or clarified in English

 8. Test taker verifies understanding of directions

Test items

 9. Items read aloud in simplified or sheltered English

10. Items read aloud in English

11. Audiotaped test items provided in English

Test directions and items

12. Key words and phrases in test highlighted

13. Simplified or sheltered English version of test provided

14. Words on test clarified (e.g., words defined, explained)

15. Language reference materials (e.g., mono- or dual-language dictionaries or glossaries) provided

16. Spelling assistance, spelling dictionaries, spell and grammar checker

tasks. For instance, a student who is given access to a dictionary or glossary will have to spend time reading the glosses or definitions and possibly referencing a separate book or section of the test. Accommodations that involve adjustments to schedule or timing include extending test time, providing breaks, and administering the test at a time of day most beneficial to the test taker.

Test environment accommodations involve adjustments to the physical and sociocultural features of the testing situation. Taking a test in an unfamiliar room or with an unfamiliar test administrator might heighten the stress caused by assessment and increase test anxiety and inhibit ELLs'

TABLE 1.21

Indirect Linguistic Support Accommodations

Test schedule

1. Time increased

2. Schedule extended

3. Subtests flexibly scheduled

4. Test administered at time of day most beneficial to test taker

5. Breaks during test sessions

Test environment

6. Test individually administered

7. Test administered in small group

8. Teacher faces test taker

9. Test administered in location with minimal distraction

10. Test taker provided preferential seating

11. Test taker tested in separate location (or carrel)

12. Person familiar to test taker administers test

13. ESL or bilingual teacher administers the test

14. Additional one-to-one support during test administration in the general education classroom (e.g., instructional assistant, special test administrator, LEP staff, etc.)

15. Test administered in familiar room

16. Test administered in ESL or bilingual classroom

17. Special test preparation provided

Note. $n = 17$ of 75 accommodations.

ability to process the language of the test, and therefore content, of the test. Adjustments to test environment, such as allowing small-group or individual testing or testing in a familiar room or with familiar personnel, can help minimize the stress of assessment. Another hurdle that some ELLs face during assessment is unfamiliarity with the nature and form of a standardized test. Providing special test preparation to ELLs could help minimize the potential stress and confusion likely to accompany assessment.

Forty-four states' policies addressed the use of indirect linguistic support accommodations. As Fig. 1.12 shows, the policies of all 44 states allowed the use of at least one indirect linguistic support accommodation for at least one content area. Ten states' policies prohibited at least one of these accommodations for some content areas, and Tennessee's was the only policy to prohibit the use of an indirect linguistic support accommodation for all content areas.

Of the 44 states with policies addressing the provision of indirect linguistic support for ELLs, 42 addressed at least one of the five test schedule accommodations, and 42 addressed at least one of the 12 test environment accommodations. Table 1.22 lists states with policies addressing accommodations involving indirect linguistic support. Table 1.22 shows the number of states with policies allowing indirect linguistic support for at least one content area (A), prohibiting at least one of these accommodations for some content areas (PS), and prohibiting indirect linguistic support for all content areas (PA).

Figure 1.13 shows the frequency with which states' policies addressed content with regard to indirect linguistic support accommodations—test schedule and test environment. Of the 42 states addressing test schedule accommodations, 41 allowed at least one of these accommodations for at least one content area. Ten prohibited this accommodation for some content areas, and the policy of one state, Tennessee, prohibited at least one test schedule accommodation for all content areas. The test schedule ac-

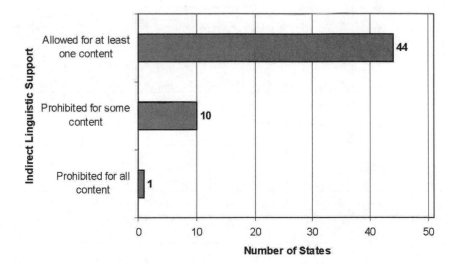

FIG. 1.12. Overview of accommodations providing indirect linguistic support allowed or prohibited by states' policies.

TABLE 1.22

Frequency With Which Indirect Linguistic Support Accommodations Were Allowed or Prohibited in States' Policies

Column groups: *Test Environment* spans "Test Time Increased" through "Breaks Provided During Test Sessions." *Test Schedule* spans the columns beginning with "Test Taker Provided Preferential Seating."

State	Policy Addressed Indirect Linguistic Support	Test Time Increased	Test Schedule Extended	Subtests Flexibly Scheduled	Test Administered at Time of Day Most Beneficial to Test Taker	Breaks Provided During Test Sessions	Test Individually Administered	Test Administered in Small Group	Teacher Faces Test Taker	Test Administered in Location With Minimal Distraction	Test Taker Provided Preferential Seating	Test Taker Tested in Separate Location (or Carrel)	Person Familiar With Test Taker Administers Test	ESL or Bilingual Teacher Administers Test	Additional One-to-One Support Provided	Test Administered in Familiar Room	Test Administered in ESL or Bilingual Classroom	Special Test Preparation Provided
AK	—	—	—	—	—	—	—	—	—	—	—	—	—	—	—	—	—	—
AL	✓	A	A	—	A	PS	A	A	A	—	A	—	—	A	—	—	A	—
AR	✓	—	—	—	—	A	A	A	—	—	A	—	—	—	—	—	—	—
AZ	✓	A	A	—	—	—	A	A	—	—	A	—	—	—	—	—	—	—
CA	✓	A	A	A	—	A	A	A	—	—	A	A	—	—	—	—	—	—
CO	✓	A	A	—	A	A	A	A	—	—	A	—	—	—	—	—	A	—
CT	✓	A	A	—	—	A	A	—	—	—	A	—	—	—	—	—	—	—
DC	✓	A	A	A	—	A	A	A	—	A	—	—	—	—	—	—	—	—
DE	✓	A	A	—	—	A	A	A	—	—	A	—	—	—	—	—	—	—
FL	✓	A	A	—	—	—	—	—	—	—	A	—	A	—	—	—	—	—
GA	—	—	—	—	—	—	—	—	—	—	—	—	—	—	—	—	—	—
HI	✓	A	—	—	—	PS	A	A	—	—	—	A	A	—	—	—	—	—
IA	—	—	—	—	—	—	—	—	—	—	—	—	—	—	—	—	—	—
ID	—	—	—	—	—	—	—	—	—	—	—	—	—	—	—	—	—	—
IL	—	—	—	—	—	—	—	—	—	—	—	—	—	—	—	—	—	—
IN	✓	PS	—	A	A	A	A	A	—	—	A	—	A	—	—	—	—	—
KS	✓	A	—	A	—	—	—	A	—	—	A	—	—	—	—	—	—	—
KY	✓	—	—	—	—	—	—	A	—	—	—	—	—	—	—	—	—	—
LA	✓	A	A	—	—	A	A	A	—	—	—	A	A	A	—	—	—	—
MA	—	—	—	—	—	—	—	—	—	—	—	—	—	—	—	—	—	—
MD	✓	A	A	—	A	A	A	A	—	—	A	A	—	A	A	—	—	—

State																		
ME	✓	A	A	—	A	A	A	A	A	—	A	A	A	—	—	—	—	—
MI	✓	A	—	—	—	—	—	—	—	—	—	—	—	—	—	—	—	—
MN	✓	A	A	—	A	—	A	A	—	—	—	A	—	—	—	—	—	—
MO	✓	A	—	—	—	—	A	A	—	—	—	—	—	—	—	—	—	—
MS	✓	A	A	—	A	A	A	A	A	—	A	A	A	—	—	A	—	—
MT	✓	A	A	A	A	—	A	A	—	—	—	—	A	—	—	—	—	—
NC	✓	A	A	—	—	PS	A	A	—	—	—	A	—	—	—	—	—	—
ND	✓	A	A	A	A	A	A	A	—	A	—	A	—	—	—	—	—	—
NE	✓	A	A	A	A	A	—	A	—	—	—	A	—	—	—	—	—	—
NH	✓	A	A	—	A	A	A	A	A	—	A	A	A	—	—	—	—	—
NJ	✓	PS	—	—	—	—	—	—	—	—	—	A	—	—	—	—	—	—
NM	—	—	—	—	—	—	—	—	—	—	—	—	—	—	—	—	—	—
NV	✓	PS	—	—	A	A	A	A	—	—	—	A	—	A	—	—	—	—
NY	✓	A	—	—	—	—	A	A	—	—	—	A	—	—	—	—	—	—
OH	✓	A	—	—	—	—	—	—	—	—	—	—	—	—	—	—	—	—
OK	✓	—	A	A	A	—	A	A	—	A	—	A	—	—	—	—	—	—
OR	✓	A	A	A	A	A	A	A	—	A	—	A	—	—	—	A	—	—
PA	✓	A	—	A	—	A	—	A	—	A	A	A	—	—	—	—	A	—
RI	✓	A	A	A	A	A	A	A	—	A	A	—	—	—	A	—	—	—
SC	✓	A	—	—	—	—	A	A	—	—	—	—	A	—	—	—	—	—
SD	✓	A	A	—	A	A	A	A	—	A	A	—	—	—	—	—	—	—
TN	✓	—	PA	A	—	—	A	A	—	—	—	—	A	—	—	A	A	—
TX	✓	—	—	—	—	—	A	—	—	—	—	—	—	—	—	—	—	—
UT	✓	—	—	—	—	A	A	A	—	—	—	—	—	A	—	—	—	A
VA	✓	A	A	A	A	PS	A	A	—	A	A	A	—	—	—	—	—	—
VT	✓	A	A	—	—	PS	A	—	—	—	A	A	—	—	—	—	—	—
WA	✓	PS	PS	A	A	A	A	A	—	A	A	A	—	—	—	A	—	—
WI	✓	A	—	—	—	—	A	A	—	—	—	—	A	—	—	—	—	—
WV	✓	A	A	A	A	A	A	A	—	A	A	—	—	—	—	—	—	—
WY	✓	A	A	—	A	PS	A	A	—	A	—	A	—	—	A	—	—	—
Total A		34	26	15	20	22	36	37	4	10	15	28	6	10	3	4	4	1
Total PS		4	1	0	0	6	0	0	0	0	0	0	0	0	0	0	0	0
Total PA		0	1	0	0	0	0	0	0	0	0	0	0	0	0	0	0	0
Total	44	38	28	15	20	28	36	37	4	10	15	28	6	10	3	4	4	1

Note. A = allowed; PS = prohibited; PA = prohibited always.

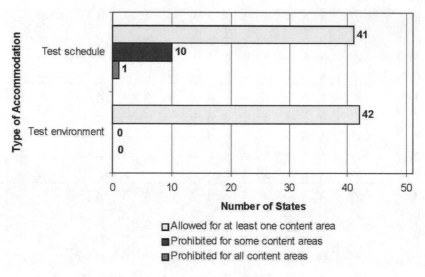

FIG. 1.13. Overview of indirect linguistic support accommodations allowed or prohibited by states' policies.

commodation addressed most frequently in states' policies, increased test time, was allowed for at least one content area by the policies of 34 states and prohibited for some content areas by the policies of 4 states (Indiana, New Jersey, Nevada, and Washington); no states' policies prohibited this accommodation for all content areas.

As Fig. 1.13 shows, all 42 states' policies addressing test environment accommodations allowed the use of at least one of these accommodations for one or more content areas. No test environment accommodation was prohibited. The two most frequently addressed test environment accommodations involved the size of the group in which an ELL was to take the assessment. Thirty-six states' policies allowed the assessment to be administered individually for at least one content area. The frequency with which states' policies allowed the administration of the assessment in a small group was similar: The policies of 37 states allowed this accommodation for at least one content area.

Some accommodations were designed to mitigate the effects of the test environment by facilitating interaction between test taker and test administrator: Ten states' policies allowed the assessment to be administered by the ELL's ESL or bilingual teacher for at least one content area. The policies of six states (Hawaii, Louisiana, Maine, Mississippi, New Hampshire, and Tennessee) allowed the person most familiar with the test taker to administer the test, and the policies of four states (Alabama, Maine, Mississippi, and New

Hampshire) allowed ELLs to be accommodated for at least one content area by having the test administrator face the student, presumably to enable them to note when a student might not be comprehending test instructions.

One accommodation designed to mitigate ELLs' difficulties negotiating the test environment is the provision of special test preparation for ELLs. This accommodation was allowed for at least one content area by Utah's assessment policy.

Comparison of the Frequency With Which Direct and Indirect Linguistic Support Accommodations Were Allowed or Prohibited in States' Policies. As shown in Fig. 1.14, on the whole, the frequency with which accommodations were allowed for at least one content area was slightly higher for indirect linguistic support accommodations (44) than for direct linguistic support accommodations (41), whether they were native or English language (31 and 38, respectively). Direct linguistic support accommodations were more likely to be prohibited for some content areas (26) than were accommodations providing indirect linguistic support (10). This contrast appears to be due to states' reticence to allow English language accommodations for ELA. Finally, direct linguistic support accommodations were more likely to be prohibited for all content areas than were indirect linguistic support accommodations. It is likely that the low frequency of prohibiting the use of indirect linguistic sup-

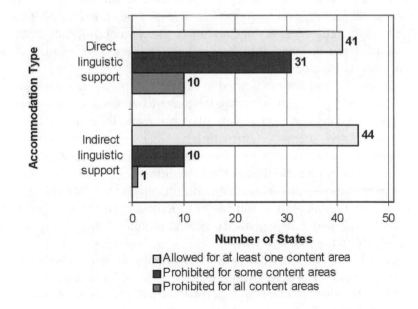

FIG. 1.14. Number of states' policies allowing or prohibiting accommodations involving direct or indirect linguistic support.

port is a result of a perception on the part of states that these accommodations pose a minimal threat to validity.

The Accommodations Decision-Making Process

To ensure that ELLs are provided with appropriate accommodations, states must determine (a) which ELLs should take accommodated versions of state assessments, and (b) which accommodations would be appropriate for particular ELLs. A majority of 47 states' policies addressing accommodations addressed some aspect of the decision-making process by designating criteria or individuals (decision makers) to facilitate the accommodation of ELLs. This section examines in detail the extent to which states' policies addressed elements of the accommodation decision-making process.

Criteria Used to Support the Decision-Making Process

Criteria named in states' polices addressed which students were eligible to be accommodated and which accommodations could or should be made available to eligible students, or both. In some cases it was clear that a particular criterion was adopted to determine eligibility of a student, whereas another was adopted to determine which accommodations should be used. In other cases, however, the precise role of a criterion was unclear in the policy. Criteria found in states' policies that might be used either to determine eligibility of students or to select appropriate accommodations were grouped into four categories: language-related, academic-related, time-related, and opinion-related.

Language-related criteria named in states' policies included language proficiency in English and the native language as well as all external educational conditions such as program placement and language of instruction. *Time-related criteria* pertain to the length of exposure a student has to an English speaking academic environment. *Academic-related* criteria relate to students' prior schooling and academic achievement as measured by test performance. *Opinion-related* criteria address teacher and parent inputs to the identification of eligible ELLs to be accommodated in state assessments. Table 1.23 lists the 10 criteria identified in states' policies grouped within the four categories.

Figure 1.15 shows the frequency with which types of criteria were adopted in states' assessment policies. Figure 1.15 shows that 27 states' policies supported the use of at least one language-related criteria; the policies of 4 states (those of Nebraska, Oregon, West Virginia, and Wyoming) supported the use of at least one academic-related criterion; 8 states' policies, at least one

TABLE 1.23

**Criteria Found in States' Policies to Facilitate Inclusion of ELLs
in Accommodated Assessments**

Language-related

1. English language proficiency
2. Student's native language proficiency
3. Language program placement
4. Primary language of instruction

Academic-related

5. Academic background in home language
6. Performance on other tests

Time-related

7. Time in United States or in English-speaking schools
8. Time in state's schools

Opinion-related

9. Parent or guardian's opinion or permission
10. Teacher observation and recommendation

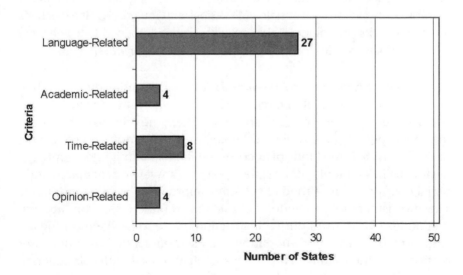

FIG. 1.15.   Types of criteria cited in states' assessment policies.

time-related criterion, and 4 states' policies (those of the District of Columbia, Florida, Mississippi, and Oregon) at least one opinion-related criterion.

As shown in Fig. 1.15, the most frequently designated criteria were those related to language. The policies of 27 states listed at least one language-related criterion. Among language-related criteria, by far the most frequently cited was English language proficiency (designated in the policies of 23 states). Seven states' policies cited students' proficiency in native language; 5 (those of Connecticut, Florida, Massachusetts, Maryland, and Wyoming) cited students' placement in a language program; and 2, Arizona's and Nevada's, cited the primary language of instruction as a criterion.

The policies of 4 states (Nebraska, Oregon, West Virginia, and Wyoming) supported the use of academic-related criteria: Three (Nebraska, West Virginia, and Wyoming) cited the student's academic background in home language; two, Oregon and Wyoming, cited performance on tests. Eight states' policies indicated that time might play a role in the decision-making process: Five states' policies (those of Arkansas, Massachusetts, Minnesota, West Virginia, and Wyoming) cited the consideration of the time an ELL has spent in the United States or in English-speaking schools, and three states' policies (those of Arizona, California, and Nebraska) cited student's time in the state's school system. The policies of 4 states (the District of Columbia, Florida, Mississippi, and Oregon) indicated that the inclusion of an ELL in an accommodated assessment should be based on opinion-related criteria: Three states' policies (those of the District of Columbia, Florida, and Oregon) cited the test taker's parents' or guardian's opinion or permission; the policies of two states, Mississippi and Oregon, cited the teacher's recommendation or opinion. Table 1.24 lists criteria (grouped by categories) named in states' policies for use in the decision-making process.

Selection of Appropriate Accommodations.   Examination of states' policies revealed a number of considerations regarding the selection of accommodations for particular students. Often, the criteria listed under the four categories (see Table 1.23) were used to determine the eligibility of ELLs as well as the kinds of accommodations that might be appropriate for eligible students. Many states' policies, however, articulated additional considerations aimed at selecting appropriate accommodations. These considerations included (a) that only routine classroom accommodations (those used during instruction) were to be used during assessment, (b) that accommodations be used only if their use does not compromise the validity of the assessment, and (c) that the selection of accommodations should be based on the needs of each individual eligible student.

TABLE 1.24

**Criteria for Determining Inclusion of ELLs
in Accommodated Assessment**

State	Policy Specified Criteria	Language				Time		Academic		Opinion	
		English Language Proficiency	Student's Native Language Proficiency	Language Program Placement	Primary Language of Instruction	Time in United States or English-Speaking Schools	Time in State's Schools	Academic Background in Home Language	Performance on Other Tests	Parent or Guardian's Opinion or Permission	Teacher Observation or Recommendation
AK	—	—	—	—	—	—	—	—	—	—	—
AL	—	—	—	—	—	—	—	—	—	—	—
AR	✓	✓	✓	—	—	✓	—	—	—	—	—
AZ	✓	—	✓	—	✓	—	✓		—	—	—
CA	✓	—	—	—	—	—	✓	—	—	—	—
CO	—	—	—	—	—	—	—	—	—	—	—
CT	✓	—	—	✓	—	—	—	—	—	—	—
DC	✓	✓	—	—	—	—	—	—	—	✓	—
DE	✓	✓	✓	—	—	—	—	—	—	—	—
FL	✓	—	—	✓	—	—	—	—	—	✓	—
GA	—	—	—	—	—	—	—	—	—	—	—
HI	—	—	—	—	—	—	—	—	—	—	—
IA	✓	✓	✓	—	—	—	—	—	—	—	—
ID	—	—	—	—	—	—	—	—	—	—	—
IL	—	—	—	—	—	—	—	—	—	—	—
IN	✓	✓	—	—	—	—	—	—	—	—	—
KS	✓	✓	✓	—	—	—	—	—	—	—	—
KY	✓	✓	—	—	—	—	—	—	—	—	—
LA	—	—	—	—	—	—	—	—	—	—	—
MA	✓	✓	✓	✓	—	✓	—	—	—	—	—
MD	✓	✓	—	✓	—	—	—	—	—	—	—
ME	✓	✓	—	—	—	—	—	—	—	—	—
MI	—	—	—	—	—	—	—	—	—	—	—
MN	✓	✓	—	—	—	✓	—	—	—	—	—

(continued)

TABLE 1.24 *(continued)*

State	Policy Specified Criteria	Language				Time		Academic		Opinion	
		English Language Proficiency	Student's Native Language Proficiency	Language Program Placement	Primary Language of Instruction	Time in United States or English-Speaking Schools	Time in State's Schools	Academic Background in Home Language	Performance on Other Tests	Parent or Guardian's Opinion or Permission	Teacher Observation or Recommendation
MO	—	—	—	—	—	—	—	—	—	—	—
MS	✓	✓	—	—	—	—	—	—	—	—	✓
MT	✓	✓	—	—	—	—	—	—	—	—	—
NC	—										
ND	—										
NE	✓	✓	—	—	—	—	✓	✓	—	—	—
NH	✓	✓	—	—	—	—	—	—	—	—	—
NJ	—										
NM	—										
NV	✓	—	—	—	✓	—	—	—	—	—	—
NY	—										
OH	—										
OK	—										
OR	✓	✓	✓	—	—	—	—	—	✓	✓	✓
PA	—										
RI	—										
SC	✓	✓	—	—	—	—	—	—	—	—	—
SD	—										
TN	—										
TX	—										
UT	✓	✓	—	—	—	—	—	—	—	—	—
VA	—										
VT	✓	✓	—	—	—	—	—	—	—	—	—
WA	✓	✓	—	—	—	—	—	—	—	—	—
WI	✓	✓	—	—	—	—	—	—	—	—	—
WV	✓	✓	—	—	—	✓	—	✓	—	—	—
WY	✓	✓	—	✓	—	✓	—	✓	✓	—	—
Total	28	23	7	5	2	5	3	3	2	3	2

The explicit allowance of only those accommodations used routinely during instruction was indicated in the policies of 25 states. The use of routine classroom accommodations for assessment is a consideration usually applied to special education students. Accommodations used during instruction are tracked as part of the IEP. However, because ELLs do not have IEPs there is no mechanism to track any accommodations that might have been used in classroom assessment or to modify instruction. Hence, although knowledge of these strategies might be helpful in determining appropriate accommodations, it is unrealistic to assume that test administrators have access to such information for ELLs. It should be acknowledged, however, that in cases where teachers are involved in the decision-making process their knowledge of the language of instruction and instructional modifications that support the language needs of ELLs will be invaluable for informing the selection of appropriate accommodations for these students.

Another consideration articulated widely in states' policies was whether the use of a given accommodation would compromise the validity of an assessment. Some states' policies addressed this concern directly, others did so indirectly. For instance, Louisiana policy indicated that "accommodations must never compromise the purpose of the test." Similarly, Texas policy stated that "test administration procedures that do not invalidate test results may be used." Other states addressed validity with less direct language. Pennsylvania policy simply stated that "the accommodation should not provide the student with an unfair advantage" and that "the testing contractor must be able to score the test." Arizona policy stipulated that "Accommodations must not alter the content of the test or provide inappropriate assistance to the student within the context of the test." In some states' policies, districts were required or encouraged to use accommodations accepted as valid by the test publisher. Hence, with regard to accommodations, Montana policy stated, "Riverside Publishing has identified accommodations that have been found to have no impact on the validity of the test score," and Colorado's assessment policy indicated that the "Test Publishers provide instructions and recommendations for ensuring that results of the test are reliable and valid." Concerns over validity were often expressed in terms of whether an accommodation was considered standard or nonstandard, where standard accommodations are those that preserve the validity of the test and nonstandard accommodations are those that compromise the validity, and hence the results, of the test.

Finally, a consistent theme among states' policies was that the selection of accommodations should be based on the needs of each individual eligible student. The designation of criteria and decision makers can support this imperative.

Decision Makers Designated in State Policies to Address the Accommodation of ELLs

Fewer than half the states' policies that addressed accommodations named decision makers (22 of 47). All but eight of these states also specified criteria.

The labels states' policies employed for individual decision makers varied, but the personnel denoted in the policies amounted to 12 different decision makers. These decision makers were grouped by the research team into five categories: (a) language acquisition specialist; (b) test coordinator or administrator; (c) general education teacher; (d) school administrator; and (e) parents, students, and community members. Table 1.25 lists the categories of decision makers and the 12 individuals identified in states' policies.

Figure 1.16 shows the frequency with which types of decision makers were cited in states' assessment policies. As shown in Fig. 1.16, 11 states' policies supported the designation of at least one language acquisition specialist, 8 states' policies supported the designation of at least one test official, 11 states' policies at least one general education teacher, 14 states' policies at least one school administrator, and 12 states' policies supported the designation of at least one parent, student, or community member. Other personnel designated as decision makers included school personnel (Kentucky and Utah), school test coordinator (Louisiana), and district test coordinator (Mississippi).

Table 1.26 provides an overview of the frequency with which the individual decision makers were named in states' policies. Among the 11 states with policies designating language acquisition specialists as a part of the decision-making process, 9 states' policies supported the designation of the student's ESL or bilingual teacher(s); 3 (Colorado, New Hampshire, and West Virginia) supported the participation of other ESL teachers or administrators; and one, Washington, the participation of an interpreter. Of the 8 states' policies supporting the designation of test officials, 5 (Alabama, Louisiana, Mississippi, Montana, and Utah) supported the participation of test administrators, 4 (Alabama, South Dakota, Virginia, and West Virginia), guidance counselor, and 3 (Alabama, Virginia, and West Virginia), reading specialist.

At least one general education teacher was listed in the policies of 11 states. Among the 14 states' policies citing a school administrator, 9 named

TABLE 1.25

Decision Makers Named in States' Assessment Policies

Language acquisition specialist

1. Student's ESL or bilingual teachers
2. Other ESL or bilingual or migrant teacher or ELL administrator
3. Interpreter

General education teacher

4. Student's classroom teachers or content teachers

Parents, students, or community members

5. Student's parents or guardians
6. Student
7. Community members

Test coordinator or administrator

8. Test administrators
9. Guidance counselor
10. Reading specialist

School administrator

11. Principal
12. School or district officials

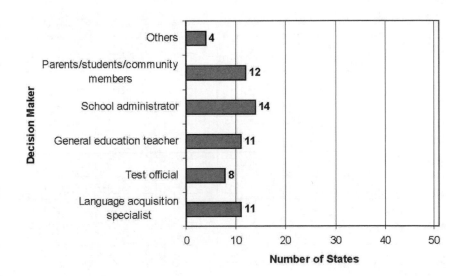

FIG. 1.16.   Types of decision makers cited in states' assessment policies.

TABLE 1.26

Decision Makers Designated in States' Policies to Determine Inclusion of ELLs in Accommodated Assessment

State	Policy Specified Accommodation Decision Makers	Language Acquisition Specialist — Student's ESL or Bilingual Teachers	Language Acquisition Specialist — Other ESL or Bilingual or Migrant Teacher or ELL Administrator	Language Acquisition Specialist — Interpreter	Test Official — Test Administrators	Test Official — Guidance Counselor	Test Official — Reading Specialist	General Education Teacher — Student's Classroom Teachers or Content Teachers	School Administrator — Principal	School Administrator — School or District Officials	Student or Parent — Student's Parents or Guardians	Student or Parent — Student	Others
AK	—	—	—	—	—	—	—	—	—	—	—	—	—
AL	✓	✓	—	—	✓	✓	✓	✓	✓	—	✓	—	—
AR	—	—	—	—	—	—	—	—	—	—	—	—	—
AZ	✓	—	—	—	—	—	—	—	—	✓	—	—	—
CA	—	—	—	—	—	—	—	—	—	—	—	—	—
CO	✓	✓	✓	—	—	—	—	✓	✓	—	—	✓	—
CT	—	—	—	—	—	—	—	—	—	—	—	—	—
DC	✓	—	—	—	—	—	—	—	—	✓	✓	—	—
DE	—	—	—	—	—	—	—	—	—	—	—	—	—
FL	—	—	—	—	—	—	—	—	—	—	—	—	—
GA	—	—	—	—	—	—	—	—	—	—	—	—	—
HI	—	—	—	—	—	—	—	—	—	—	—	—	—
IA	—	—	—	—	—	—	—	—	—	—	—	—	—
ID	—	—	—	—	—	—	—	—	—	—	—	—	—
IL	—	—	—	—	—	—	—	—	—	—	—	—	—
IN	—	—	—	—	—	—	—	—	—	—	—	—	—
KS	—	—	—	—	—	—	—	—	—	—	—	—	—
KY	✓	—	—	—	—	—	—	—	✓	—	—	—	✓
LA	✓	✓	—	—	✓	—	—	—	—	—	—	—	✓
MA	—	—	—	—	—	—	—	—	—	—	—	—	—
MD	✓	✓	—	—	—	—	—	—	—	—	✓	✓	—
ME	✓	—	—	—	—	—	—	—	✓	—	✓	✓	—
MI	—	—	—	—	—	—	—	—	—	—	—	—	—
MN	✓	✓	—	—	—	—	—	—	—	✓	✓	—	—
MO	—	—	—	—	—	—	—	—	—	—	—	—	—
MS	✓	—	—	—	✓	—	—	✓	✓	—	—	—	✓

MT	✓	—	—	—	✓	—	—	—	—	—	—	—	—
NC	—	—	—	—	—	—	—	—	—	—	—	—	—
ND	—	—	—	—	—	—	—	—	—	—	—	—	—
NE	—	—	—	—	—	—	—	—	—	—	—	—	—
NH	✓	—	✓	—	—	—	—	✓	—	✓	✓	—	—
NJ	—	—	—	—	—	—	—	—	—	—	—	—	—
NM	—	—	—	—	—	—	—	—	—	—	—	—	—
NV	—	—	—	—	—	—	—	—	—	—	—	—	—
NY	✓	—	—	—	—	—	—	✓	✓	—	—	—	—
OH	—	—	—	—	—	—	—	—	—	—	—	—	—
OK	✓	—	—	—	—	—	—	—	—	✓	—	—	—
OR	✓	—	—	—	—	—	—	✓	—	—	✓	✓	—
PA	✓	✓	—	—	—	—	—	✓	—	—	—	—	—
RI	—	—	—	—	—	—	—	—	—	—	—	—	—
SC	—	—	—	—	—	—	—	—	—	—	—	—	—
SD	✓	✓	—	—	—	✓	—	✓	✓	—	—	—	—
TN	—	—	—	—	—	—	—	—	—	—	—	—	—
TX	—	—	—	—	—	—	—	—	—	—	—	—	—
UT	✓	—	—	—	✓	—	—	—	—	—	—	—	✓
VA	✓	✓	—	—	—	✓	✓	✓	✓	—	✓	—	—
VT	✓	—	—	—	—	—	—	—	—	—	✓	—	—
WA	✓	✓	—	✓	—	—	—	✓	✓	—	✓	—	—
WI	—	—	—	—	—	—	—	—	—	—	—	—	—
WV	✓	—	✓	—	—	✓	✓	✓	—	—	✓	—	—
WY	—	—	—	—	—	—	—	—	—	—	—	—	—
Total	22	9	3	1	5	4	3	11	9	5	11	4	4

the school principal and 5 (those of Arizona, the District of Columbia, Minnesota, New Hampshire, and Oklahoma) named a school or district official. Finally, of the 12 states' policies supporting the designation of at least one parent or student, 11 cited parents or guardians and 4 (those of Colorado, Maryland, Maine, and Oregon) cited the student as a part of the decision-making process.

The policies of four states (Kentucky, Louisiana, Mississippi, and Utah) cited decision makers who, because of idiosyncrasies or lack of specificity, did not fit into the five categories listed in Table 1.25. The policies of Kentucky and Utah designated unspecified school personnel, Mississippi designated district test coordinator, and Louisiana policy indicated that the School Test Coordinator should participate in the decision-making process. As Table 1.26 shows, the individual decision makers cited with the greatest frequency, irrespective of category, were the student's classroom or content teacher (11 states), parent or guardian (11 states), ESL or LEP teacher (9 states), and principal (9 states).

States' policies addressing decision makers generally named more than one individual. Working from the data in Table 1.26, it can be shown that the policies of only 4 states (Arizona, Montana, Oklahoma, and Vermont) named a single decision maker, whereas the policies of 18 states named multiple decision makers. Slightly less than half (10 of 22 states' policies) acknowledged two to three decision makers, and slightly more than a third (8 of 22 states' policies) identified more than seven decision makers. In the policies of the 18 states designating more than one decision maker, the extent to which the activities of the decision makers were to be coordinated was unclear.

Analysis of Subgroups of States' Policies

The policies of states making up two subgroups were selected for analysis by the research team: (a) states requiring high school exit exams (19 states), and (b) states with the greatest populations of ELLs (10 states). The subgroups were selected because of their relevance to the assessment of ELLs. With regard to the first subgroup, high school exit exams have a potentially great impact on ELLs attempting to earn a high school diploma. It is therefore crucial that states' policies are clear about the use of accommodations for these assessments. With regard to the second subgroup, because top 10 states support a significant share of the ELL school-age population, data gathered about these states' assessment policies are important to consider.

States' Policies Regarding the Use of Accommodations on High School Exit Exams

High-stakes tests are tests for which scores entail significant consequences:

Schools may be judged according to the school-wide average scores of their students. High school-wide scores may bring public praise or financial rewards; low scores may bring public embarrassment or heavy sanctions. For individual students, high scores may bring a special diploma attesting to exceptional academic accomplishment; low scores may result in students being held back in grade or denied a high school diploma. (AERA, 2004)

One of the most common forms of high-stakes testing is the high school exit exam, a test that each student must pass to graduate high school. Although states were not asked to submit policies detailing the use of accommodations on high school exit exams for this study, the research team was able to cull data regarding these assessments from existing documents.

Information on high school exit exams and the accommodations available to ELLs on these tests were presented in a variety of ways in states' policies. Often, general information about the exit examinations was available in introductory sections of test administrator manuals outlining the assessments offered by the state. However, it was not always possible to establish with certainty from submitted documentation complete descriptions of exit exams, such as grade(s) during which the assessment was offered, number of times students were allowed to take the assessment, or even the content area tested. This limitation was apparent where documentation submitted by SEAs included policy pertinent only to the assessment of ELLs or extracts from policy documents. The lack of information regarding high school exit exams is not necessarily a reflection of the quality of the policies so much as their organization and the SEAs' understanding of the research team's request for documentation. Where additional information was needed to supplement states' policy documents, the research team consulted the *State Student Assessment Programs Annual Survey for SY 2000–2001* (CCSSO, 2002).

With regard to accommodations available for ELLs taking exit exams, in some cases, these were listed separately for each assessment offered by a state. For instance, Mississippi policy provides a master list of accommodations allowed or prohibited for 9 assessments. Following this list, relevant accommodations are listed for each assessment, including subject exams, such as History and Algebra I, the state's norm-referenced test (CTBS/5), as well as the Functional Literacy Examination, Mississippi's high school exit exam. Other states' policies were organized according to accommodation. In such cases, accommodations were described and information provided in the policy regarding the assessments for which the particular accommodation was to be made available. For example, under the heading "Dictionaries and Glossaries," New York policy explains that ELLs "may use foreign language dictionaries and glossaries when taking Regents examinations in subjects other than the foreign languages, when taking Regents competency tests in subjects other than reading and writing, and when taking the occupational education proficiency examinations."

Overall, 19 states reported requiring students to take a high-stakes graduation test during the 2000–2001 school year (CCSSO, 2002). Of the 19 states that self-reported high school exit exams to CCSSO, 16 provided policy documents for this study that included information on the exams. These policies indicated accommodations available to ELLs for use on the high-stakes test for particular grade levels and for particular content areas. Grade levels at which tests were administered and content areas were tested varied according to grade level. For instance, the Minnesota Basic Skills Test assessed reading and mathematics in Grade 8 and writing in Grade 10.

Table 1.27 identifies high school exit exams reported by states to CCSSO, the presence or absence of a discussion of these tests in policy documents submitted for this study, the grade level at which these tests were first administered, the content areas tested, and the states' policies regarding the use of accommodations for ELLs. Exit exams were offered as early as eighth grade. The early administration of exit exams is a result of the fact that graduation standards often were set for grades lower than 12. For instance, California's High School Exit Exam (CAHSEE) assesses Grade 9 standards in ELA and mathematics. In most cases, policy specified that students were to be allowed to take exit exams multiple times. In the case of the CAHSEE, students who did not pass the Grade 9 assessment were to be given eight more opportunities to take the exam beginning in 10th grade.

Policies of 16 of the 19 states cited by CCSSO (2002)—all but Georgia's, New Jersey's, and South Carolina's—explicitly allowed the use of direct and indirect linguistic support accommodations on high school exit exams. Georgia policy did not allow accommodations on any state assessment. South Carolina policy allowed accommodations, but was unclear regarding whether or not these accommodations applied to high school exit exams. New Jersey policy stated that accommodations were allowed on tests other than the Grade 11 High School Proficiency Test (HSPT11) and, hence, was understood to have prohibited accommodations on the HSPT11. It should be noted, however, that New Jersey policy allowed an alternate testing procedure for some ELLs to "fulfill graduation requirements." In this instance, ELLs were required to pass the Special Review Assessment process (SRA11) in the native language and "the Maculaitis with a raw score of 133 in order to graduate."

Of those states allowing accommodations on high school exit exams, Indiana, Tennessee, and Texas were alone in allowing only indirect linguistic support accommodations. Hence, a total of 13 states explicitly allowed at least one direct linguistic support accommodation for ELLs. Table 1.28 shows those direct linguistic support accommodations allowed for at least one content area in the policies of states reporting the use of high school exit exams.

TABLE 1.27

**States' Policies Regarding the Use of Accommodations
on High School Exit Exams**

State	Test Reported to CCSSO	Test Explicitly Named in Policy	Grade Test First Offered[a]	Content Tested	Accommodations Available for ELLs	
					Yes	No
AL	High School Graduation Exam	✓	10	Reading comprehension, language, math, science	✓	—
CA	High School Exit Exam	✓	9	ELA, math	✓	—
FL	Comprehensive Assessment Test	✓	10	Reading, writing, math	✓	—
GA	High School Graduation Test	✓	12	ELA, math, science, social studies	—	✓
	High School Writing Test	✓	11	Writing	—	✓
IN	Statewide Assessment	✓	10	ELA, math	✓	—
LA	Graduation Exit Examination	✓	10	ELA, math, science, social science	✓	—
MD	MD Functional Tests	✓	—	Reading, writing, math	✓	—
MN	Basic Skills Test[b]	✓	8	Reading, math	✓	—
		✓	10	Writing	✓	—
MS	Functional Literacy Examination	✓	11	Functional literacy (reading and writing)	✓	—
NC	NC Testing Program —Competency Testing	✓	9	Reading, math	✓	—
	NC Tests of Computer Skills	✓	8	Computer skills	✓	—
NJ	Grade 11 High School Proficiency Test	—	11	Reading, writing, math	—	✓
NM	NM High School Competency Exam	✓	10	Reading, language arts, writing, math, science, social studies	✓	—

(continued)

TABLE 1.27 *(continued)*

State	Test Reported to CCSSO	Test Explicitly Named in Policy	Grade Test First Offered[a]	Content Tested	Accommodations Available for ELLs	
					Yes	No
NV	High School Proficiency Examination	✓	11	Reading, writing, math	✓	—
NY	Regents Competency Tests	✓	9	Math, science	✓	—
		✓	10	Global studies	✓	—
		✓	11	Reading, writing, U.S. history	✓	—
OH	9th-Grade Proficiency Testing	✓	9	Reading, writing, math, science, citizenship	✓	—
SC	Basic Skills Assessment Program	—	10	Reading, writing, math	—	—
TN	Competency Test	—	9	Language arts, math	✓	—
TX	Texas Assessment of Academic Skills	✓	10	Reading, math	✓	—
		✓	10	Writing	✓	—
		✓	8	Science, social studies	✓	—
VA	Standards of Learning	✓	—	English—Reading, literature, research	✓	—
		✓	—	English—Writing	✓	—
		✓	—	Math	✓	—
		✓	—	History	✓	—
		✓	—	Computer, technology	✓	—
	Literacy Passport Testing	✓	9	Reading, writing, math	—	—

Note. ELA = English language arts. CCSSO = Council of Chief State Schools Officers.

[a]States' policies typically allowed students to take test on multiple administrations subsequent to the initial administration. [b] The Minnesota Basic Skills Test is referred to in state policy documents as the Basic Standards Test.

The accommodation allowed most frequently was the provision of language reference materials, allowed for at least one content area by the policies of 11 states. Six states' policies allowed directions to be read aloud in English, and 7 permitted the reading aloud of test items in English. Five states allowed the repetition of directions.

As Table 1.28 shows, the pool of direct linguistic support accommodations available for ELLs taking high school exit exams is slightly smaller than that for ELLs taking a broader range of state assessments. Whereas in the sample of 51 states 27 direct linguistic support accommodations were named (11 native language, 16 English language), in the smaller pool of states offering accommodations for high school exit exams, 21 direct linguistic support accommodations were listed (9 native language, 12 English language).

This analysis compared the policies of 19 states requiring exit exams to the total pool of 51 states' policies. Further research is necessary to determine the reasons for differences in lists of accommodations made available to ELLs in the policies of these two samples of states' policies. Some differences in accommodation lists could be a result of differences in perception about the nature of high school exit exams. On the other hand, these differences might reflect the inevitable divergences among states' policies when a cross-section of policies is drawn from a larger sample.

Policies of States With the Greatest Populations of ELLs

The policies of the 10 states with the highest populations of ELLs were examined separately. Because these states have the most ELLs, it was hypothesized that these states were likely to have more detailed and comprehensive policies regarding the assessment of ELLs.

Findings for the 2000–2001 school year did not provide strong support for this hypothesis. Instead, it was found that the policies of top 10 states varied widely and that these states' policies mirrored the characteristics found in the policies of the remaining 41 states. Nonetheless, because the top 10 states support a significant share of the ELL school-age population, data gathered from this study's analysis of these states remains a significant part of the discussion of state assessment policy. Table 1.29 shows the 10 states with the highest populations of ELLs during the time frame of this study, 2000–2001.

General Characteristics of Policies Regarding the Accommodation of ELLs.   The policies of the 10 states with the greatest numbers of ELLs were less likely to address the accommodation of ELLs than those of the remaining 41 states: 80% of the top 10 states' policies addressed accommodations as opposed to 95% of the remaining 41 states' policies. Georgia and Illinois were the only top 10 states not to address the use of accommodations. (Illinois made an alternate assessment available to ELLs in lieu of accommodations.)

As with the policies of the remaining 41 states, the organization of the policies of the top 10 states was informed by three central concerns: (a) identification of student groups eligible to take accommodated assess-

TABLE 1.28

Direct Linguistic Support Accommodations Allowed for ELLs Taking High School Exit Exams

		Accommodation	AL	CA	FL	GA
English Language Accommodations	Clarification	Spelling Assistance Provided			✓	
		Language Reference Materials (Mono- or Dual-Language Dictionaries or Glossaries) Provided	✓	✓	✓	
		Words on Test Clarified (e.g., Words Defined, Explained)			✓	
		Directions Explained or Clarified in English		✓	✓	
	Repetition	Audiotaped Test Items Provided in English				
		Test Items Read Aloud in English	✓		✓	
		Both Oral Directions and Written Directions in English Provided				
		Audiotaped Directions Provided in English				
		Directions Repeated in English		✓		
		Directions Read Aloud in English	✓			
		Key Words of Phrases in Directions Highlighted				
Native Language Accommodations	Simplification	Directions Simplified		✓		
	Sight translation	Provided Interpreter or Site Translator	✓		✓	
		Directions Explained or Clarified in Native Language			✓	
		Directions Translated Into Native Language	✓		✓	
	Scripted oral translation	Audiotaped Test Items Provided in Native Language				
		Audiotaped Directions Provided in Native Language				
		Oral Directions Provided in Native Language				
	Written translation	Written Directions Provided in Native Language				
		Translated Version of the Test Provided				
		Side-by-Side Bilingual Versions of the Test Provided				
		State	AL	CA	FL	GA

State																			
IN	—	—	—	—	—	—	—	—	—	—	—	—	—	—	—	—	—	—	—
LA	—	✓	✓	✓	—	✓	—	—	—	✓	—	—	—	—	—	—	✓	—	—
MD	—	✓	—	—	✓	✓	✓	✓	✓	—	—	—	—	—	—	✓	—	—	—
MN	✓	—	✓	✓	✓	—	—	✓	✓	—	—	—	✓	✓	✓	—	✓	—	—
MS	—	✓	—	✓	—	—	—	—	—	✓	✓	—	—	—	—	—	—	—	—
NC	—	✓	—	—	—	✓	—	—	✓	✓	—	—	—	—	—	—	—	—	—
NJ	—	—	—	—	—	—	—	—	—	—	—	—	—	—	—	—	—	—	—
NM	—	—	✓	—	—	—	—	—	—	—	—	—	—	—	—	—	—	—	✓
NV	—	—	✓	—	—	—	—	—	—	—	—	—	—	—	—	—	—	—	—
NY	—	✓	—	—	—	—	—	—	—	✓	—	✓	—	—	—	—	—	—	—
OH	—	✓	—	—	—	✓	—	—	—	✓	—	—	—	—	—	—	—	—	—
SC	—	✓	—	✓	—	—	—	—	—	—	—	—	—	—	—	—	—	—	—
TN	—	—	—	—	—	—	—	—	—	—	—	—	—	—	—	—	—	—	—
TX	—	—	—	—	—	—	—	—	—	✓	—	—	—	—	—	—	—	—	—
VA	—	✓	—	✓	—	✓	—	—	—	—	—	✓	✓	—	—	✓	✓	—	—
Total	1	11	3	4	2	7	2	2	5	6	1	2	4	1	2	1	2	1	1

Note. A check mark indicates an accommodation allowed by a state's policy for at least one content area. Some of the accommodations allowed were also prohibited for one or more content areas. Only those accommodations allowed for at least one content area are listed; hence, six direct linguistic support accommodations are not listed; two native language accommodations—test items read aloud in native language and student responds in native language—and four English language accommodations—items read aloud in sheltered English, simplified version of test provided, test taker verifies understanding of directions, and key words and phrases in test highlighted.

TABLE 1.29

Number and Percentage of ELLs Enrolled in Top 10 States

State	Total Enrollment	Number of ELLs Enrolled	% Total Enrollment
CA	6,050,895	1,511,646	25.0
TX	4,059,619	570,022	14.0
FL	2,379,701	254,517	10.7
NY	2,882,188	239,097	8.3
IL	2,048,792	140,528	6.9
AZ	875,659	135,248	15.4
GA	1,444,937	64,949	4.5
NM	320,306	63,755	19.9
CO	724,508	59,018	8.1
WA	1,004,770	58,455	5.8
Total	21,791,375	3,097,352	11.9

Note. Adapted from Kindler, A. (2002). *Survey of the States' Limited English Proficient Students and Available Educational Programs and Services, 2000–2001*. National Clearinghouse for English Language Acquisition & Language Instruction Educational Programs, p. 19.

ments (e.g., ELLs, students with disabilities), (b) identification of accommodations to be made available to eligible students within these groups, and (c) identification of content areas (e.g., mathematics, ELA) for which particular accommodations should be allowed or prohibited.

How States' Policies Designated ELLs Eligible for Accommodation.
The degree to which the needs of ELLs were addressed varied across the policies of the top 10 states. As with the policies of the remaining 41 states, those of the top 10 states tended to blur distinctions between the needs of students with disabilities and the needs of ELLs. For example, Colorado policy was organized to address all students eligible for accommodations. Similarly, in Washington, policy accommodations were organized around "special populations," defined as "special education, highly capable, 504 plan, ESL/bilingual, and migrant students."

Other states' policies focused more directly on the needs of ELLs as a group. New York policy, for instance, provided separate, detailed discussion of the administration of accommodations specifically for ELLs taking the state's Regents exams. Arizona provided separate documentation on the assessment of ELLs that included discussion of accommodations.

How States' Policies Organized Individual Accommodations Available for ELLs. The tendency among states' policies to blur the distinctions between the needs of ELLs and those of students with disabilities was evidenced in how accommodations were presented in policy documents of the top 10 states. First, some of these policies presented accommodations for ELLs according to the traditional taxonomy. Second, accommodations found in states' policies intended for ELLs were often directed at all eligible students requiring accommodation, including ELLs and students with disabilities. Figure 1.17 shows the percentages of the top 10 states compared to those of the remaining 41 states in terms of how the respective policies of these two groups organized accommodations for ELLs.

As Fig. 1.17 shows, 30% of the top 10 states' policies (those of California, Colorado, and Washington) used a taxonomy responsive to students with disabilities to organize accommodations. The percentage of the remaining 41 states' policies is somewhat higher at 56%. Among the policies of the top 10 states, Colorado's used the traditional taxonomy in its entirety. (Table 1.6 lists those states addressing the use of accommodations for ELLs and those using an ELL-responsive taxonomy to organize those accommodations.) In

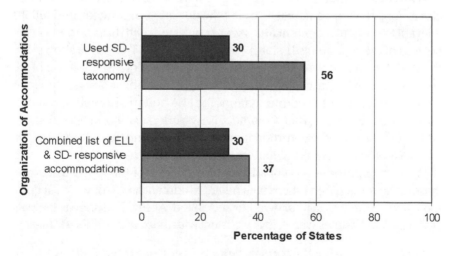

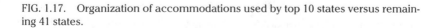

FIG. 1.17.   Organization of accommodations used by top 10 states versus remaining 41 states.

the policies of California and Washington, however, the traditional framework was adapted. California policy listed the familiar categories of timing and scheduling, presentation, and response, and appended to these categories the following accommodations: out of level testing, Braille, test read aloud, translation of directions, and use of bilingual dictionary. Washington policy offered a slightly different version of the traditional taxonomy: scheduling and timing, setting, aids or assistance, and format.

The remaining six states' policies simply provided lists of accommodations. In some cases the number of accommodations was small enough to make a taxonomy unnecessary. New Mexico, for instance, addressed only one accommodation. On the other hand, Texas policy organized accommodations according to whether they were allowable or nonallowable.

The frequency with which the top 10 states' policies cited ELL-responsive accommodations and those responsive to students with disabilities in a single list as compared to the frequency with which the remaining 41 states' policies did so was fairly close (30% and 37%, respectively). The three top 10 states with combined lists of accommodations were California, Texas, and Washington. The other five top 10 states' policies listing accommodations provided separate lists for ELLs (those of Arizona, Florida, New Mexico, New York, and Washington; see Table 1.7).

Content Areas for Which Accommodations Were Addressed. Tendencies among the top 10 states regarding the designation of accommodations relevant to particular content areas were consistent with trends found in the policies of the remaining 41 states (see Table 1.8). As Table 1.30 shows, 7 of the 10 states with the greatest populations of ELLs addressed the use of accommodations for particular content areas. Each of these 7 states' policies addressed the use of accommodations for ELA and mathematics; 5 states' policies (those of California, Colorado, New York, Texas, and Washington) addressed the use of accommodations for science, and three (those of California, New York, and Texas) addressed their use for social studies.

Figure 1.18 provides a comparison of the policies of the top 10 states and those of the remaining 41 states with regard to content areas for which accommodations were explicitly allowed or prohibited. As Fig. 1.18 shows, the policies of the top 10 states were fairly consistent with those of the other 41 states.

Analysis of Individual Accommodations Found in States' Policies

Accommodations allowed or prohibited by the policies of the top 10 states were examined using the ELL-responsive taxonomy, which categorizes accommodations for ELLs according to whether these provide direct

TABLE 1.30

**Content Areas for Which Accommodations Were Designated
in the Policies of Top 10 States**

State	Policy Explicitly Addressed Content	ELA/Literature		Math	Science	Social Studies	Other
		Reading	Writing				
CA	✓	✓	✓	✓	✓	✓	—
TX	✓	✓	✓	✓	✓	✓	—
FL	✓	✓	✓	✓	—	—	—
NY	✓	✓	✓	✓	✓	✓	—
IL	—	—	—	—	—	—	—
AZ	✓	✓	✓	✓	—	—	—
GA	—	—	—	—	—	—	—
NM	—	—	—	—	—	—	—
CO	✓	✓	✓	✓	✓	—	—
WA	✓	✓	✓	✓	✓	—	—
Total	7	7	7	7	5	3	0

Note. ELA = English language arts.

or indirect linguistic support. Overall, the policies of states with the highest populations of ELLs were comparable to those policies of the remaining 41 states. In this section, special attention is paid to contrasts between the policies of the top 10 states and those of the other 41.

Accommodations Providing Direct Linguistic Support. Accommodations providing direct linguistic support were addressed in the policies of 8 of the top 10 states. Each of these states' policies addressed at least one native language accommodation; slightly fewer (7, those of Arizona, California, Colorado, Florida, New York, Texas, and Washington) addressed the use of English language accommodations.

Native Language Accommodations. Seven of the top 10 states' policies allowed the use of at least one native language accommodation for at least one content area (70%). Fifty-nine percent of the policies of the remaining 41 states allowed the use of this accommodation for ELLs. As Fig. 1.19

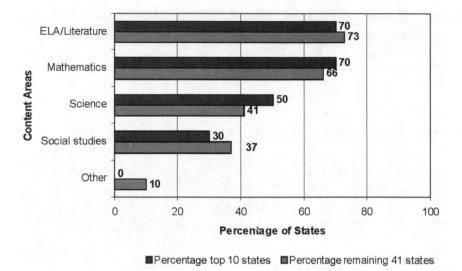

FIG. 1.18.   Percentage of top 10 states versus percentage of remaining 41 states addressing content areas for which accommodations were allowed or prohibited.

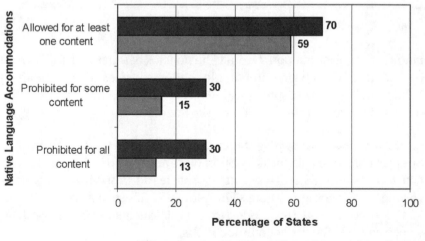

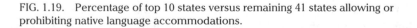

FIG. 1.19.   Percentage of top 10 states versus remaining 41 states allowing or prohibiting native language accommodations.

shows, the policies of the top 10 states were twice as likely to prohibit some native language accommodations for some content areas (30% vs. 15%) and more than twice as likely to prohibit some native language accommodations for all content areas (30% vs. 13%).

A look at particular native language accommodations broken down by state reveals that the type of native language accommodation most frequently addressed by the policies of the top 10 states was sight translation, the oral rendering of test directions, items, or both in the student's native language. As Table 1.31 shows, the type of sight translation allowed for at least one content area by the greatest number of states' policies was the translation of test directions. Sight translation also has the distinction of being the only category of native language accommodation for which an accommodation was prohibited for all content areas by the policies of the top 10 states: The policies of two states (Texas and Washington) prohibited the reading of test items aloud in the native language; Colorado prohibited the clarification of directions in native language.

It appears that the policies of the top 10 states were more likely than those of the remaining 41 states to allow the use of complete translations of tests for ELLs. As Table 1.31 shows, 4 (40%) of the top 10 states' policies (those of Texas, New York, Arizona, and Colorado) allowed either mono- or dual-language test translation for at least one content area. Among the policies of the remaining 41 states, however, only 10, or 24%, did so.

English Language Accommodations. The policies of the top 10 states roughly paralleled those of the remaining 41 states with regard to English language accommodations. The only remarkable difference between the policies of the two groups of states was in the frequency with which English language accommodations were allowed. As Fig. 1.20 shows, whereas 50% of the top 10 states allowed the use of at least one English language accommodation for one or more content areas, 80% (or 33) of the remaining 41 states did so. The percentages of states' policies prohibiting English language accommodations for some content areas was almost identical for both groups of states: 50% of the top 10 states' policies as opposed to 56% (or 23) of total states' policies. Finally, a greater percentage of the top 10 states' policies prohibited one or more accommodations for all content areas: 20% compared to 12% of the other 41 states' policies (or 5 states' policies).

As with states' policies addressing native language accommodations, policies addressing English language accommodations were fairly consistent across the two groups of states: top 10 and remaining 41. As Table 1.32 shows, the accommodation most frequently allowed by the top 10 states for at least

TABLE 1.31

Number of Top 10 States' Policies Allowing or Prohibiting Native Language Accommodations

State	Policy Addressed Native Language Accommodation	Written Translation			Scripted Oral Translation			Sight Translation				Response
		Written Directions Provided	Side-by-Side Dual-Language Versions of the Test Provided	Translated Version of the Test Provided	Oral Directions Provided in Native Language	Audiotaped Test Directions Provided in Native Language	Audiotaped Test Items Provided in Native Language	Directions Translated Into Native Language	Directions Explained or Clarified in Native Language	Test Items Read Aloud in Native Language	Interpreter or Sight Translator Provided	Student Responds in Native Language
CA	✓	—	—	—	—	A	—	A	A	—	—	—
TX	✓	—	—	A	—	—	—	A	—	PA	—	—
FL	✓	—	—	—	—	—	—	A	A	—	A	—
NY	✓	—	—	A	—	—	—	A	—	A	PS	A
IL	—	—	—	—	—	—	—	—	—	—	—	—
AZ	✓	—	—	A	—	—	—	A	—	A	PS	A
GA	—	—	—	—	—	—	—	—	—	—	—	—
NM	✓	—	—	PS	—	—	—	—	—	—	—	—
CO	✓	—	—	A	—	—	—	A	PA	—	—	A
WA	✓	—	—	—	—	A	—	A	—	PA	—	—
Total A		0	0	4	0	2	0	7	2	2	1	3
Total PS		0	0	1	0	0	0	0	0	0	2	0
Total PA		0	0	0	0	0	0	0	1	2	0	0
Total states	8	0	0	5	0	2	0	7	3	4	3	3

Note. A = allowed; PS = prohibited sometimes; PA = prohibited always.

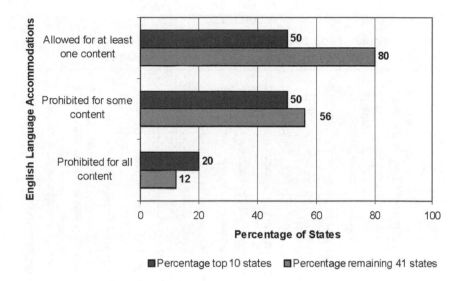

FIG. 1.20. Percentage of top 10 states versus remaining 41 states allowing or prohibiting English language accommodations.

one content area was the repeating of directions in English. This accommodation was allowed by the policies of 4 of the top 10 states (40%; Arizona, California, Colorado, and Washington) and 15 (37%) of the remaining 41 states. Similarly, the approach of the top 10 states' policies to repeating or reading test items aloud was consistent with that of the remaining 41 states: The policies of 4 of the top 10 states (40%; Colorado, Florida, Texas, and Washington) prohibited these accommodations for some content areas, as compared to 43% of total states (or 18 states' policies).

Other accommodations addressed frequently included simplification of directions, allowed by the policies of 20% of the top 10 states (those of Arizona and California) as compared to 29% (or 12) of the policies of the remaining 41 states. The explanation or clarification of directions in English for students was allowed by 30% of the top 10 states' policies (those of Arizona, California, and Florida) and by 29% (or 12) of the policies of the remaining 41 states.

Accommodations Providing Indirect Linguistic Support. Policies of the top 10 states were less likely to have addressed indirect linguistic support accommodations than were those of the remaining 41 states. As Fig. 1.21 shows, 70% of the top 10 states' policies allowed at least one indirect linguistic support accommodation for at least one content area; a higher percentage of the remaining states' policies (90%, or 37) did so. Ten percent of the policies

TABLE 1.32

Number of Top 10 States' Policies Allowing or Prohibiting the Use of English Language Accommodations

State	Policy Addressed English Language Accommodation	Simplification			Repetition								Clarification				
		Directions Simplified	*Items Read Aloud in Simplified English*	*Simplified or Sheltered Versions of Test Provided*	*Directions Read Aloud in English*	*Items Read Aloud in English*	*Directions Repeated in English*	*Both Oral and Written Directions Provided*	*Audiotaped Test Items Provided in English*	*Audiotaped Directions Provided in English*	*Key Words or Phrases in Directions Highlighted*	*Key Words and Phrases in Test Highlighted*	*Directions Explained or Clarified in English*	*Words on Test Clarified (e.g., Words Defined, Explained)*	*Language Reference Materials (Mono- or Dual-Language Dictionaries or Glossaries) Provided*	*Spelling Assistance, Spelling Dictionaries, Spell or Grammar Checker Provided*	*Test Taker Verifies Understanding of Directions*
CA	✓	A	—	—	A	A	A	—	A	A	A	A	A	—	A	A	—
TX	✓	—	—	—	—	PS	—	—	—	—	—	—	—	—	—	PA	—
FL	✓	—	—	—	—	PS	—	—	—	—	—	—	A	A	A	PS	—
NY	✓	—	—	—	—	—	—	—	—	—	—	—	—	—	PS	—	—
IL	—	—	—	—	—	—	—	—	—	—	—	—	—	—	—	—	—
AZ	✓	A	—	—	—	—	A	—	—	—	—	—	A	—	A	—	—
GA	—	—	—	—	—	—	—	—	—	—	—	—	—	—	—	—	—
NM	—	—	—	—	—	—	—	—	—	—	—	—	—	—	—	—	—
CO	✓	PA	—	—	A	PS	A	—	—	—	PA	PA	PA	PA	—	—	—
WA	✓	—	—	—	A	PS	A	—	—	A	—	—	—	—	—	—	A
Total A	—	2	0	0	3	1	4	0	1	2	1	1	3	1	3	1	1
Total PS	—	0	0	0	0	4	0	0	0	0	0	0	0	0	1	1	0
Total PA	—	1	0	0	0	0	0	0	0	0	1	1	1	1	0	1	0
Total states	8	3	0	0	3	5	4	0	1	2	2	2	4	2	4	3	1

Note. A = allowed; PS = prohibited sometimes; PA prohibited always.

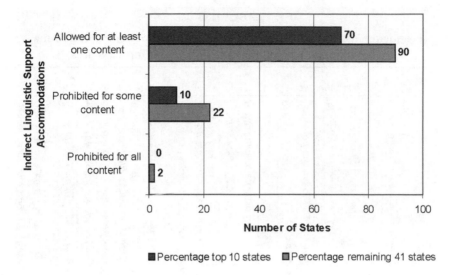

FIG. 1.21. Percentage of top 10 states versus remaining 41 states allowing or prohibiting indirect linguistic support accommodations.

of the top 10 states prohibited the use of indirect linguistic support accommodations for some content areas as opposed to 22% (or 9) for the remaining 41 states' policies. No top 10 state's policy prohibited accommodations for all content areas, whereas 2% (1) of the remaining 41 states' policies did so.

Table 1.33 provides a breakdown of the indirect linguistic support accommodations allowed or prohibited by the top 10 states. As Table 1.33 indicates, the policies of 7 states allowed the use of indirect linguistic support accommodations. Georgia and Illinois did not address the use of any type of accommodation; the only accommodation addressed in the policy of New Mexico was test translation.

The Accommodations Decision-Making Process

Like the remaining 41 states' policies, a majority of the policies of the top 10 states addressed some aspect of the decision-making process, which included the designation of criteria and decision makers to ensure that appropriate accommodations were made available to the right students.

Criteria. Figure 1.22 shows the percentage of states (top 10 and the remaining 41 states) that adopted particular kinds of criteria: language-related, academic-related, time-related, and opinion-related. As Fig. 1.22 shows, 30% of the policies of the top 10 states specified that one or more lan-

TABLE 1.33

Frequency With Which Indirect Linguistic Support Accommodations Were Allowed or Prohibited in Policies of Top 10 States

State	Policy Addressed Indirect Linguistic Support	Test Schedule					Test Environment											
		Test Time Increased	Test Schedule Extended	Subtests Flexibly Scheduled	Test Administered at Time of Day Most Beneficial to Test Taker	Breaks Provided During Test Sessions	Test Individually Administered	Test Administered in Small Group	Teacher Faces Test Taker	Test Administered in Location With Minimal Distraction	Test Taker Provided Preferential Seating	Test Taker Tested in Separate Location (or Carrel)	Person Familiar With Test Taker Administers Test	ESL or Bilingual Teacher Administers Test	Additional One-to-One Support Provided	Test Administered in Familiar Room	Test Administered in ESL or Bilingual Classroom	Special Test Preparation Provided
CA	✓	A	A	A	—	A	A	A	—	—	A	A	—	—	—	—	—	—
TX	✓	—	—	—	—	—	A	—	—	—	—	—	—	—	—	—	—	—
FL	✓	A	A	—	—	—	—	—	—	—	—	A	—	A	—	—	—	—
NY	✓	A	—	—	—	—	A	A	—	—	—	A	—	—	—	—	—	—
IL	—	—	—	—	—	—	—	—	—	—	—	—	—	—	—	—	—	—
AZ	✓	A	A	—	—	—	A	A	—	—	—	A	—	—	—	—	—	—
GA	—	—	—	—	—	—	—	—	—	—	—	—	—	—	—	—	—	—
NM	—	—	—	—	—	—	—	—	—	—	—	—	—	—	—	—	—	—
CO	✓	A	A	—	A	A	A	A	—	—	—	A	—	—	—	—	A	—
WA	✓	PS	PS	A	A	A	A	A	—	A	A	A	—	—	—	A	—	—
Total A		5	4	2	2	3	6	5	0	1	2	7	0	1	0	1	1	0
Total PS		2	1	0	0	0	0	0	0	0	0	0	0	0	0	0	0	0
Total PA		0	0	0	0	0	0	0	0	0	0	0	0	0	0	0	0	0
Total states	8	7	5	2	2	3	6	5	0	1	2	7	0	1	0	1	1	0

Note. A = allowed; PS = prohibited sometimes; PA = prohibited always.

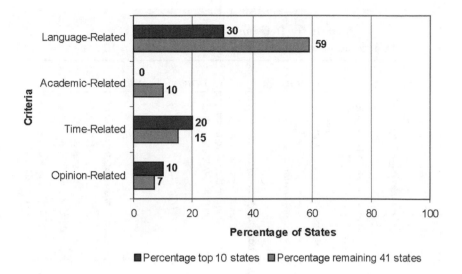

FIG. 1.22.   Percentage of top 10 states versus remaining 41 states' policies specifying types of criteria to be used in the decision-making process.

guage-related criterion should be used, as compared to 59% of those of the remaining 41 states. Whereas no top 10 state policy recommended the use of academic-related criteria, 10% (4) of the remaining 41 states' policies did so. Twenty percent of the top 10 states' policies required the use of time-related criteria, as opposed to 15% (6) of those of the remaining states. Finally, the percentage of states designating opinion-related criteria was similar for the top 10 and remaining states: 10% and 7% (3), respectively.

Table 1.34 provides a breakdown of the data for the top 10 states' policies by state, showing a fairly even distribution among criteria. This distribution is similar to that found for the remaining states. The most significant exception is found for the use of English language proficiency as a criterion. Whereas only one top 10 state (or 10%) designated this criterion, 22 of the remaining 41 states (or 54%) indicated that a student's English language proficiency should be a factor in making decisions regarding accommodations.

Decision Makers.   Figure 1.23 shows the percentage of states (top 10 and the remaining 41 states) that designated at least one of the following decision makers: language acquisition specialist; test coordinator or administrator; general education teacher; school administrator; and parents, students, or community members. As Fig. 1.23 shows, 20% of the top 10 states' policies designated a language acquisition specialist, compared to 22% (9) of the other 41 states' policies. A greater contrast can be found in the frequency with

TABLE 1.34

Criteria for Determining Inclusion of ELLs
in Accommodated Assessment in Policies of Top 10 States

State	Policy Specified Criteria	Language				Time		Academic		Opinion	
		English Language Proficiency	Student's Native Language Proficiency	Language Program Placement	Primary Language of Instruction	Time in United States or English-Speaking Schools	Time in State's Schools	Academic Background in Home Language	Performance on Other Tests	Parent or Guardian's Opinion or Permission	Teacher Observation or Recommendation
CA	✓	—	—	—	—	—	✓	—	—	—	—
TX	—	—	—	—	—	—	—	—	—	—	—
FL	✓	—	—	✓	—	—	—	—	—	✓	—
NY	—	—	—	—	—	—	—	—	—	—	—
IL	—	—	—	—	—	—	—	—	—	—	—
AZ	✓	—	✓	—	✓	—	✓	—	—	—	—
GA	—	—	—	—	—	—	—	—	—	—	—
NM	—	—	—	—	—	—	—	—	—	—	—
CO	—	—	—	—	—	—	—	—	—	—	—
WA	✓	✓	—	—	—	—	—	—	—	—	—
Total	4	1	1	1	1	0	2	0	0	1	0

which states' policies designated test officials: No top 10 state policy designated this decision maker, whereas 20% of the other states (8) did so. General education teachers were designated more frequently, with 30% of the top 10 states' policies designating these personnel as decision makers and 20% of the other states' policies (8) doing so. School administrator was selected with the most frequency by the top 10 and the remaining 41 states' policies, 40% and 22% (9 of 41 states' policies), respectively. Twenty percent of the top 10 states' policies indicated that parents, students, or community members should participate in the decision-making process, compared to 24% of policies of those states with smaller populations of ELLs (10 states).

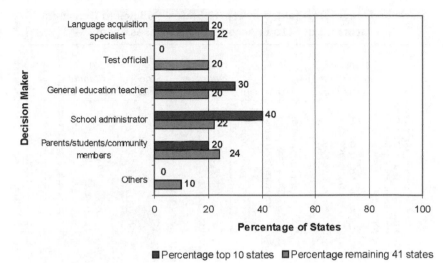

FIG. 1.23.   Percentage of top 10 states versus remaining 41 states' policies designating personnel to participate in the decision-making process.

Table 1.35 provides a breakdown of the data for the top 10 states' policies by state, showing a fairly even distribution among decision makers.
This distribution is similar to that found for the remaining 41 states' policies. The most significant exception is that whereas total states' policies
designated a variety of test officials—test administrator, guidance counselor, and reading specialist—none of these three personnel were designated in the policies of the top 10 states. Another difference can be seen in
the designation of students' parents or guardians. These individuals were
designated as decision makers in the policy of only one of the top 10 states
(Washington), whereas parents or guardians were designated in the
policies of 10 (or 24%) of the remaining 41 states.

Conclusion

Data presented in this section have shown that, taken as a whole, states'
policies for school year 2000–2001 addressed a number of key elements
for the accommodation of ELLs on state assessments. First, a variety of accommodations (75) available to ELLs were listed in states' policies. Of
these accommodations, 44 were responsive to the needs of ELLs. The
kinds of accommodations addressed in states' policies varied and included those directly addressing the linguistic needs of ELLs in their native
language or in English and indirectly, through accommodations that adjust
the test schedule or environment.

TABLE 1.35

Decision Makers Designated in Top 10 States' Policies to Determine Inclusion of ELLs in Accommodated Assessment

State	Policy Specified Accommodation Decision Makers	Language Acquisition Specialist			Test Official			General Education Teacher	School Administrator		Student or Parent		
		Student's ESL or Bilingual Teachers	Other ESL, Bilingual, or Migrant Teacher or ELL Administrator	Interpreter	Test Administrators	Guidance Counselor	Reading Specialist	Student's Classroom Teachers or Content Teachers	Principal	School or District Officials	Student's Parents or Guardians	Student	Other(s)
CA	—	—	—	—	—	—	—	—	—	—	—	—	—
TX	—	—	—	—	—	—	—	—	—	—	—	—	—
FL	—	—	—	—	—	—	—	—	—	—	—	—	—
NY	✓	—	—	—	—	—	—	✓	✓	—	—	—	—
IL	—	—	—	—	—	—	—	—	—	—	—	—	—
AZ	✓	—	—	—	—	—	—	—	—	✓	—	—	—
GA	—	—	—	—	—	—	—	—	—	—	—	—	—
NM	—	—	—	—	—	—	—	—	—	—	—	—	—
CO	✓	✓	✓	—	—	—	—	✓	✓	—	—	✓	—
WA	✓	✓	—	✓	—	—	—	✓	✓	—	✓	—	—
Total	4	2	1	1	0	0	0	3	3	1	1	1	0

Second, data show that states' policies addressed the process by which eligible ELLs are identified and given accommodations appropriate for their individual needs. The policies of 28 states identified criteria to be used in the decision-making process, and policies of 22 states identified personnel who should participate in this process.

Finally, there were fairly minor differences between the overall set of 51 states and two subgroups of states selected by the research team for further analysis—those states offering high school exit exams and those states with the greatest populations of ELLs.

Analysis of school year 2000–2001 data from state assessment policies provides insight into the complexity of the task facing state policymakers attempting to employ accommodation as an inclusion strategy for ELLs. Although many important considerations for accommodating ELLs are addressed in the assessment policies examined, few states' policies provided comprehensive guidance. The discussion that follows examines the extent to which states' assessment policies provided guidance for the selection of appropriate accommodations and makes recommendations regarding how policies might better serve ELLs.

DISCUSSION

One of the primary goals of states' accommodations policies is (or should be) to provide districts with sufficient guidance to make good decisions regarding the inclusion of ELLs in state assessment. To accomplish this goal, states' policies must help districts determine which ELLs should be accommodated and which accommodations are most likely to benefit each of these students. As the findings suggest, this is a complex task. States' policies must provide guidance regarding which of the many available accommodations are most likely to provide support that will result in valid and comparable test scores. They must designate criteria and personnel to match eligible ELLs with appropriate accommodations. Finally, to be effective, states' policies must be comprehensive and accessible to district and school personnel.

In examining state assessment policies and research on accommodations and second language acquisition, the research team attempted to identify factors that contribute to effective policy: policy that provides adequate guidance to districts using accommodations for ELLs. Findings presented earlier indicate that the comprehensiveness and clarity of states' assessment policies varied greatly. Indeed, many of these policies fell short of providing effective guidance to districts regarding the use of accommodations. The following points summarize findings in relation to key elements of assessment policy for ELLs:

- In addressing the use of accommodations, states' assessment policies often did not focus adequately on the unique linguistic needs of ELLs.

  - ELLs and students with disabilities were addressed simultaneously.
  - A variety of approaches were taken to listing accommodations available to ELLs, including the use of a taxonomy developed to

classify accommodations for students with disabilities rather
than for ELLs.

*   States' policies often did not make clear which accommodations
    were appropriate to particular content areas.
*   A total of 75 accommodations for ELLs were identified in states'
    policies; only 44 of these were responsive to the needs of ELLs.
*   States' policies were vague and inconsistent in providing guidance
    for the selection of suitable accommodations for appropriate ELLs.

    ○   Criteria often were not indicated.
    ○   Decision makers often were not designated.

*   Findings from analyses of two subgroups of states' policies—the
    19 states requiring high school exit exams and the 10 states with
    the greatest populations of ELLs—had roughly the same charac-
    teristics as the policies of the 51 states taken as a whole.

How States' Policies Addressed Accommodations for ELLS

Most states' assessment policies for the 2000–2001 school year (47) addressed the use of accommodations for ELLs. States' policies regarding accommodations were generally organized around three considerations
central to accommodation policy: (a) which student groups were eligible to
take accommodated assessments (e.g., ELLs, students with disabilities),
(b) which accommodations were to be made available to eligible students
within these groups, and (c) which content areas were relevant for particular accommodations. Each consideration should form a part of any accommodation policy. In the judgment of the research team, states' policies often
succeeded or failed according to the degree to which they focused on the
needs of ELLs as they addressed each of these three considerations.

How ELLs and Students With Disabilities Were Grouped
in States' Policies

One strategy adopted by states was to organize policy explicitly around
the needs of two student groups: ELLs and students with disabilities. Some
states' policies treated these two groups as entirely separate, whereas others combined these groups in providing guidance on accommodations. In
some cases, states' policies adopted special nomenclature to describe this
combined group of ELLs and students with disabilities, such as "special
populations" or "special needs students." In other cases, policies simply ad-

dressed both student groups in the same document. This strategy of grouping ELLs and students with disabilities has served as an expedient for organizing state policy and addressing the needs of students for whom the SEA is accountable. For instance, drawing from state and federal legislation, Wisconsin policy defined students with special needs as

> students with limited English proficiency under Wis. Stats. 115 and Title VII of IASA, students with disabilities under Subchapter V of Wis. Stats. 115 and the Individuals with Disabilities Education Act (IDEA), and students covered by Sec. 504 of the Vocational Rehabilitation Act of 1973.

In most cases, guidelines for individual assessments for which accommodations were offered were subordinated to considerations of student groups (ELLs and students with disabilities). Some states' policies, however, addressed student groups within the context of particular state assessments. For example, much of Oregon's policy regarding accommodations was found in the state's administration manuals for the Statewide Knowledge and Skills Assessments. The manuals addressed two areas: (a) reading and literature, math, and science, and (b) writing and mathematics problem solving. Each manual contained guidelines for including ELLs and students with disabilities in each content area tested in Oregon's Statewide Knowledge and Skills Assessments.

Irrespective of how particular states' policies were organized—addressing ELLs and students with disabilities together in the same document or providing separate documentation for each group—there was a significant variation in the comprehensiveness of guidance provided in these policies regarding the accommodation of ELLs. Whereas some states offered separate and extensive policy documents identifying accommodations appropriate for ELLs, some states provided only cursory guidance that was sometimes restricted to one or two pages.

In some cases, states' policies both grouped ELLs and students with disabilities and provided detailed guidance for both groups, indicating that grouping of these students need not preclude thoughtful, comprehensive policy. However, examination of states' policies indicates that, in some instances, policy for ELLs might have been simply grafted onto policy previously developed for students with disabilities (Rivera et al., 2000). Although not entirely representative of states' assessment policies regarding accommodations for ELLs, Connecticut's policy provides a compelling example of how some states' policies seem to be written from the perspective of students with disabilities.

In its Assessment Guidelines, the Connecticut State Department of Education addressed the use of accommodations for testing all eligible students. In a discussion providing "General Information About Accommodations," the document cites Section 504 of the Rehabilitation Act of 1973 and the Americans With Disabilities Act of 1990 as entitling "students with disabilities the opportunity to participate in and receive the benefits to be derived from statewide testing efforts." When describing accommodations the document continues in the same vein, suggesting that accommodations are "provided to allow students with disabilities the opportunity to demonstrate their aptitude and achievement in testing situations." No mention is made of ELLs in this introductory material. In fact, ELLs are not mentioned explicitly until the section entitled "Who May Receive Accommodations." Here, ELLs are referenced in the last sentence of the first paragraph, almost as an aside: "Additionally, limited accommodations are available for bilingual and ESL students." So, although this part of the document purports to provide general information about accommodations for all students, it does so from the perspective of students with disabilities.

Because policy regarding students with disabilities is more developed than that regarding ELLs, providing policy documents that attempt to address the combined needs of ELLs and students with disabilities has the potential to obscure the needs of ELLs. It seems likely that states' policies written to address the accommodation of ELLs separately from the accommodation of students with disabilities would help districts and schools focus more effectively on the linguistic needs of ELLs.

How Accommodations for ELLs Were Organized in States' Policies

The second major strategy used in states' policies to provide guidance for the accommodation of ELLs was the listing of accommodations. Forty-seven of the 51 states' policies addressed the use of accommodations for ELLs; 46 states' policies named particular accommodations to be made available to ELLs. The research team found that the policies of these states tended to blur distinctions between ELLs and students with disabilities in two ways: (a) by organizing lists of accommodations according to a taxonomy developed for students with disabilities, and (b) by providing lists of accommodations meant to address the combined needs of ELLs and students with disabilities.

States adopted a variety of strategies for organizing accommodations in policies for the 2000–2001 school year. Some states' policies simply listed available accommodations; other states' policies listed accommodations available to ELLs according to particular assessments. A majority of states (27 of 47), however, arranged accommodations within the traditional taxonomy developed for students with disabilities. Within the traditional taxonomy, available accommodations are sorted into the following categories: (a) timing and scheduling, (b) setting, (c) presentation, and (d) response. This taxonomy was used in states' policies to organize many of the 75 accommodations available to ELLs. Forty-four are relevant to ELLs. The remaining 31 are relevant only to students with disabilities and include such accommodations as the use of Braille and special lighting conditions.

Accommodations appropriate for ELLs can be found in every category of the traditional taxonomy, which suggests that this taxonomy is broad enough to encompass nearly all available accommodations for "special needs students." The inclusiveness of this taxonomy is its primary shortcoming. Policies relying on such an inclusive taxonomy run the risk of obscuring differences in accommodations appropriate for ELLs and those appropriate for students with disabilities.

Whether adopting the traditional taxonomy or some other means of classification, many states' policies listed individual accommodations available for ELLs alongside those available for students with disabilities. For instance, among the accommodations listed in Mississippi's policy, those involving reading test directions and test items aloud could also have involved the use of sign language or text scanners and voice synthesizers. Maryland policy lists "accompany oral directions with written directions" alongside "cue the student to remain on task." Wyoming policy listed 56 accommodations available to all eligible students. As was the case with the policies of Maryland and Mississippi, the majority of these accommodations are clearly intended for students with disabilities; only a handful are relevant to ELLs (e.g., extra time, reading directions aloud), and none address ELLs' needs exclusively. Wyoming policy provided an additional list of six accommodations directed toward ELLs specifically. Some of these accommodations, such as the individual administration of the assessment, the reading aloud of the math assessment in English, and clarification of words (in English), were also represented on the primary list. Other accommodations addressed ELLs by offering support in the native language, such as the reading aloud of instructions.

In some cases, the distinctions among accommodations relevant to ELLs, as opposed to those relevant to students with disabilities, are obvious. For instance, it is fairly clear that use of enlarged print would be of little help to ELLs and that providing a side-by-side bilingual version of a test would apply only to ELLs instructed in their native language. However, by adopting the traditional framework to organize accommodations or by listing ELL-responsive accommodations and those responsive to students with disabilities in a single list, states' policies ignore important differences between ELLs and students with disabilities and encourage the perception that the needs of all "special populations" can be met through the same assessment strategies.

Content Areas for Which Accommodations Were Addressed

States' policies were inconsistent in addressing the relationship between content areas and accommodations. Overall, the most noticeable trend with regard to states' treatment of content areas is that accommodations providing direct linguistic support to ELLs were more likely to be prohibited for ELA (writing and reading) than for other content areas. This is most likely due to the perception that accommodations to the language of a test are more likely to compromise the validity of an ELA assessment than other assessments, such as those in math or science.

Most states explicitly addressed the content areas for which accommodations could be made available to ELLs. For instance, Wyoming policy listed six accommodations designated exclusively for ELLs. Of these accommodations, two were allowed only for the mathematics test (reading aloud in English and reading aloud in the student's native language). Wisconsin's policy recommended the use of six accommodations for the Wisconsin Knowledge and Concepts Examinations. However, the state's policy explicitly prohibited the use of accommodations on the Wisconsin Reading Comprehension Test because this test "addresses specific English language-based skills (reading comprehension) and is administered in an untimed format." Kansas policy listed nine accommodations that were "allowed on Kansas Assessments" with only one caveat: Reading aloud to ELLs was not permitted for reading comprehension tests.

A few states, however, did not explicitly reference content areas in their policies. For example, Kentucky policy listed eight accommodations available specifically to ELLs but made no mention of prohibitions for particular assessments, even though some of the accommodations involved translation (e.g., "oral word-for-word translation of text to student's primary language"). Similarly, policies of the District of Columbia, Kentucky, New Jersey, South Dakota, Virginia, and West Virginia did not indicate which tests were to be administered along with particular accommodations.

Despite the fact that some states' policies did not explicitly identify content areas for which particular accommodations were appropriate, it is often clear from context which content areas are allowed to be administered with partic-ular accommodations. Often, by knowing the assessment addressed in the state's policy one can determine the content areas for which accommoda-tions are allowed. For instance, South Carolina policy made five accommo-dations available to ELLs taking the Palmetto Achievement Challenge Test (PACT). Of the five accommodations, one (oral administration) was explicitly allowed only for the PACT mathematics test. Because PACT consists of ELA and mathematics assessments, it is assumed that the other four accommo-dations were available for both ELA and mathematics.

In many cases, knowing the relevant state assessments might provide readers of states' policies with enough information to administer accom-modations appropriately. However, by not explicitly identifying content ar-eas for which accommodations can be allowed, states' policies introduce an unnecessary level of ambiguity regarding which tests are eligible to be accommodated and which specific accommodations can be used.

Accommodations Available to ELLs

A total of 75 accommodations were cited in states' assessment policies as be-ing available to ELLs. However, only 44 of these accommodations addressed the needs of ELLs. In response to the relative lack of focus on ELLs in state policy, the research team developed an ELL-responsive taxonomy linking the use of accommodations more directly to the linguistic needs of ELLs. As dem-onstrated earlier, second language acquisition research offers a helpful per-spective from which to identify, organize, and analyze accommodations likely to be appropriate for ELLs. The ELL-responsive taxonomy classifies ac-commodations according to whether they provide direct or indirect linguistic support. Both forms of accommodation address ELLs' linguistic needs, help-ing these students access the academic construct being measured by the as-sessment. Within the taxonomy, accommodations for ELLs listed in states' assessment policies are organized into the following categories:

- Direct linguistic support.

    - Native language.
        ◦ Written translation.
        ◦ Scripted oral translation.
        ◦ Sight translation.
        ◦ Student allowed to respond in native language.

    - English language.

      ○ Simplification.
      ○ Repetition.
      ○ Clarification.

- Indirect linguistic support.

  - Test schedule.
  - Test environment.

Of the 44 accommodations classified by the research team as ELL-responsive, 27 provided direct linguistic support (11 in native language, 16 in English) and 17 provided indirect linguistic support. Direct linguistic support accommodations involve the use of oral and written strategies to make the language of the test more accessible to ELLs; they include native language and English language accommodations. Indirect linguistic support accommodations address the unique needs of ELLs by adjusting the conditions under which the test is administered so that ELLs are freed from distractions that inhibit access to their developing linguistic resources.

As noted in the review of literature, native language accommodations are most appropriate for ELLs participating in native language instruction and for ELLs who are literate in the native language but in early stages of learning English. English language accommodations are most appropriate for students receiving grade-level instruction in the content being tested in English.

Little research has been conducted on the effects of indirect linguistic support accommodations—either adjustments to test schedule or environment. However, these accommodations are commonly allowed because they do not pose a significant threat to test validity. Adjustments to test schedule might help enhance ELLs' performance on tests. For instance, it seems likely that, used in conjunction with direct linguistic support accommodations, extra time could help maximize the cognitive resources at ELLs' disposal in a testing situation. Adjustments to test environment might help maximize the cognitive resources at ELLs' disposal in a testing situation. For the most part, these accommodations are innocuous and are not considered a threat to score comparability. More research is necessary, however, before firm conclusions can be drawn regarding the effectiveness of accommodations providing indirect linguistic support.

The Accommodation Decision-Making Process

Most states' policies acknowledge that the identification of accommodations appropriate to ELLs should be made on an individual basis. States' policies for the 2000–2001 school year provided guidance to help districts determine (a) which ELLs should take accommodated versions of state assessment, and (b) which accommodations are appropriate for particular ELLs. This guidance included criteria to be used in the decision-making process and individuals responsible for making decisions. Not all policies included both considerations. Furthermore, often the relationship between criteria and decision makers was unclear and the coordination of the decision-making process was unguided.

Criteria

Overall, criteria for determining which students are eligible for ELL-responsive accommodations address two points: (a) when ELLs might be ready to take the same assessments as their English-speaking peers, and (b) when ELLs might take other-than-standard versions of the assessment (August & Hakuta, 1997; Rivera & Stansfield, 1998). Taken as a whole, states' policies addressed these concerns by providing criteria of the following types:

1. *Language-related:* Level of English language proficiency or placement in a language-related program of instruction.
2. *Time-related:* Length of time a student has been in an academic environment in which English was the primary language of instruction.
3. *Academic-related:* Student's prior schooling and academic achievement as measured by test performance.
4. *Opinion-related:* Judgment of school personnel or family of student (including student).

As school year 2000–2001 data indicate, most states (27) listing criteria specified language-related criteria (specifically, level of English language proficiency). Significantly fewer states cited academic-related, time-related, or opinion-related criteria (4, 8, and 4 states, respectively). Although language proficiency is probably the most important of the criteria, it addresses only one aspect of ELLs' needs. Academic-related criteria can be helpful in taking into account important aspects, such as the kind of education a student has received before coming to the United States, as well as the language in which he or she has received instruction in the United States.

Another consideration found in many states' policies is the use during assessment of only those accommodations used for instruction. This consideration is more pertinent to students with disabilities than to ELLs. Indeed, states' assessment policies regarding the use of "routine classroom accommodations" for ELLs is premised on policy developed for students with

disabilities, like the use of the traditional taxonomy for organizing accommodations available to ELLs. In this instance, the use of a framework developed
for students with disabilities results in a misapplication of what seems to be a
commonsensical requirement that students not be subjected to new procedures when taking a state assessment. However, this requirement falls short
of its objective because it is based on the premise that there is a system in
place to track the use of routine classroom accommodations. The IEP of a
student with disabilities provides such an apparatus, and the accommodations used during assessment are more likely to be those used routinely during instruction. In the case of ELLs, however, there is no such apparatus.

Rather than focusing on the use of routine classroom accommodations,
state policy would be better serve the needs of ELLs by requiring educators to take into account these students' programs of instruction, including
language of instruction, curriculum, and resources available to students in
English and in native languages.

Decision Makers

In addition to criteria, states' assessment policies often indicated which
individuals were to participate in decisions regarding how to accommodate ELLs and which ELLs to accommodate. In school year 2000–2001
states' policies designated the following individuals to participate in the
decision-making process: (a) language acquisition specialists, (b) test officials (those administering the test), (c) general education teachers, (d)
school administrators, and (e) students or students' family.

In designating decision makers, states' policies for the 2000–2001 school
year appear to have been shaped by a number of factors, including, no
doubt, expedience. Two particularly significant considerations were addressed inconsistently in states' policies: coordination of the decision-making process and designation of individuals with appropriate qualifications.

Most states listing decision makers designated more than one individual,
implicitly acknowledging that more than one perspective should be considered in decisions regarding inclusion. However, many states' policies did
not address how these individuals should interact in the decision-making
process. Indeed, only 12 states specified that decision makers would work
together as a team during the decision-making process.

With regard to qualifications of decision makers, Rivera et al. (2000) observed, "state policies should also encourage professionals with knowledge of language learning processes to participate in the decision-making
process" (p. 69). Although most state policy documents on accommoda-

tions policies designated decision makers likely to have appropriate expertise (e.g., principal, ESL or bilingual teacher, parent, local committee), the designations of many policies were vague. Vague designations, such as "school personnel" or "district officials," leave important personnel decisions up to districts and schools.

It seems appropriate for states' policies to provide guidance for appointing and coordinating the efforts of personnel with appropriate qualifications to determine which ELLs should receive particular accommodations. A classroom teacher with intimate knowledge of an ELL's English language proficiency and academic background could contribute greatly to the decision-making process. Other qualified personnel include staff familiar with the administration of tests for particular content areas (e.g., reading specialist). Appointing and coordinating the efforts of individuals with appropriate expertise helps ensure that each ELL will be provided with the best possible accommodations.

Analysis of Subgroups of States' Policies

The policies of states making up two subgroups were selected for analysis by the research team: (a) states requiring high school exit exams (19 states), and (b) states with the greatest populations of ELLs (10 states). The subgroups were selected because of their relevance to the assessment of ELLs. With regard to the first subgroup, high school exit exams have a potentially great impact on ELLs attempting to earn a high school diploma. It is therefore crucial that states' policies are clear about the use of accommodations for these exams. With regard to the second subgroup, because the top 10 states support a significant share of the ELL school-age population, data gathered from the current study's analysis of these states should be considered carefully.

Policies of states requiring high school exit exams varied in the amount of guidance provided to local educators. Overall, these states' policies addressed fewer direct linguistic support accommodations (21 as opposed 27 on the part of the larger group of 51 states). This difference might be the result of the fact that states tended to offer a variety of accommodations and that, therefore, any group of states larger than the group of 19 states requiring high school exit exams collectively would be likely to offer a greater number of accommodations. It seems less likely that the differences are based on perceptions that different accommodations are appropriate for high school exit exams than are appropriate for other assessments. However, before such a conclusion can be drawn, a careful examination of states' assessment policies regarding the use of particular accommodations for exit exams as opposed to other state assessments is necessary.

By addressing the policies of the 10 states with the greatest populations of ELLs, this analysis focuses on states with very different ELL population sizes. In school year 2000–2001, for instance, California, the most populous top 10 state, had a population of more than 1.5 million ELLs, whereas Wisconsin, the top 10 state with the least number of ELLs, had fewer than 60,000 ELLs. Given the looseness of this grouping, it is beyond the scope of this study to draw a direct correlation between population size and the use of particular accommodations or types of accommodations. Nonetheless, some observations can be made. Overall, although it might be expected that the policies of states with relatively large ELL populations would be at a significantly more advanced state of development with regard to ELLs, these states' policies were fairly consistent with the policies of the remaining 41 states. Only a few differences were apparent. Among these differences, three points of contrast between the policies of the 10 states and those of the remaining 41 states suggest that the 10 states identified in this analysis as having relatively large ELL populations might be demonstrating more sensitivity to the needs of ELLs.

First, with regard to general characteristics of states' policies, it appears that the policies of the top 10 states were less likely to organize accommodations for ELLs and students with disabilities in a single list than were the policies of the remaining 41 states and more likely to list accommodations for ELLs and students with disabilities separately (compare 30% of the top 10 states' policies to 56% of other states' policies). In addition, the top 10 states' policies were considerably less likely than those of the other states to use the traditional taxonomy to organize accommodations for ELLs (compare 30% to 56%). These data suggest that states with larger ELL populations tend to draft policy that addresses the needs of this demographic more directly.

Another point of contrast that might be related to ELL population size is the use of translated versions of entire tests. The policies of the top 10 states were more likely than those of the remaining 41 states to allow the use of complete translations of tests for ELLs. Forty percent of the top 10 states' policies (those of Texas, New York, Arizona, and Colorado) allowed either mono- or dual-language test translation for at least one content area, as opposed to 24% of the remaining 41 states' policies. Most of the translated tests were offered in Spanish, and it seems likely that states with larger Hispanic populations are more inclined to provide accommodations in these students' native language (refer to Table 1.31).

Finally, policies of the top 10 states were less likely to rely on indirect linguistic support accommodations than were those of the remaining 41 states. As Fig. 1.21 shows, whereas only 70% of the top 10 states allowed the use of indirect linguistic support for one or more content areas, 90% of the remaining states' policies did so. Indirect linguistic support accommodations are less likely to be tailored to the needs of ELLs. Hence, this finding might indicate that the top 10 states relied less on accommodations that are applicable to all students and more on accommodations that address ELLs' linguistic needs directly. By contrast, the policies of the remaining 41 states appear to rely more on accommodations that attempt to address the needs of all students, ELLs as well as those with disabilities.

RECOMMENDATIONS

Given the mandate under NCLB to include ELLs in state assessment systems and in NAEP, a discussion of effective accommodations is more important than ever. Findings from state policy documents along with the review of available accommodations studies highlight two important aspects of accommodation that require the attention of policymakers at the state and national levels. First, analysis of states' policies has revealed the need to provide strong guidance for the selection of appropriate accommodations. Such guidance must focus on the needs and characteristics of particular student groups. Second, review of accommodations studies has shown that more research must be conducted on the impact of particular accommodations or groups of accommodations on the scores of ELLs.

Guide Selection of ELL-Responsive Accommodations Through Clear and Comprehensive Policy

1. Provide detailed and accessible policies that directly address ELLs' linguistic needs. Detailed, comprehensive, and accessible policies at the state level are needed to ensure that district and school personnel are provided enough guidance to select appropriate accommodations for ELLs. Policies should identify and describe accommodations that address the linguistic needs of ELLs.

2. Use student background variables to inform selection of accommodations. Background variables should be taken into consideration in identifying appropriate accommodations for each ELL. Decisions regarding the use of accommodations for ELLs need to be made on an individual basis, and variables affecting these decisions should be discussed explicitly in policy. Policies should:

- Provide a definition of ELL (or LEP student).
- Recommend that districts and schools consider the English language proficiency level of ELLs when selecting accommodations.
- Recommend that districts and schools consider the extent to which ELLs have been instructed in the content of the test when selecting accommodations.
- Recommend that districts and schools take into account the language of instruction when determining which accommodations are most appropriate for students.

3. Designate appropriate decision makers for determining which accommodations are to be used for particular assessments. Policies should explicitly recommend that a team of individuals make decisions about which accommodations to allow ELLs at different levels of English language proficiency and with different academic backgrounds. Decision-making teams should include school leadership, assessment personnel, and ESL or bilingual and general education teachers familiar with the overall school program and specific academic program of the ELL.

4. Use an ELL-responsive framework as a tool to organize accommodations and guide appropriate selection of accommodations for ELLs. Currently the most often used taxonomy is one developed to classify accommodations for students with disabilities. Because the assessment needs of ELLs and students with disabilities differ significantly, it is recommended that policymakers distinguish the needs of these two student groups. State policies should use an ELL-responsive framework to organize accommodations appropriate to address ELLs' need to access the language of a test. At a minimum, the framework should recognize accommodations providing linguistic support. The framework used for this study acknowledges the unique linguistic needs of ELLs, categorizing accommodations as direct linguistic support and indirect linguistic support. Such a tool can be used to examine the appropriateness of an existing list of accommodations for ELLs found in states' policies.

5. Indicate clearly which accommodations are appropriate for use with particular content areas. State policies should provide specific guidance on the assessment and content area for which an accommodation is allowed or prohibited. For instance, policymakers should indicate that native language translation is allowed for the state mathematics and science exams but prohibited for the ELA exams.

6. Use accommodations supported by research. Although research on accommodations for ELLs is inconclusive, two kinds of accommodations appear to have potential to support ELLs' access to test content: native lan-

guage and linguistic simplification. Combining specific direct linguistic support accommodations (e.g., bilingual glossaries) with specific indirect linguistic support accommodations (e.g., extra time) also appears to support ELLs' performance on assessments.

- *Native language accommodations.* The limited number of studies focused on native language accommodations suggests that decisions about the use of accommodations should be based on the students' language of instruction. A student who has not been schooled in his or her native language in mathematics, for example, should not be accommodated on assessments of mathematics in the native language. Furthermore, research on the effectiveness of native language in instructional contexts points to its usefulness as a tool for helping ELLs access content.
- *Linguistic simplification accommodations.* Research suggests that linguistic simplification of test items or directions might have a positive effect on the performance of ELLs on mathematics and possibly science tests. However, it should be kept in mind that this accommodation appears to be useful for students at lower and intermediate levels of English language proficiency. Further research needs to be conducted to examine the effects of this accommodation on ELLs who are at more advanced stages of English language proficiency.
- *Combinations of direct and indirect linguistic support accommodations.* Finally, combinations of direct and indirect linguistic support accommodations support ELLs on state assessments. For example, there is a strong rationale for combining the use of bilingual glossaries with extra time to complete the assessment. If bilingual glossaries are to be used effectively, it is reasonable to expect the student to need extra time to access the glossary and to read the glossary and use it when decoding the test items.

Develop the Accommodations Knowledge Base Through Research

Given the importance and complexity of fairly and accurately assessing ELLs on state and national assessments, it is crucial that more research be conducted to inform the understanding of accommodations. These recommendations call for an increased understanding of accommodations for ELLs.

1. Develop a 5-year national research agenda to study the effect of individual accommodations on the performance of ELLs in state assessment.

Because state policy on accommodating ELLs is evolving and the research that can inform this policy is not yet at a stage where it can provide conclusive guidance, it is advisable that a national agenda for research on accommodations for ELLs in state assessment be established. The following steps should be included in setting this agenda:

- *Support research on accommodations.* The U.S. Department of Education should provide research funding to examine the effects of ELL-responsive accommodations. The Department should also encourage states to systematically collect data from schools on accommodated tests and to design studies using these data that will provide information about the usefulness and effectiveness of individual accommodations. The Department should support the publication and dissemination of research findings from the individual state efforts. For example, the Department could support the dissemination of these studies by establishing a national repository of research on accommodations and other related aspects of assessment for ELLs.
- *Set agenda.* It would be appropriate for the U.S. Department of Education to provide leadership in this area by convening a panel comprising leading researchers in assessment and second language acquisition, SEA leaders involved in policy development around ELL assessment, and teachers. Focused on the accommodation of ELLs as part of a systematic research program, the panel would be charged with setting priorities. The panel would examine existing accommodations and research on accommodations to establish priorities for studying the effects of single and multiple accommodations on ELLs' performance on state assessments and NAEP.
- *Bridge research–practice gap.* The panel should encourage partnerships between the research community and SEA leaders charged with developing policy for ELLs and assessment. In particular, the panel should provide guidance on how to systematically investigate single accommodations that seem most promising for ELLs, including but not necessarily limited to native language and linguistic simplification accommodations, and interactions between combinations of direct linguistic and indirect linguistic support accommodations.
- *Carry out research on specific accommodations to determine which have a positive effect on ELLs' test scores without posing a threat to test validity.* The goal of accommodations research should be to determine which accommodations have a positive effect on ELLs' test scores without being a threat to score comparability or validity. Researchers should consider examining the effect on scores of differ-

ent direct linguistic and indirect linguistic support accommodations on monolingual English speakers and ELLs. Accommodations found to pose no threat to score comparability should be provided routinely to ELLs participating in state assessment.

- *Include considerations of students' academic and background characteristics in accommodations research.* The more students' academic and background characteristics are taken into consideration, the better we will be able to align particular accommodations with individual students' needs.

2. Develop a research agenda for accommodating ELLs participating in NAEP. Research priorities regarding accommodations used for NAEP overlap those of accommodations used on state assessments. However, because of the unique requirements of NAEP it is recommended that NAEP officials:

- Identify promising accommodations to be used in assessing ELLs and provide these accommodations routinely to ELLs participating in NAEP.
- Systematically study those accommodations provided to ELLs taking NAEP.
- Review and critique criteria for administering all NAEP accommodations.
- Periodically review the criteria for administering accommodations and the extent to which individual accommodations appear promising in supporting ELLs participating in NAEP.

3. Continue study of states' assessment policies. The study of how state policies are evolving in providing guidance on accommodations for ELLs is a crucial component to developing an understanding of how ELLs' assessment needs are being met. Such research should be a funding priority for the Department of Education and other agencies invested in the equitable assessment of ELLs.

4. Analyze policy–practice gaps. Additional research in the area of state policy should investigate how policy is understood and carried out in practice. Case studies in districts and schools should examine how state policy on accommodations for ELLs is interpreted and how accommodations are actually selected and implemented.

REFERENCES

Abedi, J. (2001). *Assessment and accommodations for English language learners: Issues and recommendations* (Policy Brief 4). Los Angeles: University of California, Center for the Study of Evaluation/National Center for Research on Evaluation, Standards, and Student Testing.

Abedi, J., Courtney, M., & Leon, S. (2003). *Research-supported accommodation for English language learners in NAEP* (CSE Tech. Rep. No. 586). Los Angeles: University of California, National Center for Research on Evaluation, Standards, and Student Testing.

Abedi, J., Courtney, M., Mirocha, J., Leon, S. & Goldberg, J. (2003). *Language accommodations for English language learners in large-scale assessments: Bilingual dictionaries and linguistic modification* Unpublished manuscript. Los Angeles: National Center for Research on Evaluation, Standards, and Student Testing.

Abedi, J., Hofstetter, C., Baker, E., & Lord, C. (2001). *NAEP math performance and test accommodations: Interactions with student language background* (CSE Tech. Rep. No. 536). Los Angeles: National Center for Research on Evaluation, Standards, and Student Testing.

Abedi, J., & Lord, C. (2001). The language factor in mathematics tests. *Applied Measurement in Education, 14,* 219–234.

Abedi, J., Lord, C., Boscardin, C. K., & Miyoshi, J. (2001). *The effects of accommodations on the assessment of limited English proficient students in the National Assessment of Educational Progress* (Publication No. NCES 2001–13). Washington, DC: National Center for Education Statistics.

Abedi, J., Lord, C., & Hofstetter, C. (1998). *Impact of selected background variables on students' NAEP math performance* (CSE Tech. Rpt. No. 478). Los Angeles: University of California, National Center for Research on Evaluation, Standards, and Student Testing.

Abedi, J., Lord, C., & Plummer, J. R. (1995). *Language background as a variable in NAEP mathematics performance*. Los Angeles: University of California, National Center for Research on Evaluation, Standards, and Student Testing.

Abedi, J., Lord, C., & Plummer, J. R. (1997). *Final report of language background as a variable in NAEP mathematics performance* (CSE Tech. Rep. No. 429). Los Angeles: University of California, National Center for Research on Evaluation, Standards, and Student Testing.

Adams, M. J. (1990). *Beginning to read: Thinking and learning about print.* Cambridge, MA: MIT Press.

Albus, D., Bielinski, J., Thurlow, M., & Liu, K. (2001). *The effect of a simplified English language dictionary on a reading test* (LEP Project Rep. No. 1). Minneapolis: University of Minnesota, National Center for Educational Outcomes.

American Educational Research Association, American Psychological Association, & National Council on Measurement in Education. (1999). *Standards for educational and psychological tests.* Washington, DC: American Psychological Association.

American Educational Research Association. (2000). Position statement concerning high-stakes testing in pre-K–12 education. Washington, DC: Author. Retrieved September 29, 2004, from http://www.aera.net/about/policy/stakes.htm

Anderson, M., Liu, K., Swierzbin, B., Thurlow, M., & Bielinski, J. (2000). *Bilingual accommodations for limited English proficient students on statewide reading rests: Phase 2* (Minnesota Rep. No. 31). Minneapolis, MN: National Center for Educational Outcomes.

August, D., & Hakuta, K. (Eds.). (1997). Improving schooling for language-minority children: A research agenda. Washington, DC: National Academy Press.

Blair, D., & Harris, R. (1981). A test of interlingual interaction in comprehension by bilinguals. *Journal of Psycholinguistic Research, 10,* 457–467.

Butler, F. A., & Stevens, R. (1997). *Accommodation strategies for English language learners on large-scale assessments: Student characteristics and other considerations* (CSE Tech. Rep. 448). Los Angeles: University of California, Center for the Study of Evaluation, Standards, and Student Testing.

Castellon-Wellington, M. (2000). *The impact of preference for accommodations: The performance of ELLs on large-scale academic achievement tests* (Tech. Rep. No. 524). Los Angeles: University of California, National Center for the Study of Evaluation, Standards, and Student Testing.

CCSSO. (1997). *Annual survey of state student assessment programs* (Vols. I & II). Washington, DC: Author.

CCSSO. (2002). *Annual survey of state student assessment programs* (Vols. I & II). Washington, DC: Author.

Celce-Murcia, M., & Larsen-Freeman, D. (1983). *The grammar book: An ESL/EFL teacher's book.* Rowley, MA: Newbury House.

Cervantes, R. (1983). *Say it again Sam: The effect of repetition on dictation scores.* Unpublished term paper, University of Hawaii at Manoa.

Chaudron, C. (1988). *Second language classrooms: Research on teaching and learning.* New York: Cambridge University Press.

Dornic, S. (1979). Information processing in bilinguals: Some selected issues. *Psychological Research, 40,* 329–348.

Elliott, S. N., Kratochwill, T. R., & Schulte, A. G. (1998). The assessment accommodations checklist: Who, what, where, when, why, and how? *Teaching Exceptional Children, 31*(2), 10–14.

Ellis, N. (1996). Sequencing in SLA: Phonological memory, chunking, and points of order. *Studies in Second Language Acquisition, 18,* 91–126.

Ellis, N. (1999). Cognitive approaches to SLA. *Annual Review of Applied Linguistics, 19,* 22–42.

Ellis, N., & Schmidt, R. (1997). Morphology and longer distance dependencies: Laboratory research illuminating the A in SLA. *Studies in Second Language Acquisition, 19,* 145–171.

Ellis, N., & Sinclair, S. (1996). Working memory in the acquisition of vocabulary and syntax: Putting language in good order. *The Quarterly Journal of Experimental Psychology, 49*(A), 234–250.

Forster, K. I., & Olbrei, I. (1973). Semantic heuristics and syntactic trial. *Cognition, 2,* 319–347.

Garcia, T., with del Rio Paraent, L., Chen, L., Ferrara, S., Garavaglia, D., Johnson, E., Liang, J., et al. (2000, November). *Study of a dual language test booklet in eighth grade mathematics: Final report.* Washington, DC: American Institutes for Research.

Hafner, A. L. (2000). *Evaluating the impact of test accommodations on test scores of LEP students and non-LEP students.* Dover: Delaware Department of Education.

Halliday, M. A. K., & Martin, J. R. (1993). *Writing science: Literacy and discursive power.* Pittsburgh, PA: University of Pittsburgh Press.

Hofstetter, C. H. (2003). Contextual and mathematics accommodation test effects for English language learners. *Applied Measurement in Education, 16,* 159–188.

Hoosain, R., & Salili, F. (1987). Language differences in pronunciation speed for numbers, digit span, and mathematical ability. *Psychologia, 30*(1), 34–38.

Improving America's School Act, Public Law 107-110 (1994).

Jensen, E. D., & Vinther, T. (2003). Exact repetition as input enhancement in second language acquisition. *Journal of Learning Language, 53,* 373–428.

Jones, P. L. (1982). Learning mathematics in a second language: A problem with more and less. *Educational Studies in Mathematics, 13,* 269–287.

Kindler, A. (2002). *Survey of the states' limited English proficient students and available educational programs and services, 2000–2001 summary report.* Washington, DC: National Clearinghouse for English Language Acquisition & Language Instruction Educational Programs.

Kiplinger, V. L., Haug, C. A., & Abedi, J. (2000, June). *A math assessment should test math, not reading: One state's approach to the problem.* Paper presented at the 30th annual National Conference on Large-Scale Assessment, Snowbird, UT.

Koenig, J. A., & Bachman, L. F. (Eds.). (2004). *Keeping score for all: The effects of inclusion and accommodation policies on large-scale educational assessments.* Washington, DC: National Research Council.

LaCelle-Peterson, M., & Rivera, C. (1994). Is it real for all kids? A framework for equitable assessment policies for English language learners. *Harvard Education Review, 64,* 55–75.

Laufer, B., & Hadar, L. (1997). Assessing the effectiveness of monolingual, bilingual, and "bilingualized": Dictionaries in the comprehension and production of new words. *The Modern Language Journal, 81,* 189–196.

Long, M. (1980). Inside the "black box": Methodological issues in classroom research on language learning. *Language Learning, 30*(1), 1–2.

Long M. (1983). Native speaker/non-native speaker conversation in the second language classroom. In M. Clarke & J. Handscombe (Eds.), *On TESOL '82: Pacific perspectives on language learning and teaching* (pp. 207–225). Washington DC: TESOL.

Long, M. (1996). The role of the linguistic environment in second language acquisition. In W. C. Ritchie & T. K. Bhatia (Eds.), *Handbook of second language acquisition* (pp. 413–468). San Diego: Academic.

Lutkus, A. D., & Mazzeo, J. (2003). *Including special-needs students in the NAEP 1998 Reading Assessment. Part I: Comparison of overall results with and without accommodations.* Jessup, MD: U.S. Department of Education.

Mack, M. (1986). A study of semantic and syntactic processing in monolinguals and fluent early bilinguals. *Journal of Psycholinguistic Research, 15,* 463–488.

McLaughlin, B. (1990). "Conscious" versus "unconscious" learning. *TESOL Quarterly, 24,* 617–634.

McLaughlin, B., Rossman, T., & McLeod, B. (1983). Second language learning: An information processing perspective. *Language Learning, 33,* 135–158.

Messick, S. (1989). Validity. In R. L. Linn (Ed.), *Educational measurement* (3rd ed., pp. 13–103). New York: Macmillan.

Messick, S. (1994). *Standards-based score interpretation: Establishing valid grounds for valid inferences.* Princeton, NJ: Educational Testing Service.

Miyake, A., & Friedman, N. (1998). Individual differences in second language proficiency: Working memory as language aptitude. In A. F. Healy & I. E. Bourne (Eds.), *Foreign language learning: Psycholinguistic studies on training and retention* (pp. 339–364). Mahwah, NJ: Lawrence Erlbaum Associates.

National Center for Educational Statistics. (2003). *What Is NAEP?* Retrieved April 28, 2003 from http://nces.ed.gov/nationsreportcard

National Center for Educational Statistics. (2004). *NAEP inclusion policies.* Retrieved January 10, 2004 from http://nces.ed.gov/nationsreportcard/about/inclusion.asp#accom_table

National Research Council. (1999). *Testing, teaching, and learning.* Washington, DC: National Academy Press.

Naveh-Benjamin, M., & Ayres, T. J. (1986). Digit span, reading rate, and linguistic relativity. *Quarterly Journal of Experimental Psychology, 38A,* 739–751.

No Child Left Behind Act, Public Law 103-383 (2002).

Olson, J., & Goldstein, A. (1997). *The inclusion of students with disabilities and limited English proficient students in large-scale assessments: A summary of recent progress.* Washington, DC: National Center for Education Statistics.

Pica, T., Lincoln-Porter, F., Paninos, D., & Linnell, J. (1996). Language learners' interaction: How does it address the input, output, and feedback needs of language learners? *TESOL Quarterly, 30,* 59–84.

Rivera, C., & Stansfield, C. (1998). Leveling the playing field for English language learners: Increasing participation in state and local assessments through accommodations. In R. Brandt (Ed.), *Assessing student learning: New rules, new realities* (pp. 65–92). Arlington, VA: Educational Research Service.

Rivera, C., & Stansfield, C. (2004). The effects of linguistic simplification of science test items on the performance of limited English proficient and monolingual English speaking students. *Educational Assessment, 9*(3&4), 79–105.

Rivera, C., Stansfield, C. W., Scialdone, L., & Sharkey, M. (2000). *An analysis of state policies for the inclusion and accommodation of English language learners in state assessment programs during 1998–1999.* Arlington, VA: The George Washington University Center for Equity and Excellence in Education.

Rivera, C., & Vincent, C. (1997). High school graduation testing: Policies and practices in the assessment of English language learners. *Educational Assessment, 4,* 335–335.

Robinson, P. (1995). Attention, memory, and the "noticing" hypothesis. *Language Learning, 45,* 283–331.

Robinson, P. (2001). Attention and memory during SLA. In C. Doughty & M. Long (Eds.), *Handbook of research in second language acquisition* (pp. 631–678). Oxford, England: Blackwell.

Schachter, P. (1983). *On syntactic categories.* Bloomington: Indiana University Linguistics Club.

Shepard, L., Taylor, G., & Betebenner, D. (1998). *Inclusion of limited-English proficient students in Rhode Island's grade 4 mathematics assessment performance assessment* (CSE Tech. Rep. No. 486). Boulder, CO: Center for the Study of Evaluation, Standards, and Student Testing.

Sireci, S. G. (2003, December). *Test accommodations for English language learners: A review of the literature.* PowerPoint presentation at the annual summit of the Office of English Language Acquisition, U.S. Department of Education, Washington, DC.

Sireci, S. G., Li, S., & Scarpati, S. (2002). *The effects of test accommodations on test performance: A review of the literature* (CEA Research Rep. No. 485). Amherst: School of Education, University of Massachusetts.

Skehan, P. (1998). *A cognitive approach to language learning.* Oxford, England: Oxford University Press.

Soares, C., & Grosjean, F. (1984). Bilinguals in a monolingual and a bilingual speech mode: The effect on lexical access. *Memory and Cognition, 12,* 380–386.

Stansfield, C. W. (2002). Linguistic simplification: A promising test accommodation for LEP students? *Practical Assessment, Research & Evaluation, 8*(7). Retrieved September 26, 2005, from http://pareonline.net

Swain, M. (1985). Communicative competence: Some roles of comprehensible input and comprehensible output in its development. In S. Gass & C. Madden (Eds.), *Input in second language acquisition* (pp. 235–252). Rowley, MA: Newbury House.

Swain, M. (1995). Three functions of output in second language learning. In G. Cook & B. Seidlhofer (Eds.), *Principle and practice in applied linguistics: Studies in honour of H.G. Widdowson* (pp. 125–144). Oxford, England: Oxford University Press.

Thurlow, M. L., McGrew, K. S., Tindal, G., Thompson, S. J., Ysseldyke, J. E., & Elliott, J. L. (2000). *Assessment accommodations research: Considerations for design and analysis* (Tech. Rep. No. 26). Minneapolis: University of Minnesota, National Center on Educational Outcomes.

Tindal, G., & Fuchs, L. S. (1999). *A summary of research on test accommodations: An empirical basis for defining test accommodations*. Lexington, KY: Mid-South Regional Resource Center.

Van Patton, B. (1990). Attending to form and content in the input: An experiment in consciousness. *Studies in Second Language Acquisition, 12,* 287–301.

APPENDIX I-A:

OVERVIEW OF ACCOMMODATIONS RESEARCH

Review of Individual Studies

Each of the 15 studies examined one or more of the following types of accommodations: (a) linguistic simplification, (b) customized English dictionaries and glossaries (e.g., English-to-Spanish glossary, Spanish/English glossaries, simplified English glossaries, computer test with pop-up glossary), (c) use of the native language (e.g., dual-language tests), (d) reading items or directions, or both aloud, and (e) providing extra time in combination with other accommodations. These studies are discussed here in the context of the accommodations examined in the study.

Linguistic Simplification

Abedi, Courtney, Mirocha, et al. (2003) used NAEP science items to compare the effects of administering a test to ELLs and non-ELLs with and without linguistically simplified items, a customized English dictionary, and an English-to-Spanish glossary. The student sample consisted of 611 fourth- and eighth-graders, of whom 317 were ELLs. ELLs and non-ELLs were randomly administered test items with no accommodation or with one accommodation. The study results revealed that fourth-grade ELLs performed better on accommodated items as compared to nonaccommodated items. (It did not compare the performance of fourth-graders on items administered with different accommodations.) Among eighth-grade ELLs, the study reported that ELLs taking the linguistically simplified items scored highest, and ELLs

TABLE 1.A.1

Studies Examining the Effectiveness of Accommodations for ELLs

Study	Accommodations					Content				Sample			
	Linguistic Simplicity	Dictionary/ Glossary	Native Language	Read Aloud	Extra Time	Reading	Math	Science	Social Science	ELLs	Non-ELLs	Total	Grade(s)
Abedi, Courtney, Mirocha, et. al (2003)	✓	✓						✓		317	294	611	4, 8
Abedi, Courtney, & Leon (2003)	✓	✓			✓		✓			535	614	1,149	4, 8
Abedi, Hofstetter, Baker, & Lord (2001)[a]	✓	✓			✓		✓			501	445	946	8
Abedi & Lord (2001)	✓						✓			372	802	1,174	8
Abedi, Lord, Boscardin, & Miyoshi (2001)		✓						✓		183	236	419	8
Abedi, Lord, & Hofstetter (1998)[a]	✓		✓				✓			864	530	1,394	8
Abedi, Lord, & Plummer (1997)	✓						✓			320	711	1,031	8
Albus, Bielinski, Thurlow, & Liu (2001)		✓				✓				133	69	202	Middle school
Anderson, Liu, Swierzbin, Thurlow, & Bielinski (2000)			✓		✓	✓				105	101	206	8
Castellon-Wellington (2000)					✓				✓	106	0	106	7
Garcia (2000)			✓	✓			✓			320	82	402	8
Hafner (2000)			✓	✓	✓		✓			82	288	370	4, 7
Hofstetter (2003)	✓		✓				✓			676	173	849	8
Kiplinger, Haug, & Abedi (2000)[a]	✓	✓					✓			152	1,046	1,198	4
Rivera & Stansfield (2004)	✓								✓	109	11,306	11,415	4, 6

Note. In describing student samples some researchers used the terms LEP and non-LEP rather than ELL and non-ELL.

[a]Because ELL and non-ELL sample sizes were not reported, values were calculated from percentages of total sample.

given access to the bilingual dictionary scored lowest. In second and third position, respectively, were ELLs provided with an English dictionary and ELLs administered test items under standard conditions. The researcher concluded that "some of the accommodation strategies employed were effective in increasing the performance of ELL students and reducing the performance gap between ELL and non-ELL students" (p. xiii).

Abedi, Hofstetter, et al. (2001) used NAEP mathematics items to examine four accommodations: (a) simplified linguistic structures, (b) glossaries, (c) extra time, and (d) extra time plus glossaries. "One of five test booklets [four under accommodated conditions, one under standard conditions] were administered randomly to eighth-grade students in intact math classrooms" (p. 16). The sample included 946 students, about half of whom were categorized as LEP students (primarily Spanish-speaking). For most students, regardless of LEP status, performance on NAEP math items was higher under all accommodated conditions. The authors concluded that, in particular, the use of the modified or linguistically simplified English version of the assessment narrowed the score difference between LEP and non-LEP students. However, in a review of the study, Sireci et al. (2002) noted that "this 'narrowing' was due to the fact that the non-LEP students performed poorest on this version, not that the LEP group did much better than other conditions" (p. 51).

Abedi and Lord (2001) simplified 20 NAEP eighth-grade mathematics items and randomly administered both the original and simplified items to 1,174 students, 372 of whom were designated as ELLs. The researchers found that linguistic simplification was beneficial to ELLs in the lowest level mathematics classes as well as for non-ELLs of lower socioeconomic status. In a subsequent analysis of students' performance by mathematics achievement levels, it was found that the simplified items positively affected performance of students in low- and average-level mathematics classes yet had a slightly negative effect on students in more advanced mathematics classes (i.e., algebra and honors mathematics). The researchers concluded that for students in the lowest levels of mathematics classes certain linguistic features, such as unfamiliar words and passive verb constructions, appeared to contribute to the difficulty of text interpretation irrespective of ELL status.

Abedi, Lord, and Hofstetter (1998) compared the performance of LEP students and non-LEP students on mathematics items taken from the eighth-grade portion of the NAEP 1996 Mathematics State Assessment Program. The researchers constructed three test booklets: (a) the original English version, (b) a linguistically simplified version, and (c) a version translated into Spanish. The student sample consisted of 1,394 eighth-graders, 864 of whom were designated LEP. Non-LEP students included 530 students classified as initially fluent in English or fully English proficient. Test booklets were administered randomly to each student in the sample. Students designated as non-LEP performed better than LEP students across all three test booklets. LEP students scored highest on the simplified items, followed by the regular English test items, and lowest on the Spanish items. These findings led the researchers to reason that "the modified English accommodation enabled the LEP students to achieve scores most comparable to those of non-LEP students" (p. viii).

Abedi et al. (1997) simplified 20 eighth-grade NAEP mathematics items considered linguistically complex and randomly administered original and simplified test items to 1,031 students, 320 of whom were designated as eligible for placement in an ESL program. Findings from the study suggested that linguistic simplification was more effective for ELLs in lower level mathematics classes than for ELLs in more advanced mathematics classes.

Hofstetter (2003) conducted an examination of "contextual factors, particularly at the classroom level, that influence Latino students' performance on the NAEP mathematics assessment generally and by test accommodation" (p. 164). Her sample consisted of 849 eighth-grade students, 676 of whom were ELLs. Three test booklets were developed from eighth-grade NAEP mathematics items: (a) a nonaccommodated test, (b) a linguistically simplified test booklet, and (c) a Spanish language test booklet. Each student was randomly administered one of the booklets. Results showed slightly higher performance for ELLs and non-ELLs on the linguistically simplified test than on the standard test booklet.

Kiplinger, Haug, and Abedi (2000) experimented with Grade 4 NAEP items from the 1996 NAEP mathematics assessment. The test was designed to meet the specifications of the Grade 4 mathematics Colorado State Assessment Program. The researchers administered three test forms—a nonaccommodated version, a simplified version, and a version with an English glossary containing definitions of nontechnical words. Using matrix sampling, the test forms were administered randomly to a total sample of 1,198 fourth-graders, of whom 152 were identified as ELLs and 156 as special education students. The researchers found no significant difference in student performance across the three versions of the test. Moreover, no student group performed significantly better on any test form. The researchers attributed this finding to the general difficulty of the test items. With the exception of students with the lowest English proficiency, all students benefited from use of the glossary and the simplified test conditions, with students performing best under the glossary condition. The researchers concluded that glossaries and linguistic simplification might benefit all students, and therefore should be used.

Rivera and Stansfield (2004) carried out a study in which either a simplified or nonsimplified test of science was administered to eight groups of fourth- and sixth-graders, with approximately 1,400 students in each group. Only 109 of the students were ELLs and these were spread across all groups. The linguistically simplified test items were randomly assigned through spiraling of test booklets on the Delaware Student Testing Program. Rivera and Stansfield found that linguistic simplification did not pose a threat to score comparability for monolingual English-speaking students. Unfortunately, the sample size for ELLs ($n = 109$) was too small to generalize widely from students' performance on the simplified and nonsimplified versions of the test. Although the researchers found that some of the linguistically simplified versions were slightly easier for ELLs to comprehend than the original items, the difference in difficulty was not statistically significant due to the lack of statistical power inherent with a small sample size.

Dictionaries and Glossaries

Abedi, Courtney, and Leon (2003) compared the use of four accommodations on a mathematics assessment: a customized English dictionary, a computer test with pop-up glosses, extra time, and small-group testing. Accommodations were randomly distributed within intact classrooms to two student samples: 607 fourth-grade students (including 279 ELLs) and 542 eighth-grade students (including 256 ELLs). The fourth-grade students were tested under standard conditions and with four accommodations. The eighth graders were administered the test under standard conditions and with two accommodations (customized dictionary and computer test with pop-up glossary).

Fourth-grade ELLs who took the computer test or received extra time had significantly higher scores than did ELLs who were tested under standard conditions. For ELLs, performance on the computerized test using the pop-up glossary was statistically significant; test performance for ELLs using the customized dictionary accommodation was not statistically significant.

For eighth-grade ELLs, performance on the computerized test with the pop-up glosses was significantly higher than performance with the customized dictionary or the test taken under standard test conditions alone. At both grade levels, non-ELLs did not perform significantly better on any of the accommodated conditions than on the standard test condition.

In interpreting their findings, Abedi, Courtney, and Leon (2003) noted that students who received the computerized test made extensive use of the pop-up glosses, which were activated simply by using the mouse to move the cursor over a word. Despite the fact that "students expressed enjoyment of the computer delivery of the test," Abedi and his colleagues cautioned that the use of computers for testing might prove logistically challenging. The researchers also noted that few students provided with a customized English dictionary indicated that they had availed themselves of this accommodation.

Abedi, Courtney, Mirocha, et al. (2003) compared the effect of three accommodations including the use of a commercially published English and bilingual dictionary on a science test built with NAEP fourth- and eighth-grade items Although fourth-grade non-ELLs outperformed ELLs by approximately 2 points, ELL students in both the English and the bilingual dictionary conditions scored significantly higher than ELL students in the standard condition. Although an achievement gap between ELL and non-ELL student performance remained evident, eighth-grade ELLs scored highest under the linguistically simplified condition, ELLs under the English dictionary condition scored the next highest, and students under the bilingual dictionary condition scored the lowest. Use of the dictionary did not affect the performance of non-ELLs, providing evidence that validity was not compromised.

Abedi, Courtney, Mirocha, et al. (2003) concluded that the findings show that different accommodations might be effective at different grade levels. In this case the dictionary condition seemed to help fourth-graders more than eighth-graders. Although the linguistic simplification mode was more effective for eighth-graders, Abedi speculated that this finding is reasonable given the linguistic complexity of the science test in the higher grades.

Abedi, Hofstetter, et al. (2001), described earlier, examined the effect of glossaries as well as glossaries with extra time among several other accommodations for eighth-graders. The glossary consisted of "brief explanations" of potentially difficult terms that were written specifically for the test and printed in the margin of the test booklet alongside relevant test items (p. 22). Participants in the study were either taking eighth-grade math, prealgebra, or algebra and integrated math. Overall, the findings indicated that for all students, the "most effective form of accommodation was the standard test booklet with Glossary plus Extra Time" (p. 54). Although LEP student performance overall was lower than that of non-LEP students by 5 to 6 points, LEP students appeared to benefit from all accommodations, with glossary and extra time being of most benefit. Glossary plus extra time was also the most beneficial accommodation for non-LEP students. Glossary only was least beneficial for LEP students and moderately beneficial for non-LEP students.

Abedi, Lord, et al. (2001) administered 20 original NAEP science items to a sample of 422 eighth-grade students, including 183 ELLs (158 of whom were identified as Hispanic). The researchers developed three test booklets that were randomly distributed to students: (a) a standard test booklet, (b) a test booklet with a customized English dictionary appended to the end of the booklet, and (c) a booklet containing bilingual marginal glosses. The items on the customized dictionary were excerpted from an available published dictionary and included only words found on the test. The English and Spanish marginal glosses provided definitions or explanations of key terms in the test. English glosses appeared in the right margins, and Spanish translations of these glosses appeared in the left margins.

Non-ELLs performed similarly under accommodated and unaccommodated conditions, indicating that the accommodations did not affect the construct tested. ELLs performed better under all accommodated conditions than under the unaccommodated condition, but performed significantly better under the English dictionary condition. The mean of students under the English and Spanish glossary conditions was nearly the same as the mean for the nonaccommodated test, indicating that the accommodation was of minimal benefit.

Albus et al. (2001) sampled 202 middle school students, two thirds of whom were native Hmong speakers (133). The researchers examined the impact on students' reading performance of using a simplified English dictionary. The dictionary was commercially published and designed for ELLs. Four reading passages were designed to match to the Minnesota's Basic Standards Reading Test and were administered to ELLs ($n = 133$) and non-ELLs ($n = 69$). On two of the passages, students were allowed to use the dictionary. For students who self-reported dictionary use, no significant differences in reading comprehension were found for either the experimental or control students (ELL or non-ELL). However, ELLs at the self-reported intermediate level of English proficiency showed a moderately significant gain. Overall, the researchers found that students with intermediate levels of English proficiency can make better use of an English dictionary than can students at lower levels of English proficiency.

Kiplinger et al. (2000), described earlier, examined the use of glossaries (as well as linguistic simplification) on NAEP math items. Glossaries were written by the researchers and consisted of short explanations of words considered unnecessarily difficult for ELLs (or students with disabilities). Glosses were placed directly on the test booklet near the relevant terms. Kiplinger et al. found that fourth-grade ELLs with intermediate or higher English language proficiency performed better using a glossary on a mathematics test. However, when test difficulty was controlled, the researchers found that "all but the most limited English proficient students, including students with disabilities, performed best on the Glossary form of the test" (p. 12).

Native Language

Abedi et al. (1998), described earlier, compared performance on an original mathematics test in English with a Spanish version of the original test. Test books with eighth-grade NAEP mathematics items were randomly assigned to 1,394 students, 864 of whom were LEP students. Overall, students (LEP and non-LEP) performed best under the linguistically modified condition, followed by the standard condition, and least well under the Spanish language condition. In general, performance of non-LEP students was higher than that of LEP students. LEP students performed somewhat better under standard conditions than under the Spanish language condition.

In considering the study findings, it is important to note that the sample was not explicitly delineated. That is, it is not clear from the study whether only Spanish-speaking students versus Asian and other language background students were assigned the Spanish language accommodation. In addition, the researchers acknowledged that data on students' various levels of Spanish language proficiency were not available. Such data are essential background information that helps to target an appropriate native language accommodation. Also, the authors noted that most students in the study were receiving mathematics instruction in English, not Spanish. The poor performance of students on the Spanish test led the researchers to conclude that "the language of instruction is an important consideration in identifying suitable test accommodations for LEP students" (pp. 28–29).

Anderson et al. (2000) conducted a study to examine the effects of providing a translated version of test questions. The test was intended to approximate an English language reading comprehension test based on the Minnesota Basic Standards Assessment. Although not noted or examined as separate accommodations, the researchers also provided an audiotaped Spanish rendition of the test directions and questions. (This was the same type of accommodation offered on the state mathematics assessment.) Also, although not explicitly allowed as an accommodation, test takers also were provided with extra time if it appeared it was needed (i.e., the test was scheduled for 2 hours, but students appearing to need extra time were offered additional time to complete the test).

A group of 206 eighth-graders participated in the study. The main content of the test—presented in the form of 4 reading passages—was provided only in English. Students were divided into three groups: an accommodated ELL group ($n = 53$), a nonaccommodated ELL group ($n = 52$), and a control group of general education students ($n = 101$). As in other studies, ELL performance levels were below those of the general population of students. Overall, Spanish-speaking students did not benefit from the provision of instructions and test questions in Spanish. However, it is important to note that the level of Spanish language proficiency was not controlled for in the student population tested. Also, students in the study had not received academic instruction in Spanish.

Garcia (2000) studied the effects of a bilingual Spanish–English or dual-language test. Garcia's sample consisted of 402 eighth-graders delineated as follows: (a) non-ELLs, or native English speakers ($n = 82$); (b) native Spanish speakers who had received 3 or more years of instruction in English ($n = 193$); and (c) native Spanish speakers who had received less than 3 years of academic instruction in English ($n = 127$). The researchers randomly administered two versions of NAEP mathematics items: a Spanish–English bilingual version and an English-only version. Students in one group (native English speakers) received the standard, English-only test booklet; students in the second group (native Spanish speakers with 3 or more years of English instruction) received either the standard or dual-language version of the test; and students in the third group received only the dual-language version.

As part of a postassessment cognitive lab, students reported finding the dual-language test booklet useful. Yet the extent to which students actually utilized the two languages represented in the test booklet varied. Findings indicated that students using the dual-language test booklet were likely to use one language only—students with 3 or fewer years of English instruction tended to use Spanish exclusively, whereas those with 3 or more years of instruction used the Spanish items as a way to cross-check their understanding of an item. After controlling both for English proficiency and language used to respond to test items, the researchers found no differences in mathematics test performance across the English and dual-language test booklet.

Students less proficient in English performed better on the dual-language test booklet. Native Spanish speakers who had received instruction in English for 3 or more years did not perform better on the dual-language test than they did on the standard test. In fact, their performance was slightly worse on the dual-language version of the test booklet. Although all students were allowed extra time, just slightly over 4% (17 of 402) of students utilized the option. The outcome for Spanish speakers instructed in English for 3 or more years suggests that extended instruction in English and level of English language proficiency were factors affecting performance. The researchers also concluded that the outcome "indicated psychometric equivalence between the dual language and English-only test booklets" (p. 6). In other words, the dual-language booklet did not pose a threat to test validity.

Hafner (2000) studied "extended oral presentation" in the native language, which, at the test administrator's discretion, included simplifying test directions, rereading test directions, providing additional examples, or reading directions in a student's native language. However, because Hafner did not track the particular aspects of "oral presentation" it is not possible to determine the effect of reading directions in a student's native language as an accommodation. (Further discussion of this study can be found in the next section.)

Hofstetter (2003), described earlier, conducted an examination of "contextual factors, particularly at the classroom level, that influence Latino students' performance on the NAEP mathematics assessment generally and by test accommodation" (p. 164). Results showed that, generally, students taking the Spanish version of the test scored slightly lower than students using the standard booklet. However, Hofstetter noted that students using the Spanish booklet who also received math instruction in Spanish performed better than students who received math instruction in Spanish but took the standard version of the test. She concluded that this provides "strong evidence that students perform better when the language of the mathematics test matches the students' language of instruction" (p. 183).

Reading Test Items or Directions Aloud

Castellon-Wellington (2000) examined the effect on scores of reading aloud items on the seventh-grade social studies test of the Iowa Test of Basic Skills. The sample consisted of ELLs ($N = 106$) only.

Castellon-Wellington provided a read-aloud accommodation that involved oral repetition of the actual text and did not involve any form of simplification. For the study, seventh-grade ELLs were offered a choice between receiving extra time to complete a test or having the items read aloud. First, students took a form of the Iowa Test of Basic Skills under standard conditions. Next, they were asked which accommodation they preferred for a retest (i.e., oral presentation or extra time). The allocation of accommodations was split into thirds: One third of the sample received the accommodation of their preference, another third received the accommodation not preferred, and the other third received an accommodation at random. The data indicated that neither preferred nor nonpreferred accommodations benefited the performance of ELLs.

According to Castellon-Wellington (2000), this accommodation is beneficial because "some students may be more prone to respond to both visual and oral stimuli than ... to visual stimuli alone" (p. 3). She also pointed out that the provision of read-aloud accommodations can be accomplished without the burden of providing additional testing materials or modifying existing materials.

Hafner (2000) studied the provision of extended oral presentation and extra time. The study examined reading aloud test directions for the mathematics component of the Terranova for fourth- and seventh-grade students. Hafner's sample included 82 ELLs and 288 non-ELLs; approximately a third of the students also were designated as students with disabilities. Oral presentation included, at the administrators' discretion, simplifying test directions, rereading test directions, providing additional examples, or reading directions in a student's native language. The data on Terranova mathematics items for fourth- ($n = 248$) and seventh-grade ($n = 122$) students indicated that those who received extra time had significantly higher scores than those who had been provided with extended oral presentation of directions only, regardless of ELL status. Hafner did not consider the interaction of ELL status and accommodation condition.

Extra Time

Abedi, Courtney, and Leon (2003), discussed earlier, compared the use of extra time on a mathematics assessment along with three other accommodations: a customized English dictionary, a computer test with pop-up glosses, and test administration in small groups. Accommodations were randomly distributed within intact classrooms to fourth-grade and eighth-grade students. The fourth-graders were the only group to be administered a test with extra time or with the pop-up glosses. Fourth-grade ELLs performed better with extra time than they did under most other conditions: standard condition, customized dictionary, or small-group administration. However, they performed less well with extra time than when given the computer version of the test with the pop-up glosses.

Abedi, Hofstetter, et al. (2001), discussed earlier, used NAEP mathematics items to examine the effect of extra time, either as a single accommodation or paired with the use of a glossary. Other accommodations included linguistic simplification and the use of glossaries without extra time. The sample included 946 students, half of whom were categorized as LEP students (primarily Spanish-speaking). Overall, students (LEP and non-LEP) performed best when given extra time and the use of a glossary and next best when given extra time only. This trend also was true for LEP students. The effect of allowing extra time on LEP students' performance was inconclusive.

Castellon-Wellington (2000), introduced earlier, examined the use of extra time for seventh-grade ELLs who were offered a choice between receiving extra time to complete a test or having the items read aloud. One third of the sample received the accommodation of their preference, another third received the accommodation not preferred, and the other third received an accommodation at random. The data indicated that neither accommodation benefited the performance of ELLs, even when the accommodation was preferred.

Hafner (2000) studied the provision of extra time only and the provision of extra time along with extended oral presentation. The data indicated that on mathematics items of the Terranova, fourth- ($n = 248$) and seventh-grade ($n = 122$) students who received extra time had significantly higher scores than those who had been provided with extended oral presentation of directions only. As Sireci et al. (2002) observed, however, Hafner did not consider whether the accommodations were more beneficial to ELLs in particular.

APPENDIX I-B:

POLICY DOCUMENTS SUBMITTED BY STATES

Alaska	Guidelines	December 2000
	Participation Guidelines for Alaska Students in State Assessments	
	Guidelines	January 2000
	Participation Guidelines for Alaska Students in State Assessments	
Alabama	Policy	July 2000
	Alabama Student Assessment Program Policies and Procedures for Students of Special Populations Bulletin 1998, No. 11 Revised 2000 Replacement pages, Appendix B, pages 26–27	
	Policy	1998
	Alabama Student Assessment Program Policies and Procedures for Students of Special Populations	
	Revisions	1998
	Alabama Student Assessment Program Policies and Procedures for Students of Special Populations, Appendix A—Replacement pages	
Arkansas	Handbook	August 2000
	Arkansas Alternate Portfolio Assessment System for Students With Limited English Proficiency	

	Handbook	June 2000
	Arkansas Comprehensive Testing, Assessment, & Accountability Program	
	Report	June 1999
	Technical Report for the Arkansas Comprehensive Testing & Assessment Program	
	Manual	February 1999
	Appendix B: Test Coordinators' Manuals & Test Administrator's Manuals	
Arizona	Memo	July 1997
	Attorney General Opinion I97-008	
	Memo	April 2000
	LEP Students and High School AIMS	
	Policy/Web Site	Downloaded July 2001
	Title 7. Education (from Arizona Secretary of State Web site)	
	Guidelines/Web Site	Downloaded July 2001
	LEP Guidelines Arizona Student Achievement Program Accountability for All Students (from Arizona Department of Education Web site)	
	Guidelines	No Date
	Guidelines for Administering AIMS to Special Education and LEP Students: Students to Be Tested/Not Tested	
	Manual	Spring 2001
	Arizona's Instrument to Measure Standards Test Administration Manual Spring 2001 High School	
	Manual	Spring 2001
	Arizona's Instrument to Measure Standards District/Charter School Coordinator's Manual, Grades 3, 5, and 8	
	Manual	Spring 2001

	Arizona's Instrument to Measure Standards Test Administration Manual and Scripts English and Spanish, Grades 3, 5, and 8	
	Manual	Spring 2001
	Arizona's Instrument to Measure Standards District/Charter School Coordinator's Manual, High School	
	Memo	July 2001
	Participation and Accommodation of LEP Students in State Assessment Programs Survey	
California	Handout	No Date
	STAR 2001	
	Handout	Spring 2001
	Standardized Testing and Reporting (STAR)	
	Handout	December 1998
	Standardized Testing and Reporting Program	
	Report	August/October 2001
	Report	August/October 2001
	Peer Review Report on California: Evidence of Final Assessment System Under Title I of the Elementary and Secondary Education Act	
	Report	September 2001
	STAR—Spring 2001 Technical Report	
	Report	September 2001
	Technical Report: California Standards Tests	
	Summary	April 2001
	California Department of Education— Response Summary to Title I Issues Raised by the U.S. Department of Education	
	Handout	Spring 2001

	Special Instructions for Testing Students Requiring Special Accommodations	
	Memo	September 2001
	Memo to Michael Cohen	
	Report	September 2001
	The 1999 Base Year—Academic Performance Index	
	Policy	April 1999
	California Code of Regulations—Subchapter 3.75: Standardized Testing and Reporting Program	
	Report	April 1999
	Reporting 1999 STAR Results to Parents/Guardians	
	Memo	January 19, 2001
	Memo To Delaine A. Eastin	
	Other	No Date
	CEEE study: An Analysis of State Policies for the Inclusion and Accommodation of English Language Learners in State Assessment Programs During 1998–1999 (Rivera, Stansfield, Scialdone, & Sharkey, 2000).	
	Memo	1999
	English Learner (EL) and Fluent English Proficient (FEP) Students	
	Policy	No Date
	Section Four Inclusion Issues—California Department of Education Responses to Title 1 Issues Raised by the U.S. Department of Education in April 2001	
Colorado	Handbook	March 1997
	Handbook on Planning for LEP Student Success	
	Other	June 2001
	E-mail re: Preparing students for the tests	

	Guidelines	August 2000
	Colorado Department of Education Reading Assessment Frameworks (Grades 3–10)	
	Memo	No Date
	Colorado Department of Education 2000–01 ELLs Elementary/Middle-Jr. High/High/ harter Schools/Alternative Programs	
	Guidelines	June 1997
	Rules for the Administration of the Colorado Basic Literacy Act	
	Guidelines	August 1997
	Rules for the Administration of the English Language Proficiency Act	
	Handbook	2001
	Colorado Programa de Evaluacion del Estudiante—2001 Manual para Administrar el Examen Grados 3 y 4	
Connecticut	Policy	July 2000
	State of Connecticut Department of Education Public Act 99-211	
	Revisions/Updates	September 2000
	Connecticut Department of Education Memo: Important Updates to Annual Assessment of Bilingual Students	
	Guidelines	March 2001
	Connecticut Department of Education Memo: English Mastery Standard to Assess the Linguistic and Academic Progress of Students in Programs of Bilingual Education	
	Guidelines	2000
	Connecticut Department of Education Assessment Guidelines	
	Letter	April 2001
	State of Connecticut Department of Education: Letter on Arrival	
	Report	No Date

	2001 Connecticut Academic Performance Test: CAPT Disaggregation Report	
Delaware	Guidelines	April 2000
	Delaware Student Testing Program Guidelines for the Inclusion of Students With Disabilities and Students With LEP	
	Manual	No Date
	Language Minority Student Data Entry Manual, 1999–2000	
	Guidelines	No Date
	Directions for Entering/Correcting DTSP Accommodations for LEPs	
	Memo	January 2001
	Revised Section III of the Inclusion, Guidelines, LEP and Bilingual Regulations, LEP Web Page, Revised Manual of Instructions	
	Handbook	Fall 2000
	Delaware Student Testing Program Test Coordinator's Handbook	
	Report	June 2000
	Delaware Student Testing Program State Summary Report	
	Guidelines	December 2000
	Delaware Student Testing Program Guidelines for the Inclusion of Students With Disabilities and Students With LEP	
	Guidelines	April 2001
	Delaware Student Testing Program Guidelines for the Inclusion of Students With Disabilities and Students With LEP	
	Handout	No Date
	Procedures for the Annual Spring Administration of the Language Assessment Scales	
	Memo	April 2001

Participation and Accommodation of LEP Students in State Assessment Programs Survey

Washington, DC	Handbook	Summer 2000
	Office of Bilingual Education Handbook, SY 2000–2001	
	Policy	No Date
	Standardized Testing for Special Population	
Florida	Manual	October 2001
	FCAT: Test Administration Manual Reading and Mathematics	
	Report	May 2001
	FCAT: Understanding FCAT Reports	
Georgia	Policy	March 1999
	Georgia 160-3-1.07 Testing Programs: Student Assessment	
	Handbook	No Date
	Georgia Statewide Student Assessment Handbook, 1999–2000	
Hawaii	Letter	October 2001
	Letter from Mr. Selvin Chin-Chance, Administrator, State of Hawaii Department of Education	
	Guidelines	August 2001
	Hawaii Content and Performance Standards State Assessment (Draft)	
	Assessment	2002
	HCPS II Hawaii State Assessment—Reading and Writing: Directions for Administering	
	Handbook	Spring 2002
	Hawaii Content and Performance Standards State Assessment Grades 3, 5, 8, and 10 (Test Coordinators Handbook Spring 2002, Draft)	
Idaho	Guidelines	No Date
	State Test Coordinators Guide	
	Policy	1997

Idaho State Board Administrative Rules

| Illinois | Handbook | January 1999 |

The Language Proficiency Handbook: A Practitioner's Guide to Instructional Assessment

| Handout | October 1996 |

Introduction to Illinois Assessment Initiatives for Bilingual/ESL Students

| Handout | 1996 |

IMAGE: Illinois Measure of Annual Growth in English, 1996 Sample Materials

| Handout | No Date |

Evidence of Final Assessment System Under Title I of the Elementary and Secondary Education Act (table)

| Handout | February 2001 |

Extended Questions and Answers: The Illinois Measure of Annual Growth in English for Students in TBE/TPI Programs

| Manual | 2001 |

Illinois Measure of Annual Growth in English District Coordination Manual

| Policy | No Date |

Title 23: Educational and Cultural Resources, Subtitle A, Subchapter F, Part 228: Transitional Bilingual Education

| Manual | No Date |

Illinois Standards Achievement Test: Test Administration Manual Grades 3, 4, and 5 Census Test

| Manual | No Date |

Illinois Standards Achievement Test: Test Administration Manual Grades 7 and 8 Census Tests

| Handout | No Date |

IMAGE or ISAT? Which to Administer, School Year 2000–2001

	Memo	2000
	Illinois School Code, 2000 Edition	
Indiana	Memo	September 2000
	ISTEP + Policies for Temporary and Limited English Proficient (LEP) Students	
	Handout	Fall 2000
	Limited English Proficient (LEP) Students	
	Manual	2000
	ISTEP and Indiana Statewide Testing for Educational Progress Program Manual, 2000–2001	
	Pamphlet	No Date
	Serving Language Minority Students	
	Memo	No Date
	Participation and Accommodation of LEP Students in State Assessment Programs Survey	
Iowa	Guidelines	March 2000
	Guidelines for the Inclusion of ELLs in Your District-Wide Assessment Program	
	Policy	July 1999
	Chapter 12 General Accreditation Standards: Iowa Administrative Code School Rules of Iowa	
Kansas	Handout	November 2000
	Inclusion of ELLs in the Kansas State Assessment Program	
	Handout	November 2000
	Decision Making Tool for Including ELLs in the Kansas State Assessments	
Kentucky	Policy	September 1999
	Inclusion of Special Populations in the State-Required Assessment and Accountability Programs	
Louisiana	Policy	April 2001

LEAP for the 21st Century High Stakes Policy Memo

Policy   December 2000

LEAP for the 21st Century High Stakes Testing Policy

Guidelines   No Date

Guidelines for Selecting Test Accommodations for Students With Limited English Proficiency / LA Educational Assessment Program

Manual   Spring 2001

LEAP District and School Test Coordinators' Manual Grades 4, 8, and 10

Policy/Update   No Date

Notice of Intent: LEAP for the 21st Century High Stakes Testing Policy

Maine   Policy   March 2001

Maine Educational Assessment: Policies and Procedures for Accommodations for the Maine Educational Assessment

Manual   March 2001

Maine Educational Assessment: The Maine Educational Assessment Test Administrator's Manual, Grade 8

Maryland   Manual   July 2000

Requirements for Accommodating, Excusing, and Exempting Students in Maryland Assessment Programs

Massachusetts   Guidelines   June 2000

Approved Bilingual Dictionaries for Use on the MCAs by Students With Limited English Proficiency

Guidelines   Spring 2000

Requirements for the Participation of Students With Limited English Proficiency

	Policy	September 2000
	Release of Spring 2000 Spanish-Language Test Items	
	Policy	September 2000
	Release of Spring 2000 Test Items	
	Report	November 2000
	Spring 2000 MCAS Tests: Report of State Results	
	Report	October 2000
	The Performance of Limited English Proficient Students on the 1998 and 1999 MA Comprehensive Assessment Program	
Michigan	Guidelines	March 1995
	Michigan High School Proficiency Tests	
	Manual	Winter 2001
	Michigan Education Assessment Program Coordinator and Test Administrator Manual, Grades 4, 5, 7, and 8	
	Memo	April 2001
	Participation and Accommodations of LEP Students in State Assessment Program (Survey)	
	Manual	Spring 2001
	Michigan Education Assessment Program Coordinator and Test Administrator High School Tests Manual	
Minnesota	Handout	January 2001
	BST Math Practice Tests in Other Languages (MN Department of Children, Families and Learning—Web site)	
	Guidelines	March 2001
	Basic Standards Test: Guidelines for Students With Limited English Proficiency	
	Guidelines	November 2000

	Basic Standards Test: Guidelines for Students With Limited English Proficiency	
Mississippi	Policy	August 1998
	Mississippi Assessment System: Students With Disabilities and LEP Students	
	Guidelines	Fall 2000
	Mississippi Assessment System: Guidelines for Students With Disabilities and ELLs	
Missouri	Manual	Spring 2000
	Missouri Assessment Program Examiner's Manual	
	Manual	Spring 2001
	Missouri Assessment Program Test Coordinator's Manual	
	Manual	April 2000
	Missouri School Improvement Program: Integrated Standards and Indicators Manual	
	Handbook	1995
	Missouri Department of Elementary and Secondary Education: Educating Linguistically Diverse Students Requirements and Practices	
Montana	Manual	No Date
	Montana Alternate Assessment Scale Directions for Administration and Rating Scales, Grade 11	
	Manual	No Date
	Montana Alternate Assessment Scale Directions for Administration and Rating Scales, Grade 8	
	Manual	No Date
	Montana Alternate Assessment Scale Directions for Administration and Rating Scales, Grade 4	
	Handbook	January 2001
	Montana Office of Public Instruction Assessment Handbook, Volume 2	
	Presentation	February 2001

	Montana Comprehensive Assessment System: A Statewide MetNet Teleconference (PowerPoint)	
	Manual	2001
	A Component of the Montana Comprehensive Assessment System MontCAS Test Coordinator Manual	
	Supplement	No Date
	Montana Supplement to the Directions for Administration	
Nebraska	Guide	October 1999
	STARS: A Planning Guide for Nebraska Schools	
	Assessment	May 2000
	STARS: Update #1 Moving Forward with Assessment	
	Assessment	August 2000
	STARS: Update #2 A STARS Summary	
	Assessment	September 2000
	STARS: Update #3 Writing Assessment	
	Assessment	December 2000
	STARS: Update #4 Planning for Writing Assessment, Assessment Reporting, Model Assessments	
	Assessment	March 2001
	STARS: Update #5 Statewide Writing Assessment	
	Assessment	Spring 2001
	ELLs in STARS Assessment	
	Memo	January/April 2001
	Participation and Accommodation of LEP Students in State Assessment Programs Survey	
Nevada	Guidelines	2000–2001

	Guidelines for the Conduct of the Nevada Proficiency Examination Program	
	Manual	1999–2000
	99–00 Nevada High School Proficiency Examinations in Math, Reading, and Writing	
	Manual	2000–2001
	00–01 Nevada 4th and 8th Grade Proficiency Examinations in Writing	
	Letter	January 2001
	Letter from Thomas W. Klein, Evaluation Consultant, State of Nevada Department of Education	
New Hampshire	Memo	January 2001
	Revised Student Procedures for the NH Educational Improvement and Assessment Program	
	Procedure	No Date
	Procedures for Determining How Each Student Will Participate in the New Hampshire Educational Improvement and Assessment Program	
	Guidelines	January 2001
	Equal Education Access for Students With Limited English Proficiency: A Compliance Guide	
New Jersey	Memo	January 1999
	State of New Jersey Department of Education: LEP Students and State Wide Assessment	
	Policy	No Date
	New Jersey Department of Education Procedures for the Assessment of Limited English Proficient Students	
	Handout	No Date
	LEP Students Receiving Alternative Assessments	
New Mexico	Handbook	June 2000
	New Mexico State Department of Education Handbook Statewide Student Assessment Program	

	Memo	February 2001
	Update on Bilingual Assessment Issues	
New York	Memo	February 2000
	State of New York Department of Education: Progress Report on the English Language Learners Advisory Group	
	Guidelines	February 2000
	New Standards and Assessments: Status of Accommodations for LEP/ELL Students	
	Memo	January 2001
	Administration of the January 2001 Regents Examinations, Regents Competency Tests, and Occupational Education Proficiency Examinations	
	Guidelines	No Date
	Guidelines for Administering Regents Competency Tests	
	Memo	January 2001
	Reporting Procedures for the Grade 4 English Language Arts Assessment	
	Manual	January 2001
	An Implementation Manual for Schools With Elementary and Middle Level Grades	
	Report	January 2001
	The New York State School Report Card for and Overview of Academic Performance	
	Manual	2001
	New York State Testing Program: School Administrator's Manual	
	Memo	Fall 2000
	Procedures for Ordering, Shipping, and Storing of Materials for the 2001 Administration of the NYS Elementary and Intermediate Level Tests	
	Memo	February 1999
	Granting Credit for Foreign Language Study Outside the Regular Classroom	

	Memo	January 2001
	Administration of the January 2001 Regents Examinations, Regents Competency Tests	
	Memo	February 2001
	Procedures for Requesting and Storing the June 2001 Regents Examinations	
	Memo	April 2001
	Spring 2001, Grade 4 Elementary—Science, Grade 8 Intermediate—Science and Social Studies and Intermediate Technology Tests	
	Manual	2001
	Regents Examinations, Regents Competency Tests, Proficiency Examinations School Administrator's Manual	
	Memo	January 2001
	Participation and Accommodation of LEP Students in State Assessment Programs Survey	
North Carolina	Memo	February 2001
	Public Schools of North Carolina State Assessment	
	Memo	August 1999
	Public Schools of North Carolina State Assessment	
	Guidelines	March 1998
	Guidelines for Testing Students With Limited English Proficiency: NC Statewide Testing Program, Grades 3–12	
	Guidelines	August 1999
	Testing Accommodations for Students With Disabilities and Students Identified as Limited English Proficient	
	Guidelines	Summer 1999
	Public Schools of North Carolina Assessment Brief	
	Guidelines	No Date

	North Carolina Statewide Student Accountability Standards	
	Guidelines	No Date
	Student Accountability Standards (from NCPublicSchools.org)	
	Memo	April 2001
	Current Testing Policy for LEP Students in North Carolina	
	Table	February 2001
	Illustration of Transition to One Statewide English Language Proficiency Test	
	Flow Chart	February 2001
	Navigating Limited English Proficient Student Participation in Statewide Assessment	
North Dakota	Handout	No Date
	State Assessment Strategy	
	Report	1998
	North Dakota 1998 Research Results for State-Wide CTBS/5 (TerraNova) Testing Grade 8	
	Memo	March 2001
	Department of Public Instruction Memo: 2001 Spring CTBS/5—TerraNova Test Interpretation Workshops	
	Manual	2000
	Test Coordinator's Manual 2001 North Dakota Statewide Testing Program	
	Memo	No Date
	Participation and Accommodation of LEP Students in State Assessment Programs Survey	
Ohio	Guidelines	September 2000
	Conclusion Guidelines for Conducting Alternate Assessment Implementation Year: 2000	
	Guidelines	September 2000

	Alternate Assessment and the IEP Team	
	Policy	No Date
	District Accountability	
	Handbook	November 2000
	Rules Book	
	Guidelines	1999
	EMIS-Education Management Information System: Definitions, Procedures and Guidelines for FY2001	
	Not Specified	January 2001
	Update on "English-Limited Students" and the Proficiency Tests	
	Not Specified	February 1995
	ODE's Response Regarding Translating Directions for LEP/ESL Students	
Oklahoma	Manual	Spring 2001
	Oklahoma School Testing Program Spring 2001 Test Preparation Manual	
	Memo	December 2000
	Sandy Garrett, State Superintendent of Public Instruction, Oklahoma State Department of Education	
	Memo	January 2001
	Sandy Garrett, State Superintendent of Public Instruction, Oklahoma State Department of Education	
	Policy	No Date
	Subchapter 13, Student Assessment 210:10-13-2	
	Policy	No Date
	Subchapter 13, Student Assessment 210:10-13-1–210:10-13-14	
	Directions	No Date

	Oklahoma School Testing Program: Directions for Coding on Student Answer Documents	
	Report	No Date
	State Summary Report for All Student Populations—Draft	
	Memo	February 2001
	State Department of Education: Documentation Pertaining to Participation of LEP Students in Statewide Assessments	
Oregon	Memo	January 2001
	Oregon Migrant Education Service Center: Oregon Migrant Education Personnel Directory	
	Directory	No Date
	Oregon Migrant Education Program, 2000–2001 Personnel Directory	
	Memo	March 2000
	Clarification Regarding Inclusion of Non-English Students in Oregon Statewide Assessment	
	Not Specified	No Date
	2000–2001 Oregon Statewide Assessment Benchmark Level of Assessment	
	Policy	March 2001
	Oregon School Boards Association Selected Sample Policy	
	Report	2001
	District Report Card	
	Report	1999
	1999 Oregon Statewide Assessment Program Performance of Selected Subgroups	
	Manual	2001
	Administration Manual 2001: Benchmarks 1, 2, 3	
	Manual	December 2000

Administration Manual 2001: CIM Benchmark
in Reading and Literature, Math and Science

Manual   December 2000

Administration Manual 2001: Benchmarks 2,
3, & CIM

Manual   2001

Administration Manual 2001: CIM Benchmark
in Writing and Math

Manual   2000

2000 Oregon Statewide Writing and Math
Problem-Solving Assessment: Administration
Manual

Manual   2000

2000 Oregon Statewide Reading and Literature,
Math, Science, and Social Science Multiple
Choice Assessment: Administration Manual

Manual   2001

Oregon Department of Education Juried
Assessment Manual 2001

Pennsylvania   Handbook   2001

The PA System of School Assessment
Handbook for Assessment Coordinators

Policy   December 2000

Testing Accommodations for the
Pennsylvania System of School Assessment

Handbook   November 2000

The PA System of School Assessment
Mathematics Assessment Handbook

Handbook   2000

The PA System of School Assessment Writing
Assessment Handbook Supplement, Grade 11

Handbook   August 2000

The PA System of School Assessment
Reading Assessment Handbook

Letter   July 2001

	Letter from R. Jay Gift, Assessment Advisor, Commonwealth of Pennsylvania Department of Education	
Rhode Island	Guidelines	2001
	Requirements for Student Participation and Assessment Accommodation	
South Carolina	Guidelines	Spring 2001
	Appendix B from PACT Spring 2001—Test Coordinator's Manual: Guidelines for Testing Students With LEP	
	Report	2000
	School Demographic Report	
	Memo	No Date
	Participation and Accommodation of LEP Students in State Assessment Programs Survey	
	Manual	Spring 2001
	(Palmetto Achievement Challenge Tests) Test Administrator's Manual Spring 2001	
	Manual	Spring 2001
	Test Coordinator's Manual for the South Carolina Palmetto Achievement Challenge Tests (PACT)	
South Dakota	Handbook	Spring 2001
	South Dakota Handbook for Test Coordinators State Assessment Program Spring 2001, Grades 2, 4, 8, 11	
Tennessee	Manual	2001
	Tennessee Comprehensive Assessment Program Testing Coordinator's Manual	
	Manual	2001
	TCAP Achievement Test 2001 Administration Manual	
	Manual	January 2001
	Tennessee High School Subject Matter Assessment Program Manual for System Testing Coordinators	

	Guidelines	2001
	English as a Second Language Resource Guide	
Texas	Manual	2001
	Texas Student Assessment Program District and Campus Coordinator Manual 2001	
	Memo	April 2001
	State Testing Requirements for LEP Students in Grades 3–8	
	Policy	Downloaded July 2001
	Student Assessment Division (from Texas Education Agency Web site)	
	Policy	No Date
	S.B. No. 676, An Act Relating to Assessment of Academic Skills of Certain Students of Limited English Proficiency	
	Report	No Date
	Summary Report: Test Performance and Group Performance (from Interpreting Assessment Reports document)	
	Report	2001
	Texas Assessment of Academic Skills 2001 Optional Reports	
	Policy	September 1999
	Education Code: Chapter 29 (from Texas Legislature Web site)	
	Policy	April 2001
	Questions and Answers Relating to the Implementation of Senate Bill 676	
	Policy	May 30, 1995
	Education Code: Chapter 29 (from Texas Legislature Web site)	
	Memo	July 2001

Participation and Accommodation of LEP Students in State Assessment Programs Survey

Utah	Policy	April 2001

53A-3-602. School District Performance Report—Elements—Annual filing

	Procedure	April 2001

Rule R277-473. Testing Procedures

	Guidelines	May 2001

Guidelines for Participation of Students With Special Needs in the Utah Performance Assessment System for Students

Vermont	Memo	October 2000

E-mail re: Alternate Assessment Training

	Memo	October 2000

Alternate Assessment Implementation and Training for State Assessments from Vermont Department of Education Web site

	Memo	March 2001

E-mail re: Communication Portfolio for ELLs

	Guidelines	Spring 2001

Participation Guidelines for Students With Special Assessment Needs

	Guidelines	Downloaded June 2001

Documentation of Eligibility for Alternate Assessment

	Guidelines	Downloaded June 2001

Allowable Accommodations Grid for the State Component Standards-Based Assessments

	Guidelines	Downloaded June 2001

State of Vermont Alternate Assessment of ELLs Communication Portfolio

	Guidelines	Downloaded June 2001
	Individualized Instructional Plan for ELLs	
	Memo	April 2001
	E-mail re: Notice Regarding New ESL Students/Vermont DRA	
	Memo	July 2001
	Participation and Accommodation of LEP Students in State Assessment Programs Survey	
Virginia	Policy	May 1999
	Board of Education Resolution on Accommodations for Testing Students With LEP and School Accountability	
	Guidelines	October 1997
	Limited English Proficient Students: Guidelines for Participation in the Standards of Learning Assessments	
	Handbook	July 1999
	English as a Second Language Handbook for Teachers and Administrators	
	Memo	January 2001
	Participation and Accommodation of LEP Students in State Assessment Programs Survey	
Washington	Guidelines	June 2000
	Guidelines for Participation and Testing Accommodations for Special Populations on the Washington Assessment of Student Learning	
	Policy	June 1999
	Education Reform and Assessment Laws, June 1999: Statewide Reporting of Assessment Results	
Wisconsin	Guidelines	September 1999
	English Language Proficiency Levels (from Wisconsin Department of Public Instruction Web site)	

		Downloaded
	Guidelines	August 2001
	Examples of Test Accommodations for Students With LEP for the Wisconsin Knowledge and Concepts Exams (WDPI Web site)	
	Guidelines	2000–2001
	DPI Guidelines to Facilitate the Participation of Students With Special Needs in State Assessment (WDPI Web site)	
West Virginia	Guidelines	No Date
	Guidelines: Limited English Proficient Students for Testing in the SAT-9	
	Policy	Downloaded July 2002
	Title 126—Legislative Rule—Board of Education Series 14: The Statewide Assessment Program (2340) (http://wvde.state.wv.us/policies/p2340.html)	
Wyoming	Policy	January 2000
	Policies for the Participation of All Students in District and Statewide Assessment and Accountability Systems	

Study 2

Test Translation and State Assessment Policies for English Language Learners

Charles W. Stansfield and Melissa Bowles

The first study in this volume examined state assessment policies regarding the use of accommodations for ELLs[1] participating in state assessment. The study was designed to provide a broad perspective on the priorities set by SEAs during the 2000–2001 school year. However, an examination of states' policies does not show how schools and districts interpreted and implemented the policies. This study bridges the policy–practice gap by examining in depth one accommodation—test translation—and analyzing in detail policies and practices supporting the use of this accommodation.

As categorized in Study 1 of this volume, test translation is one of 11 native language accommodations. The authors further classified the 11 native language accommodations cited in states' assessment policies for school year 2000–2001 into four categories: (a) written translation, (b) scripted oral translation, (c) sight translation, and (d) student response in the native language. (A detailed discussion of these categories of accommodations and of the relevant state data can be found in Study 1.)

This study examines the use of written translation and sight translation. *Written translation* involves the use of two strategies for providing ELLs access to the content of the test: the provision of dual-language reference materials, such as dictionaries and glossaries, and the translation of the test or test parts. Written translation was the native language accommodation cited by the largest number of states (19) in their assessment policies for the 2000–2001 school year. Most of these states allowed the use of bilingual ref-

[1]Because many states' policies refer to English language learners (ELLs) as limited English proficient (LEP) students, the terms "ELL" and "LEP" are used interchangeably throughout this study.

erence materials. Translation of tests or test parts was allowed by fewer states. Nonetheless, written translation of complete tests is an increasingly frequent and significant accommodation: The policies of 16 states indicated that this accommodation is either allowed for all content areas or prohibited for only some content areas. As Stansfield (1996) suggested, formal assessment in the native language can be accomplished through the use of a written translation or adaptation of the original version of the test.

Sight translation involves spontaneous oral rendering of test content in the student's native language and therefore can vary depending on the skills of the translator, making it difficult to determine if all students provided sight translation received equal assistance from this accommodation. Sight translation is an informal accommodation, and as such is problematic. However, because several states (29) were identified as allowing the use of sight translation in Study 1 on accommodations policies, it is one of the focuses of this study.

Test translation is widely used by states and has been identified by researchers as among the most promising means of providing ELLs access to test content (see Study 1). However, to date there has been no comprehensive review and description of state policies and practices concerning this accommodation. This study attempts to fill the policy–practice gap by examining not only state policy but also the practices of the 12 states that use test translation. The result is a study that provides an overview of states' policies regarding test translation and juxtaposes these onto actual practice.

The study is presented in five parts: The first part outlines the purpose of the study and the methodology used. The second part reviews key issues pertaining to test translation. The third part presents an overview of state policies related to two kinds of test translation—sight translation and written translation. The next part presents findings from case studies conducted for the 12 states—Arizona, Colorado, Delaware, Massachusetts, Minnesota, New Mexico, New York, Oregon, Rhode Island, Texas, Utah, and Vermont—using test translation as an accommodation for ELLs in school year 2000–2001. The final part provides a discussion of findings and offers recommendations to states regarding the development and implementation of sight and written test translation.

PURPOSE AND METHODOLOGY

Purpose

The study is designed to contribute to our understanding of how SEAs develop translated tests and the policies guiding the development and implementation of these tests throughout the 50 states and the District of Columbia. Four research questions guided the study:

1. What are states' policies regarding the translation of state assessment?
2. What is the process for the development and implementation of translated state assessments?
3. To what extent do states allowing test translation attempt to determine the validity and effectiveness of translated tests?
4. What translated materials are available to stakeholders regarding state assessment?

Methodology

The research questions posed for the policy and practice parts of the study (Questions 1 and 2–4, respectively) required the use of different methodologies. The policy analysis required the examination of state policy documents, whereas the analysis of practice involved the interviewing of key state assessment personnel. The methodologies employed for each part of the study—policy analysis and case studies—are described next.

Policy Analysis

All of the information concerning states' policies in this study is based on data drawn directly from states' official written policy documents regarding testing and accommodations. Initial data collection was conducted by The George Washington University Center for Equity and Excellence in Education (GW/CEEE) research team using the procedures outlined in Study 1 of this volume. This process involved collection of policy documents from the state assessment directors of the 50 states and the District of Columbia. Documents included state assessment handbooks, policy memoranda, and other guidance communicated to districts and schools by the SEA. (For a complete list of state policy documents used in this study, see Appendix B.) Data were entered into a framework that was then submitted to SEAs for verification. Changes made to state reports were supported by documentation.

Data provided by the GW/CEEE team were used to guide an in-depth examination of states' policies regarding sight translation and written translation.

Case Studies

In developing the case studies, a pool of appropriate states was selected. To accomplish this, data from the policy analysis phase of the study were used to identify states with policies allowing translations of state-wide assessments. Next, we confirmed states' use of test translation during the 2000–2001 school year by contacting state leaders knowledgeable about the assessment of ELLs in each state. Typically, these were state assessment directors or bilingual coordinators.

Data for the case studies were gathered from two principal sources: (a) SEA policy documents and Web sites, and (b) telephone interviews. SEA policy documents and Web sites were examined to provide background information regarding, for instance, overviews of statewide testing programs, numbers of ELLs enrolled in the state, and primary non-English languages in the state.

More detailed information was gathered from telephone interviews using a questionnaire developed with input from a test accommodations advisory committee convened by GW/CEEE. The committee developed a 36-question protocol designed to generate data beneficial to educators and state officials who wanted to learn more about test translation practices across the country. These questions addressed a range of issues regarding test translation, such as the history of test translation in the state, the translation process, translated ancillary materials, and publications in languages other than English on the Web. Investigation of these issues was designed to provide insight into the psychometric qualities of the translated tests, district translation, and the future of test translation in their state. (The complete interview protocol is provided in Appendix A.)

Each interviewee signed and returned a consent form to participate in the study and received a copy of the questionnaire that formed the basis of the interview. Typically, we interviewed the state assessment director and the bilingual or ESL coordinator. In some cases, however, the state assessment director nominated the assessment staff member who knew most about the subject to speak with us, and sometimes both the director and that person spoke with us at the same time. In other cases, we also interviewed former SEA staff who had been involved in the translation of the tests. At times, SEA personnel permitted us to speak with their test contractor or the manager of the translation company that conducted the translation. This person provided us with more detailed information about the translation process and psychometric analyses performed on the tests. On several occasions, the state or the state's test contractor was also able to provide us with formal reports about the translated tests.

Finally, based on the data gathered from the case studies, we drafted a report on each of the 12 states. To verify our findings, we sent a draft case study to each person we interviewed for review. Case studies were revised based on input from these individuals.

KEY ISSUES AFFECTING TEST TRANSLATION

The use of test translation as an accommodation for state assessment is affected by a number of issues. First, state contexts are complex. SEA decisions regarding whether or not to use translated tests are informed by the size and makeup of their respective student populations, as well as political and budgetary considerations. In addition to these practical concerns, more theoretical issues also should be taken into consideration when translating tests. The most pressing of these concerns is whether or not the English version and the translated version of a test are equivalent. Psychometricians have recommended methods of establishing test equivalence; however, to date, the most reliable means to ensure test equivalence are found among practitioners and involve the selection of appropriate translators and the use of rigorous and recursive methods of checking translation accuracy.

Before offering an overview of these issues, however, it is first essential to distinguish among the translation of tests, the adaptation of tests, and the development of alternate assessments in students' native languages. A translated test is one in which content originally in English is rendered into a non-English language. The original English version of the test and the translated test differ only in the language, not in the constructs being measured. However, it is not always feasible to translate a test directly into another language without modification. In fact, most translated tests normally require minor adjustments or *adaptations* to accommodate the language of the non-English version. For example, a math or science test translated into Spanish might reverse the use of commas and periods in the translated version (the number 10,215.64 is written 10.215,64 in Spanish). Such minor changes make the translated version more suitable and do not affect score comparability.

Adaptation, however, might involve more substantial changes, such as the replacement of particular items with other items that are more appropriate for the native language or valid for the examinee population or for the language of the new test (Stansfield, 2003). Because this level of change affects the ability to compare scores across the standard and adapted versions, such tests are most accurately characterized as adaptations rather than translations. The change in test content raises validity concerns, especially if a substantial number of items are changed. As a result, it becomes necessary to demonstrate the equivalence of the constructs measured by the standard and adapted instruments. Because this process takes time and is expensive, adaptation is rarely used in state assessments in the United States (Stansfield, 2003).

On the other hand, because examinee populations speak (and in some cases write) in a non-English language and come from different cultural and educational contexts, it might be assumed that an entirely new test, or alternate assessment, should be developed in the students' native language. However, for an alternate assessment to be effective in including ELLs in the state assessment system, two criteria must be addressed. First, the alternate test must assess the same constructs as the regular state assessment it is designed to replace. Second, the alternate assessment must produce scores that are comparable to those produced by the regular state assessment. Although the first criterion might be fulfilled, the second is much more difficult to satisfy because it involves sophisticated statistical adjustments to scores to ensure that the alternate can be scored on the same scale as the regular state assessment. Nonetheless, so long as the content of alternate assessments can be aligned to the standards and the scores of ELLs participating in the alternate assessment can be made comparable to those of students taking regular state assessment, alternate assessments could be a viable option for states.

Factors Affecting States' Decisions to Translate State Assessments

Typically, the decision of SEAs regarding whether or not to translate a test depends on a number of factors, including cost efficiency, suitability of a written test in the non-English language for the targeted population, and political and attitudinal concerns (Stansfield, 2000). Each of these factors is addressed next.

Cost Efficiency

The cost of translating or adapting a test is a major issue states face in deciding whether or not to provide a native language version of a test. Translation and adaptation can be costly processes because of the meticulous reviews that the tests must undergo. Furthermore, once a test has been rendered into another language, the resulting product is subject to the same rigorous item reviews applied to the English version of the test. Two factors affecting cost efficiency include subject area and size of student population benefiting from the translation.

Tests in subject areas such as mathematics and science can be translated without much alteration, as the fundamental concepts being tested are independent of language. Hence, these subject areas can be cost effective, given a large enough target population.

Occasionally, however, states might want to provide native language versions of tests in subject areas that are less amenable to translation, such as reading. In these cases, some items on the test might be translated to the native language, whereas others will need to be replaced with entirely new items in the native language. For instance, adaptation of an ELA test to Spanish to test native Spanish speakers' knowledge can be complicated. First, the state would have to create new test specifications for the Spanish test, identifying the grammar points that should be tested. Some of those points (e.g., subject–verb agreement) might be the same for the two tests, but others would not. Once the new specifications are developed, some completely new items would have to be written, and these must then undergo a review process similar to that of the ELA test. Because the test specifications must be modified and new items written, the cost of an adaptation could easily approach the cost of developing a completely new test. A state might nevertheless choose adaptation over the development of a new test because the presence of items common to the English version and the native language adaptation might facilitate statistical linking of test scores on the two versions. An entirely new test would present the disadvantage of having no items in common with the English test, making linking more difficult.

A second consideration regarding cost efficiency is the number of students that might benefit from translated or adapted tests. Until very recently, the cost of translated or adapted tests and the small numbers of students these tests benefit have restricted the creation of translated versions in languages other than Spanish. Some states have developed policies allowing for native language versions of tests, but then abandoned development after determining that, relative to the number of students who would be served by the translated or adapted test, the cost of test development is too high. Other states have developed non-English versions of their assessments only to find that fewer students than expected opt to take them instead of the English version. Thus, such states cease to develop non-English versions of such tests.

Suitability for Targeted Population

When policymakers are considering whether or not to translate state assessments, they must determine which students will benefit from the translation. Two factors can influence the choice to translate or adapt a state test: (a) students' language proficiency and literacy in English and in the native language, and (b) students' academic background and current instructional program.

The impact of language proficiency on test performance must be considered when evaluating the suitability of a translated or adapted test for a given examinee. Since 1975, nonnative English-speaking students in the United States have been classified into three groups: students not proficient in English, LEP students, and students who are fully proficient in English. A translated or adapted test is normally more appropriate for an examinee not proficient in English, because the regular English version would simply not be accessible to the student.

A translated or adapted test might also appear to be an appropriate assessment for the LEP student. However, this is not always the case. The appropriateness of either the regular or the translated or adapted version depends on a number of factors, most prominently the student's proficiency in the two languages for which the test is available and the language in which the student has been instructed in the content tested.

Language proficiency varies according to the domain in which it might be used and the kind of language skill required by the situation. Cummins (1984) distinguished between language use that is cognitively undemanding and that which is cognitively demanding. He also contrasted language situations that are rich in supporting context with those that are decontextualized. According to Cummins's classifications, the tasks associated with a test are often cognitively demanding, and both the tasks and the language occur in situations of reduced contextual support. Therefore, testing situations place examinees under cognitive strain, and, for ELLs, the reduced contextual support that characterizes the language of a test might make it harder to comprehend than common language, which is highly contextualized.

In addition to the fact that the testing situation and context could affect an examinee's ability to comprehend language, a given examinee's proficiency might vary from one domain of language to another. This means that an individual might have complete proficiency in one domain of language and only partial proficiency in another. For example, the examinee might have good speaking proficiency, but poor reading proficiency in the native language. Thus, if the LEP examinee does not have the kind of native language proficiency required by the test, then the native language version will not produce a score that reflects the examinee's true ability. Indeed, if the examinee has stronger reading proficiency in the language of the regular version of the test, that version might even provide a more accurate score.

Another factor affecting the suitability of translated and adapted tests is the examinee's academic background in the language of the test. Although an LEP examinee might have greater proficiency in the language of the translated version of the test, most of his or her knowledge of the subject matter might have been acquired in an English-medium instructional setting. This instruction will develop the examinee's knowledge of content-relevant vocabulary and expression in English, but not in the native language. Thus, through English-medium instruction in the subject matter, the examinee might acquire the ability to interact with an achievement test in English, but this ability might not transfer readily to the examinee's native language. Thus, decoding test stimuli and items in the native language could be more difficult for the examinee. In such a case, the regular version might provide a more accurate measure of the student's true ability in the construct being assessed. Studies have shown that background knowledge affects performance on language tests (Alderson & Urquhart, 1983, 1985; Hale, 1988). Similarly, the acquisition of academic knowledge in a language can alter the appropriateness of tests of that discipline in two different languages for a bilingual examinee. Those who are considering using translated or adapted tests for LEP examinees need to be sensitive in judging the role of language proficiency in the discipline and the role of content knowledge in each test version when determining which version will be more appropriate.

Attitudes and Politics

A final influence on the decision of whether to offer a non-English version of a state assessment is the attitude of SEA officials toward the role of language in the state's education system. Some officials might feel that use of non-English tests sets a bad precedent, whereas others might fear that offering such tests will generate public criticism of the assessment program. In states where a specific ethnic group wields considerable political influence in state government, the language of that group is more likely to appear on state assessments. Although attitudes toward English and non-English languages play a role in some programmatic decisions, such considerations are less influential than matters of cost and numbers.

Factors Affecting Test Equivalence

There are many approaches to ensuring the accuracy of translated tests. Psychometricians tend to approach this process as a science, whereas practicing translators often consider translation as an art that requires translators with knowledge of the content and the target language. Both camps are concerned about determining the equivalence of the test.

There are two major issues in test translation: (a) the psychometric equivalence of native language and English language tests, and (b) the accuracy and appropriateness of the language used in the native language version of the test. The focus of this study is on the second of these concerns. However, before moving to a discussion of steps that can be taken in the translation process to ensure accuracy of translated tests, it is important to acknowledge the psychometric difficulties facing test developers.

Psychometric Concerns

Test translation has been criticized on purely psychometric grounds: The constructs assessed by the original and target language tests might not be equivalent, and statistical adjustments must be made to ensure that the resulting test scores are equivalent.

In the 1990s, an international effort to develop guidelines for the translation and adaptation of tests was conducted by a group of psychometricians with a strong orientation to using statistical methods to ensure equivalence (Hambleton, 1993, 1994). The resulting guidelines included discussion of three research designs for testing the comparability of scores: (a) having bilinguals take both the original and adapted versions, (b) having monolingual speakers of the source language take both the original and back-translated (i.e., retranslated from the target language back into the source language) versions of a test, and (c) having monolingual speakers of each language take the version of the test that corresponds to their language. In each design the two sets of scores are compared and statistical adjustments made based on the assumption that the adjustments correct error in measurement introduced by the use of different languages in the assessment.

Each of the three research designs discussed by Hambleton has flaws that make the design difficult or impossible to execute. For example, the bilingual groups design (the first design) requires the identification of individuals who are equally bilingual. Most sociolinguists insist that such individuals are extremely rare, and some claim that it is impossible to be equally bilingual in two languages. Sireci (1997) identified a major practical problem with this design: Bilingual participants are not generally representative of the examinee population they are supposed to represent.

The second design, the use of back-translation, is problematic because it does not allow for the examination of the translated test. Rather, monolingual English speakers of the source language take the original test and a version of it that has been translated from English to the target language and then back to English. Even Hambleton, who originally described this method, called it a very weak design.

The third design requires two different groups of students—English speakers and monolingual speakers of the native language—to take the tests. In this design, the examinees represent two different populations with different educational backgrounds. As a result, differences in item difficulty and in mean test scores could be due to variation in the two test populations in the mastery of the educational content and constructs assessed. Elder (1997) noted that group differences can be explained in two ways: (a) There is a real difference in the ability being tested, or (b) there are confounding variables within the test that systematically mask or distort the ability being tested. Similarly, Sireci (1992) identified the major drawback of this third design to be the inability to separate group ability differences from differences due to the two different versions of the tests. He argued that the design could be improved by a matching procedure that would select participants for the two groups on some related criteria, such as intelligence or socioeconomic status. However, he noted that the results of studies on the effects of using related criteria as opposed to random selection are mixed. He also noted that such designs are usually impractical. That is, either data on related criteria are not available or the researcher has a limited ability to sample from each group.

It is rarely possible to collect data that permit us to know whether mean differences are due to differences in language of the test or to differences in content mastery in the two examinee populations taking the test. Therefore, test program administrators cannot legitimately make statistical adjustments to compensate for these differences. As a result, translated versions of state assessments are normally scored on the same scale as the English versions.

Although solutions to creating equivalent tests are both psychometrically demanding and problematic, educational tests continue to be translated. In the development of a translated test, psychometric concerns cannot be overarching. Linguistic concerns about the accuracy of the translation must also be addressed: To what extent does the translated test measure the intended content and address the linguistic needs of the students? Test translation is not something that should be taken lightly, but rather entered into with careful consideration of linguistic and psychometric issues and the needs of the students or examinees for such an instrument.

The Translation Process

Under the authority of ESEA, SEAs continue to develop test translations as a means of providing ELLs access to test content. Although practical methods to guarantee test score equivalence are rare, certain translation practices can ensure that the greatest possible equivalence between English and translated versions of state assessments is achieved. The first step is to employ an appropriate method to translate the test. The second step is to choose translators with appropriate qualifications. Finally, a translated test must be presented in an appropriate format (e.g., in a monolingual or bilingual test booklet).

Ensuring the Accuracy of the Translation. A number of methods can be used to verify the accuracy of a translation. Two of the most common are (a) side-by-side comparison of the original and translated versions, either by professional translators or a team of educators or community members in the state in question, and (b) back-translation. In the first option, either professional translators or bilingual educators and community members compare the original and translated versions item by item and line by line to ensure equivalence between the two forms. The second potential verification tool, back-translation, has been the subject of much debate in the literature. This process entails retranslating a document from the target language back into the source language, on the premise that if the original translation was accurate, the translation back into the source language should be nearly identical to the original document.

Cross-cultural psychologist Richard Brislin wrote extensively about back-translation (1970, 1976, 1986; Brislin, Lonner, & Thorndike, 1973). Brislin recommended back-translation as a method that produces a high-quality translation of a test instrument. He claimed the instrument could be used to examine traits and constructs across cultures. Following his lead, a number of other authors (Bernard, 1988, 1994; McKay et al., 1996; Warner & Campbell, 1970) have written about it as well. As described in the literature on cross-cultural research, back-translation involves having a bilingual translate the original test to the target language and then having a different bilingual translate it back to English. The two English versions are then compared, and points of disagreement are used to identify problems in the initial forward translation. The forward translation is then corrected. Sometimes the process of creating a back-translation and comparing it with the source document is repeated until the source document and back-translation agree (Marin & Marin, 1991).

Although back-translation is viewed in the test translation literature as a method for drafting, reviewing, and revising a translation, its primary function is to identify and correct errors in the forward translation. However, relying exclusively on the back-translation to examine the quality of the translated document could be risky. First, the lack of agreement between the original document and the back-translation might be due to problems with the back-translation, not problems with the forward translation. That is, the back-translation is as likely to contain translation errors (mistranslations, omissions, insertions) as is the forward translation. Hence, once the back-translation has been conducted, the test program administrator is provided with two translations (forward and back) but no verification of the quality of either.

Second, a translator's knowledge that the initial forward translation will be validated by a back-translation procedure might influence his or her approach to forward translation. By producing a very literal forward translation, the translator can ensure that the back-translation will produce a document that is very similar to the source document. Unfortunately, such a translation is likely to produce stilted rather than natural expression and result in a test that is difficult to read and hence less accessible to the examinee.

Despite these shortcomings, back-translation can be a useful procedure. Indeed, it is a method of quality control that can be especially useful to the test program manager who does not have knowledge of the target language and does not have confidence in the translation reviewers who are available. Normally, however, other methods, such as successive reviews and revisions of a forward translation by other professional translators and by representatives of the examinee population, are available to identify and correct problems with the forward translation. For this reason, professional translation agencies do not use back-translation as a quality control procedure unless specifically requested to do so by their clients.

Nevertheless, some states have used back-translation in the development of state assessments for ELLs. Minnesota, for instance, experimented with back-translation to obtain feedback on its translation of one of several state assessments to Spanish (Liu, Anderson, & Swierzbin, 1999). A full year was devoted to the translation and pilot testing of the test. In the real world of state assessment, however, only 2 to 4 weeks typically are available for translating, reviewing, revising, typesetting, proofing, and correcting a test. Although back-translation proved successful in Minnesota, Liu, Anderson, and Swierzbin (1999) noted the high cost of the process. Successive iterations of forward translation and revision would work just as well, and the translation equivalence of the two versions can be assured more quickly at less cost. In subsequent years, Minnesota has not used back-translation to verify its translated assessments, but has relied instead on forward translation with iterative rounds of review and revision.

Identifying Translators With Appropriate Qualifications.

There has been relatively little guidance provided regarding the qualifications necessary to conduct effective test translation. One major issue surrounding translator qualifications involves the use of professional translators as opposed to "bilinguals"; that is, representatives of different linguistic communities who also speak English.

Much of the support for the use of bilinguals in test translation stems from Brislin's discussions of the procedures he used for translating measures to carry out cross-cultural research (Brislin, 1970, 1976, 1986; Brislin et al., 1973). In his work, Brislin (1970) relied on the use of bilinguals rather than professional translators, possibly because he was translating tests into Micronesian languages and was unable to identify professional translators. Although Brislin stated that the quality of test translation will differ across languages due to the nature of the relationships between the particular target language and English, he conceded that translator competency in English might also play a role in translation quality.

Largely because of Brislin's work, there has been a marked preference for employing bilingual members of linguistic minority groups as translators. In fact, teams of bilinguals have often been convened to work jointly on translations because of their familiarity with the language and cultural context of the students. Such teams of translators typically do not include professional translators. The tendency to select individuals to translate tests solely on the basis of being bilingual members of a linguistic minority group is unfortunate. Although these individuals might have strong linguistic skills in the target language, and an understanding of its cultural context, they do not necessarily have a broad understanding of the translation process or knowledge of regional variations in vocabulary in the target language.

On the other hand, credentialed professional translators can add much to the translation process. Professional translators are fluent in the languages they translate. Because most professional translators limit their work to translating into their native language they are themselves often members of a linguistic minority and hence are familiar with linguistic and sociocultural factors that affect the appropriateness of a translation. In addition, they normally have outstanding writing skills in the target language.

In addition to a high degree of literacy in the target language, knowledge of the culture of both languages, and knowledge of the translation process, test translators need to have a solid knowledge of the subject or content of the test, and how it is expressed in the target language. Finally, test translators need to have a knowledge of good item-writing guidelines and be able to apply them with at least the same level of skill as the authors of the original test that is being translated.

Since Brislin's work in the 1970s and 1980s, there have been a number of attempts to establish more defined guidelines for translator qualifications. The Guidelines for Adapting Educational and Psychological Tests recommends that translators have familiarity with both cultures, the subject area of the test, and test development principles (Hambleton, 1994, p. 235). The Guidelines also support the use of teams of individuals to conduct test translations.

In 1996, the GED Testing Service used five criteria in selecting translators to translate different subtests of the high school equivalency battery into Spanish: (a) accreditation by the American Translators Association, (b) near-native reading and writing skills in the source language, (c) educated native writing skills in the target language, (d) experience as an item writer, and (e) academic specialization in the subject area of the test (Stansfield & Auchter, 2001). In the GED project, translators received extensive orientation to the test specifications and to the language backgrounds of the students in the examinee population. However, translators and reviewers worked independently, and their work was supervised by a translation manager, who was also a test developer.

A paper prepared for the NAEP Governing Board by the American Institutes for Research (Garcia, 2000) also addressed the issue of translator competency. The paper, which was a preliminary task to the translation of a mathematics assessment for the proposed Voluntary National Test, recommended similar qualifications for translators and a similar approach to that presented in Stansfield and Auchter (2001).

These guidelines emphasize the need for translators with the highest professional qualifications. Based on these guidelines, it is recommended that translators be selected to translate state assessments not merely on the basis of their being bilinguals, but on the basis of their professional qualifications. It is advisable to select translators who have been certified by the American Translators Association or another such licensing board. This ensures that the translator meets high standards in both languages and introduces a degree of quality control not possible with self-selected groups of bilinguals.

Test Booklet Options. There are two basic options when administering a translation or adaptation of a test in another language. One is to produce test booklets in both languages and then allow either the teacher or the student to determine which booklet should be used by the examinee. Another is to produce the test booklet in a format that puts the two languages on facing pages. A variant of this option uses parallel columns with, for example, the left column in English and the right column in Spanish. Other variations are also possible, including having students take the test in both languages and giving the student the higher of the two scores. The allotment of additional time might also be a consideration for examinees taking the test in the parallel column or facing pages format. Several studies of the effects of various presentation formats have been conducted and are reviewed here. On the basis of these studies, a general recommendation regarding presentation format is provided at the end of the section.

Stansfield (1997) conducted an informal survey concerning test booklet formats using the Internet to collect descriptions of practices around the world. The results showed that different approaches were used in different countries and that, regardless of the approach used, test program administrators expressed confidence in the effectiveness of their approach. However, these same test program administrators believed that competing test booklet formats were flawed in ways that might affect the validity of the test score. For example, test program administrators who did not use a bilingual test booklet felt strongly that this format was not authentic because students are not typically presented with bilingual texts to process. They also expressed the belief that format affects the cognitive processes tapped in taking the test, and therefore the validity of the score.

Perhaps the most interesting finding of the Stansfield (1997) study involved a report from Mexico regarding translated tests in Maya and Spanish. The test program administrators felt that if students were allowed to choose one test or the other, their choice would be influenced by the expectation that they should take the test in Spanish because it is the dominant language of the larger society. Students therefore were asked to take a test in both languages. To avoid any order effect (effect on performance attributable to the order in which the tests were administered), the students were given the higher of the two resulting scores, regardless of which form they took first.

To evaluate the effects of different test booklet formats, the Massachusetts Department of Education used two different formats when field testing its state assessments in the fall of 1997 (Stansfield & Kahl, 1998). Spanish-speaking ELL students were given either a bilingual test booklet, with Spanish and English on facing pages, or a Spanish-only booklet, but were also told that, if they wished to, they could consult the English booklet during the test. Each student's teacher made the decision as to which test booklet format the student would receive, and the teacher administered the tests.

After the field test administration, three staff of the Massachusetts Department of Education interviewed 97 students and 17 teachers. The results indicated that students who received bilingual test booklets relied mostly on the Spanish version of the items. However, in some cases they also read the English version and felt that they gleaned some additional meaning from this version. As a result, it was decided that in the future, only a bilingual version of the test would be printed in addition to the English version (Stansfield & Kahl, 1998).

A similar study in Minnesota (Liu, Anderson, Swierzbin, & Thurlow, 1999) involved a bilingual version of the state reading assessment in which English and non-English versions of the test were placed on facing pages of the test booklet. In interviews conducted after field testing, project staff found that although some students used both languages in taking the test, most relied exclusively on a single language. The impact of the format on the former group was positive; the impact on the latter group was neutral; that is, students relying on a single language were able to take the test in the bilingual booklet without any negative effects.

A recent study conducted by Garcia (2000) in preparation for a national assessment of mathematics investigated how groups of students with different background characteristics reacted to bilingual test booklets. After taking an eighth-grade mathematics test in a bilingual test booklet format, students were interviewed by the researchers. Through these interviews it was determined that native Spanish speakers with more than 3 years of instruction in the United States focused on the English pages the majority of the time. Those with less than 3 years of instruction focused on the Spanish pages the majority of the time. Twelve of the 70 students with more than 3 years of instruction in the United States used the Spanish pages to check their understanding of the English item or to look for the meaning of specific words and phrases (e.g., *bisector*). Of 181 bilingual students who took the assessment with a bilingual test booklet, 85% rated the bilingual format as useful or very useful for them, in comparison with an English test booklet. Regression analyses with other variables showed that the dual-language format did not differ in the validity of the assessment when compared to a similar analysis of response data obtained with an English test booklet.

Research studies (Liu et al., 1999; Stansfield, 1997; Stansfield & Kahl, 1998) have shown another advantage to bilingual test booklets as well. Given the choice to receive either a test booklet in their native language or in English, not all ELLs actually choose the native language version over the standard test in English. As noted earlier in the discussion regarding the suitability of translations and adaptations for target populations, this is largely because an ELL might not be fully literate in his or her native language; hence, a translated test alone might not prove to be a useful accommodation. Bilingual test booklets, on the other hand, are often used because these formats can help ELLs grasp the context of the items in their native language and the content area terms in English.

The bilingual format seems to be gaining acceptance in state assessment programs in the United States. When considered as a potential test accommodation, there is a growing belief that it "does no harm," at the same time relieving the examinee and the test administrator from having to decide the language of the test. Because many examinees who take translated tests have some degree of bilingualism, making the test available in both languages might actually reduce construct-irrelevant variance due to the influence of test language for such examinees.

Conclusion

With the increase in the number of ELLs in public schools and the recent emphasis placed on inclusion in statewide assessment by federal legislation, states are attempting to find accommodations that will provide ELLs access to test content without compromising the scores obtained from these assessments. As all states are required to test all students on what they know and can do under NCLB, native language accommodations are increasingly important as a means to comply with federal legislation. Among the native language accommodations selected by states, test translation offers an important means of accommodating ELLs while still maintaining validity. However, as this overview demonstrates, many factors must be taken into consideration if states are to develop and administer translations that provide accurate information regarding what ELLs know and can do.

First, states must determine which format is appropriate for students. Options include the use of a single translated version of the test or a dual-language version, which places the English and non-English versions side by side (either on facing pages or in adjacent columns). As our review has shown, students at different levels of language proficiency and academic backgrounds have different needs. A bilingual format might accommodate these diverse needs more effectively than formats using only the non-English language.

Second, SEAs developing translated tests must select a method to ensure accuracy. Two of the most common are side-by-side comparison of the original and the translation and back-translation. Although back-translation can be a useful procedure, successive iterations of forward translation along with revision can be more cost effective and just as fruitful.

Finally, the qualifications of translators must be considered in the translation process. There have been a number of recent efforts to establish criteria for test translators that can be consulted by state assessment personnel interested in developing translated versions of tests. Whichever criteria are used, reliance on bilinguals who are not professional translators might be problematic.

Overall, research has only begun to address the issues affecting the translation of state assessments. Given the lack of knowledge about test translation and its increasing use in state assessment, it is clear that more research is needed. This study is designed to contribute to our understanding of how SEAs develop translated tests and the policies guiding the development and implementation of these tests throughout the states. As the knowledge base for test translation is further developed, state education officials will be able to learn from one another and develop more effective strategies for testing ELLs.

ANALYSIS OF STATE POLICIES REGARDING TEST TRANSLATION

Before examining the practices of states using test translation as an accommodation, we first developed an understanding of the policy context by examining state assessment policies with regard to translation. The analysis of states' policies is based on policy documents submitted by the SEAs of all 50 states and the District of Columbia for the 2000–2001 school year. Like the analysis in Study 1 of this volume, this study is based on data from official state policy documents; no self-reported or word-of-mouth data are included. However, whereas Study 1 examined these policies with regard to a broad range of ELL-responsive test accommodations, this study provides a more in-depth analysis of these policies as they relate to native language accommodations and the translation of state assessments for ELLs. For a detailed description of the methodology used for the policy analysis, see the introduction to this study.

The presentation of findings regarding states' assessment policies is divided into four sections. The first section addresses the states' policies regarding native language accommodations at the broadest level, indicating which states had policies allowing or prohibiting the use of these accommodations for state assessment.

The next two sections examine the policies in greater detail. First, policies regarding sight translation are examined to show which states' policies allowed sight translation of assessments, which specified content areas to be sight translated, which prohibited sight translation in some content areas, and which listed qualifications for sight translators. Next, policies regarding written translation are examined to show which states' policies allowed the written translation of statewide assessments, which formats (e.g., side-by-side translation) and languages were specified in states' policies, and for which content areas translations were provided.

The fourth section focuses on the issue of student eligibility to receive translated assessments. First, states with policies listing criteria for determining which students were eligible to receive a statewide assessment in their native language are identified. Next, states with policies specifying a maximum amount of time for which students can receive translated tests are discussed.

Finally, caveats are discussed and conclusions offered.

General Policy

Native language accommodations are intended to provide direct linguistic support to ELLs. According to the taxonomy of Study 1, native language accommodation comprises four categories of accommodation: (a) written translation, (b) scripted oral translation, (c) sight translation, and (d) student response in the native language (see Study 1). As the primary focus of this study is on sight translation and written translation, these two accommodations are also the focus of this policy analysis.

States' policies address the provision of native language accommodations less frequently than other accommodations. As a result, many states simply do not address the issue in states' policies. Data from Study 1 indicate that of the 47 states with policies addressing the accommodation of ELLs, 41 specifically addressed native language accommodations (see Table 1.14).

Although sight translation—the oral rendition of a test into a non-English language—is in many ways problematic, it is a form of accommodation cited frequently in states' policies and therefore merits discussion. Formal written translation of tests (i.e., a translation of the test or test directions in a dual- or single-language format) has been noted here and elsewhere as a promising accommodation and it is used by a number of states. It therefore receives the greatest attention.

In the 2000–2001 school year, 32 states had policies addressing sight translation. Of these, 29 states allowed the use of sight translation on all components, 7 states prohibited sight translation on some components, and 7 prohibited the use of this accommodation on all test components. With regard to the formal written translation of tests, the policies of 19 states addressed the use of this accommodation; 2 states had policies prohibiting formal written translation for all content areas.

Although these numbers indicate in a general way states' attentiveness to the provision of native language accommodations, and test translation in particular, for ELLs, it is important to keep in mind that there was great variability in the degree to which state policies addressed various aspects of test translation. Some states provided detailed guidelines, whereas others provided no specific guidance whatsoever. Finally, however, it is important to note that even states that allow translation of statewide assessments do not usually allow translation for all content areas. Most commonly, translation of the ELA component is not allowed because the underlying construct (English language skills) would be altered if the test were translated into another language.

Sight Translation

As defined in Study 1, sight translation comprises four types of accommodations: (a) directions translated into native language, (b) directions explained or clarified in the native language, (c) test items read aloud in native language, and (d) interpreter or sight translator provided.

In this section we examine states with policies addressing sight translation and identify the test components or content areas explicitly prohibited from being sight translated. We also discuss the qualifications some states included for selecting sight translators. Finally, we suggest ways in which competent sight translators can be identified to ensure equity for ELLs receiving this accommodation.

States Allowing Sight Translation

As Fig. 2.1 shows, in the 2000–2001 school year, 32 states' policies addressed the use of sight translation of test directions or content. Test directions were the most frequent target of sight translation: Twenty-eight states

196

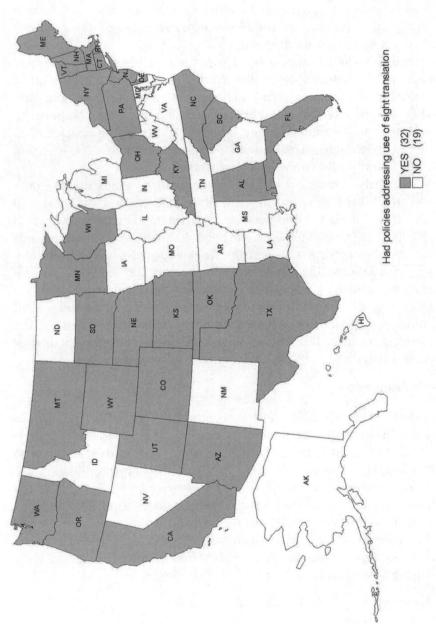

FIG. 2.1.   States with policies addressing sight translation.

had policies allowing the translation of directions into a non-English language or explanation and clarification in a non-English language. The policies of 17 states allowed test items from at least some content areas to be read aloud (sight translated) in the students' native language. Eight states' policies allowed students to respond to the test in their native language. (See Study 1, Table 1.14.)

States With Policies Prohibiting Sight Translation for Particular Components

Of the 32 states that allowed components of the state assessments (directions or items) to be sight translated, 10 states' policies specified components for which translation was prohibited. Relevant text from these policies is provided in Table 2.1.

As shown in the language of state policy, sight translation was frequently prohibited on measures of English language, such as tests of ELA, reading, and writing. In New York and New Jersey during school year 2000–2001, sight translation was prohibited on a particular high-stakes test: the state's high school graduation exam.

Qualifications for Sight Translators

Of the 32 states with policies regarding sight translation, only 6 specified qualifications for sight translators. The qualifications listed varied in content and focus, and none specified that translators be certified in either the content area of the test or target language. Table 2.2 reproduces the language used in each state's policy.

Successful sight translation requires the literacy associated with a competent translator and the rapid rendering skills associated with an experienced interpreter. Hence it requires specialized skills associated with interpretation in courtrooms and hospitals. Court interpreters, for instance, are normally tested on their sight translation skills, which usually make up 20% to 25% of a state or federal court interpreter certification test.

The lack of criteria in states' policies for sight translator qualifications, therefore, is notable. In no state did the list of qualifications adequately define the skills or background expected of a professional interpreter performing a sight translation. For instance, the only qualification noted in Delaware's policy was that the sight translator be proficient in the student's native language. However, to produce accurate translations, a sight translator must also be proficient in English. Kansas policy stipulated that the sight translator must be a paraprofessional. Yet, sight translation skills

TABLE 2.1

States' Policies Specifying Components for Which Translation Was Prohibited

State	Policy
Connecticut	"The test examiner may read and clarify, in English or the student's native language, as appropriate, all test directions to the students. It is not allowable to translate and read math test questions to students due to difficulties in standardizing those translations" (CT-4, p. 26).
Delaware	Passages on the reading test may not be translated (DE-8, p. 23; DE-7, p. 25).
New Jersey	Accommodations are not permitted for the HSPT 11 (Grade 11 High School Proficiency Test). Translation of directions only is permitted on other assessments (NJ-3, p. 1).
New York	Services of a translator cannot be provided to ELLs for the Native Language Writing Test or the Regents Competency Tests in reading and writing (NY-14, p. 13).
Ohio	"LEP students may ... qualify for a state-provided translator in the test areas of mathematics, citizenship, and science." Reading and writing tests cannot be translated (OH-4, p. 27).
Oklahoma	Both questions and directions can be sight translated, except on reading tests (OK-1, p. 18).
Rhode Island	Only the general directions for the English Language Arts assessment can be read to the student in the native language. The actual test content itself cannot be sight translated (RI-1, p. 15).
Texas	Items on the reading and writing tests of the Texas Assessment of Academic Skills (TAAS) must not be translated (TX-1, p. 9).
Utah	"Reading test passages cannot be read to the student or translated" (UT-3, p. 18).
Wisconsin	No accommodations are allowed for ELLs on the Wisconsin Reading Comprehension Test (WRCT) because "the WRCT assesses specific English language-based skills (reading comprehension) and is administered in an untimed format." In addition, "translating the English language arts test, while not currently prohibited by rule, is also open to the criticism that the test validity has been compromised." State policy suggests that if a student is exempted from WRCT, he or she should also be exempted from the Language Arts test (WI-2, p. 1).

TABLE 2.2

Qualifications Required for Sight Translators in Six States' Policies

State	Policy
Delaware	"Test administrator must be proficient in the native language" (DE-7, pp. 25, 27).
Kansas	A "paraprofessional" must translate questions/directions (KS-1, p. 4).
Maine	"Translation must be done by local personnel" (ME-1, p. 29).
Nebraska	"Staff must be adequately prepared and trained in the native language assessment procedures" (NE-7, p. 5).
Utah	Only "licensed bilingual educators" can perform sight translations (UT-3, p. 18).
Wisconsin	A "qualified translator" is defined as "a person who has a high proficiency in both English and the child's native language, and who also has some familiarity with the instructional and assessment context before working with the child and the test" (WI-2, p. 1).

are not generally required of paraprofessionals (e.g., teacher aides). Utah policy required sight translators to be licensed bilingual educators. However, there is no evidence that sight translation skills are taught in Utah teacher training programs or that teacher certification candidates are required to demonstrate sight translation skills on the state's teacher certification tests.

Nebraska had a minimal, although reasonable, statement of qualifications in its assessment policy, requiring sight translators to be adequately prepared in native language assessment procedures. We can infer that such procedures might include sight translation. Wisconsin defined a qualified translator as someone who has high proficiency in English and the child's language and knowledge of the instructional and assessment context. Wisconsin's qualifications might be the most extensive in terms of identifying the prerequisite background characteristics of a sight translator working in a testing context. However, these are only background knowledge and abilities. They are not the actual skills required to perform sight translation.

Nothing was included in any state's policy about the training that the person doing the sight translation should receive, nor was any advice given about allowing sight translators the opportunity to prepare and rehearse for the task before actually administering the test. Implicit in the policies of Wisconsin and Nebraska is a recognition that the sight transla-tor should know something about assessment, probably as much the per-son who administers the test in English. Rather than provide a set of qualifications, Utah's and Kansas's policies supplied a definition of who should conduct the sight translation. Although the policies of Delaware and Wisconsin mentioned that the sight translator must have native lan-guage proficiency, only Wisconsin's policy stated that the sight translator must have proficiency in two languages, English and the target language. Overall, no states' policies adequately specified the technical competen-cies required for sight translation and none provided criteria for how the competencies should be verified.

At the most basic level, the sight translator must have all the competencies of a test administrator in English and in the target language. In addition, the in-dividual must be an experienced translator or interpreter. However, even these qualifications are not enough to ensure accurate sight translation. The ability to read a text aloud, in a different language than the language of the text, is a specialized skill that even most professional translators do not have. The skill involves rapid decoding of the printed word and rapid encoding of a precise translation of it. The non-English rendering of it must be smooth, not halting, and clearly pronounced, just as test directions read aloud by the test administrator are clearly pronounced.

To complicate matters further, the accuracy and consistency of sight translations is open to serious question because interpreting is never fully accurate, even when performed by expert interpreters. For example, court interpreter and medical interpreter certification tests, such as those available to state judicial systems through the National Center for State Courts, typically require only 70% accuracy to pass, and the percentage of candidates who can pass such tests is usually less than 20%. Among bilin-gual teachers, teacher aides, and community volunteers, the quality of sight translation is likely to be less than it would be among practicing or as-piring professional interpreters. Thus, although sight translation might fa-cilitate the inclusion of additional students in the state assessment system, it also introduces inconsistency and inaccuracy into the measurement.

Written Translation

As Fig. 2.2 shows, during the 2000–2001 school year, 16 states' policies (those of Arizona, Colorado, Delaware, Massachusetts, Maine, Minnesota, Nebraska, New Mexico, New York, Oregon, Rhode Island, South Dakota, Texas, Utah, Vermont, and Wyoming) allowed written translations of at

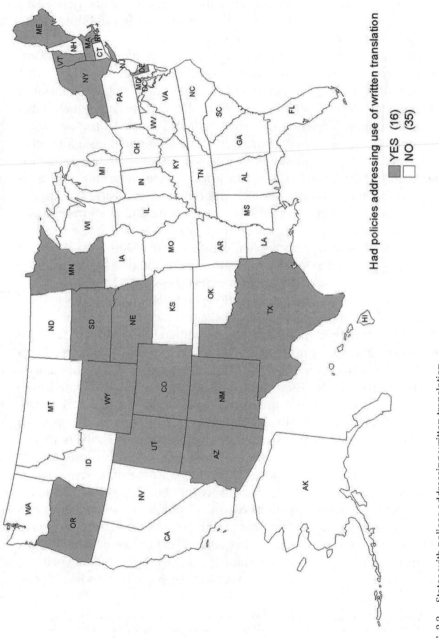

Had policies addressing use of written translation

■ YES (16)
□ NO (35)

FIG. 2.2. States with polices addressing written translation.

least some components of the state assessments.[2] However, not all of these states conducted the translations. For instance, both Maine's and Nebraska's policies allowed local development of test translation but did not provide translated versions of the state assessment.

Four of the 16 states (Delaware, Massachusetts, Minnesota, and Oregon) allowed bilingual test versions to be administered, with the original English test on one page or column of the test booklet and the translated test on the facing page or in the adjacent column. However, not all states with policies allowing written versions actually developed translated assessments. Of the 16 states with policies allowing written translations, only 11 actually developed and administered written translations of state assessments in 2000–2001. It is likely that among the reasons for the discrepancy are that the assessment office did not plan, set aside funding, or schedule the development of a translated test or the state determined that the number of ELLs in a specific language group was not large enough to warrant the expense of translation. (See the review of literature earlier for a more in-depth discussion of issues surrounding the decision of whether or not to develop a translated version of an assessment.)

Detailed descriptions of the translation practices of the 11 states that developed and administered written translations are provided later.

Of the 16 states with policies allowing written translations of state assessments, 12 specified the language for which translation is provided. Text from the policies of these 12 states is represented in Table 2.3. As shown in Table 2.3, Spanish was the language most commonly cited, with all 12 states' policies allowing written translations in Spanish. The language cited with the next greatest frequency was Russian, with two states (New York and Oregon) allowing written translations. The policies of only three states (New York, Minnesota, and Oregon) allowed the translation of tests into more than one language. The remaining nine states had policies that indicated only Spanish translations were to be used. New York policy allowed translation of some of its assessments into three languages and others into five languages. New York is the only state that administered a written translation of assessments in Chinese, Haitian Creole, and Korean. Minnesota is the only state that administered a written translation of its assessments in Hmong, Somali, and Vietnamese. New York provided writ-

---

[2]Although Colorado policy is included here as allowing the use of translated tests, the case study revealed that these tests were not translations but tests separately developed in Spanish for Spanish-speaking ELLs. The only tests translated into Spanish are the Colorado alternate assessments for Spanish-speaking students with special needs. (See the case study for Colorado later in this study.)

TABLE 2.3

States with Policies Specifying Languages for Which Written Translations Could Be Provided

	Chinese	Haitian	Hmong	Korean	Russian	Somali	Spanish	Vietnamese
AZ							✓	
DE							✓	
MA							✓	
MN			✓		✓		✓	✓
NM							✓	
NY	✓	✓		✓	✓		✓	
OR					✓		✓	
RI							✓	
TX							✓	
UT							✓	
VT							✓	
WY							✓	
Total	1	1	1	1	2	1	12	1

ten translation into more languages (five) than any other state. Minnesota was next with four languages, followed by Oregon with two.

Student Eligibility to Receive Translated Assessments

Criteria for Determining Which Students Receive Native Language Versions. The policies of 10 states specified the criteria to be used to determine which students receive native language versions of the statewide assessments. The criteria most frequently cited were (a) the student's enrollment in an ESL or bilingual education program, (b) the student's proficiency in English, (c) the student's proficiency or literacy in the native language, (d) the length of time the student has been in the United States, (e) the language the student speaks at home, and (f) the student's immigration status. These criteria have been synthesized and are listed in Table 2.4; a more extensive description of these states' policies follows.

As Table 2.4 shows, proficiency or literacy in the native language was the most frequently used criterion to determine whether students re-

TABLE 2.4

**Ten States' Criteria for Determining Which Students Receive Native
Language Versions of Tests**

State	Instructional Program	English Proficiency[a]	Native Language Proficiency or Literacy[b]	Time in United States	Language Spoken at Home	Immigration Status
AZ			✓			
MA	✓	✓	✓	✓		
ME	✓					
MN				✓		
NE	✓		✓			
NY		✓				
OR	✓	✓	✓		✓	
TX	✓	✓	✓	✓		✓
UT		✓	✓			
WY	✓	✓	✓			
Total	6	6	7	3	1	1

[a]Most states left it to the discretion of the districts to determine which instrument(s) to use in assessing students' English proficiency. None of the policies specified that a specific instrument be used, although some (e.g., WY) listed a number of assessments that could be used (i.e., IPT, LAS, Woodcock-Muñoz). [b]Terminology used in state policies varied considerably, with some (e.g., AZ and MA) indicating simply that the student must be "literate" or must be able to "read and write" in the native language, and others (e.g., TX and WY) indicating that the student's literacy and oral proficiency in the native language must be assessed. However, none of the state policies made reference to any specific assessment instrument to be used in assessing native language literacy or proficiency.

ceived native language versions of the statewide assessments. Seven of the 10 states listed this as a criterion, but no state specified one unique measurement instrument to be used in assessing students' proficiency or literacy across the state.

Proficiency in English and instructional program (most often, participation in a native language or bilingual education program) were the second most frequently used criteria, with 6 of the 10 states mentioning each as a factor in determining which students should receive assessments written in their native language. Although some states' policies (e.g., Wyoming) provided a list of English proficiency assessments that could be used, none specified a particular measurement instrument to be used in assessing

English proficiency across the state. Rather, decisions about which measurement instruments to choose were often left to districts; hence, there was no single common yardstick against which all students in the state were measured.

It is important to acknowledge, however, that the majority of states (31) did specify that level of English proficiency is a criterion for inclusion in or exemption from the statewide assessment program. However, as previously noted, there was no clear indication of the English language proficiency test to which this level applied. Although many of the state policy documents examined here did not explicitly indicate that language proficiency was a criterion for provision of accommodations (e.g., assessments in the student's native language), it is possible that the proficiency tests used for inclusion–exemption decision making were also used in that capacity. Time in the United States was a criterion in three states (Massachusetts, Minnesota, and Texas), whereas language spoken at home (Oregon) and immigrant status (Texas) were criteria in just one state each. The text of states' policies outlining criteria for determining eligibility of ELLs to receive translated versions of tests are provided here.

- *Arizona*. Spanish-speaking ELLs can receive the Spanish version of the AIMS (statewide assessment) provided that they are literate in Spanish and have never taken the AIMS in Spanish before. (ELLs are allowed to take the test in Spanish only once. Then, in subsequent years, they must take the test in English.)
- *Massachusetts*. Spanish-speaking ELLs who have been in the United States for 3 or fewer years can participate in the Spanish MCAS (statewide assessment program) if they meet all of the following criteria:

1. They do not have sufficient fluency in English to participate in the English versions.
2. They will continue to receive instruction in a transitional bilingual education program or receive ESL support during the school year in which they will be tested.
3. They can read and write in Spanish.

- *Maine*. For an ELL to receive a native language version of the statewide assessment, the student must be participating in a native language instruction program, and the translation must be performed by local personnel.
- *Minnesota*. To determine whether an ELL will receive the English or native language version of the statewide math test, the following factors are taken into account:

1. The length of time the student has been in the United States.
2. The length of time the student has been enrolled in schools where English is the primary language of instruction.
3. The determination of whether math performance would be best demonstrated in a language other than English.

• *Nebraska*. An ELL can receive a native language version of the state-wide assessments if the student is literate and has had the opportunity to learn the material being assessed in the native language.

• *New York*. All ELLs who score at or above the 30th percentile on an approved test of reading in English must take the state assessments in ELA and math, and they can choose to take the math assessment in their native language, if available. Any ELL who scores below the 30th percentile on an approved test of reading in English must take the appropriate math assessment for the grade level, if that assessment is available in the native language. (The student can also opt to take it in English, but can be exempted if there is no test in his or her native language.)

• *Oregon*. Spanish- or Russian-speaking ELLs can take the bilingual math assessment. Receiving instruction in Spanish or Russian is not a prerequisite for taking the bilingual assessment. ELLs who are not literate in English or the native language can take a modified assessment or be exempted. That decision is made with teacher, parent, and an instructional team on the basis of work samples that represent an appropriate English reading level, native language literacy, the language spoken at home, enrollment in language support programs, including first and second language development support.

• *Texas*. Receipt of the Spanish or English version is determined by the Language Proficiency Assessment Committee (LPAC), on the basis of:

1. The student's immigration status.
2. Number of years enrolled in U.S. schools.
3. Literacy in English, Spanish, or both.
4. Oral proficiency in English, Spanish, or both.
5. Academic program participation, language of instruction, and planned language of assessment.
6. Previous testing history and level of academic achievement.

Texas policy stipulated that a student does not necessarily have to receive every subject (content area) test in the same language. That is, based on the student's academic background and proficiency, the LPAC can decide that it would be best for the student to take one subject in English and another in the native language.

- *Utah*. Receipt of the Spanish version of the statewide assessment is determined on the basis of level of proficiency in English and level of literacy in the native language, as determined at the district level.
- *Wyoming*. To determine whether an ELL should receive the English or Spanish version of the statewide assessment, students must be tested in English proficiency as well as native language proficiency to determine language dominance. The state does not require that any specific instrument be used to assess either English or Spanish proficiency. The state's policy documents list examples of English proficiency tests that can be administered (e.g., the IPT, LAS, and Woodcock-Muñoz). The student must also have received or currently be receiving formal instruction in Spanish.

Maximum Time Limits for Native Language Testing.   Both IASA, which was in effect in 2001, and NCLB permit the student to be tested in the native language for 3 years following arrival in the district or state. NCLB allows the states to waive the 3-year limitation for an additional 2 years for individual students, so that some students can receive native language versions of state assessments for a total of 5 years after arrival in the district (U.S. Congress, 2002, Section 1111 [3][c][x]).

As of the 2000–2001 school year, the policies of only three states (Arizona, Massachusetts, and Texas) specified a maximum amount of time for which ELLs were allowed to receive tests in their native languages. In Arizona, ELLs could take the Spanish version of the statewide assessment on one occasion, during 1 year only. So, for instance, if a Spanish-speaking ELL took the Spanish version of the assessment in Grade 3, he or she could not receive the test in Spanish at the next tested level (Grade 5), despite eligibility according to the previously mentioned criteria. In both Massachusetts and Texas, ELLs were allowed to receive the Spanish version of the statewide assessment for a maximum of 3 years.

Caveats

Caution should be taken in interpreting the findings in this section of the study. It is important to keep in mind that these findings are a result of analysis of assessment policies provided by the states for the 2000–2001 school year. Further information might be present in documents that were not provided to us. In addition, although findings reported in this section represent as closely as possible requirements addressed explicitly in the policy documents provided, these findings do not necessarily reflect actual practices within states. It is possible that some states or districts provided ELLs with translation accommodations not mentioned in the policy documents examined here.

Summary and Conclusion

Detailed analysis of states' policies regarding test translation in the 2000–2001 school year reveals that more than two thirds of states had a policy addressing translation of statewide assessments. However, policies vary a great deal in terms of the nature and amount of guidance they provide.

A close examination of the policies regarding both sight translation and written translation shows that in virtually all states there were components for which translation was prohibited. Typically, states prohibited both written and sight translation of ELA assessments because translation would necessarily modify the underlying construct being measured. In general, test directions were the most likely candidates for sight translation among states whose policies provide specific details about sight translation.

According to states' policies, written translations were permitted for a number of languages. Spanish was clearly the most common target language for test translation in the United States; however, seven other languages— Chinese, Haitian, Hmong, Korean, Russian, Somali, and Vietnamese—were also cited in state policy documents as allowable languages for test translation.

Examination of state policy documents revealed two major areas in need of further development. One gap in the states' policies concerns qualifications stipulated for sight translators. Although a few states did specify criteria for selection of translators, these were exceedingly vague and lenient. Appropriate minimal criteria for sight translator qualifications might include knowledge of the test being administered, experience rendering sight translations, and high proficiency in both English and the target language. It would also be helpful for sight translators to be certified by the American Translators Association or certified as an interpreter by the National Center for State Courts.

Another gap in state policy was the lack of rigorous criteria for determining which students were eligible to receive translated tests. Not all states had policies listing such criteria. Those that addressed this issue typically used one or more of the following three: English language proficiency, instructional program, and amount of time in the United States. These criteria are certainly necessary. However, states' policies often failed to make clear which tests were to be used to measure English language proficiency, and so there is no guarantee that students, even within a given state, were being uniformly classified. Finally, an additional criterion that would help ensure that students receive the most beneficial test accommodation is proficiency and literacy in the native language. States' policies in the 2000–2001 school year provided very little guidance regarding this criterion.

CASE STUDIES OF STATES' TEST TRANSLATION PROCEDURES

The 12 case studies presented in this part of the study are designed to be read in the context of the earlier policy study. Whereas the policy study provides an overview of states' test translation programs, the case studies offer in-depth descriptions of the policies and practices of the 12 states identified by the research team as using test translation during school year 2000–2001 (Arizona, Colorado, Delaware, Massachusetts, Minnesota, New Mexico, New York, Oregon, Rhode Island, Texas, Utah, and Vermont). In designing the study, the research team felt that the value of the case studies lay more in the presentation of each particular state context than in a synthesis of findings across the 12 states. Hence, in presenting findings from the case studies, analysis of each individual state context is given priority over synthesis of the findings regarding the test translation programs of the 12 states.

The 12 states were selected for the case studies from an initial list of 16 states identified in Study 1 as allowing, or potentially allowing,[3] written translation of statewide assessments for some content areas in the 2000–2001 school year (see Study 1, Table 1.14). To gather data for the case studies, the researchers examined state documents and state department of education Web sites. The team contacted either the state assessment director or the bilingual coordinator in each of the 16 states to determine whether written translations were indeed offered during the 2000–2001 school year. Through this process, it was determined that 12 of the 16 states identified in the policy study offered translated assessments in the 2000–2001 school year. Hence, these states were selected as the subjects of the case studies. Colorado is a special case, as the state offers parallel versions of assessments in Spanish and not written translations. Because parallel development is a valuable tool for assessing ELLs, the research team felt that it was important to include details on this state's procedure.

---

[3]These 16 states were those addressing test translation and were coded in Study 1 as A (allowed for all content areas) and PS (prohibited for some content areas). (For an explanation of the coding used, see Study 1.) For the purposes of the case studies it was assumed that states with policies prohibiting test translation for some content areas were likely to allow this practice for others.

Having conducted this initial examination of the state context and narrowed down the pool of states to be examined for the case studies, the researchers interviewed SEA personnel—typically state assessment directors and bilingual and ESL coordinators—regarding test translation procedures. In some cases other SEA personnel were interviewed, and sometimes the researchers were able to speak directly to test contractors or the manager of the translation company responsible for conducting the translation. (For a more in-depth description of the process of data collection for these 12 case studies, see the earlier Methodology section.)

Each case study addresses the seven major categories represented in the Interview Protocol—background of testing program, test translation process, other forms of communication in the non-English language, use of technology, research and analysis of translated tests, test translation at the district level, and the future of test translation in the state (see the full protocol in Appendix A). Findings for each state are organized into 15 sections:

1. Overview of the State Testing Program
2. Number of ELLs in the State
3. History of Test Translation
4. What Tests Are Translated
5. Other Translated Materials
6. Commercially Available Tests
7. How Many Students Take Translated Tests
8. The Translation Process
9. Reaction to Translated Tests
10. Translation in Districts
11. Test Presentation Format
12. Translated Tests and Score Reporting
13. Technology
14. Research and Statistical Analyses of Translated Tests
15. Future of Test Translation

Each case study addresses only those issues for which information was available. Hence, whereas case studies for some states, such as Texas, include all 15 sections, some have fewer (e.g., the Arizona case study is divided into only 4 sections because of limited information available from the state).

Following the case studies, a discussion is provided that synthesizes information from earlier parts of the study—the review of key issues related to test translation, the policy study, and the case studies. The discussion reviews findings from the study and provides guidance for states to follow in developing native language accommodations for ELLs participating in state assessment, including preliminary considerations for selecting accommodations for ELLs and guidelines for the developing and implementing common native language accommodations: written translation, audiotaped translation, sight translation, and student response in native language.

Arizona

Overview of the State Testing Program

The Arizona statewide assessment system is composed of four unique assessment components: (a) Arizona's Instrument to Measure the Standards (AIMS), (b) AIMS–Equivalent Demonstration (AIMS–ED), (c) Arizona's Instrument to Measure the Standards–Alternate (AIMS–A), and (d) the Alternate State Achievement Test (ASAT). In addition, the NAEP and the SAT-9 are administered statewide.

AIMS is a standards-based assessment of reading, writing, and mathematics administered in Grades 3, 5, 8, and 10. It is based on the Arizona Academic Standards, which were adopted by the state Board of Education in 1996. There are multiple-choice and short-answer questions on all three content areas, in addition to an extended writing prompt on the writing test.

The AIMS–ED is an alternative to the standard AIMS test. The AIMS–ED provides students with various ways of demonstrating achievement of the reading, writing, and mathematics standards. It is designed to meet the needs of students who might not perform their best on a single, comprehensive assessment like the AIMS.

The AIMS–A is a statewide standards-based achievement test for special needs students.

The ASAT is offered in Arizona in place of the SAT-9.

Number of ELLs in the State

Data from Kindler (2002) indicate that during the 2000–2001 school year, 875,659 students were enrolled in Arizona public schools.[4] As Fig. 2.3 shows, of the total number of students enrolled in Arizona schools, 740,411 (84.6%) were non-ELLs, whereas 135,248 (15.4%) were classified as ELLs. Data regarding primary languages of ELLs in Arizona were not available.

---

[4]If not otherwise indicated, demographic data for ELL and non-ELL enrollment in each state discussed in these case studies are from Kindler (2002).

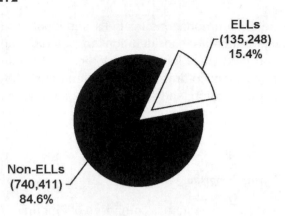

ELLs
(135,248)
15.4%

Non-ELLs
(740,411)
84.6%

FIG. 2.3.   Total number of ELLs in Arizona, as a percentage of overall student population.

History of Test Translation

During the 2000–2001 school year, all three components of the AIMS test (reading, writing, and mathematics) were translated into Spanish and administered at the four tested grade levels (3, 5, 8, and 10).

However, Proposition 203 (English Language Education for Children in Public Schools) was adopted by Arizona voters in November 2000, to take effect in school year 2001–2002. The bill establishes English as the official language of Arizona and requires that all public school education in the state be conducted in English. ELL students are to be placed in a structured English immersion program for not more than 1 year, at which point they are mainstreamed into English classrooms. Furthermore, the bill also mandates that all students take statewide achievement tests in English, regardless of their English proficiency. So, at the time this study was conducted (2002), Arizona was not offering assessments in any language other than English.

Technology

The Arizona Department of Education's Web site has links to documents in Spanish relating to the 2000–2001 assessment program, which was offered in Spanish. As previously indicated, the state no longer offers any statewide assessments in Spanish.

Colorado

Overview of the State Testing Program

The Colorado Student Assessment Program (CSAP) requires that all students enrolled in Grades 3 through 10 in Colorado public schools be assessed annually in one or more content areas according to the Colorado Model Standards. The CSAP includes assessments in reading, writing, math, and science based on the statewide standards. In Grades 3 through 10, students are assessed in reading and writing; in Grades 5 through 10 they are assessed in math; and in Grade 8 they are assessed in science. The testing window for the different assessments occurs between February and April.

Number of ELLs in the State

According to Kindler (2002), during the 2000–2001 school year, 724,508 students were enrolled in Colorado public schools. As Fig. 2.4 shows, of the total number of students, 665,490 (91.9%) were non-ELLs and 59,018 (8%) were classified as ELLs.

Data collected by the Colorado Department of Education (CDE) indicate that the primary language of the vast majority (approximately 81%) of ELLs is Spanish. The second most common primary language background in the state, Vietnamese, accounts for only about 2.6% of ELLs. A number of languages rank just below Vietnamese in frequency, with between 1% and 2.5% of the ELL population being native speakers of Korean, Russian, Hmong, and Chinese. Figure 2.5 shows the major native languages of ELLs enrolled in Colorado schools.

History of Test Translation

In 1996–1997, Colorado ELLs who were being instructed in reading and writing in Spanish had the option to take CTB/McGraw-Hill's commercially available Spanish language assessment Supera.™ However, Colorado first developed and administered its own assessments (the CSAPs) in Spanish in

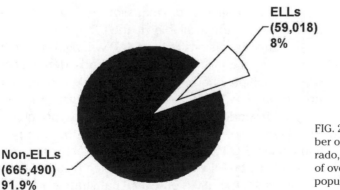

ELLs
(59,018)
8%

Non-ELLs
(665,490)
91.9%

FIG. 2.4. Total number of ELLs in Colorado, as a percentage of overall student population.

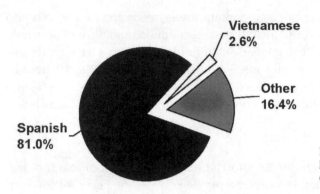

FIG. 2.5.   Primary
languages of ELLs in
Colorado.

1997–1998. That year, one form of the Grade 3 and 4 Spanish reading tests
and Grade 4 Spanish writing test were developed. This form was administered every year until 2001–2002, when new test forms were developed.

Which Tests Are Translated

During the 2000–2001 school year, Spanish versions of the Grades 3 and
4 reading and Grade 4 writing CSAP assessments were administered.
These were not translations of the English reading and writing assessments, but rather independently developed assessments in Spanish based
on the Colorado Model Standards. The Standards were used to create a series of assessment frameworks, which list the knowledge and skills that
the CSAP should test at each grade level. Then, these assessment frameworks were used as a guide for test construction by developers of the tests
in both English and Spanish.

Both the Spanish and English versions of the CSAP reading assessment
consist of multiple-choice and constructed response items based on authentic fiction and nonfiction passages. Item maps for the English version
of the CSAP reading assessment are available via the CDE Web site.

Both the Spanish and English versions of the CSAP writing assessment
consist of multiple-choice, short constructed response, and extended constructed response items. Multiple-choice items are designed to test subject–verb agreement, vocabulary, and selected points of grammar and
usage based on the Colorado Model Standards. There are two types of short
constructed response items, the first prompting students to write para-
graph-length text about a familiar topic, and the second a paragraph-level
error identification and editing task. Extended constructed response items
prompt students to write longer narratives of several paragraphs. Released

items for the Grade 4 Spanish and English writing assessments are provided on the CDE Web site. Colorado also provides a direct translation into Spanish of one set of assessments—the reading and writing alternate assessment (CSAP–A) for special needs Spanish-speaking ELLs.

Other Translated Materials

The CDE provides some ancillary materials in Spanish. In addition to the tests and test booklets, the CDE also produces scoring guides in Spanish, as well as Spanish translations of the read-aloud prompts in the test administration manual.

The CDE provides a Spanish translation of the parent guide on its Web site and sends a translated score report to parents of Spanish-speaking ELLs.

Commercially Available Tests

Colorado does not use any commercially available assessment tools in Spanish as part of the statewide assessment program.

How Many Students Take Translated Tests

The CDE Web site lists the yearly results of all CSAP assessments. In the 2000–2001 school year, 1,721 students took the Grade 3 reading assessment, 1,288 students took the Grade 4 reading assessment, and 1,375 students took the Grade 4 writing assessment. (In 2000–2001 a writing assessment for Grade 3 was not administered in Spanish. It was administered for the first time in 2003.)

The Translation Process

Colorado's test development contractor, CTB/McGraw-Hill, works in collaboration with the CDE to develop both the English and Spanish versions of the CSAP. Both the test specifications and the actual test items are developed by CTB/McGraw-Hill, in collaboration with the CDE, and with the Colorado Model Standards and Assessment Frameworks in mind. In developing the CSAP, Colorado content area specialists, language arts teachers, and assessment experts work with CTB/McGraw-Hill to select a pool of items that measure Colorado's Model Content Standards. Some test materials come from CTB/McGraw-Hill's test bank of previously field tested reading passages, writing prompts, and items. Some of these items are further revised so that they are more closely aligned with the assessment frameworks. Additional items are developed as needed and reviewed by Content Review, Bias Review, Community Sensitivity Review, and Instructional Impact committees composed of Colorado teachers, community members, CDE personnel, and SADI (Standards and Assessments Development and Implementation) council members. These reviewers' suggestions are then incorporated and used to form the final pool of items from which the reading and writing assessments are constructed.

Authentic materials are used for the reading passages in both languages, and come from a variety of sources, including periodicals and storybooks.

Once materials are developed, standard setting is conducted to set cutpoints to define the four performance levels on the CSAP (unsatisfactory, partially proficient, proficient, and advanced). The cutpoints for the English version of the Grade 4 reading and writing assessments were determined in 1997. The purpose of standard setting is to determine cutpoints for the English and Spanish versions of the third-grade reading assessment and the Spanish version of the Grade 4 reading and writing assessments. The CSAP standard setting took place in Denver on August 18–20, 1998, following the first administration of these assessments. Standard setting was conducted in accordance with the Bookmark Standard Setting Procedure (Lewis, Green, Mitzel, Baum, & Patz, 1998; Lewis, Mitzel, & Green, 1996). In the Bookmark Standard Setting Procedure, a group of judges consisting of teachers and other interested stakeholders independently examines the test items, which are ordered by difficulty in a binder. They determine the item that corresponds to a criterion-referenced level of performance in the subject being assessed. Then the average logit difficulty value for the items selected by the judges is used to determine the examinee ability level that will be associated with each performance level.

Item difficulty data from several thousand examinees were used in the standard setting of the English versions (approximately 16,000 for writing and 48,000 for reading), whereas the item difficulty data available for the standard setting for the Spanish versions was based on only a few hundred examinees (approximately 850–900 for both reading and writing).

To maintain the comparability of the English and Spanish standards, the participants in the Spanish standard setting for Grades 3 and 4 followed these steps:

1. Participants studied the English version of the performance level descriptors.
2. Participants studied the specific set of items that students taking the English version of the corresponding test would be expected to master to be classified in each of the performance levels.

3. Participants identified a comparable set of items in the Spanish version of the assessment.
4. The cut score associated with the comparable set of items was determined.

The results of the standard setting are summarized in Table 2.5. The percentage beside each cutpoint represents the percentage of the tested population in each performance level. Notice that the range of scale scores is

TABLE 2.5

Results of Standard Setting for Colorado Reading, Grades 3 Through 5

English Version	Spanish Version
Grade 3	
Scale: 300 to 700	Scale: 300 to 740
Unsatisfactory (12%)	Unsatisfactory (28%)
Partially Proficient Cutpoint: 445 (20%)	Partially Proficient Cutpoint: 482 (29%)
Proficient Cutpoint: 482 (58%)	Proficient Cutpoint: 513 (37%)
Advanced Cutpoint: 561 (8%)	Advanced Cutpoint: 576 (5%)
Grade 4	
Scale: 300 to 720	Scale: 300 to 790
Unsatisfactory (10%)	Unsatisfactory (48%)
Partially Proficient Cutpoint: 445 (31%)	Partially Proficient Cutpoint: 506 (27%)
Proficient Cutpoint: 496 (52%)	Proficient Cutpoint: 537 (22%)
Advanced Cutpoint: 562 (6%)	Advanced Cutpoint: 592 (1%)
Grade 5	
Scale: 300 to 720	Scale: 300 to 790
Unsatisfactory (21%)	Unsatisfactory (41%)
Partially Proficient Cutpoint: 469 (41%)	Partially Proficient Cutpoint: 496 (32%)
Proficient Cutpoint: 522 (30%)	Proficient Cutpoint: 532 (21%)
Advanced Cutpoint: 588 (6%)	Advanced Cutpoint: 596 (3%)

not the same for English and Spanish versions of the tests. The range of scale scores is affected by the difficulty of the items on the assessment and the performance of the students. The larger range for the Spanish assessments indicates that the items on the Spanish assessments were somewhat more difficult for the students. For example, mean p values were somewhat lower for the Spanish test than for the English test, making it possible to score higher on the Spanish test, although on average students taking the Spanish test scored lower.

For further technical information about the development of the CSAPs (e.g., item analyses, scaling, and calibration) please refer to the 1998 Final Technical Report on the Colorado Student Assessment Program, available on request from the CDE.

Reaction to Translated Tests

Although the CDE has not conducted any formal studies to gather feedback on the Spanish versions of the tests, there is an overall sense that teachers in the state are glad to have the Spanish versions as a measurement tool for their Spanish-speaking ELLs.

Translation in Districts

CDE policy allows most components of the Grades 5 through 10 CSAPs except reading and writing to be sight translated at the district level.

Bilingual classroom teachers provide sight translations of these assessments and, in the case of constructed response items, then translate students' oral answers into English and record them in the test booklet. The back of the test booklet is marked to indicate that the test was administered with the oral presentation of test accommodation, but otherwise the test is treated like any other for scoring purposes. The test is sent to the state to be scored, and scores are reported on the same scale as the English equivalents.

However, although Colorado policy allows sight translation, the state does not encourage its use because the resulting translations are not standardized (i.e., the sight translations are not uniform but vary from translator to translator and even from one administration to the next). The number of sight translations provided each year is small, and the CDE does not have exact figures because sight translation is not disaggregated from other types of oral test presentation accommodations, such as those provided to special needs students, which do not involve translation.

Test Presentation Format

Colorado publishes separate monolingual test booklets in English and Spanish because the tests are developed separately.

Translated Tests and Score Reporting

The Spanish versions of the reading and writing assessments are reported on a slightly different scale than the English assessments, to compensate for the fact that the items on the Spanish assessment were slightly more difficult for the examinees. All CSAPs (both English and Spanish) are scored by CTB/McGraw-Hill.

Technology

The CDE has one parent publication on the Web in Spanish, a parent guide to the state's assessment program. Sample items and prompts for the administration manual are also available on the Web site in Spanish.

Research and Statistical Analysis of Translated Tests

The Spanish versions of the tests are not equated to their English version counterparts. Rather, they are calibrated and scored as separate tests. However, when cutoffs were set for the various performance level categories in 1998, care was taken to ensure that the performance standards for the English and Spanish versions are comparable. For example, as part of the standard setting process, participants in the standard setting committee for the Spanish tests had to study specific sets of items that students taking the English version of the corresponding test would be expected to master to be classified in each of the performance levels. The participants then had to identify a comparable set of items in the Spanish version of the assessment. The statistics on the comparable set of items were then used to set the Spanish performance levels.

Whenever new forms of the Spanish tests are administered, CTB/McGraw-Hill conducts several types of statistical analysis. CTB/McGraw-Hill compiles a technical report on the basis of these analyses that contains a description of the test configuration; raw score descriptive statistics; item response theory (IRT) scale score descriptive statistics, both for the entire test and for subscales; raw score descriptive statistics for subscales; correlations between IRT scale scores for subscales; classical-test-theory item analyses (p values, item–test correlation, percentage of omits, percentages for each score level); IRT item parameters and fit summary statistics; IRT differential item functioning analysis results; estimates of standard error of measurement; and raw-to-scale score conversion tables. This information on the most recent round of test development can be found in the CSAP Technical Report, available on request from the CDE.

The CDE Web site lists the reliabilities (as calculated by Cronbach's alpha) of all CSAP assessments. Overall, reliabilities of the Spanish assessments were only slightly lower than the English assessments. For the 2000–2001 school year, the reliability of the English Grade 3 Writing assessment was .89, as compared to .87 for the Spanish version. The reliability of the English Grade 4 Reading assessment was .93 compared to .92 for the Spanish assessment. The reliability of the English Grade 4 Writing assessment was .90 as compared to .84 for the Spanish version. Generally, these differences in reliability are minor. The reliability of the Spanish assessments is good, especially when one considers their modest length. For example, the Grade 3 Spanish Reading assessment has only 41 items, and the Grade 4 Spanish Writing assessment has only 44 items. The Grade 4 Reading assessment has 67 items. CSAP results for school year 2000–2001 are presented in Table 2.6.

TABLE 2.6

CSAP Results

	Number of Examinees	Number of Items	Reliability (Cronbach's Alpha)	% Proficient or Above
Third Grade Reading (English)	55,207	42	.89	72
Third Grade Reading (Spanish)	1,795	41	.87	56
Fourth Grade Reading (English)	55,216	69	.93	63
Fourth Grade Reading (Spanish)	1,373	67	.92	31
Fourth Grade Writing (English)	55,212	42	.90	38
Fourth Grade Writing (Spanish)	1,375	44	.84	36

Future of Test Translation

Due to funding concerns, the CDE does not plan to expand its native language assessment program in the near future. At this time, there are no indications that additional grade levels of the CSAP will be offered in languages other than English.

Administrators in the English Language Acquisition division of the CDE have expressed a desire to have a test of English proficiency that measures the ability to use English in an academic context. Such a test of the language that is used in the classroom would be useful for placement and instructional purposes.

Delaware

Overview of the State Testing Program

The Delaware Student Testing Program is based on approved content standards for the teaching of ELA, mathematics, science, and social studies. State assessments in ELA and mathematics were administered for the first time in the spring of 1998 and again in the spring of 1999 to students in Grades 3, 5, 8, and 10. Assessments in science and social studies for Grades 4 and 6 were field-tested in the fall of 1999. The results of the field-testing were used to assemble the final forms of the tests and the first operational administration occurred in the fall of 2000.

Number of ELLs in the State

During the 2000–2001 school year 114,676 students were enrolled in Delaware public schools (Kindler, 2002). As Fig. 2.6 shows, of the total number of students, 2,371 (2%) were classified as ELLs.

As Fig. 2.7 shows, the most recent data published by the Delaware Department of Education (DDE; for the 1999–2000 school year) indicate that the three most populous non-English primary language backgrounds in the state are Spanish, Haitian Creole, and Korean. During the 1999–2000 school year, the DDE reported that approximately 72% of ELL students ($n = 1,656$) spoke Spanish as their primary language, followed by 5.1% ($n = 118$) Haitian Creole and 3.8% ($n = 88$) Korean.

History of Test Translation

Delaware first administered translated tests during the 1999–2000 school year, as a result of recommendations by a Governor's Council on Hispanic Affairs, which raised awareness about the growing needs of the

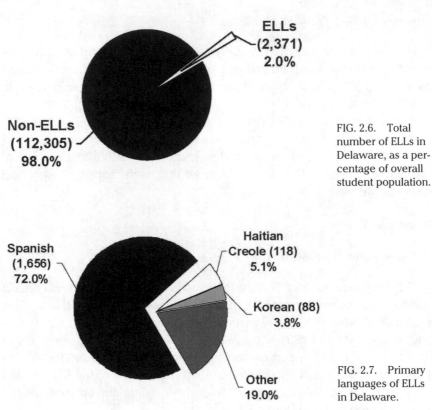

FIG. 2.6. Total number of ELLs in Delaware, as a percentage of overall student population.

FIG. 2.7. Primary languages of ELLs in Delaware.

Spanish-speaking population in the state. In response, Delaware's assessment director implemented a plan to begin offering Spanish language versions of the state's assessments.

Which Tests Are Translated

Delaware currently translates into Spanish one form per year of its on-grade assessments (math, science, and social studies tests in Grades 3, 5, 8, and 10). It does not translate off-grade assessments and does not provide written translations of the assessments in languages other than Spanish. It does not provide a written translation of its ELA assessment or offer a test of Spanish language ability.

Other Translated Materials

Delaware translates two ancillary documents into Spanish. Every year, a letter is sent to parents prior to the statewide assessments informing them of the upcoming testing. The state provides a translation (in Spanish) of this letter and sends it to districts, where it can be reproduced in the necessary quantity. In addition, after testing, a packet is sent out to parents of students who have taken the Spanish version of the statewide assessment. The packet contains a score report (in English) and an explanation of the scores (in Spanish). The state provides this translation and sends it to districts in quantity.

Although the state does not translate any other ancillary materials, Delaware's districts have the option of translating other materials when necessary. Districts are then responsible for identifying translators and making all arrangements for the translation.

Commercially Available Tests

Delaware uses a portion of the Stanford Achievement Test (9th ed., SAT-9; for norming purposes) in conjunction with its translated standards-based tests. In fact, the first 30 items of all of Delaware's statewide tests are in English and come directly from the SAT-9. Therefore, even those students who take the Spanish version of the statewide assessment take the first 30 items of the SAT-9 in English.

Delaware does not use any commercially developed tests in Spanish. All of the Spanish assessments are direct translations based on the state's original standards-based tests in English.

How Many Students Take Translated Tests

Typically, a few hundred students per year take the Spanish version of the state assessments. The state does not actively collect and archive data on the students who take the translated tests. The state has a database that records what accommodations have been applied for, but there is no system in place for tracking students to see that they have had the opportunity to take advantage of the accommodations.

The Translation Process

Harcourt Educational Measurement, the state's test development contractor, manages the test translation process. The state essentially has little interaction with them regarding the details of the translation process, and most of the state's dealings with Harcourt are to discuss administrative matters. The state provides Harcourt with the English version of the tests and then allots them an average of 10 to 15 weeks to translate the tests and do the desktop publishing.

Most of the translators and reviewers are staff members at Harcourt, although some are from translation companies or are bilingual educators from the community. Harcourt uses a mix of speakers representing different Latin American countries, especially speakers of the countries commonly represented by students in the state. The specific qualifications vary by translator, but Harcourt chooses personnel for the project based on a number of factors: the country of origin of the translator, the translator's proficiency in Spanish, the amount of education in the home country, and the amount of translation experience.

Harcourt uses forward translation, with a series of reviews and revisions, to translate the state assessments. Back-translation is not performed for Delaware. The stages involved in the translation process are detailed below.

- *Step 1*. A specialized team of translators with sound knowledge of the subject area prepares a draft translation. For instance, to translate a math assessment, Harcourt assembles a team of native Spanish speakers with math content knowledge.
- *Step 2*. Another team, representing different Spanish-speaking countries, then performs a review of the draft. The team checks to ensure that the Spanish faithfully reflects the English original and identifies any areas where cultural assumptions could be problematic. For instance, the stimulus for one item on the English assessment involved children walking dogs to earn extra money, and another involved children washing cars for a fundraiser. These two activities would probably never occur in a Spanish-speaking country and do not represent an authentic cultural context in Spanish. As such problems are identified, decisions are made about how best to handle them. Delaware gives Harcourt freedom to make adaptations where necessary, and typically in cases like the ones just mentioned, the stimulus is not translated directly but modified just enough to present a more authentic cultural context in Spanish. The final translated version is based on this review.
- *Step 3*. A final read-through is conducted, with attention to the way the text flows, and a senior editor reads the text to see if it reads as if it were originally written in Spanish. Proofreaders take a last look at the text to ensure that all of the conventions of the Spanish language are followed (e.g., accents, punctuation, capitalization, formatting). Typically, after two rounds of this type of editing, the document is sent to the layout department, where it is put in desktop publishing format using Quark.

Harcourt tries to translate the tests into Pan-American Spanish, or Spanish that can be understood by Spanish speakers from all parts of Latin America. They accomplish this by using translators and reviewers from various parts of Latin America. In addition, they carefully consider any words that have more than one translation in Spanish and make a decision about which to use. Typically, they try to use a "standard" Spanish word rather than a word that is specific to a particular region. For instance, there are numerous words in Spanish for lawn—*sacate, patio, grama,* and *césped,* to name a few. Harcourt has made a decision to translate lawn as *césped.* They do not provide glosses for words with multiple possible translations or place alternate translations in parentheses (e.g., *césped [sacate/patio/grama]*). They select a standard word and, unless they receive feedback indicating that the word was not comprehensible, they continue to use that standard word from year to year. In some cases, Harcourt makes a decision to modify a word in an item to avoid any confusion that could result from regional differences. For instance, an item on the English assessment used the word *cookies,* which in Spanish has multiple translations. Harcourt examined the item and determined that the word *sweets* (universally translated in Spanish as *dulces*) could substitute for *cookies* without altering the content being tested and simultaneously avoiding confusion.

During the translation process, Harcourt also looks at textbooks that are currently being used in the United States to teach the various subject areas in Spanish. They strive to use language that is consistent with that found in textbooks. Harcourt is also in the process of creating Spanish–English and English–Spanish glossaries of terms commonly found on the Delaware assessments, to ensure consistency from year to year.

Reaction to Translated Tests

Delaware has not conducted any formal studies to obtain systematic feedback on the translated tests. The DDE has received some informal feedback from classroom teachers, however. The most common comment from teachers is that some of the students have difficulty understanding the test. Teachers have expressed some concern over the Spanish that is being used in the test, because they feel that the translators are not tailoring the test to the target population, which is mostly Mexican and Guatemalan. However, state administrators also indicated that the students' inability to understand certain parts of the test could have to do with their limited proficiency and literacy in Spanish.

Translation in Districts

The state provides written translations of the statewide assessments into Spanish only. However, districts have the discretion to offer sight translations of the assessments to speakers of languages other than Spanish. It is entirely up to the districts to identify the need, find a translator, and make all necessary arrangements. The state is not involved at all, unless the district contacts the state asking for a list of potential translators for the given language. It is then still up to the district to contact and choose a translator.

The translators are almost always volunteers from the community who indicate that they are fluent in the target language. For Spanish, the state has a list of certified court interpreters to choose from, but for other languages, lists are made up of volunteers with no specific qualifications. The only restriction that the state imposes is that the translator not be a parent or friend of the student.

Sight translations can be provided for all portions of the math, social studies, and science assessments. However, for the language arts assessment, sight translators are allowed to translate only the directions, items, and options (but not passages on which the items are based). They can also translate the writing prompts.

The state does not look at sight translators' qualifications and never performs any evaluations of translators' performance. Therefore, there is no information about the quality of the translations or any safeguarding measure to ensure that all of the students receive translations of similar quality.

Test Presentation Format

Delaware publishes separate test booklets in English and Spanish. Delaware does not publish bilingual test booklets, with English and Spanish versions in a single document. Students can request an accommodation to use the Spanish test booklet, or, alternatively, they can request to have access to both the English and Spanish test booklets and use them side by side.

Delaware pilot-tested one other presentation format, bilingual audiocassettes. A section of the test was read aloud on the tape, first in English, and then in Spanish. However, neither students nor teachers responded well to this format, and it has since been discontinued.

Teachers and school administrators collaborate to make the decision about providing test accommodations to ELLs. Once a decision has been reached, the school must request the accommodation in advance to receive the appropriate materials from the state.

The state has not conducted research to evaluate the effectiveness of the two presentation formats currently in use. They have also received little, if any, feedback from teachers about which format students prefer.

Translated Tests and Score Reporting

Scores from translated tests are reported on the same scale as scores from the English version of the test. There is an assumption that the translated tests and the originals are equivalent, so there is no separate reporting procedure or scale.

Technology

Delaware does not have any publications on the Web in languages other than English.

Research and Statistical Analysis of Translated Tests

Little research has been done on the translated tests. The items that are translated and used on the Spanish language versions have previously been field-tested in English. Beyond that, there is no effort to examine the psychometric qualities of the translated test. There is an assumption that the two versions are equivalent, so no separate linking or equating procedures are performed.

Future of Test Translation

Delaware has no plans to translate any off-grade assessments, and does not plan to provide written translations of assessments into languages other than Spanish. The DDE feels that translating into other languages would be cost prohibitive, especially in light of the small number of students who would benefit from those translated tests.

After Spanish, the two next largest linguistic minority groups in Delaware are speakers of Haitian Creole and Korean. If the number of ELLs from those language backgrounds increased substantially, the state could envision providing written translations in those languages as well. Such a dramatic increase is not likely in the foreseeable future, and for now the state feels that it is more cost effective to provide sight translations for those languages.

The DDE is now beginning to look into a number of issues surrounding test translation. The comments from teachers about regional differences in the Spanish used on the test have sparked the interest of the state's Assessment Group. As a result, the state plans to begin learning more about the translation procedures that Harcourt uses.

The DDE is also concerned over the lack of communication with the school districts and is looking to get more feedback on all test accommodations. Right now, the districts do not send the state information about the numbers of students who benefit from the native language accommodations, and the state is interested in finding out how many of the students who request native language accommodations actually receive them.

Massachusetts

Overview of the State Testing Program

The current statewide assessment program in Massachusetts, the Massachusetts Comprehensive Assessment System (MCAS), was implemented following the Education Reform Law of 1993, which required the inclusion of all Massachusetts public school students in state assessments. The MCAS, based on learning standards from the Massachusetts Curriculum Frameworks, is administered annually in grades 3, 4, 5, 6, 7, 8, and 10, and consists of four content area tests—English Language Arts, Mathematics, Science & Technology, and History & Social Science.

All public school students enrolled in Grades 3, 4, 5, 6, 7, 8, and 10 are required to participate in the MCAS, including those with limited English proficiency. Students with limited English proficiency are required to take the MCAS in English if they (a) have been enrolled in U.S. schools for more than 3 years, or (b) have been enrolled in U.S. schools for 3 or fewer years but will no longer be enrolled in a bilingual education program or receive ESL support during the school year following testing. However, Spanish-speaking ELL students who have been enrolled in U.S. schools for 3 or fewer years must be administered the Spanish-language versions of the Mathematics, Science & Technology, and History & Social Science MCAS tests if they (a) do not have sufficient proficiency to take the English version of the tests, (b) will continue to receive either instruction in a bilingual education program or ESL support during the school year following testing, and (c) can read and write in Spanish. Only if students do not meet these criteria to take either the English or Spanish version of the MCAS are they exempted from the assessments.

Number of ELLs in the State

According to the Massachusetts Department of Education (MDE), during the 2000–2001 school year, there were 979,593 students enrolled in Massachusetts public schools. As Fig. 2.8 shows, of those, 44,080 (approximately 4.5%) were classified as ELLs.

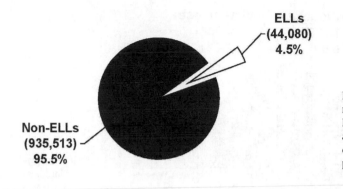

ELLs
(44,080)
4.5%

Non-ELLs
(935,513)
95.5%

FIG. 2.8.   Total number of ELLs in Massachusetts, as a percentage of overall student population.

Data from the MDE for the 2000–2001 school year indicate that the five most populous non-English primary language backgrounds in the state are Spanish, Portuguese, Vietnamese, Khmer, and Russian, in that order. During the 2000–2001 school year, the MDE reported that approximately 58% of ELL students ($n = 25,598$) spoke Spanish as their primary language, followed by 9.6% ($n = 4,236$) Portuguese, 3.7% ($n = 1,666$) Vietnamese, 3.1% ($n = 1,395$) Khmer, and 2.4% ($n = 1,058$) Russian. These percentages are represented in Fig. 2.9.

History of Test Translation

The Education Reform Law of 1993, which spurred the creation of the MCAS, called for a standards-based assessment program with tests administered not just in English but in other languages as well. The MDE looked to student demographic data for guidance about which languages the tests should be translated into. The MDE found that approximately 60% of the state's ELL population was Spanish-speaking, followed by single-digit percentages of speakers of other languages. On this basis, the MDE determined that it would only be feasible to translate the MCAS into Spanish, because there was a sizable population of Spanish-speaking students who could benefit from the translated assessment. It simply was not practical to translate MCAS into any other languages because of the small number of students who would potentially take the assessments in those languages in a given year.

The first operational administration of the Spanish version of the MCAS occurred during the 1997–1998 school year. At that time, the MCAS was administered annually in Grades 4, 8, and 10 in four content areas—English Language Arts, Mathematics, Science & Technology, and History & Social Science. The MDE translated all MCAS components except the ELA test,

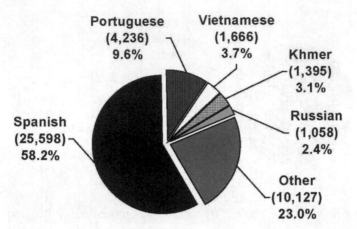

FIG. 2.9. Primary languages of ELLs in Massachusetts.

because translating the test would alter the underlying construct being measured. Massachusetts determined that it would not be valid to translate this test because there were no Spanish language arts standards to guide test construction.

Which Tests Are Translated

During the 2000–2001 school year, the MCAS program was expanded to include annual testing of students, not just at Grades 4, 8, and 10, but at Grades 3, 5, 6, and 7 as well. Accordingly, beginning in the 2000–2001 school year, Massachusetts translated into Spanish one form of the Mathematics, Science & Technology, and History & Social Science tests at each of the seven tested grade levels (3, 4, 5, 6, 7, 8, and 10). In addition, both the answer booklet in which students record their answers to MCAS questions and math manipulatives used during test administration were translated into Spanish.

Other Translated Materials

The MDE translates a number of ancillary materials into languages other than English. To ensure that instructions to examinees are uniform across test sites, MDE translates the read-aloud prompts in the test administration manual into Spanish.

Each year, the MDE also releases a set of translated MCAS items for each tested grade level to help familiarize students with the Massachusetts Curriculum Framework standards and the way in which they are tested. The set contains six items from each of the content areas tested (Mathematics, Science & Technology, and History & Social Science), for a total of 18 items per grade level.

Each year the state translates a parent interpretive guide (the Guide to the MCAS Parent/Guardian Report) into 10 languages—the native languages of the highest numbers of ELL students in the state. From 1997 to 2000, the Guide to the MCAS Parent/Guardian Report was published in eight languages. In 2001, a ninth language, French, was added. During the 2000–2001 school year, the parent guide was translated into Cape Verdean, Chinese (separate editions for simplified and traditional characters), French, Haitian Creole, Khmer, Portuguese, Russian, Spanish, and Vietnamese. This guide can be found on the Massachusetts Department of Education Web site.

In addition, parents receive their child's score report (in English) accompanied by a score report template (a sample score report), which has been translated into one of the 10 languages previously mentioned. That way, the state avoids the expense and time required to produce and print each individual score report in any of the 10 languages, while still offering a way for parents to follow along with the report in their native language.

Commercially Available Tests

Massachusetts does not use any commercially available native language assessment instruments.

How Many Students Take Translated Tests

The number of students taking the Spanish version of the MCAS during 2000–2001 was quite small, and Spanish versions accounted for less than 1% of the total number of tests administered. Table 2.7 shows the total numbers of students, by grade, who were administered Spanish versions of the MCAS in the 2000–2001 school year.

The Translation Process

Starting in 1997, when the MCAS was first being developed, the MDE contracted with Advanced Systems in Measurement and Evaluation (now Measured Progress) to develop and score the MCAS assessments. From 1997 until 2000, Measured Progress subcontracted the translation to Second Language Testing, Inc. (SLTI), which specializes in test translation.

SLTI selects educated native speakers of the target language to translate and review all assessments. All are professional translators with knowledge of item-writing procedures, experience in test translation and test translation review, and a strong background in the content area being

TABLE 2.7

Spanish Versions of the MCAS Administered

Grade and Subject	Number of Spanish Versions	Number of Total Tests Administered (English & Spanish)
Grade 4 Mathematics	526	78,576
Grade 6 Mathematics	529	78,452
Grade 8 Mathematics	441	75,471
Grade 8 Science & Technology	440	75,471
Grade 8 History & Social Science	438	75,471
Grade 10 Mathematics	415	68,118
Grade 10 History & Social Science	417	68,118
Total	3,206	519,677

tested. SLTI uses forward translation, with a series of iterative reviews and revisions, to translate assessments. The stages involved in the process are detailed next.

First, the translation manager at SLTI examines the English file to ensure that all items and options are in the correct sequential order and are formatted properly. Then, the translation manager makes initial decisions about how to handle specific terms found in the assessment, as well as in the instructions, headers, footers, item stems, and so forth.

Before beginning the translation, translators and reviewers are oriented to the project. The orientation typically includes information on the state's assessment program and the most frequent countries of origin of examinees who will take the assessment in Spanish.

Subsequently, the translator begins work on the first draft. During this process, the translator identifies any culturally loaded items or items that would not be logical in the context of the target language. If such items are found, necessary adaptations are made to the item so that the content tested in the English item can be tested in the translation.

Once the translator completes a draft of the translation, it is sent to the reviewer. The reviewer is instructed to evaluate the draft translation by comparing it line by line and item by item with the English version. The reviewer examines the translation to ensure that it is an accurate representation of the English version and that the content being tested is the same in both languages. Thus, the reviewer will look for words or ideas that have been omitted in the translation, and for words and ideas that are found in the translation, but not found in the English version. The reviewer also looks for words and ideas that have been mistranslated; that is, for which the exact meaning has been altered. The reviewer also ensures that the language of the translation is consistent; that is, the same words have been translated in the same way throughout the document and across assessments, and that any structural features specific to any item in English remain the same in the target language. The reviewer ensures that parallel language is used on both the English and Spanish versions so that test takers in the target language will neither be favored nor prejudiced. Furthermore, the reviewer identifies any words that might be expressed differently in other Spanish-speaking countries, and places alternate translations in parentheses after each such word. The reviewer makes changes, comments, and suggestions on the translated test document using the Track Changes feature of Microsoft Word.

The digital file containing the reviewer's revisions is sent back to SLTI, where it is reviewed, and then forwarded to the original translator, along with observations and recommendations. The translation manager then works with the translator to determine which comments to incorporate. On average, about 80% of the reviewer's suggestions are incorporated. In some cases, however, the translator might come up with improvements other than those suggested by the reviewer.

Once this revision has been completed, the translation is sent to a second reviewer, of Puerto Rican descent. This step is deemed necessary because of the relative size of Massachusetts's Puerto Rican population. The Puerto Rican reviewer examines the translation with particular emphasis on identifying words or phrases that would be expressed differently in Puerto Rican dialect.

In 1997, at this stage the MDE convened a community review of the translation, bringing together six educators from different Latin American countries to examine the translation item by item. There were some disagreements among reviewers about lexical items (largely because of certain differences in usage between speakers from different countries). However, in the end, agreement was reached and the committee's suggested changes were incorporated into the translation.

This community review process was discontinued the following year, and beginning in 1998, the MDE contracted with an external company, Linguistic Systems, Inc., to conduct an external review of the translations before sending them for desktop publishing.

Once the review is complete and all disagreements are resolved, final changes are made to the translation and the file is sent to the state's test contractor, where page layout is done in PageMaker. Once page layout or desktop publishing is complete, the test is sent back to SLTI for proofreading. After errors are identified and corrected, a final version is sent to Linguistic Systems, which verifies that no errors exist, and the test is ready for printing.

During the 2000–2001 school year, the MDE's contract with Measured Progress ended and the state contracted with Harcourt Educational Measurement to manage the translation of the MCAS assessments administered in the spring of 2001. We were unable to interview Harcourt about the procedures they use, but the MDE understands that Harcourt performs a forward translation of the English version, followed by iterative reviews. As of 2000–2001, the MDE was still contracting Linguistic Systems to perform external reviews of the translations.

Reaction to Translated Tests

Although Massachusetts has not conducted any formal surveys to gather systematic feedback about the translated tests, the MDE believes that parents, students, and teachers have responded positively to the Spanish version overall. Some evidence of reactions to the translated version was obtained in the study of test presentation format, described later.

Translation in Districts

MDE policy does not allow districts to perform either sight or written translations of any assessments. All students must take either the English or Spanish version of the MCAS that has been prepared by the state. In the case that neither test version is suitable (i.e., the student is proficient or literate in neither English nor Spanish), the MCAS is not administered to the student during that year.

Test Presentation Format

In spring 1997, when both English and Spanish versions of the MCAS were being field-tested, the MDE was faced with making a decision about test presentation format. At that point, the MDE commissioned SLTI to prepare a paper reviewing practices concerning test presentation format, timing, and related matters. The review (Stansfield, 1997) found strong support and a rational basis for both monolingual and bilingual test booklets. Because there had been little empirical research into the effects of monolingual versus bilingual test booklets at that time, the state decided to study the effects of test presentation format during field-testing (for a discussion, see Stansfield & Kahl, 1998). Spanish test booklets were printed in two formats. One format was a monolingual (Spanish only) test booklet, and the other was a bilingual (Spanish/English) test booklet, with the English text and its Spanish translation on facing pages. Classroom teachers determined which students should receive which format, based on their knowledge of the student's degree of literacy in English and Spanish.

Following test administration, three staff members of the MDE interviewed both teachers and students to gauge their reactions to the two test booklet formats. In all, 97 students and 17 teachers from a number of districts were interviewed. Most students indicated that they preferred the bilingual test booklet format. Although most students who received bilingual test booklets reported that they had relied mostly on the Spanish version of the items, in some cases they also reported referring to the English version and felt that they were able to glean some additional meaning from the English. The conclusion was that the bilingual versions "do no harm" and might in fact help some students.

As a result of these interviews, the MDE decided to offer the Spanish version of the MCAS using a bilingual test booklet format only. That is, no operational administrations of the MCAS have used a monolingual (Spanish) test booklet in favor of a bilingual booklet with English and Spanish on facing pages.

Translated Tests and Score Reporting

Massachusetts views the Spanish version of the MCAS as directly parallel to the English, so the scores from the Spanish version are reported on the same scale as those from the English administration. Even in the state's annual reports of MCAS results, scores from both versions are reported together, not separated on the basis of language. The bilingual booklet is not even viewed as an accommodation, and no records are kept as to which students received a bilingual booklet. The view of MDE is that this is an alternate form of the same exact test designed for specific students. To the state, the fact that it differs in language is no more consequential than a difference in font. The MDE does not view the bilingual booklet as an accommodation, and it does not disaggregate the scores of students who receive it. Therefore, no data are available on the performance of students who receive the bilingual booklet.

All MCAS items (multiple-choice, constructed response, and open response) are scored by Massachusetts's test development contractor. The Spanish version is scored by bilingual staff because they must be literate in Spanish to accurately score open response and constructed response items.

Technology

The MDE provides parents interpretive materials in English and 10 other languages on its Web site. When the MDE first published these guides on the internet, there were technical difficulties in accessing the Chinese document over the web. However, these problems have since been resolved. In addition, the MDE Web site also provides access to 100% of the released MCAS test items (in English and Spanish) each year. The released items consist of all items that counted toward a student's score, but not field test or equating items. The released MCAS items for the most recent administration can be found on the MDE's Web site.

Research and Statistical Analyses of Translated Tests

The MDE does not routinely perform any psychometric analyses on the Spanish MCAS, because the Spanish and English tests are assumed to be equivalent.

Future of Test Translation

The MDE plans to make a few changes to the test translation program, which should ensure greater quality control over the finished product. Beginning with the 2002–2003 school year, the English forms of the MCAS will be finalized earlier than in the past, allowing more time for the Spanish version to be translated and reviewed. (In previous years, the total time allowed for translation was just 2–3 weeks.) In addition, the MDE plans to add another round of quality control to the translation process. Bilingual educators and professional translators will be hired by the MDE on a contract basis to perform a second external, independent review of the translation, in addition to the existing external review currently being performed, to ensure that the final version of the translation and the printed test are entirely accurate.

MDE staff are also in the process of developing a new English Language Development assessment, to be used statewide to assess students' English proficiency in relation to state standards. As of the 2000–2001 school year, Massachusetts did not have a single instrument that was uniformly used to measure students' proficiency and literacy in English. Instead, the decision about which instruments to use was made at the district level. However, in the 2002–2003 school year, the state required all ELL students to take the Language Assessment Scales–Oral and Language Assessment Scales–Reading and Writing as a measure of their English proficiency.

Minnesota

Overview of the State Testing Program

Prior to 1994, there was no requirement in Minnesota for any kind of statewide assessment. Although individual school districts generally collected data in the past, the nature of the assessment varied from one district to another, and there was no attempt to provide a statewide picture of student performance. The first component of the Minnesota Statewide Assessment system, the Basic Skills Tests (BSTs), was implemented in 1994. Since then the system has expanded to include three additional programs: the Minnesota Comprehensive Assessments (MCAs), the Test of Emerging Academic English, and the Alternate Assessments for Special Education.

The BSTs are high-stakes tests of basic math and reading skills that a student is required to pass to graduate from high school. A student must take these tests for the first time in eighth grade and must pass the reading and math tests by 12th grade to receive a Minnesota state diploma. Students must also pass a mandatory writing test that is administered in the tenth grade.

The MCAs are standards-based assessments of reading, mathematics, and writing. Students do not pass or fail these tests. Instead, results are used by teachers to determine how well students are learning the concepts defined in Minnesota's High Standards. Scores on MCAs also influence decisions about curriculum and instructional practices. MCAs are administered in reading at Grades 3, 5, 7, and 10; in math at Grades 3, 5, 7, and 11; and in writing at Grade 5.

The Minnesota Test of Emerging Academic English is given to ELLs in Grades 3 through 12. These tests help teachers evaluate student progress in learning English. Scores on these tests are used to determine the effectiveness of curriculum and instructional practices to help students make successful transitions into English language classrooms.

The Alternate Assessments for Special Education are given to students with significant disabilities when the student's IEP or 504 teams determine that the BST or MCA assessments are not appropriate.

Number of ELLs in the State

The Minnesota Department of Children, Families, and Learning (CFL) reported that during the 2000–2001 school year, there were 845,065 students enrolled in Minnesota public schools. As Fig. 2.10 shows, approximately 7% ($n \approx 59{,}154$) were classified as ELLs. Figure 2.11 shows the most commonly spoken languages of ELLs in Minnesota schools: Hmong (37%), Spanish (35%), Somali (9.2%), Vietnamese (4.7%), Lao (3.8%), Russian (3.5%), and Cambodian (3.1%).

History of Test Translation

In 1995 CFL and the NCEO received a grant from the U.S. Office of Educational Research and Improvement (OERI) to evaluate the development and implementation of the BSTs. Specifically, the grant served to examine the ways in which ELL students and students with disabilities could be included in the state's Basic Standards Exams in reading, mathematics, and writing.

Minnesota first administered translated assessments in the 1997–1998 school year, primarily to include ELLs from various language backgrounds in the state accountability system. However, Minnesota state law requires that reading skills be assessed in English, so mathematics was the prime candidate for translation. Accordingly, the mathematics sections of the BSTs and MCAs were translated into Spanish, Hmong, and Vietnamese and administered in the 1997–1998 school year. Translated versions were offered in these languages in each consecutive year and then in the

ELLs (59,154)
6.5%

Non-ELLs
(785,911)
93.5%

FIG. 2.10. Total number of ELLs in Minnesota, as a percentage of overall student population.

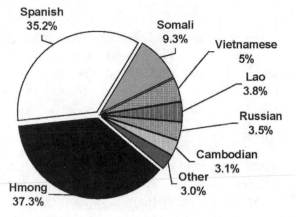

FIG. 2.11. Primary languages of ELLs in Minnesota.

2000–2001 school year, Somali was added to accommodate the growing Somali population in the state.

Which Tests Are Translated

Each year, Minnesota translates into Spanish, Hmong, Vietnamese, and Somali one form of the mathematics section of the MCA at each of the four tested grade levels (3, 5, 7, and 11). In addition, the state also translates three forms of the mathematics section of the BST into these four languages each year.

Other Translated Materials

Minnesota does not translate any ancillary materials into languages other than English. Districts are, however, given the discretion to translate any materials they deem necessary.

Commercially Available Tests

Minnesota does not use any commercially available native language assessment instruments.

How Many Students Take Translated Tests

For the 2000–2001 school year, we were only able to obtain the number of students who took translated assessments in the elementary grades. In third grade, 337 translated assessments were administered, and in fifth grade 255 were administered.

The Translation Process

Betmar Languages, a Minnesota-based translation company, manages the state's test translation process. The CFL granted us permission to speak with a representative of Betmar about the procedures used to translate the Minnesota assessments; however, despite numerous attempts we were unable to interview anyone from Betmar.

Reaction to Translated Tests

In 1996 when Minnesota was in the initial stages of developing its statewide assessments, the NCEO conducted a study to gather feedback from Cambodian-, Hmong-, Lao-, Spanish-, and Vietnamese-speaking parents about what means they felt would be best to include their children in the testing program (Quest, Liu, & Thurlow, 1996). Focus groups were conducted to provide a forum for parents and students to relate their experiences from the early administrations of the BSTs.

Participants in all groups thought that translation of the directions could help some students. Feedback from students clearly indicated that some had not understood certain parts of the directions. Some students, for instance, did not realize that they could make marks in the mathematics test booklet, using it as a place to calculate. Because they had no other scrap paper, some students reported having taken the entire test by performing all of the calculations either in their heads or with calculators.

Most participants believed that some, but probably not all, students would benefit from a translation of the writing prompt or the math test (which consists entirely of word problems). However, many were concerned about the potentially negative consequences of receiving a notation on their records indicating that they had taken a translated version of the test. Also, Cambodian and Hmong parents expressed concern that because their children had never attempted to solve math word problems in their native language, translation probably would not be of much benefit. Other parents further indicated that written translations might be futile, because many ELL students, particularly Hmong and Cambodian, were not literate in their first languages. They therefore suggested that oral (sight) translations might be more beneficial.

Simultaneously, although many parents expressed a desire for their children to maintain and develop skills in their native language, many also expressed a strong desire for their children to become fluent in English.

Apart from the study by the NCEO, the CFL has not conducted formal studies to gather systematic feedback about the translated tests. However, the state believes that parents, students, and teachers have reacted positively to the translated versions overall.

Translation in Districts

Minnesota policy allows districts to perform sight translations of the mathematics portions of the BST and MCA only. It is the districts' responsibility to identify qualified translators, who must then sign a nondisclosure agreement before seeing the test. In addition, all translators must follow the script the state provides. That is, they are not permitted to render into the non-English language anything that is not explicitly stated in the script.

All district-translated tests are scored by the state, and the scores are aggregated with all others. The only difference is that district-translated tests are marked as having been presented orally with accommodations.

The state does not examine sight translators' qualifications and does not perform any evaluations of translators' performance. Therefore, there is no information about the quality of the translations or any safeguarding measure to ensure that all of the students receive translations of similar quality. State officials have expressed some concern over the use of sight translation for this reason, as there is no way to ensure that quality control standards are consistently being met. However, the state believes that the availability of sight translations is essential to allow for maximum inclusion of ELLs into the state accountability system, as many ELLs might not be literate in their first language and therefore would not be able to benefit from a written translation of the tests. This point is particularly relevant for Hmong students in the United States, because the Hmong writing system was developed only recently, in the 1970s. As a result, many Hmong parents might not be literate in Hmong and their children will have had little or no contact with the writing system, despite the fact that they regularly speak Hmong with family members and others in their community (Liu, Thurlow, Erickson, Spicuzza, & Heinze, 1997).

Test Presentation Format

In 1998–1999 and 1999–2000, a two-part study was conducted to investigate the effects of a bilingual (side-by-side English and Spanish) test booklet for ELL students on the statewide BST reading test (Anderson, Liu, Swierzbin, Thurlow, & Bielinksi, 2000; Liu, Anderson, Swierzbin, & Thurlow, 1999). In the first phase of the study, 9 eighth-grade Spanish-speaking ELL students completed a portion of a bilingual version of the BST (with reading passages from newspaper feature articles) in their original English and all test items translated into Spanish and presented side-by-side with the original English. In addition, students also had the option to listen to test directions and items in Spanish on an audiocassette during the test. After completing the test, students met with researchers one-on-one to answer a series of survey questions about (a) how difficult they perceived the test to be, (b) which question formats they relied on, and (c) which format they would prefer in future administrations of the BST. Students' responses varied widely, potentially because of the range of English proficiency levels represented in the sample. Responses relating to the difficulty of the test were not extremely informative, but many students indicated that they found the test to be difficult. Again, students' responses about which item format they had relied on varied considerably, with students at higher proficiency levels reporting that they relied mostly on the English and students at lower levels reporting their opposite reliance on Spanish. For the most part, students reported using one form and referring to the other when they encountered an unknown term or wanted to check their understanding of what was being asked. Crucially, no students reported that the format of the test was confusing or bothersome. Apparently, students did not take advantage of the audiocassette, tending to rely exclusively on the written stimuli.

In the second phase of the study, 206 eighth-grade students participated in an administration of the reading BST. The control group (composed of general education [non-ELL] students) took the English version of the test with no modifications, as did the unaccommodated ELL group. However, the accommodated ELL group took the test under the same conditions as in Phase 1 (reading passages in English, items presented side by side in English and Spanish, availability of an audiocassette recording of test directions and items). This phase was guided by three research questions:

1. Does giving students reading test questions in both English and Spanish (both aurally and in writing) enable them to better demonstrate their understanding of the text?
2. How do students use these accommodations?
3. Will students use the accommodations if they are made available?

To answer the first research question, mean test scores of the three groups were submitted to a one-way analysis of variance (ANOVA). The means were found to be statistically different, and a post hoc Tukey test indicated that the general education mean (30.09) was significantly higher than that of the other two groups, and that the accommodated ELL mean (17.70) was not significantly different than the unaccommodated ELL mean (15.85). That is, the accommodations did not produce a large boost in ELL students' test scores. However, the scores for the accommodated group did correlate better to their self-reported evaluations of English reading ability than the scores of the unaccommodated group. This could be an indication that the provision of accommodations allowed students to demonstrate their reading proficiency better than students who received no accommodations.

To answer the second research question, ELL students in the accommodated group were asked to report the extent to which they used the written English version, written Spanish version, or spoken Spanish versions of the test items. Results revealed that two thirds of the students reported using one or more accommodations some of the time. Perhaps surprisingly, approximately one third of the students reported not having used accommodations even though they were available. Students' responses about the context in which they used the accommodations varied. Again, this is in large part because of the range of proficiency levels in the sample. Most students reported using them as a reference, typically when they did not understand a word in English. Only a small number (those who were least proficient in English) reported using the Spanish accommodations on all questions.

Responses from an exit questionnaire were used to answer the third research question, which investigated students' test format preferences. Students were asked which form of the test they would choose to take if given the choice during an operational administration of the BST: (a) a version with questions in spoken Spanish and written Spanish and English, (b) a version with only written Spanish and English questions, or (c) a version with questions written only in English. Responses were almost evenly distributed across the three options, with about one third of the students preferring each format. From this we can see that some, but not all, students felt that they had benefited from the accommodations.

However, this study was conducted for research purposes only, to "push the envelope" in terms of accommodations for LEP students. Minnesota has never used bilingual test booklets during operational administration of statewide assessments. The translated tests in Hmong, Somali, Spanish, and Vietnamese are published in separate monolingual booklets.

Translated Tests and Score Reporting

Scores from translated tests are reported on the same scale as scores from the English version of the test. There is an assumption that the translated tests and the originals are equivalent, so there is no separate reporting procedure or scale.

Technology

Minnesota does not have any publications on the Web relating to the statewide assessments in languages other than English.

Research and Statistical Analysis of Translated Tests

Because it is assumed that the English and translated versions are equivalent, the state does not conduct any formal studies on the psychometric quality of translated tests. Therefore, no separate linking or equating procedures are performed.

However, the NCEO has published a number of reports on the implementation of the Minnesota accountability testing system, specifically concerning accommodations made for ELLs. All of the reports are available online at NCEO's Web site.

Future of Test Translation

Barring a change in the refugee populations in the state, Minnesota does not plan to offer written translations in any other languages in the near future.

Staff at the Department of Education stress that they would like to be in a position to exert more quality control over the translations, but currently do not have staff members who are bilingual in Spanish, Hmong, Vietnamese, and Somali to review the translations.

New Mexico

Overview of the State Testing Program

The New Mexico Statewide Student Assessment System consists of four major components. Each component serves a different purpose and targets specific grade levels.

The statewide reading assessment is an instruction-based assessment, individually administered for Grades 1 and 2. Its purpose is to determine reading proficiency. Each local school district determines the method that will be used to assess student progress in reading, but districts are required to report aggregate data to the New Mexico State Department of Education (NMSDE) on reading achievement using one of two formats. The first option, the Report of Students' Reading Achievement, consists of reporting the number of students who have mastered "essential competencies" and the number of students who are emergent, competent, and fluent readers. The second option, the Optional Reading Assessment of Progress, involves reporting on the fall and spring progress students have made in the four skills (reading, speaking, listening, and writing).

The New Mexico Achievement Assessment Program is administered to students in Grades 3 through 9 in the content areas of reading and language arts, mathematics, science, and social studies. For this assessment, the state uses the commercially produced TerraNova and Supera.

The New Mexico Writing Assessment Program is a direct, on-demand assessment that is administered to students in Grades 5 and 7. Students spend approximately 1 hour a day, over a 3-day period, engaged in the writing process in response to a specific writing prompt or topic. On the first day, after receiving the writing prompt for the appropriate grade level and a prewriting checklist, students work on prewriting activities and then are instructed to write a rough draft of their composition. On the second day students receive a guide for revisions and are instructed to use the guide to help them think about how to improve their writing and to revise their rough drafts as necessary. On the third day the students make last-minute changes and transcribe their final drafts into the Final Composition Booklet. The composition is scored holistically on a 6-point scale (6 being the highest score) using a set of criteria that measures a student's ability to communicate in a particular mode of discourse. A score of 4 or higher is the goal for satisfactory student attainment. Analytic scores are also provided for each student's composition in the areas of sentence formation, mechanics, word usage, and development.

The New Mexico High School Competency Examination is a criterion-referenced test that measures student performance against the New Mexico content standards and benchmarks. It assesses competencies in the content areas of reading, language arts, mathematics, science, social studies, and writing. Passing the examination is a graduation requirement for public high school students in New Mexico. Students take the test for the first time in the 10th grade and must pass all six subtests to receive a high school diploma. Sophomores who fail any part of the examination have another chance in their junior year and two chances in their senior year to successfully pass all six subtests before graduation. Seniors who do not pass the examination but fulfill the other course and credit requirements are given the option of exiting with a certificate of completion (or "attendance") and can return within the next 5 years to retake the examination, pass it, and receive a diploma. A student can participate through an alternate assessment based on bilingual education or special education program guidelines.[5]

---

[5]During the 2000–2001 school year, New Mexico did not have a policy regarding accommodations. Spanish language versions of tests were considered alternate assessments.

Number of ELLs in the State

According to Kindler (2002), during the 2000–2001 school year 320,306 students were enrolled in New Mexico public schools. As Fig. 2.12 shows, 63,755 (19.9%) of those students were classified as ELLs.

Home Language Surveys are collected by the school districts and reported to the NMSDE on every student with a primary or home language other than English. Results of those surveys for the 2000–2001 school year were not available at the time this report was written. However, data from the 2001–2002 school year indicated that the most common non-English languages in the state were Spanish (28.5%), Navajo (4.5%), Vietnamese (1.9%), Korean (0.56%), Laotian (0.25%), and Cantonese (0.22%). Tagalog, Hmong, and Cambodian followed, each comprising less than 0.22% of the population, as shown in Fig. 2.13.

History of Test Translation

New Mexico allows for Spanish language versions of state-mandated tests because of the nature of the state's population. Bilingual education is integral to the state—the state's first constitution in 1911 provided for the use of both Spanish and English in all government publications and in 1973, the New Mexico Legislature passed a Bilingual Multicultural Education law, which is still in effect. By providing funding to schools for bilingual education, this law supports the view held by the framers of the New Mexico state constitution and encourages cultural diversity and linguistic bilingualism.

Which Tests Are Translated

The current High School Competency Test has been translated for more than a decade. (The English edition became operational in 1987 and a Spanish edition was added a year or so later.)

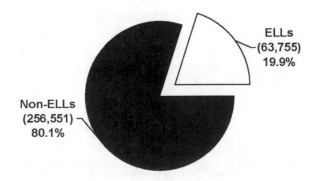

ELLs
(63,755)
19.9%

Non-ELLs
(256,551)
80.1%

FIG. 2.12. Total number of ELLs in New Mexico, as a percentage of overall student population.

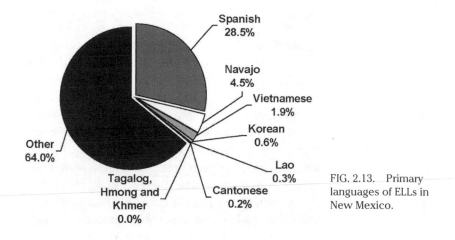

FIG. 2.13. Primary languages of ELLs in New Mexico.

Unfortunately, during that period, the one translated form has never been updated. The pass rate on the Spanish version is very high. The cut score was originally set near the chance level so that the pass rate among first-time test takers was 87%. The cut score on both tests was reset in spring of 2000 to establish higher standards, and the new cut score was implemented for the 2000–2001 school year. Some people expect the pass rate on the Spanish version to decline considerably as a result of the new cut score.

Other Translated Materials

For assessments presented in the Spanish language, the read-aloud portions of the test administration manuals are translated into Spanish by the state. Districts have the discretion to translate certain other ancillary materials, such as letters and information to parents.

Commercially Available Tests

In addition to the assessments developed at the state level, New Mexico students are also required to take one of two CTB/McGraw-Hill standardized tests, either the TerraNova (in English) or the Supera (in Spanish).

How Many Students Take Translated Tests

At the time of publication, exact numbers of students who took each assessment in Spanish in 2000–2001 were not available. However, the state estimates that approximately 10,000 students in Grades 3 through 9 take the Supera in Spanish each year, and fewer than 500 take the High School Competency Exam in Spanish annually.

The Translation Process

CTB/McGraw-Hill is New Mexico's main test development contractor. In addition to creating the commercially available TerraNova and Supera, CTB/McGraw-Hill is also in charge of developing the New Mexico High School Competency Exam. The English version of the test was first developed in the mid-1980s and became operational in either the 1986–1987 or 1987–1988 school year. The NMSDE then decided to translate the test into Spanish. Staff at NMSDE were in charge of the translation project, not CTB/McGraw-Hill. Educators and administrators in the state reviewed the English test, making small changes to make the test more conducive to translation. Then personnel within the state translated the test. More precise details are not known about the process because of the amount of time that has elapsed since the translation was conducted. CTB/McGraw-Hill proofread, typeset, and printed the tests for the state.

The English version of the test has been updated multiple times since its original creation, largely to reflect the changes in the curriculum that have taken place since the 1980s. However, another Spanish translation has not been done, in large part because the state does not believe translation of the test to be cost effective, as fewer than 500 students a year take the Spanish version. Thus, the English and Spanish versions are currently quite different from each other.

At present, CTB-McGraw/Hill still plays a role in the dissemination of the Spanish version. Each year the school districts fill out orders for the number of Spanish versions they anticipate needing, and CTB-McGraw/Hill prints the necessary booklets. However, no other modifications are made to the test from year to year.

Also, because of the small number of students taking the Spanish version, CTB-McGraw/Hill has not performed any psychometric analyses on the Spanish test, as they have for the English version.

Reaction to Translated Tests

Historically, teachers, students, and the public have appreciated having the tests translated into Spanish. However, recently demand for the development of alternate versions of tests in Spanish has become evident. These would not be translations, but parallel original assessments constructed in Spanish. The development of alternate tests would be carried out simultaneously with the development of the regular assessments. One possible advantage is that the parallel tests could be ready at the same time that the English versions are ready. The development of the regular tests often falls behind schedule, and when this happens there is not enough time to do a careful translation of the final version. It is thought that the development of parallel forms could relieve some pressure on the test development process.

Another concern is the type of Spanish that is used on the test. Standard Spanish has been used on the state assessment. However, whereas the Spanish of southern New Mexico is close to standard Mexican Spanish, a unique dialect of Spanish with many archaisms is spoken in northern New Mexico.

Translation in Districts

Although there was no accommodation policy in the state in 2000–2001, districts had the option to do a portfolio assessment in the native language for students who were not eligible to take the statewide tests. The composition of the portfolio assessment was left up to the districts (i.e., there was no consistent system or guidance for portfolio assessment across the state).

Districts are allowed to translate tests into other languages. The Albuquerque school district, for instance, translates tests into Vietnamese and several other Asian languages to accommodate the large Asian population in that part of the state. Typically, school district employees in the bilingual and ESL programs translate the tests. Apparently, this is a case of practice without policy: In the 2000–2001 school year there was no official accommodations policy in the state, although one was implemented in 2002–2003.

Test Presentation Format

New Mexico uses monolingual test booklets. That is, students receive either the English or Spanish version of a test in one discrete test booklet. The determination regarding the language in which the student is tested is made by the district and based on the student's English language proficiency test scores.

Translated Tests and Score Reporting

In the past, scores earned on the Spanish versions of statewide assessments were not included in school, district, and state totals. This policy has since changed, and in 2001 the Spanish versions of the tests were incorporated into the state accountability system. Student scores were derived from either the Spanish test or the English test, but not from both.

Technology

The NMSDE Web site does not include any sample tests or test-related publications in Spanish.

Research and Statistical Analysis of Translated Tests

CTB-McGraw/Hill sends a separate item analysis on the Spanish version of the High School Competency Test to the NMSDE. Despite the history of translating tests into Spanish, there has never been enough money to support research on these tests.

Future of Test Translation

Currently, there is a debate over whether the new standards-based high school test currently being developed should be translated into Spanish. Some people feel that a high school diploma should be dependent on knowing English. Others feel that the Spanish version should only be available to students who have been in the state for 1 year or less. The state will probably translate the test, given the traditional support for bilingualism in New Mexico.

In the 2002–2003 school year, New Mexico implemented a policy on accommodations for ELLs. Accordingly, a guidance document entitled Appropriate Accommodations for English Language Learners has been made available via the Web site.

New York

Overview of the State Testing Program

The New York state assessment program consists of two main types of statewide tests: (a) a series of standards-based tests of ELA, mathematics, science, and social studies, administered at the elementary and middle school levels, and (b) a series of high-stakes tests that students must pass to receive a high school diploma (the New York State Regents Exams).

At the elementary and middle school levels, there are three tested grade levels (4, 5, and 8). All content areas are not tested at each level; rather certain tests are administered to students in certain grades. In Grade 4, students take tests in ELA, mathematics, and science. In Grade 5, students take a social studies test, and in Grade 8, students take the full battery of content area tests (ELA, mathematics, science, and social studies).

At the high school level, students must pass a series of Regents Exams as a graduation requirement. At a minimum, students must pass the Regents Exams in English, Mathematics, Global History & Geography, U.S.

History & Government, a foreign language, and two fields of science (from Living Environment, Earth Science, Biology, Chemistry, or Physics).

The older, non-standards based Regents Competency Tests (RCTs) are used as alternate assessments for students with special needs who have an IEP.

To allow students multiple opportunities to pass the exams, one new form of each Regents Exam is administered in June, one in August, and one in January. The Grade 8 assessments in math, science, and social studies are administered in June. The Grade 5 assessment in social studies is administered in November. The Grade 4 assessments are administered in January and May.

Teachers score all of the New York tests. That is, districts, not the state, score all tests. The state provides the districts with rubrics and training materials and the districts train teachers to do the scoring.

Number of ELLs in the State

Data from Kindler (2002) indicate that during the 2000–2001 school year, 2,882,188 students were enrolled in New York public schools. As shown in Fig. 2.14, 239,097 (8.3%) were classified as ELLs. The five most common home languages of students in New York are Spanish, Haitian Creole, Russian, Chinese, and Korean. Data regarding the percentages of ELLs who speak each of these languages were not available.

History of Test Translation

The New York State Education Department (NYSED) has a long history of translating state-mandated tests. The state's experience in this area goes back to the practice of translating the RCTs. The RCTs are tests that were created as end-of-course measures, but unlike similar tests, they did

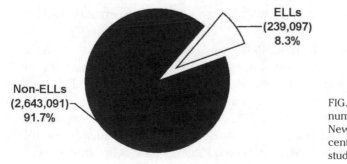

ELLs
(239,097)
8.3%

Non-ELLs
(2,643,091)
91.7%

FIG. 2.14. Total number of ELLs in New York, as a percentage of overall student population.

not serve for validating studies for college entrance purposes. The number of languages into which the RCTs were translated eventually grew to 29. The state bilingual education director indicated that New York translates tests because the NYSED wants to test the specific competency the test is testing, not the student's English skills. Translation maintains equity and the integrity of the testing process.

In 1997, when the New York legislature and the State Board of Education moved to require students to take the Regents Exams in order to obtain a high school diploma, the NYSED agreed to translate the required exams to the five languages with the greatest number of speakers in the schools. Consequently, those exams were translated to Spanish, Haitian Creole, Chinese (using the traditional characters still used in Taiwan, Hong Kong, and Singapore), Russian, and Korean. The fifth language in terms of student population has changed several times since then. However, it is not politically practical to eliminate Korean, and there is not the money to translate the tests into a sixth language. Currently, the fifth language in terms of student population is Arabic; however there are no plans to begin translating the Regents or other exams to Arabic.

The first tests to be translated were the Regents math tests. These were followed by the two Regents social studies tests (Global History and Geography and U.S. History and Government), then two science tests (Earth Science and Living Environment).

Following the decision to translate the Regents Exams required for high school graduation, the NYSED then decided to translate the Grade 4 and 8 math, science, and social studies exams. When the statewide, standards-based, Grade 4 social studies assessment was moved to Grade 5, the practice of translating this test continued. Originally, the state wanted to translate these tests to five languages, as was being done for the Regents Exams. However, due to funding constraints, the state decided to begin translating them to the top three languages in terms of population (Spanish, Haitian Creole, and Chinese). The program continues in this manner today; that is, the fourth and fifth languages have not been added and there are no plans to add them.

The state allows the older RCTs to be used as alternate assessments for students with IEPs. However, the oldest RCT forms that have been translated sometimes have obsolete items and content. As a result, translated RCT forms are used only in 14 languages. Occasionally, the NYSED will translate a new form of an RCT, because an old form is no longer considered acceptable. In this case, the translation is most frequently conducted in one of the five languages to which Regents Exams are translated.

Which Tests Are Translated

Among the Regents Exams, the state translates the Living Environment (biology and environmental science), Earth Science, U.S. History and Government, Global History and Geography, and Math A or Course 1 into five languages. Math A is the standards-based math assessment, whereas the Course 1 exam is an old non-standards-based RCT. Both assessments were used until January 2002, and students could meet the high school graduation requirement in math by passing either test. The Course 1 exam was discontinued after January 2002. Each new Regents Exam is translated into five languages. However, the August administration is translated to Spanish only.

The state also translates the Grade 4 and Grade 8 Math and Science assessments into three languages—Spanish, Haitian Creole, and Chinese. The state also translates the Grade 5 Social Studies exam into those languages. Finally, an Intermediate Technology Exam is translated into the five Regents languages.

Other Translated Materials

The state does not translate other materials to non-English languages. Test administration manuals are not translated. Staff at the NYSED say that bilingual teachers can do an oral translation of the instructions that are read aloud when they administer the tests.

An interesting aspect of the NYSED program is the availability of official glossaries in the required subject areas. The glossaries are published by the NYSED and distributed to schools with bilingual programs. This helps to ensure that the terms students are learning in the bilingual education programs in the state match those that appear on the exams in the given language. Initially, the NYSED tried to create the glossaries prior to introducing the translated tests. However, this was not always possible. Glossaries for the math and social studies tests were created first, followed by glossaries for the science tests. The first glossaries to be completed were in Spanish, followed by Haitian Creole.

Glossaries were also created as a way to standardize the translations. Until 1999, teachers in the state translated the exams. The teacher translators often disagreed among themselves and used different terminology when translating the tests. Thus, a glossary was viewed as a way to standardize the language used on the tests. To prepare students for the language of the tests, glossaries are distributed to teachers. In this way, it is expected that teachers will employ the same terminology in teaching that is employed on the tests. Students also have access to these glossaries while taking the tests.

As of 2001, glossaries existed in the following languages and subject areas:

- Sequential Math A and Math B Regents Examinations—Spanish, Haitian Creole, Russian.
- Global History and Geography (draft)—Spanish, Haitian Creole, Russian.
- United States History and Government (draft)—Spanish, Haitian Creole, Russian.
- Earth Science Reference Tables—Spanish, Haitian Creole, Chinese, Russian, Korean.
- Biology (draft)—Spanish, Haitian Creole.

The glossaries are developed in the following manner. Two teachers are contracted to carry out the work in one of two ways: (a) One translates English terms on a test and the other reviews the translation of the terms, or (b) both teachers work together as a team. When the translation is complete, a third teacher is brought to the NYSED to review their glossary.

Initially, the NYSED publishes the glossary as a draft, inviting comments from teachers, schools, or other individuals. Based on the comments, the glossary is finalized, and then after 1 year a final version is published. Draft versions of glossaries are free. The NYSED sells the final version of the glossaries for $4 each. The NYSED is willing to share the final glossaries with other states.

In the summer of 2001, the NYSED commissioned glossaries for Regents math and social studies exams in Bosnian, Vietnamese, Arabic, Polish, and Serbo-Croatian. The New York City Board of Education has also commissioned glossaries in a variety of subjects and languages, and these are used widely in New York City public schools.

Commercially Available Tests

Commercially available tests can be used by districts for off-year testing, for progress testing, or for capturing norm-referenced information, but they cannot be used in lieu of a state assessment. Several districts use them within their bilingual education programs.

How Many Students Take Translated Tests

It is estimated that only about 50% of ELLs in New York receive instruction in their native language.

The Translation Process

Prior to the translation of the Regents Exams, the RCTs were translated by or under the supervision of the NYSED Bilingual Education office. However, eventually responsibility for this was shifted to the Student Assessment office. The Bilingual Education office translated the RCTs in math, social studies, and science; the first RCTs translated were in math. The Bilingual Education office brought in bilingual teachers and language specialists for 15 languages. As a group, they began evaluating the items, their translatability, and their cultural relevance. Some items were eliminated immediately based on these discussions. Acceptable items were those that tested the subject area, could be translated without problems, and did not exhibit cultural bias. The Bilingual Education office utilized teachers as translators, but allowed reviewers to be translators or some other individual with strong language credentials (e.g., language specialists).

Initially, teachers were selected because they were respected as teachers. However, it soon became apparent that not all good teachers were good translators. In selecting new translators, the NYSED eventually began to ask the teachers to submit a sample translation, which the NYSED evaluated before inviting them to come to NYSED offices in Albany.

The standardization of language was a major concern at the time when the RCTs were first translated. Glossaries initially were prepared because of concerns about which translations were the most appropriate given terms or ideas and the need to standardize the language used. As time went on, the NYSED brought in a teacher to translate the test and a different teacher to review the translation.

As indicated previously, the Bilingual Education office used teachers to translate the RCTs. These teachers were brought to the state capital, mostly from New York City, to do the work at the NYSED to maintain test security. To maintain standardization of language across test forms, the same teachers typically were employed. When the stakes were low and there was less testing in the schools, this worked well. However, as the number of tested subjects increased, and the tests had high stakes for students and districts, the teachers either tired of coming to Albany or they wanted to remain with their classes to prepare them for the tests. The schools also began to object to lending the teachers to the state so often. Thus, it became more difficult to recruit teachers to participate in the translation process.

After translation responsibilities were passed to the Student Assessment office, a decision was made to use professional translators to translate the tests. However, it was decided that teachers should continue to review and approve the translations.

When the NYSED expanded translation to five languages, it became impossible to continue using teacher translators. Based on that experience, the NYSED published a request for proposals in 1999 calling for vendors to bid on the translation of the state assessments. Vendors bid and contracts were awarded. The NYSED is currently working with five translation vendors. The state continues to use teachers as reviewers of the vendors' work. In some cases, the teacher reviewers are former translators of earlier forms of the test. On occasion, when no teacher is available, the NYSED has used students at the State University of New York at Albany to review the test.

Staff in the Student Assessment office estimate that going to outside vendors has cost more, but that it works better, given the heavy demands on the NYSED, which suffered a one-third reduction in its professional staff between 1996 and 2001. The vendors also provide the NYSED with more support and more resources, particularly when they understand education and assessment.

Since 1999, the NYSED has contracted with translation companies to meet most of their test translation needs. The companies involved are SLTI, CS Tech, A + A Korean Translations, and TransPerfect. SLTI does the majority of translation for the NYSED. It currently translates two Regents Exams into five languages and two more Regents Exams into three languages. It also translates the Grade 4, 5, and 8 science and social studies exams into three languages.

The current process for doing the translations has evolved through negotiation between the translation vendors and the relevant staff of the Student Assessment office of the NYSED. In 2000–2001, the process took 6 weeks, but it was reduced to 4 weeks in 2002. When the English version of a test is ready, it is sent via a secure lockbox to the translation vendors. The vendors receive a hard copy of the test, a PDF file, and all the files and graphics that went into the English version. The test is reviewed for errors, translation problems, and cultural problems. Any concerns are then communicated to the NYSED and a solution is found. The tests are then given to a lead translator who begins translating the test into a Microsoft Word file. Using the Track Changes feature of Word, a second translator then reviews the file. The revised file is given to the first translator, who goes through each suggested change and either accepts or rejects it. A test translation manager monitors the process.

At this stage, the translation is sent back to the NYSED, which has previously set up a teacher review. Within a few days, teachers review the translation. Usually, two teachers review each test. Their comments, written on a paper copy of the translation, are sent back to the translation vendor, which implements the majority of the suggested changes. The test is then published using Quark Xpress, a professional desktop publishing program. Graphics are produced in Photoshop, Freehand, and Illustrator (industry-standard applications). The translator, who identifies any errors, missing words, missing diacritics, and so forth, then proofs the Quark version. Subsequently, the test is printed and shipped to the NYSED for a second teacher review. This review normally consists of proofreading and approving the final version. The translation vendor mostly implements changes suggested, and a new Quark version is prepared. Another desktop publishing specialist proofs this version for any inconsistencies in layout. The final version is then delivered to the NYSED in a secure lockbox. The delivery includes a camera-ready copy of the test, and a Zip disk or CD containing the Quark files and a PDF file. Once received by the NYSED, the test is sent to its internal print shop, which prints the required number of copies of the test, either from the camera-ready copy or from the PDF file. The copies are then distributed to schools. The copies sent to schools are shipped after the English versions are shipped, because the number of tests involved is much smaller.

Although the teacher review continues to be a strength of the program, it is not without problems. Some teachers insist on rewriting the translation using a different style of language. The translation vendors have come to an agreement with the NYSED that teacher reviews should only identify errors in translation (mistranslations, insertions, and omissions). Nonetheless, some teachers either ignore or fail to understand this agreement. When teacher reviews come to the translation vendor, each comment or correction must be evaluated for its appropriateness. Otherwise, new errors or problems could be introduced into the translation. The translation vendor makes a list of teacher comments and corrections, showing how the vendor handled them. The list is then sent to the NYSED.

Reaction to Translated Tests

Reactions to the translated tests are positive. The biggest complaint is that the tests are only translated into five languages, and these comments usually come from teachers who speak a language other than those five. Whenever this complaint is made, the SEA encourages the local education agency to provide an oral translation in languages that are not translated.

Teachers also complain that when instruction is not provided in the language, the student often does not have sufficient skills in the language.

However, in this case, the state points out that translated tests, be they written or oral translations, are usually taken by students who have recently arrived in the United States.

Occasionally, a teacher will claim that a term was used that is not in one of the NYSED distributed glossaries. There are also disagreements over the terminology that appears in the glossaries. Sometimes translators disagree with the translation that appears in the glossary; other times teacher reviewers disagree with the glossary.

Translation in Districts

The districts are allowed (and encouraged) to carry out oral translations for languages for which the state does not provide a written translation. Teachers typically conduct the oral (sight) translation, although in some cases the translation might be done by paraprofessionals or even community members. The oral translator is not allowed to look at the test until 1 hour prior to the scheduled administration time. The oral translator is allowed to prepare a written translation but there is not adequate time to do so, and therefore it is recognized that the oral translation will be somewhat impromptu. The requirement is that the translation be word for word, with no clarifications or explanations. Student answer sheets and test booklets resulting from oral translations are locally scored by district personnel, just as with the standard versions in English.

Reaction to oral translation in districts is generally positive, although no formal survey of district reactions has been conducted. Some districts complain that they cannot find sight translators for the languages they need; others are pleased to be able to offer the accommodation and thereby include more students in the assessment program. Most teachers are glad to have this accommodation available.

Test Presentation Format

As indicated previously, the tests are prepared using Quark Xpress, along with Photoshop, Freehand, and Illustrator. Thus, the foreign language versions show the same quality of graphics and layout as the English version. Once the Quark version is finalized, it is printed on 11 × 17-inch paper, saddle-stitched, and folded. Sometimes the student is supposed to respond in the test booklet. However, if the student is expected to respond using an answer sheet, a translated answer sheet is inserted in each test booklet. It is then shipped to the testing coordinator at the school. On rare occasions, if a test has not reached a school, the NYSED will fax a copy of it to the school on the day of the test.

Translated Tests and Score Reporting

Scores on translated tests are aggregated with scores on English versions.

Technology

During the 2000–2001 school year, the NYSED did not make use of its Web site to publish previously administered foreign language versions of the tests, nor did it produce a parent guide or other information on the non-English versions that are available on its Web site. English versions of the tests were made available on the Web site. Plans called for non-English versions to be published on the site, too, but this did not take place during the 2000–2001 school year.

Research and Statistical Analyses of Translated Tests

Because the tests are locally scored, the NYSED does not have item-level data with which to carry out psychometric analyses of the translated versions. The English versions are field-tested, and the field-test data are used to equate new forms. Non-English versions are generally not field-tested. The NYSED did field-test the Grade 4 and 8 math assessments, and CTB, one of its test development contractors, did statistical analyses of these tests. However, these data have not been made public. Measurement, Inc., which makes the Math A component retest forms, also field-tested a form in Spanish. Again, these data have not been released.

Future of Test Translation

New York plans to continue translating the same tests into the same languages. Due to the costs involved, there are no plans to expand the program. The state plans to continue using test translation contractors to do this work. There is no desire to have teachers translate the tests, as this proved impractical in the past. There is a desire to field-test the Spanish version of the tests, and to separately equate the Spanish versions, but this practice has not been implemented. The primary reasons are lack of staff time and psychometric concerns about the comparability of the resulting scores with the English versions of the tests. There is occasional talk of transferring the management of the translated versions from the Student Assessment office back to the Bilingual Education office of the NYSED, but this is not likely to happen.

Oregon

Overview of the State Testing Program

Oregon's state assessment system consists of untimed, standardized, criterion-referenced tests in English (reading and writing), mathematics, and science. The tests contain a variety of item types, including multiple-choice, essay, and mathematics problem-solving questions. Each test is administered at Grades 3, 5, 8, and 10.

The multiple-choice portions of the reading and mathematics tests are level tests. There are three levels—Level A, Level B, and Level C—of each reading and math multiple-choice test at each grade level tested, with Level A being the lowest level of difficulty and Level C being the highest. Level tests are used because the state believes that they enable more precise measurement than other types of group-administered tests. They extend the range of the test to measure more accurately student achievement at the high and low ends, while allowing teachers to match more closely the achievement level of each student with the test the student takes.

All districts in the state award a Certificate of Initial Mastery to students who meet Grade 10 performance standards in state and local assessments. During the 2000–2001 school year, students had to meet the standards on the English, mathematics, and science assessments to receive this credential. By 2003–2004, however, the program was to be finalized and require students to achieve the standards on the English, mathematics, science, social sciences, arts, and second or foreign language assessments.

Number of ELLs in the State

Data from Kindler (2002) indicate that during the 2000–2001 school year, 545,545 students were enrolled in Oregon public schools. As shown in Fig. 2.15, of those, 47,382 (8.7%) were classified as ELLs. In Oregon,

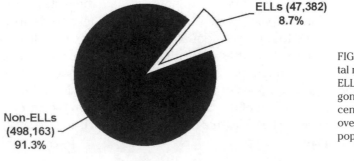

ELLs (47,382)
8.7%

Non-ELLs
(498,163)
91.3%

FIG. 2.15. Total number of ELLs in Oregon, as a percentage of overall student population.

school districts conduct a home language survey, but currently are not required to report the data to the Oregon Department of Education. However, informal counts indicate that the most populous non-English primary language backgrounds of school-age children in the state are Spanish and Russian, followed by smaller concentrations of Hmong and Vietnamese.

History of Test Translation

Oregon first began offering translated assessments in the 1996–1997 school year. Prior to that time, many ELL students were exempted from the statewide assessments. State legislators saw that expenditures were higher for the ELL population than for the general school population, yet they had no way to assess these students' progress. They asked that the Oregon Department of Education find some way to include all students in the statewide accountability system. In 1995–1996 Oregon applied for federal funding to determine how best to assess the ELL population. When the grant was awarded, the state opted to provide linguistic accommodations to ELL students on the statewide assessments, translating the mathematics (multiple-choice and problem-solving) and writing assessments into Spanish in 1996–1997. The translated tests were offered in a bilingual (dual-language) test booklet format, with each page divided in half and identical items presented in English on one side and in Spanish on the other.

In 1998–1999, Oregon began translating the mathematics tests into Russian as well, also using the bilingual (dual-language) test booklet format. However, the state decided not to translate the writing prompt into Russian, in part because the state had not conducted any psychometric studies at that time to assess the validity of translating its tests into Russian.

Psychometric studies have shown, however, that the English and Spanish/English tests are equivalent, so Oregon has continued to translate writing into Spanish and mathematics (multiple-choice and problem-solving) into both Spanish and Russian. (The mathematics tests are being translated into Russian so that an equating study can be conducted.) Also, starting in 2002–2003, science was to be translated into Spanish as well.

Which Tests Are Translated

During 2000–2001, Oregon offered bilingual (dual-language) test booklets (English/Spanish) for the writing and mathematics portions of the statewide assessment, and English/Russian booklets for the mathematics portion only. The multiple-choice portion of the mathematics test was offered in Spanish and Russian at Grades 3, 5, 8, and 10; mathematics problem solving was offered in Spanish and Russian at Grades 5, 8, and 10. The writing portion was available only in the English/Spanish format at Grades 3, 5, 8, and 10.

One form per year, per achievement level (A, B, and C), per grade level of the mathematics multiple-choice tests is translated into Spanish and Russian. In addition, one form of the mathematics problem-solving test is translated into Spanish and Russian, and all of the English writing prompts are translated into Spanish each year.

For the multiple-choice portion of the mathematics test, three achievement levels per tested grade (3, 5, 8, and 10) are translated into Spanish each year. All three levels must be translated because the state has determined (via an equating study, discussed later in this case study) that the English and Spanish tests are equivalent; hence, students can take the Spanish version of the mathematics assessment to qualify for a Certificate of Initial Mastery in mathematics.

One form (Levels A and B) of the multiple-choice mathematics test has been translated into Russian, and that same form has been administered every year since 1999–2000. That same test has been administered year after year for the state to have large enough numbers to run an equating study. The equating study was projected to be finished by December 2002, at which point the state was to determine whether the English and English/Russian tests are equivalent (and correspondingly, whether the English/Russian test will be considered a standard or modified accommodation).

The Spanish/English administration of both mathematics tests (multiple-choice and problem-solving tasks) is considered to be a standard administration with accommodations, as is the Russian/English administration of the mathematics problem-solving tasks. Because these are considered standard administrations, students who take these tests qualify to meet the benchmark standards. However, currently the Russian/English version of the mathematics multiple-choice test is undergoing psychometric analysis and therefore the administration of this test is considered to be modified. Students cannot currently take this test and qualify to meet the benchmark standards. However, once the psychometric study is completed, this version will be considered a standard administration with accommodations, just like the other tests and students will be able to take the test and qualify to meet the benchmark standards.

The administration of the Spanish/English version of the writing test is considered standard (with accommodations) so long as the student responds in English. If the student responds in Spanish, the test is then considered modified and accordingly the student cannot qualify to meet the benchmark standards.

Other Translated Materials

The Oregon Department of Education offers as many ancillary materials in languages other than English as its budget allows each year. The state translates the read-aloud student directions in the test administration manual into Spanish and Russian, and a parent flyer discussing level tests and assessments, which is posted on the department's Web site along with the bilingual (dual-language) format of the mathematics sample multiple-choice tests (both Spanish/English and Russian/English). In addition, whenever a student takes the bilingual (dual-language) version of a test, his or her score report is sent home in bilingual (dual-language) format (English on one side and Spanish or Russian on the other).

When funding is available, the state publishes a support package with sample test items and student responses to mathematics problem-solving tasks and writing prompts in Spanish. This allows students to become familiar with the test format, types of items, and response format. This package was initially distributed in paper format to schools, but since 2000–2001 it has been available on the Web as well. The state also publishes scoring guides for mathematics problem solving in Spanish and Russian and for writing in Spanish.

Glossaries of mathematics test item terms are posted in English, Spanish, and Russian on the state's Web site so that students will have a chance to familiarize themselves with the terms that they will see on the tests. This terminology is translated consistently from year to year. The glossaries were initially developed when the tests were first translated. An advisory committee of 20 to 25 bilingual educators was formed to examine both the Spanish and the Russian tests and identify terms that should be incorporated into the glossary. Since then, that common core of words has been added to each year as the state's translation contractors identify new terms to add to the list.

Commercially Available Tests

Other than the NAEP, Oregon does not use any national assessments. All items on assessments in Oregon are created (written, edited, reviewed, revised, and prepared for test layouts) within the state.

How Many Students Take Translated Tests

In 2000–2001, 3,522 students took the Spanish/English version of the multiple-choice mathematics test, and 400 took the Russian/English version.

The numbers are smaller for the mathematics problem solving, with approximately 700 students taking the Spanish/English test each year and about 100 per year in Russian/English.

Approximately 1,000 students take the Spanish/English version of the writing assessment each year. (This figure includes both students who responded in English and those who responded in Spanish.)

The Translation Process

Each year, the Oregon Department of Education sends out a request for proposals soliciting bidders for the translation of its state assessments. Each year the state has increased its efforts to recruit proposals from a wide range of companies. Contractors have changed annually as the skill levels of proposers increased and Oregon's selection process became more sophisticated. During the 2000–2001 school year, Translation Solutions, based in Portland, Oregon, was under contract with the state to translate the state assessment.

At Translation Solutions, translations are performed by translators who have specialized knowledge in the content area of the test. The draft translation is prepared through a process of forward translation, with a series of iterative reviews and revisions. The draft is prepared in Microsoft Word and sent to the state to be reviewed.

In the 2000–2001 school year, the state convened a group of 20 to 25 bilingual teachers from around the state to review the translated test item by item and line by line, in the presence of representatives from the translation team. Teachers came as a group to check the translation for accuracy and consistency and to identify any potential problems.

The teachers discussed their doubts and concerns and agreed on the translations to be used by the translation company. In some cases, the committee review revealed items that were difficult to translate and subsequently altered the English item (a procedure known as *decentering*). For instance, one item testing probability asked, "John has 3 dimes and 2 quarters in his pocket. If he reaches into his pocket and pulls out a coin, what is the probability that it will be a dime?" This problem became clumsy and excessively long when translated because the value of each coin had to be included in the verbiage. Accordingly, the committee decentered the item, changing the dimes and quarters in the English stem to yellow and red chips. This small modification allowed the same construct to be tested but facilitated translation.

After the committee review was completed, the translation company analyzed the comments and incorporated the changes. The final document was prepared in Word and sent to the state for printing.

Oregon has always used Word to format the mathematics assessments for the general population. One of the companies contracted to do the translations used Quark to do the desktop publishing 1 year. However, there were difficulties in importing graphics and formatting the document using the Cyrillic alphabet, so Word has since been a requirement of the contracts.

Reaction to Translated Tests

The overall student reaction to the dual-language tests has been positive. Follow-up surveys conducted by the state revealed that students "thoroughly enjoyed" the tests and even felt that they learned new words (both in English and in their native language) from taking the tests. Some students commented that the format was ideal, indicating that the English academic language they learned in school allowed them to understand the content of the test and their knowledge of their home language provided context for them to understand the content being tested.

Teachers' reactions were more mixed initially. At first, teachers disagreed about the selection of words used in the translations. The state addressed these concerns by doing a better job of communicating the process used and by sharing the bilingual glossaries of tested terms.

State administrators indicated that teachers had different concerns over language for Spanish as opposed to Russian tests. For the tests, some teachers wanted to choose words that would not prejudice any student; that is, that would not be biased toward one dialect or another. The Spanish teachers compromised, attempting to use the most "standard, correct" words in the translations. For Russian, the style is closer to that of spoken discourse.

Translation in Districts

The Oregon Department of Education does not favor translations done at the district level because of the inability to assure quality and consistency. Oregon allows districts to provide both sight and written translations of state assessments, but those are considered modified administrations, and students who take those tests do not qualify to meet the benchmark standards. For translation services, districts typically contract with local translation companies.

The scores from district-translated tests are not aggregated. The district-translated multiple-choice items are scored by the state, just like all other multiple-choice items. However, district-translated problem-solving sections are not scored at all because of the difficulty in finding bilingual scorers with the necessary language and content knowledge.

Test Presentation Format

All translated tests in Oregon are presented in a bilingual (dual-language) test booklet format. For the mathematics multiple-choice test, each page is divided into two columns, with the English text printed in the left column and the translated text printed in the right column. For the mathematics problem-solving and writing tests, each page is divided in half, with the translated text in the top half of the page and the English text in the bottom half.

Translated Tests and Score Reporting

The Spanish/English and Russian/English versions of the statewide multiple-choice assessments are scored by the state. The student responses to the writing assessments, whether in English or in Spanish, are scored. However, as mentioned previously, only those responses written in English can be used as evidence of meeting the state standard. The student responses to the mathematics problem-solving tasks are scored by the state whether in English, Spanish, or Russian. Any response in one of those three languages can be used as evidence of meeting the state standard. All responses are aggregated and included in participation reports, and those responses that are used as evidence of meeting state standards are included in summary reports. The only test scores not aggregated are writing test scores from students who responded in Spanish, as this is considered a modified administration and the scores cannot be used as evidence of meeting the standard.

Technology

The Oregon Department of Education posts a number of documents related to the statewide assessment program on its Web site, both in English and in translation to Spanish and Russian.

The department provides a parent brochure ("Achievement Level Tests Brochure") in Spanish on its Web site. Sample multiple-choice mathematics tests and problem-solving tasks are available online in Spanish and Russian. Samples of student responses to problem-solving tasks are also available, but only in English or Spanish.

Glossaries of mathematics test item terms (English/Spanish and English/Russian) are also available on the Web site. The glossaries are in column format, with the English term in the leftmost column, the translation in the middle column, and an example of the term used in context in the right column. The translations of these mathematics terms are used consistently from year to year and from grade to grade, and the glossaries are provided to familiarize students with the technical language prior to the day of the test.

All of the scoring guides, including the mathematics problem-solving guides in Spanish and Russian and the writing scoring guide in Spanish, can be found on the department's Web site.

There is no tracking system in place for the state's Web site, however, so the Oregon Department of Education does not have information regarding the number of hits per language or per document.

Administrators report that users occasionally have difficulties in accessing the Russian documents from the Web site because the Cyrillic alphabet is not supported by some browsers. In such cases, the state will supply a paper copy of the documents to the user on request.

Research and Statistical Analyses of Translated Tests

In 1998, Oregon conducted a three-part equating study on the Spanish/English version of the multiple-choice portion of the mathematics test. The state used an IRT common item equating procedure to link the Spanish/English version to the scale established for the English version.

The state chose to use separate groups of monolingual examinees to link the different language versions of the test to a common scale. In this procedure, the source language test is translated into the target language, and each version is administered separately to the corresponding language group. Oregon preferred this to the alternative—administering both tests to a group of bilinguals—because true bilinguals are not likely to be a representative sample of the population to be tested. That is, in Oregon the student population is not typically fluently bilingual, so equating the test by using a group of true bilinguals would not be appropriate.

Teachers and instructional teams selected students to participate in the testing, choosing suitable students to take the Spanish/English version. The tests were administered at four grade levels—3, 5, 8, and 10—but only the third and fifth grades had large enough numbers of Spanish-speaking students to conduct the necessary statistical analyses. All together, 314 third-graders and 308 fifth-graders took Form A of the Spanish/English test, and 8,895 third-graders and 8,762 fifth-graders took the corresponding English version.

In the first part of the study, items were examined for differential item functioning (DIF). An item is said to exhibit DIF "if the probability of a correct response is affected by group membership" (Choi & McCall, 2002, p. 320). A series of LR chi-square tests was used to identify DIF in the translated test, and some items were found to function differently on the two versions.

The second part of the study focused on identifying a set of anchor items that could be used to equate the Spanish/English and English tests. Anchor items were selected on the basis of three criteria: (a) all English items, (b) items identified by bilingual educators as being free from translation errors, and (c) items that exhibited little DIF on Lord's chi-square test. Calibration was performed three times, using each of these sets of common items. All of the calibrations were similar.

Once the tests had been equated under the three common linking designs, little difference was found on the overall score of the Spanish/English group as compared to the English group. In addition, the order of difficulty for both versions was found to be almost identical. Therefore, the study reported that the English and Spanish/English tests were similar enough to be used equitably in assessing students' mathematical knowledge.

The Oregon Department of Education planned to complete a similar equating study of the Russian/English version of the mathematics multiple-choice test by 2002–2003, pending large enough numbers.

Future of Test Translation

The Oregon Department of Education plans to expand its test translation program to include Spanish translations of the science component of the statewide assessments. The department also plans to offer Russian translations of the science component as well, pending the results of the ongoing validity study of the Russian/English mathematics multiple-choice test. Furthermore, the Spanish mathematics and science tests were to be field-tested on the state's Technology Enhanced Student Assessments system in the 2002–2003 school year. Also during the 2002–2003 school year, the state had planned to expand the period of the test translation contract from 1 year to 3 years, therefore assuring that the same translation company would work with the state over a period of time rather than for just a year at a time.

At the same time, Oregon has also started to work on developing plain language (linguistically simplified English) assessments in reading, mathematics, and science at the three benchmark grades (3, 5, and 8) and at the 10th-grade Certificate of Initial Mastery level. The plain language reading items would be based on the benchmark standards but would be aimed at a lower level of difficulty than the preexisting items. The plain language format would "minimize language-processing demands that are unrelated to the English reading standard targeted for assessment by an item" and would also enable more precise assessment of students at the lowest ability levels (Durán, Brown, & McCall, 2002, p. 392). The plain-language mathematics and science items would also be based on the benchmark standards and would be "attractive for use with ELLs in place of or as an alternative to the existing assessments, especially given that these students are more likely to be receiving their mathematics [or science] instruction solely in English as they progress through the grades" (Durán et al., 2002, p. 392). In addition, the plain-language format would be an option for ELLs who are not speakers of Spanish or Russian, students for whom there is currently no appropriate assessment tool.

Rhode Island

Overview of the State Testing Program

The Rhode Island State Assessment Program consists of three components—Rhode Island Performance Assessments, New Standards Reference Exams, and the nationally normed NAEP. Rhode Island Performance Assessments are administered in Writing at Grades 3, 7, and 10, and in Health Education at Grades 5 and 9. Rhode Island's content-based standards exams, the New Standards Reference Exams, are administered in ELA and Mathematics at Grades 4, 8, and 10. In addition, all students in Rhode Island public schools are required to take the NAEP in Grades 4 and 8.

Number of ELLs in the State

According to Kindler (2002), there were 156,292 students enrolled in Rhode Island public schools during the 2000–2001 school year. As shown in Fig. 2.16, of those, 10,161 (6.5%) were classified as ELLs. Results of demographic questionnaires collected by the Rhode Island Department of

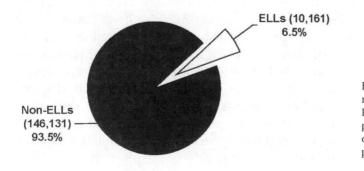

ELLs (10,161)
6.5%

Non-ELLs
(146,131)
93.5%

FIG. 2.16. Total number of ELLs in Rhode Island, as a percentage of overall student population.

Education (RIDE) indicate that the languages most commonly spoken in students' homes (after English) are Spanish, Portuguese, and Cambodian (Khmer), in that order. No data regarding the percentages of students with particular native language were available.

History of Test Translation

Rhode Island first translated assessments in 1996, largely as a result of a movement to include all students in the state accountability system. The state decided that by offering translated assessments they could attain a more accurate and complete measure of ELLs' knowledge. In 1996, math at Grades 4, 8, and 10, and health at Grades 5 and 9 were translated into Spanish, Portuguese, Lao, and Khmer. However, there were few requests for the assessments in Portuguese, Lao, and Khmer. Despite the fact that many ELLs were native speakers of those languages, few were literate enough to benefit from the written translations.

As a result, the following year Rhode Island discontinued providing written translations of the assessments into Portuguese, Lao, and Khmer, and since has translated assessments into Spanish only.

Which Tests Are Translated

In 1996, RIDE decided to translate only those assessments that could be translated into another language without changing the construct being tested. On that basis, RIDE initially decided to translate one form per year of its math assessment at Grades 4, 8, and 10, and its health assessment at Grades 5 and 9. RIDE decided early on that it would not provide translations of its ELA assessment, because this instrument was designed to measure English reading ability. During that same period, however, RIDE experimented with translating the prompts on the writing assessment, although still requiring that students respond in English. However, this practice was discontinued after a few years because it was deemed unnecessary. RIDE decided that if a student could write an essay in English, it was not necessary to translate the simple one- or two-sentence prompts for that student.

During the 2000–2001 school year, RIDE offered ELLs the Spanish version of the New Standards Reference Examinations: Mathematics at Grades 4, 8, and 10, and had its health assessment at Grades 5 and 9 translated into Spanish. However, because of budgetary concerns, during the 2002–2003 school year Rhode Island curtailed the program slightly, translating only one grade level of the health assessment, Grade 9, instead of two grade levels, as in previous years.

Other Translated Materials

RIDE does not publish any ancillary materials in languages other than English, and has no plans to do so in the near future because of budgetary limitations. However, districts can publish ancillary materials in other languages as they see fit. Typically, only larger districts with higher numbers of ELLs (e.g., Providence and Bristol) translate ancillary materials to send to parents.

Commercially Available Tests

RIDE does not develop and translate a local mathematics assessment. Instead, Rhode Island administers the English and Spanish versions of the New Standards Reference Examinations: Mathematics, published by Harcourt Educational Measurement, at Grades 4, 8, and 10. In addition, all Rhode Island students must take the NAEP in Grades 4 and 8.

How Many Students Take Translated Tests

At the time of publication, RIDE was unable to provide data about the number of students who took the Spanish versions of the math and health assessments in 2000–2001.

The Translation Process

RIDE has separate contracts for its math and health assessments, and different test development contractors are in charge of each.

Measured Progress, one of the state's test development contractors, manages the translation of Rhode Island's health assessment. Measured Progress in turn subcontracts the translation to SLTI, which specializes in test translation.

SLTI selects educated native speakers of the target language to translate and review all assessments. All are professional translators with knowledge of item-writing procedures, experience in test translation and test translation review, and a strong background in the content area being tested. SLTI uses forward translation, with a series of iterative reviews and revisions, to translate assessments. The stages involved in the process are detailed here.

First, the translation manager at SLTI examines the English file to ensure that all items and options are in correct sequential order, formatted properly, with no obvious errors or spelling mistakes. Then the translation manager makes initial decisions about how to handle specific titles and terms found in the assessment, as well as in the instructions, headers, footers, item stems, and so on.

Before beginning the translation, both translators and reviewers are oriented to the project. The orientation typically includes information on the state's assessment program and the most frequent countries of origin of examinees who will take the assessment in Spanish.

Subsequently, the translator begins work on the first draft. During this process, the translator identifies any culturally loaded items or items that would not be logical in the context of the target language. If such items are found, necessary adaptations are made to the item so that the content tested in the English item can be tested in the translation.

Once the translator completes a draft of the translation, it is sent to the reviewer. The reviewer is instructed to evaluate the draft translation by comparing it line by line and item by item with the English version. The reviewer examines the translation to ensure that it is an accurate representation of the English version and that the content being tested is the same in both languages. Thus, the reviewer will look for words or ideas that have been omitted in the translation, and for words and ideas that are found in the translation, but not found in the English version. The reviewer also looks for words and ideas that have been mistranslated. The reviewer also ensures that the language of the translation is consistent; that is, that the same words have been translated in the same way throughout the document and across assessments and that any structural features specific to any item in English remain the same in the target language. The reviewer ensures that parallel language is used on both the English and Spanish versions so that test takers in the target language will neither be favored nor prejudiced by the translation. Furthermore, the reviewer identifies any words that might be expressed differently in other Spanish-speaking countries, and places alternate translations in parentheses after each such word. The reviewer makes changes, comments, and suggestions on the translated test document using the Track Changes feature of Microsoft Word 2000.

The digital file containing the reviewer's revisions is sent back to SLTI, where it is reviewed, and then forwarded to the original translator, along with observations and recommendations. The translation manager then works with the translator to determine which comments to incorporate. Generally, about 80% of reviewer suggestions are incorporated. In some cases, the translator might generate an improvement based on a reviewer's comment.

Once revision has been completed, the translation is sent to a second reviewer, of Puerto Rican descent. This step is deemed necessary because of the relative size of Rhode Island's Puerto Rican population. The Puerto Rican reviewer examines the translation with particular emphasis on identifying words or phrases that would be expressed differently in the Puerto Rican dialect.

Once the translation manager is satisfied with the resulting translation, the document is then forwarded to Measured Progress, where the page layout is done in PageMaker. Once page layout or desktop publishing is complete, the test is sent back to SLTI for proofreading. After errors are identified and corrected, a final version is sent to SLTI, which verifies that there are no errors and that the test is ready for printing.

Harcourt Educational Measurement publishes English and Spanish versions of the New Standards Reference Examinations: Mathematics for commercial sale. RIDE purchases these assessments under contract with Harcourt.

The Spanish version of the test is a translation of the English, and contains both open-ended and short-answer items. All items are linked to a set of standards, the New Standards Performance Standards, which were compiled as part of an educational collaborative at the University of Pittsburgh, on the basis of input from professional organizations and mathematics teachers nationwide.

The English version of the assessment is translated at Harcourt. Once the English document is finalized, outside translators are contacted to perform the draft translation. The translators are selected from a pool of experienced professional translators that Harcourt has used in the past. The translators selected must be experienced in translating math assessments, but are not necessarily experts in the content area themselves. The translators are instructed to make the language of the translation as universally understandable as possible, avoiding any regional words that would bias the test toward one group or another. The translation is then sent for review by staff at Harcourt, who make comments and suggestions and send the document back to the translators for consideration. Necessary adjustments are made to the translation, and once the translators and reviewers agree that the translation is polished, it is sent to a bilingual test developer at Harcourt, who performs a back-translation. The specialist translates the test from Spanish back into English, identifying any errors, omissions, or unnecessary additions that have been made in the translation that were not in the English version. Any problems are then discussed with the translator and corrected.

The test is then reviewed again by staff at Harcourt, this time from an editorial standpoint, and any typographical errors, formatting problems, and so forth, are corrected. Then the final proofread version of the New Standards Reference Exam: Mathematics is forwarded to the production department where it is desktop published on a Macintosh platform using XyVision, a desktop publishing program used widely before Quark was introduced.

After the desktop publishing process has been completed, the test is reviewed again and any errors from the production phase are corrected. The document is then printed and packaged for distribution.

Reaction to Translated Tests

RIDE has not conducted any formal studies to gather feedback on the translated tests, but there is an overall sense that teachers in the state appreciate having an assessment tool in Spanish that can be used by some of their ELL students.

Translation in Districts

Because RIDE provides written translations of its assessments only into Spanish, districts have the discretion to offer sight translations of the math and health assessments to students whose primary language is other than Spanish. RIDE allows, but does not recommend, district-level sight translations, because there is no way to ensure quality: As there is no certification procedure for sight translators, there is no way to ensure that all students are receiving quality, accurate translations.

If a sight translation is requested by a district, RIDE might assist the district in locating a bilingual teacher in Rhode Island to do the translation. If a teacher is not available, RIDE might assist the district in searching for a bilingual parent.

District-translated tests are sent to the state to be scored. The state then finds a suitable translator to translate the student's responses into English and then scores the test and reports the scores on the same scale as the English versions of the assessments.

Test Presentation Format

Since it began translating its tests in 1996, Rhode Island has always published monolingual test booklets. Students do not have the option of requesting both an English and a native language test booklet to use side by side during test administration. They must either take the test in English or in translation. RIDE has no plans to offer this option as an accommodation or to offer bilingual test booklets.

Translated Tests and Score Reporting

Scores from all translated tests (both state and district translated) are reported on the same scale as scores from the English version of the test. It is assumed that the translated tests and the originals are equivalent, as these two tests do not differ in content. Therefore, there is no separate reporting procedure or scale.

Technology

RIDE does not have any publications on the Web in languages other than English.

Research and Statistical Analysis of Translated Tests

Neither RIDE nor Measured Progress has performed any statistical analyses on the translated health assessment.

Harcourt Educational Measurement has not performed any linking or equating procedures on the Spanish version of the New Standards Reference Examinations, as the Spanish and English versions are assumed to be equivalent.

Future of Test Translation

Because of budgetary concerns and the diminishing number of bilingual programs in Rhode Island, RIDE does not have any short-term plans to expand its test translation program, except as necessary to comply with NCLB.

However, in the 2002–2003 school year, Rhode Island was to begin implementing a series of measures to ensure that all students are assessed in the most practical way, regardless of their language background. A new English language proficiency test, which measures both functional and academic proficiency, was to be administered. This would be used not only to determine ESL placement but also to determine whether students are ready to participate fully in the English assessments. In addition, the state has begun to take measures to assess students' literacy in Spanish (an informal determination of whether Hispanic ELLs are literate in Spanish) to determine what means will be most effective in teaching and assessing Spanish-speaking ELLs.

Texas

Overview of the State Testing Program

During the 2000–2001 school year, two tests were administered as part of the Texas statewide assessment program: (a) the Texas Assessment of Academic Skills (TAAS), and (b) Reading Proficiency Tests in English (RPTE).

The TAAS measures the statewide curriculum in reading, mathematics, and writing at the end of each tested grade level (3–8). In addition, an exit-level TAAS is also administered at Grade 10. Students who were enrolled in Grade 9 or higher on January 1, 2001, must pass this test to meet the high school graduation requirement.

The RPTE are designed to measure annual growth in the English reading proficiency of second language learners and are used in conjunction with other assessments to provide a comprehensive assessment system for ELL students. ELL students in Grades 3 through 12 are required to take the RPTE until they achieve a rating of advanced.

However, the state has legislated a number of changes that are being implemented gradually in the statewide assessment system. First, the TAAS is being phased out as a high school exit exam, in favor of the Texas Assessment of Knowledge and Skills (TAKS). As mandated by the 76th Texas Legislature in 1999, the TAKS would be administered beginning in the 2002–2003 school year and is to measure the statewide curriculum in reading at Grades 3 through 9; in writing at Grades 4 and 7; in ELA at Grades 10 and 11; in mathematics at Grades 3 through 11; in science at Grades 5, 10, and 11; and social studies at Grades 8, 10, and 11. The Spanish TAKS will be administered at Grades 3 through 6, and satisfactory performance on the TAKS at Grade 11 will be a prerequisite to a high school diploma.

Title 19, Part II, Chapter 101 of the Texas Administrative Code (November 2001) further stipulates that a corresponding alternate assessment be developed for students enrolled in special education programs. The State-Developed Alternative Assessment (SDAA) assesses special education students in Grades 3 through 8 who are receiving instruction in the Texas Essential Knowledge and Skills but for whom TAKS is an inappropriate measure of their academic progress. This test assesses the areas of reading, writing, and mathematics. Students will be assessed at their appropriate instructional levels, as determined by their admission, review, and dismissal (ARD) committees, rather than at assigned grade levels. The SDAA is administered on the same schedule as TAKS and will be designed to measure annual growth based on appropriate expectations for each student as decided by the student's ARD committee. The alternative assessment will be designed in such a way as to bridge into TAKS and was expected to become a part of the school accountability system in the 2002–2003 school year.

Number of ELLs in the State

Data from the Texas Education Agency (TEA) indicate that during the 2000–2001 school year, there were 4,071,433 students enrolled in Texas public schools. As shown in Fig. 2.17, of those, 570,453 (14%) were classified as ELL.

Although there are more than 100 primary languages spoken by LEP students in Texas, more than 90% of ELL students in the state speak Spanish as their primary language. As Fig. 2.18 shows, the next largest language minority groups are Vietnamese (approximately 1.8%), Chinese, and Korean (less than 1% each).

Which Tests Are Translated

The TEA translates into Spanish one form per year of its Grades 3 through 6 TAAS tests of reading and mathematics. In addition, each year the state develops a Grade 4 writing test parallel to the English TAAS writing test (although it is not a translation). The state has decided to translate these tests because Grades 3 through 6 are the only grade levels in the state for which bilingual education (English/Spanish) programs are available. Texas state law therefore mandates that tests be available in Spanish at these grade levels.

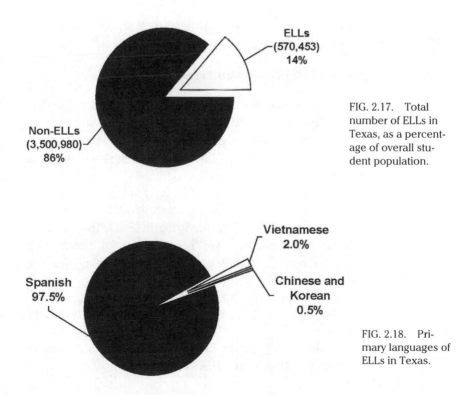

FIG. 2.17. Total number of ELLs in Texas, as a percentage of overall student population.

FIG. 2.18. Primary languages of ELLs in Texas.

Other Translated Materials

Each year, Texas publishes a number of ancillary materials in Spanish relating to the statewide assessment program. For use during test administration, the read-aloud portions of the test administration manual and the answer booklets are translated into Spanish. In addition, the state translates a number of documents pertaining to the test results including scoring guides for the writing test (including sample student work and annotations in Spanish), a parent guide to understanding the testing program (for Grades 3–6), brochures explaining the test results to accompany the score report, objectives printed on the score report, and a manual for decision-making processes for special needs students.

The state also translates a general brochure about the state education system into Spanish for parents. This Parents' Rights Guide is available in English and Spanish on TEA's Web site.

A number of other publications are available in Spanish online and are listed in the Technology section of this case study.

Commercially Available Tests

Texas does not use any commercially available native language assessment instruments as part of its statewide assessment system.

How Many Students Take Translated Tests

Data from the TEA show that the youngest students (those in the early grades of elementary school) account for the largest proportion of Spanish-speaking ELL students by grade level. Figure 2.19 shows that the number of ELL students declines steadily across increasing grade levels as students transition out of bilingual and ELL programs.

Correspondingly, in any given year, the TAAS tests are taken in Spanish by a larger number of students at the lower grade levels than at the upper grade levels. In most years, a total of approximately 45,000 to 50,000 students in Grades 3 through 6 take the TAAS in Spanish. Of those, about 22,000 to 23,000 are in Grade 3, 12,000 to 14,000 are in Grade 4, 5,000 to 7,000 are in Grade 5, and 1,000 to 2,000 are in Grade 6.

Data from the 2000–2001 State Performance Report indicating the passing rates for students taking the English and Spanish versions of the TAAS is provided in Table 2.8.

The TEA provides more information on passing rates in its annual report, which is accessible online at the TEA Web site.

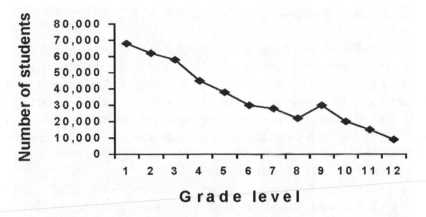

Note. Numbers are based on data collected by the Texas Public Education Information Management System (PEIMS) for the 1999–2000 school year.

FIG. 2.19.   Number of Spanish-speaking ELLs in Texas by grade.

TABLE 2.8

Passing Rates for English and Spanish Versions of the TAAS

	English	*Spanish*
Grade 3 Reading	86.8%	76.7%
Grade 3 Math	83.1%	83.5%
Grade 4 Reading	90.8%	66.4%
Grade 4 Math	91.3%	89.3%
Grade 4 Writing	89.2%	76.0%
Grade 5 Reading	90.2%	71.8%
Grade 5 Math	94.6%	87.1%
Grade 6 Reading	85.6%	50.3%

The Translation Process

In Texas, the development of the English test is influenced by the fact that it will be translated into Spanish. Once test items have been developed for the English version, a team of Spanish-speaking educators in Texas reviews the items and decenters any that they feel would be problematic to translate. Then the resulting items are field-tested in English, item analyses are run, and changes are made accordingly. The resulting English test is then reviewed externally; only after suggestions have been incorporated are the tests sent for translation.

The primary test development contractor for the TEA is NCS/Pearson. The translation of the TAAS tests, however, is subcontracted to Harcourt Educational Measurement.

Harcourt's lead content group and Spanish editors work with a specialized translation firm to adapt the assessments in Spanish. Through the years, a team of qualified reviewers and translators has been assembled. The specific qualifications vary by translator, but Harcourt selects personnel for the project based on a number of factors: the country of origin or dialect of the translator, proficiency in Spanish, amount of education in the home country, knowledge and expertise in the content area, and amount of experience translating.

Harcourt translates the tests into Pan-American Spanish, or Spanish that can be understood by Spanish speakers from all parts of Latin America. They accomplish this by using translators and reviewers from various parts of Latin America. Translations are made only after careful consideration of words having multiple translations in Spanish. Typically, Harcourt tries to use a standard Spanish word rather than a word that is specific to a particular dialect or region.

Harcourt uses forward translation, with a series of reviews and revisions, to translate the state assessments. First, a specialized team of translators with specialized knowledge of the content area prepares a draft translation. Next, another team consisting of speakers of several different dialects performs a content review of the draft translation, checking to ensure that the Spanish faithfully reflects the English original.

Once the translation has been reviewed a final time, Harcourt sends it to NCS/Pearson, where an editorial review is performed before the translation is submitted to TEA. TEA then conducts an internal review meeting at which staff from Harcourt, NCS/Pearson, and TEA are present. Revisions are made to the Microsoft Word file of the translated version on the spot. Only after those revisions are made is the file typeset in Quark at NCS/Pearson.

NCS/Pearson prepares test booklets for a second (external) review, which is conducted by bilingual teachers in Texas. Harcourt facilitates this external review, going through the test item by item with the teachers. There must be consensus for any changes to be made. Finally, NCS/Pearson makes the necessary changes and prepares the final booklets for printing.

Reaction to Translated Tests

Texas has not conducted any studies to gather formal systematic feedback on the translated tests. However, overall the response has been very positive from teachers, parents, and students, who are pleased to have an assessment tool available in Spanish. When the Spanish TAAS were first administered, students found them to be difficult and did not perform well. However, because of the feedback the test scores provided, the bilingual education program has been modified, new curriculum development materials have been provided, and bilingual education teachers have had the opportunity to participate in more professional development courses. These changes resulted in correspondingly higher test scores.

There are still some factions within the state that lobby for development of independent tests in Spanish rather than translations. However, the state does not expect to develop separate tests in Spanish in the near future because of the additional expense that such a project would incur.

Translation in Districts

Texas does not allow districts to provide either sight or written translations of the TAAS tests under any circumstances. Students not eligible to take the tests in Spanish or English are exempted from testing.

Test Presentation Format

Students have the option of taking the TAAS in English or in Spanish, and they receive the appropriate monolingual test booklet accordingly. They are not able to see both the original English and the Spanish translation simultaneously.

Translated Tests and Score Reporting

Scores from the Spanish TAAS are reported on the same scale as scores from the English version of the test. The state disaggregates English and Spanish scores in its annual State Performance Report, which is available via the TEA's Web site.

Technology

The TEA publishes many documents on the Web in both English and Spanish. Many of these are parent brochures that explain the assessment system. All of the publications listed here are available online in both English and Spanish.

- The general information brochure "Texas Essential Knowledge and Skills" *("Conocimientos y destrezas esenciales de Texas").*
- A brochure explaining the TAKS test.
- A general information brochure ("The Student Success Initiative, A Parent Guide to Testing Requirements").
- A similar brochure ("Prepare for Success, A Parent Guide to the Student Success Initiative").
- Chapter 101 of the Texas Administrative Code (which includes the recent mandates for statewide testing).
- A report to parents brochure explaining how to interpret the TAAS score report.
- A similar brochure explaining how to interpret the SDAA score report.
- A sample score report for the RPTE.
- A scoring guide to the Grade 4 writing TAAS test is also available online. However, the majority of the text is written in English, and only the sample student work is in Spanish.
- Released English and Spanish TAAS tests and English RPTE tests.

In addition, three letters explaining the recent legislation on student testing in Texas are available online:

- "Parent Notification of the Student Success Initiative"
- "Parent Notification of a Child's Progress in Grade K, 1, or 2"
- "Parent Notification of a Child's Progress in Grade 3"

Research and Statistical Analyses of Translated Tests

The TEA's test contractor, NCS/Pearson, does not use any statistical analyses to link the English and Spanish versions of the TAAS. There is a general assumption that the English version and the translated test are equivalent.

Future of Test Translation

Staff at the TEA report that the statewide assessments will not be translated into any language besides Spanish in the near future, because the idea behind translating the tests is that there has to be a bilingual program behind it.

In spring of 2003, TEA conducted the first operational administration of the TAKS, which replaced the TAAS. Also beginning in spring of 2003, TEA began field-testing the Spanish version of the TAAS and using that data to impact the development process. That advancement will make Texas the only state field-testing non-English versions of statewide tests.

Finally, over the course of the next few years, Texas will be gradually developing items in reading and science in Spanish. The goal would be to have enough items to create a Spanish test that is not a translation, but a separately developed and field-tested unit.

Utah

Overview of the State Testing Program

The Utah Performance Assessment System for Students consists of seven major assessment programs. A primary assessment tool is a series of exams based on core curriculum standards in reading and language arts, mathematics, and science. In addition, the state administers reading diagnostic instruments, a direct writing assessment, a basic skills competency test, a norm-referenced achievement test, an alternate assessment (for special needs students), and NAEP. Rather than assess students every year in every subject, tests are given in certain grade levels.

Number of ELLs in the State

During the 2000–2001 school year, 475,269 students were enrolled in Utah public schools. As shown in Fig. 2.20, 44,030 (9.3%) of these students were classified as ELLs.

Although a formal language census has not yet been completed, informal counts indicate that the most populous non-English primary language

ELLs (44,030)
9.3%

Non-ELLs
(431,239)
90.7%

FIG. 2.20. Total number of ELLs in Utah, as a percentage of overall student population.

backgrounds in the state are Spanish, Navajo, Samoan, Tongan, and Croatian. The Utah State Office of Education (USOE) estimates that about 65% of the ELLs in the state speak Spanish as their primary language, followed by 6% Navajo, and smaller percentages of Samoan, Tongan, and Croatian, as shown in Fig. 2.21. By October 2002, the USOE was to have completed a statewide language census that would provide more concrete data.

History of Test Translation

In 1999, legislation required the development of an assessment of kindergarten students' literacy development on their entry into school. An individually administered assessment of basic literacy and numeracy skills was developed to be administered to every entering kindergartner. It was determined that a Spanish version of this assessment would be necessary to accommodate Spanish-speaking students entering school. Rather than simply translating the assessment, USOE formed a committee of Spanish-speaking educators to determine which questions and supporting materials could be translated and which ones needed to be modified to reflect beginning literacy in Spanish. In addition, translation was performed by the entire committee, and there were representatives from various Spanish-speaking countries. This process resulted in an instrument that was as universal and accessible as possible for the Spanish-speaking students.

Because of the large population growth of Spanish-speakers in Utah over the past few years, in 2001 the USOE decided to implement a plan to translate its math and science standards-based assessments into Spanish. Assessments will be translated into Spanish (or Spanish versions of items created) as the English versions are developed in accordance with content-based standards. In spring of 2002, the first of the translated assess-

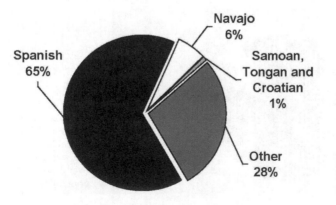

FIG. 2.21. Primary languages of ELLs in Utah.

ments, the math section of the Utah Basic Skills Competency Test, was administered.

In spring of 2003, the USOE was to provide Spanish language assessments in secondary math (Grade 7: Elementary Algebra, Algebra, and Geometry) and elementary science. Elementary math and secondary science assessments were to be translated and provided in spring of 2004.

Which Tests Are Translated

Utah plans to translate one form of each grade level of its math and science assessments into Spanish. Because of the small number of students who are projected to take the Spanish versions, the USOE feels it is not necessary to translate a new form of each assessment each year. Instead, the translated form will be used over multiple years. Utah will not provide a written translation of its ELA assessment.

Other Translated Materials

Currently, the state does not provide translations of any ancillary materials. However, districts can translate any materials they deem necessary. Districts such as Salt Lake City, which has large Spanish-speaking populations, generally have their own translators and interpreters on staff, and hence the ability to translate ancillary materials in house.

The state is currently in the process of translating parent guides to be sent to Spanish-speaking parents describing the state's accountability system. Those guides were to be ready in spring 2003, and the state is still in the process of deciding what other materials to translate.

Commercially Available Tests

Utah students in Grades 3, 5, 8, and 11 must take a nationally norm-referenced, standardized assessment. Currently, Utah offers the SAT-9 in English and the Aprenda in Spanish. Students are assigned to take either the English or Spanish test based on their English proficiency, as determined by their score on the IPT, an ESL proficiency test.

How Many Students Take Translated Tests

The USOE does not have records of the number of students who took tests that were translated at the district level. In the future, the USOE will have information about the number of students who take each of the assessments in Spanish. (All translated assessments will be administered and scored by the state.)

The Translation Process

As noted earlier, the prekindergarten assessment developed in 1999 was translated by a committee of Spanish-speaking educators who collaborated to find the most universal usage for all Spanish-speakers. Written translations performed at the district level were translated and reviewed by bilingual educators in the district in question.

Measured Progress, the state's test development contractor, manages the most recent round of translations, which started in 2002. Measured Progress in turn subcontracts the translation to SLTI, which specializes in test translation.

SLTI selects educated native speakers of the target language to translate and review all assessments. All are professional translators with knowledge of item-writing procedures, experience in test translation and test translation review, and a strong background in the content area being tested. To translate assessments, SLTI uses forward translation with a series of iterative reviews and revisions. First, the translation manager at SLTI examines the English file to ensure that all items and options are in the correct sequential order, formatted properly, with no obvious errors or spelling mistakes. Then the translation manager makes initial decisions about how to handle specific terms found in the assessment, as well as in the instructions, headers, footers, item stems, and so forth.

Before beginning the translation, translators and reviewers are oriented to the project. The orientation typically includes information on the state's assessment program and the most frequent countries of origin of examinees who will take the assessment in Spanish.

Subsequently, the translator begins work on the first draft. During this process, the translator identifies any culturally loaded items or items that would not be logical in the context of the target language. If such items are found, necessary adaptations are made to the item so that the content tested in the English item can be tested in the translation.

Once the translator completes a draft of the translation, it is sent to the reviewer. The reviewer is instructed to evaluate the draft translation by comparing it line by line and item by item with the English version. The reviewer examines the translation to ensure that it is an accurate representation of the English version and that the content being tested is the same in both languages. Thus, the reviewer will look for words or ideas that have been omitted in the translation and for words and ideas that are found in the translation, but not found in the English version. The reviewer also looks for words and ideas that have been mistranslated, and ensures that the language of the translation is consistent; that is, that the same words have been translated in the same way throughout the document and across assessments and that any structural features specific to any item in English remain the same in the target language. The reviewer ensures that parallel language is used on both the English and Spanish versions so that test takers in the target language will neither be favored nor prejudiced. Furthermore, the reviewer identifies any words that might be expressed differently in other Hispanic countries, and places alternate translations in parentheses after each such word. The reviewer makes changes, comments, and suggestions on the translated test document using the Track Changes feature of Microsoft Word 2000.

The digital file containing the reviewer's revisions is sent back to SLTI, where it is reviewed and forwarded, along with observations and recommendations, to the original translator. The translation manager then works with the translator to determine which comments to incorporate. Generally, about 80% of reviewer suggestions are incorporated. In some cases, however, the translator might come up with a better improvement than that suggested by the reviewer.

If the translation manager is satisfied with the resulting translation, the document is then forwarded to the USOE. If not, it is sent to another reviewer for a second review. In this case, the reviewer is usually from a different Hispanic country. If the translation goes out for a second review, the review process is repeated again.

Once the document arrives at the USOE, it is reviewed by a committee of bilingual educators from the state. The committee makes suggested changes and passes them to Measured Progress, which subsequently sends them to the translation manager at SLTI, where they are examined by the translation manager and lead translator of the test. Any points of disagreement are identified and sent back to the USOE for further discussion. Once disagreements are resolved, final changes are made to the translation and the file is sent to Measured Progress, where page layout is done in PageMaker. Once page layout is complete, the test is sent back to SLTI for proofreading. After errors are identified and corrected, a final version is sent to SLTI, which verifies that no errors exist. Finally, the test is ready for printing.

Reaction to Translated Tests

Since the first tests translated as part of the new program were administered in spring of 2002, the state has not yet conducted any formal studies to obtain feedback on the translated tests. They have received little informal feedback from teachers, although there has been great interest among teachers in creating Spanish assessments to better measure ELLs' knowledge.

Translation in Districts

During the 2000–2001 and 2001–2002 school years, certain districts were permitted to provide written translations of assessments. On completion of development of the new forms of the tests in math and science, this practice will be discontinued.

However, the districts still have the option to provide sight translations of assessments. State policy requires that sight translators be bilingual, certified teachers in Utah. They are allowed to provide oral translations of all components of the state assessments except for the reading passages on the ELA assessment.

Test Presentation Format

Utah publishes separate test booklets in English and Spanish. However, as an accommodation, students can be provided with both the English and Spanish test booklets to use side by side.

Translated Tests and Score Reporting

In the past, the districts scored district-translated tests and did not send the results to the state. However, with the implementation of the new translation plan at the state level, all scores will be provided to the state. Data will be reviewed to determine whether scores from translated tests can be reported on the same scale as scores from the English version. All items on the translated tests have been field-tested first in English, so there is an assumption that the two versions are equivalent. However, if sufficient numbers of students take the Spanish versions of the tests, item statistics will be generated and reviewed.

Technology

The Utah Web site does not provide publications in languages other than English.

Research and Statistical Analysis of Translated Tests

Because the test translation program is so new, Utah has not conducted any statistical analyses on the Spanish versions yet. Once sufficient data are available, the state plans to compare the item statistics and the reliability of the English and Spanish versions.

Future of Test Translation

Because the test translation program in Utah is in its infancy, the USOE believes that many refinements will be necessary along the way. There have been discussions about modifying the review procedure at the state level to include back-translation. However, this decision has not been finalized.

Administrators in the Services for At-Risk Students division have also expressed a desire to have an assessment of Spanish literacy at several grade levels for Spanish-speaking students.

Vermont

Overview of the State Testing Program

The Vermont Comprehensive Assessment System, established by the State Board of Education in 1996, was designed to evaluate student performance in the state's schools, based on Vermont's Framework of Standards and Learning Opportunities, with the goal of improving teaching and learning. Statewide assessments include the following tests: (a) Vermont Developmental Reading Assessment (DRA), administered in Grade 2; (b) New Standards Reference Exams in ELA and mathematics, administered in Grades 4, 8, and 10; and (c) VT-PASS (a science assessment), administered in Grades 5, 9, and 11.

Individual schools also assess student performance in additional subject areas and at additional grade levels using portfolios (collections of student work), norm-referenced standardized tests, and locally developed assessments. However, the three assessments just listed are the only statewide tests.

Number of ELLs in the State

The Vermont Department of Education (VDE) reported that during the 2000–2001 school year, 102,049 students were enrolled in Vermont public schools. As shown in Fig. 2.22, 1,102 (approximately 1.1%) of these stu-

FIG. 2.22. Total number of ELLs in Vermont, as a percentage of overall student population.

dents had a non-English language background (NELB) and just 936 (approximately 0.92%) were classified as ELLs.

All NELB students enrolled in 2000–2001 took part in the State of Vermont Home Language Survey conducted by the VDE. Results from the survey showed that although there are 50 languages spoken by the 1,102 NELB students, 3 languages stand out as most common: Bosnian (spoken by 21% of ELLs), Vietnamese (spoken by 15% of ELLs), and Spanish (spoken by 7% of ELLs). These percentages are shown in Fig. 2.23.

History of Test Translation

The New Standards Reference Examinations in mathematics were first offered in Spanish during the 2000–2001 school year. The impetus for offering the Spanish version was the need to include as many ELLs as possible in the state accountability system. The Spanish version of the New Standards was a logical choice because of its equivalence to the English New Standards math assessment (also used in the state) and its ready availability to the state. Because Vermont has such small numbers of ELLs, commissioning translations would simply not be cost effective.

Which Tests Are Translated

During the 2000–2001 school year, the VDE offered ELLs the Spanish version of the New Standards Reference Examinations: Mathematics at Grades 4, 8, and 10. The VDE is currently in search of means to assess all members of the ELL population in the state, and the Spanish version of New Standards was the first native language assessment to be implemented because of its availability and equivalence to the English math assessment.

Members at the VDE are grappling with the issue of how to accommodate and assess ELLs who are speakers of other languages (e.g., Bosnian and Vietnamese). Even if translations of the assessments were made

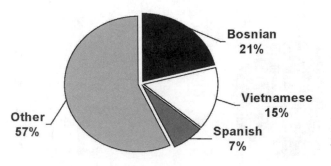

FIG. 2.23. Primary languages of ELLs in Vermont.

available in these languages, the state believes that, as instruction in these languages is not available for ELLs in Vermont, validity would be an issue. Furthermore, those students who would benefit most from such translated tests would be a group of students who were recently arrived from other countries and who had participated in their home countries in curricula that mirrored that of Vermont schools. However, given that many of Vermont's ELLs have come to the United States as refugees, such a scenario is highly improbable.

Other Translated Materials

The VDE does not publish ancillary materials in languages other than English. However, the department has had a parental consent letter for the NAEP translated into Cambodian, Vietnamese, and Bosnian. The VDE encountered such difficulty finding translators for this small document that it has not attempted to translate other ancillary materials.

Commercially Available Tests

The VDE administers only one translated assessment, the New Standards Reference Examinations: Mathematics, published by Harcourt Educational Measurement.

How Many Students Take Translated Tests

Typically, a very small number of students take the Spanish version of the New Standards in a given year. During the 2000–2001 school year, fewer than 15 students took the test in Spanish, and in some years the numbers are even smaller.

The Translation Process

Harcourt Educational Measurement publishes English and Spanish versions of the New Standards Reference Examinations: Mathematics for commercial sale. The VDE purchases these assessments under contract with Harcourt.

The Spanish version of the test is a translation of the English, and contains both open-ended and short-answer items. All items are linked to a set of standards, the New Standards Performance Standards, which were compiled as part of an educational collaborative at the University of Pittsburgh on the basis of input from professional organizations and mathematics teachers nationwide.

The English version of the assessment is translated at Harcourt. Once the English document is finalized, outside translators are contacted to perform the draft translation. The translators are selected from a pool of experienced professional translators previously employed by Harcourt. The translators selected must be experienced in translating math assessments, but are not necessarily experts in the content area themselves. The translators are instructed to make the language of the translation as universally understandable as possible, avoiding any regional words that would bias the test toward one group or another. The translation is then sent for review by staff at Harcourt, which makes comments and suggestions and sends the document back to the translators for consideration. Necessary adjustments are made to the translation, and once the translators and reviewers agree that the translation is polished, it is sent to a bilingual test developer at Harcourt, who performs a back-translation. The specialist translates the test from Spanish back into English, identifying any errors, omissions, or unnecessary additions that have been made in the translation that were not in the English version. Any problems are then discussed with the translator and corrected.

The test is then reviewed again by staff at Harcourt, this time from an editorial standpoint, and any typographical errors, formatting problems, and so forth are corrected. Then the final proofread version of the New Standards Reference Examinations: Mathematics is forwarded to the production department where it is typeset on a Macintosh platform using XyVision, a desktop publishing program used extensively before Quark was introduced.

After the desktop publishing process has been completed, the test is reviewed again and any errors from the production phase are corrected. The document is then printed and packaged for distribution.

Reaction to Translated Tests

The VDE has not conducted any formal studies to gather feedback on the translated assessment, but overall teachers have reacted positively to having an assessment tool for their Spanish-speaking ELLs.

Translation in Districts

Because the VDE provides a written translation of just the math assessment into Spanish, districts have the discretion to offer sight translations of statewide assessments. Districts are allowed to offer sight translations of both the math and science assessments but not the DRA.

It is left up to the districts to identify students who would benefit from sight translations and to contact translators. The state does not provide specific guidance on translator qualifications, and the districts can choose to use a teacher, parent, or volunteer to translate the tests.

The VDE does not receive systematic feedback from districts about sight translation, in part because the number of sight translations provided each year is quite small.

Test Presentation Format

The Spanish version of the New Standards Reference Examinations: Mathematics is published as a monolingual test booklet. Consequently, students must choose to take either the Spanish or English version of the test; they do not have the option of viewing the Spanish and English versions side by side.

Translated Tests and Score Reporting

Scores from all translated tests (both the Spanish version of the New Standards and district-translated tests) are reported on the same scale as scores from the English version of the test. Harcourt Educational Measurement scores all of the New Standards tests and does not disaggregate scores from the Spanish version. Vermont views sight translation as an accommodation; therefore, scores from district-translated tests are reported alongside other tests that were administered with accommodations.

Technology

The VDE Web site does not provide publications in languages other than English.

Research and Statistical Analysis of Translated Tests

The VDE has not performed any statistical analyses on the Spanish version of the New Standards. Harcourt Educational Measurement has not performed any linking or equating procedures on the test either, as the Spanish and English versions are assumed to be equivalent.

Future of Test Translation

The VDE is currently in the process of making a number of decisions regarding test translation. The state is investigating various ways of including all ELLs in the state assessment system. Administrators have voiced concern over the difficulty of assessing students from the diverse language backgrounds found in the state. Specifically, the VDE is concerned that translating assessments for the Bosnian and Vietnamese populations might not be practical, given (a) the difficulty in finding qualified translators in those languages, and (b) the students' lack of prior academic instruction and literacy in their native languages. Alternatively, the state is in the initial phases of developing linguistically simplified alternate assessments in English for ELLs. It is hoped that a test of this kind would accommodate students of a variety of language backgrounds and assess them equitably.

In addition, the VDE hopes to establish increased communication with individual schools. The hope is that such contact will better equip the state to make decisions regarding how to accommodate the diverse student populations in the schools.

DISCUSSION AND RECOMMENDATIONS

With the increase in the number of ELLs in schools across the United States and the recent emphasis placed on their inclusion in statewide and national assessments, states are attempting to find accommodations that will provide ELLs access to test content without compromising the scores obtained from these assessments. Educators are turning increasingly to native language accommodations to provide this access. However, as this study has shown, there is very little information available to help states and districts develop or select appropriate native language accommodations. State officials often do not have an understanding of best practices regarding the development and selection of native language accommodations. States' policies, in turn, offer a range of native language accommodations without providing crucial information regarding which students are likely to benefit from these accommodations.

This study of test translation policy and practice, which draws on policy documents from all 50 states and the District of Columbia during the 2000–2001 school year, offers guidance to states looking for appropriate accommodations for ELLs. Although the focus of this study has been primarily on the use of written or sight translation, the discussion offered in this section addresses a broader range of native language accommodations. By addressing the use of various forms of (a) written translation, (b) scripted oral translation, (c) sight translation, and (d) student response in native language, it is hoped that educators and policymakers will come to a better understanding of how to best make use of these accommodations.

This section first provides a series of preliminary considerations states should weigh in determining whether or not to adopt native language accommodations. The discussion is organized according to the four categories of native language accommodation just listed. Finally, guidelines are offered for the development and implementation of selected accommodations.

Preliminary Considerations

Before selecting appropriate accommodations for ELLs, states must consider a number of important factors regarding the ELL population to be tested. State officials must first gather basic information about ELLs' language background (e.g., native language, literacy and language proficiency in English and the native language) and prior education in the native language or culture. This information helps state officials determine ELLs' needs regarding participation in state assessment.

Language Background

A state must first identify the language background of the students. At a minimum, this requires a home-language survey of ELLs to determine (a) native language or the language spoken at home and, if applicable, (b) language in which they have previously received instruction. Other questions must also be answered if state officials are to have enough information to assess ELLs appropriately. Students' literacy and proficiency in English should be tested, preferably using a language proficiency instrument that is used across the state, so that students can be reliably compared on the same scale. This test will help the state to determine student placement in classes and will also serve as an indication of whether the student is proficient enough to demonstrate his or her knowledge on a content area assessment given in English. In addition, if possible, the students' literacy and proficiency in the native language should be probed through some measure of the student's native language. Information about native language ability will be valuable to state officials as they look to provide appropriate accommodations to ELLs. It will provide guidance for determining (a) appropriateness of testing in the native language, and (b) appropriateness of using written or oral translation.

Prior Education in the Native Language or Culture

In addition to language background, it is also necessary that information be collected regarding ELLs' prior education. A survey should be conducted inquiring about the level of formal education the students have received (e.g., number of years and subjects) and the language of instruction. Some ELLs might not have ever received formal education in their home countries, whereas others might have received a number of years of education. In addition to lacking content knowledge, ELLs who have not received formal education are also highly unlikely to be familiar with the content-specific academic vocabulary used in statewide assessments, even in their native language. On the other hand, students who have received years of education in their home country are more likely to have greater academic proficiency in their native language and are more likely to benefit from native language accommodations, such as a translated assessment in the native language.

These preliminary considerations will help states identify the linguistic needs and academic experiences of their ELL populations and will, in turn, enable states to determine which native language accommodations, if any, are appropriate for particular ELLs. Considerations regarding the four categories of native language accommodations are presented next.

Guidelines for Written Translation

Determining if Written Translation is an Appropriate Accommodation

A state should weigh a few basic considerations in determining whether or not written translation is an appropriate accommodation for ELLs. First and foremost, the information gleaned from the language and education surveys will be useful. Written translations are most appropriate for students who are literate in the native language and have had formal education in the home country or language. For these populations of ELLs, a written translation might be the best accommodation because it would be most similar to what those students would have received in their school in the home country.

States must be careful not to make assumptions about ELLs' language backgrounds or formal schooling in the home country. An early experience of the RIDE in offering written translations of statewide assessments provides a compelling example of problems that can occur when incorrect assumptions are made about ELLs' backgrounds. In 1996 Rhode Island began offering written translations of state assessments. RIDE identified the most common language backgrounds of ELLs in the state (Spanish, Portuguese, Khmer, and Lao) and chose those as the target languages of the translations. After administering tests in those languages the first year, the state discovered that the vast majority of the students from Cambodia and Laos were not literate in their native languages. Hence, it was determined only after the fact that written translation was not an appropriate accommodation for these students.

A second consideration for states considering written translation as a potential accommodation is cost efficiency (also described at length earlier in this study). Written translation is cost efficient if it can be provided to a large number of ELLs. If a state has small populations of ELLs from many different language backgrounds, it would not be cost effective to provide written translations of the statewide assessments in each native language represented in the state.

All 12 states that provided written translations of statewide assessments in school year 2000–2001 chose to provide these translations in Spanish because this represented the largest non-English language group in the state. As Table 2.9 shows, some states provided written translations in other languages, as appropriate to the demographics of the state in question.

TABLE 2.9

States Specifying Languages for Which Written Translations Could Be Provided

	Chinese	Haitian	Hmong	Korean	Russian	Somali	Spanish	Vietnamese
AZ								
DE							✓	
MA							✓	
MN			✓			✓	✓	✓
NM							✓	
NY	✓	✓		✓	✓		✓	
OR					✓		✓	
RI							✓	
TX							✓	
UT							✓	
VT							✓	
WY							✓	
Total	1	1	1	1	2	1	12	1

Developing Written Translations

A number of factors should be considered carefully before a state moves ahead with a written translation of the state assessment: translator qualifications, content areas to be translated, test format, use of ancillary materials, and statistical analyses of test results.

Translator Qualifications. The selection of a translator is crucial. Because translation is a specialized skill, and because it is essential that the original and translated versions of the assessment measure the same constructs, written translations should be performed by professional translators. Ideally, these individuals should be certified by the American Translators' Association, if they translate into a language for which the Association has a certification test. To ensure that they use appropriate content-relevant terminology in the target (non-English) language, the translators should have expertise in the content area for which they are providing translations. The first draft of the translation should be reviewed and revised at least once by another professional translator with similar expertise. The reviewer should compare the original and translated versions item by item to ensure that the two are comparable.

In addition, in states where there is instruction in the non-English language, translators should be certain to use the content area terminology presented in students' classes or textbooks, as English terms can often be translated in more than one way. For this reason, it is important for states with bilingual education programs to supply translators with the glossaries or textbooks used in those classes so that the terminology on the test matches the terminology the students have learned in class and in the textbook.

Content Areas. Once a state has decided to provide written translation as an accommodation, the state must then decide which content areas or components of the statewide assessment to translate. As discussed earlier in this study, some content areas are more amenable to translation than others. Certainly, concepts in areas such as mathematics, science, and social studies can be tested in translation without affecting the construct. Tests in these areas can be translated fairly straightforwardly. On the other hand, when tests of reading and writing are translated, the construct is altered (i.e., the test is no longer a test of reading or ELA but rather a test of reading or grammar in the target language). As a result, adaptation is necessary, and often new items must be created for the non-English version of the test. As discussed in greater detail earlier, this can represent a significant cost to the state.

Findings from states' policies indicate that a variety of content areas were offered in non-English languages. As Table 2.10 shows, mathematics was the most commonly translated content area, with 11 of 12 states providing translations of a mathematics test. In addition, science (5 of 12) and social studies (4 of 12) were frequently translated. Surprisingly, a number of states also provided written assessments of reading and writing in non-English languages, although it is important to note that usually these were not direct translations, but rather adaptations of the English test to the non-English language.

Test Format.   States must decide on the format of the printed test booklet that will be produced for the non-English language. There are two

TABLE 2.10

Content Areas for Which Written Translations Were Provided, by State

	Reading	Writing	Language Arts	Math	Science	Social Studies	Health	Reading
AZ	✓	✓		✓				✓
CO[a]	✓	✓						✓
DE				✓	✓	✓		
MA				✓	✓	✓		
MN				✓				
NM[b]	✓	✓	✓	✓	✓	✓		✓
NY[c]				✓	✓	✓		
OR		✓		✓				
RI				✓			✓	
TX[d]	✓	✓		✓				✓
UT				✓	✓			
VT				✓				
Total	4	5	1	11	5	4	1	4

[a]These tests were parallel developments in Spanish rather than direct translations from English. [b]The New Mexico High School Competency Exam consisted of six subtests—reading, language arts, math, science, social studies, and writing—that were translated into Spanish. [c]New York translated social studies and science for Grades 5 and 8, in addition to U.S. History & Government, Global History & Geography, Living Environment, Earth Science, and mathematics. [d]In Texas, the reading and math tests were translations, but the writing test was separately developed for Spanish.

basic options: a monolingual test booklet, in which test stimuli and items are presented exclusively in the non-English language, and a bilingual (dual-language) test booklet, in which stimuli and items are presented in both English and the non-English language, side by side or in facing columns in the test booklet. Based on a number of studies that have been conducted to examine the effect of presentation format on ELLs (e.g., Garcia, 2000; Liu, Anderson, & Swierzbin, 1999; Stansfield & Kahl, 1998), it seems that the bilingual test booklet format might be beneficial to many ELLs, who might wish to rely on the contextualizing information surrounding the items in their native language while referring to the English for terminology they might have learned in English in school. These studies have also found that even for ELLs who rely on just one language (either English or the native language) the bilingual format is not a hindrance. For this reason, it is advisable for states to present written translations in a bilingual test booklet format.

Case study findings revealed that four states used the bilingual test booklet format during that time period—Delaware, Massachusetts, Montana, and Oregon. It is recommended that other states follow their lead and begin to implement bilingual test booklets.

Ancillary Materials.   If a state makes the decision to provide written translations of its assessments, it is making a substantial investment in terms of time and money as well as introducing a substantial change in its assessment system. Ancillary materials, such as test administration manuals, answer sheets, and score reports, which were developed for the English versions of the tests, almost certainly do not exist in the non-English languages for which the state is providing written translations.

As revealed in the survey of 2000–2001 test translation practices, seven states—Arizona, Colorado, Delaware, Massachusetts, New York, Oregon, and Texas—translated at least some ancillary materials to accompany the written translations of assessments. More detailed information about which documents were translated can be found in the case studies of these states' policies and practices.

At a minimum, states should strive to translate ancillary materials that directly affect test administration. First and foremost, this means translating the standardized test administration procedures developed and carefully prescribed for the English test to ensure consistent administration across languages. Secondarily, this means translating other documents students must use as they complete the test, such as answer sheets or reference sheets (commonly used to provide formulas for mathematics tests).

By providing these documents in the non-English languages, states can ensure that all students are truly receiving the same test under the same conditions, thereby helping to ensure score comparability on the original and translated versions of the assessments.

Statistical Analyses. Case study findings indicate that during the 2000–2001 school year, Colorado, New Mexico, New York, and Oregon performed statistical analyses of the results of translated tests. Such analyses enable comparison of item statistics to determine if items and the test as a whole perform the same for ELLs and for non-ELLs. This information is essential for any linking of scores on the two forms. It is also helpful when making curricular decisions on the basis of test results.

Guidelines for Audiotaped Translation

A state might decide that a written translation is not an appropriate accommodation for some ELLs for a number of reasons previously discussed. For instance, if ELLs of a particular language group are not literate in their native language, a written translation would clearly not be beneficial. Similarly, if a state has small populations of speakers of a language, providing a written translation might not be cost effective.

However, the state can assess these students in their native language using an oral format. In that case, the state could provide an audiotaped translation as an accommodation. Several recommendations can ensure that all ELLs receive a standardized oral administration. First, the state should provide the script of the English version of the test to a professional translator to be translated. It is crucial that the translator receive the script of the English audio version because this script includes prompts and instructions specifically gearing the test for recorded oral administration. This translation must be performed carefully and reviewed in the same way that a written translation would be. Once the translation has been finalized, it should be read aloud and recorded for administration across the state. Having the test recorded eliminates variations between speakers, pauses, timing, and other extraneous factors that accompany a spontaneous sight translation. Once the recording has been completed, it should be compared with the script by an independent translator to verify that no item, option, or other material was inadvertently left out, and that all words are pronounced intelligibly.

Guidelines for Sight Translation

Another option states have if they wish to provide an oral translation of an assessment is to provide sight translations of the assessment to each student in the state who needs to be tested in a given language. A more detailed description of sight translation and the challenges presented by this accommodation is given earlier in this study.

Sight translation is an option that a state might choose if there were only a handful of speakers of a given language and creating a scripted oral translation would not be cost effective. In sight translation, a translator or interpreter sits with the student who is taking the test and, looking at the English test, reads the test stimuli and items aloud in the non-English language. That is, the translator or interpreter must perform a simultaneous translation on the spot.

Clearly, sight translation does not provide a standardized administration and there is variation inherent in the procedure. For this reason, it is not a preferred accommodation for ELLs. However, if a state chooses to use this accommodation, a number of precautions can help ensure a high degree of accuracy for this accommodation.

First, because of the difficulty of providing an accurate, complete rendition of the test material on the spot in another language, the person selected to perform the sight translation should be an experienced translator or interpreter. Also, the person should be familiar with the test itself and test administration procedures. Whenever possible, the sight translator should be given the test ahead of time to prepare to translate it.

Although this is not a preferred accommodation, following these basic guidelines can help ensure the equity of test administration in cases where states need to provide native language accommodations to a small number of ELLs.

Guidelines for Response in Native Language

Finally, states might choose to help include ELLs meaningfully in state assessment by allowing these students to respond to test items in their native language. This accommodation can be used on its own or in combination with any of the three native language accommodations previously discussed. Students might be allowed to respond in their native language when provided with a written translation or an oral translation (either scripted or sight translated). Alternately, a student taking a test in English might simply be allowed to record answers in his or her native language.

However, a number of factors should be taken into consideration in the implementation of this accommodation. First, if this accommodation is used along with the provision of an oral translation, the state must decide how the students' responses will be recorded. Will the student be allowed to respond orally, or must the student respond in writing? Again, depending on the literacy of the student, oral response might be the only option. If the student is going to respond orally, it is recommended that, for purposes of standardization, the responses be recorded for later transcription.

Where either written or oral responses are concerned, a speaker of the non-English language must score the responses. In addition, scoring rubrics, which were carefully crafted for the English test, would also need to be modified to suit the translated version of the assessment to ensure score comparability between the original and translated versions.

Recommendations

Based on the review of test translation literature and findings from the study, the following recommendations are provided for those involved in developing and implementing test translation for state assessments.

1. Route ELLs into appropriate test conditions.

    * Gather and analyze data ELLs' language background.
    * Gather and analyze culture and language of ELLs' prior education.
    * Ensure that ELLs tested in the native language in a particular subject have been taught the content in their native language.

2. Ensure accuracy and effectiveness of translated tests.

    * Use successive iterations of forward translation and revision (rather than back-translation).
    * Use teams of professional translators to perform translations.
    * Whenever possible, use translators certified by the American Translators Association or other reputable licensing board.
    * Use translators who are familiar with item-writing guidelines or provide training in item-writing guidelines to translators.
    * Use a dual-language test format as opposed to a monolingual test book.

3. Analyze results of assessment of ELLs and non-ELLs to inform refinement of test translations.

REFERENCES

Alderson, J. C., & Urquhart, A. H. (1983). The effect of student background discipline on comprehension: A pilot study. In A. Hughes & D. Porter (Eds.), *Current developments in language testing* (pp. 121–127). London: Academic Press.

Alderson, J. C., & Urquhart, A. H. (1985). The effect of students' academic discipline on their performance on ESP reading tests. *Language Testing, 2,* 192–204.

Anderson, M., Liu, K., Swierzbin, B., Thurlow, M., & Bielinski, J. (2000). *Bilingual accommodations for limited English proficient students on statewide reading tests: Phase 2* (Minnesota Report No. 31). Minneapolis: University of Minnesota, National Center on Educational Outcomes. Retrieved October 31, 2002, from the World Wide Web: http://education.umn.edu/NCEO/OnlinePubs/MnReport31.html

Bernard, H. R. (1988). *Research methods in cultural anthropology.* Newbury Park, CA: Sage.

Bernard, H. R. (1994). *Research methods in anthropology: Qualitative and quantitative approaches* (2nd ed.). Newbury Park, CA: Sage.

Brislin, R. (1970). Back translation for cross-cultural research. *Journal of Cross Cultural Psychology, 1,* 185–216.

Brislin, R. (1976). *Translation: Applications and research.* New York: Gardner.

Brislin, R. (1986). The wording and translation of research instruments. In W. J. Lonner & J. W. Berry (Eds.), *Field methods in cross-cultural psychology* (pp. 137–164). Newbury Park, CA: Sage.

Brislin, R., Lonner, W. J. & Thorndike, R. L. (1973). *Cross-cultural research methods.* New York: Wiley.

Choi, S. W., & McCall, M. (2002). Linking bilingual mathematics assessments: A monolingual IRT approach. In G. Tindal & T. M. Haladyna (Eds.), *Large-scale assessment programs for all students.* (pp. 317–338). Mahwah, NJ: Lawrence Erlbaum Associates.

Cummins, J. (1984). Wanted: A theoretical framework for relating language proficiency to academic proficiency among bilingual students. In C. Rivera (Ed.), *Language proficiency and academic achievement* (pp. 2–19). Clevedon, England: Multilingual Matters.

Durán, R. P., Brown, C., & McCall, M. (2002). Assessment of English-language learners in the Oregon statewide assessment system: National and state perspectives. In G. Tindal & T. M. Haladyna (Eds.), *Large-scale assessment programs for all students* (pp. 371–394). Mahwah, NJ: Lawrence Erlbaum Associates.

Elder, C. (1997). What does test bias have to do with fairness? *Language Testing, 14,* 261–277.

Garcia, T., with del Rio Paraent, L., Chen, L., Ferrara, S., Garavaglia, D., Johnson, E., et al. (2000). *Study of a dual language test booklet in 8th grade mathematics: Final report.* Washington, DC: American Institutes for Research.

Hale, G. (1988). Student major field and test content: Interactive effects on reading comprehension in the test of English as a foreign language. *Language Testing, 5,* 49–61.

Hambleton, R. K. (1993). Translating achievement tests for use in cross-national studies. *European Journal for Psychological Assessment, 9,* 57–68.

Hambleton, R. K. (1994). Guidelines for adapting educational and psychological tests: A progress report. *European Journal for Psychological Assessment, 10,* 229–244.

Kindler, A. L. (2002). Survey of the states' limited English proficient students and available educational programs and services 2000–2001 summary report, Office of English Language Acquisition, Language Enhancement and Academic Achievement for Limited English Proficient Students. Washington, DC: National Clearinghouse for English Language Acquisition & Language Instruction Educational Programs.

Lewis, D. M., Green, D. R., Mitzel, H. C., Baum, K., & Patz, R. J. (1998, April). *The bookmark standard setting procedure: Methodology and recent implementations.* Paper presented at the annual meeting of the National Council on Measurement in Education, San Diego, CA.

Lewis, D. M., Mitzel, H. C., & Green, D. R. (1996, June). Standard setting: A bookmark approach. In D. R. Green (Chair), *IRT-based standard setting procedures utilizing behavioral anchoring.* Symposium conducted at the meeting of the Council of Chief State School Officers National Conference on Large Scale Assessment, Phoenix, AZ.

Liu, K., Anderson, M. E., Swierzbin, B., & Thurlow, M. (1999). *Bilingual accommodations for limited English proficient students on statewide reading tests: Phase 1* (Minnesota Report No. 20). Minneapolis: University of Minnesota, National Center on Educational Outcomes. Retrieved October 31, 2002, from the World Wide Web: http://education.umn.edu/NCEO/OnlinePubs/MnReport20.html

Liu, K., Thurlow, M., Erickson, R., Spicuzza, R., & Heinze, K. (1997). *A review of the literature on students with limited English proficiency and assessment* (Minnesota Report No. 11). Minneapolis: University of Minnesota, National Center on Educational Outcomes. Retrieved October 26, 2002, from the World Wide Web: http://education.umn.edu/NCEO/OnlinePubs/MnReport11.html

Marin, G., & Marin, B. V. (1991). *Research with Hispanic populations.* Newbury Park, CA: Sage.

McKay, R. B., Breslow, M. J., Sangster, R. L., Gabbard, S. M., Reynolds, R. W., Nakamoto, J. M., et al. (1996). Translating survey questionnaires: Lessons learned. *New Directions for Evaluation, 70,* 93–105.

No Child Left Behind Act, Public Law 103–383 (2002).

Quest, C., Liu, K., & Thurlow M. (1996). *Cambodian, Hmong, Lao, Spanish-speaking and Vietnamese parents and students speak out on Minnesota's Basic Standards Tests* (Minnesota Report No. 12). Minneapolis: University of Minnesota, National Center on Educational Outcomes. Retrieved October 26, 2002, from the World Wide Web: http://education.umn.edu/NCEO/OnlinePubs/MnReport12.html

Sireci, S. G. (1997). Problems and issues in linking assessment across languages. *Educational Measurement: Issues and Practice, 16,* 12–19.

Stansfield, C. W. (1996). *Content assessment in the native language.* Washington, DC: ERIC Clearinghouse on Assessment and Evaluation. (ERIC/AE Digest Services EDO-TM-96-02)

Stansfield, C. W. (1997). *Experiences and issues related to the format of bilingual tests.* (ERIC Document Reproduction Service No. ED 423 306).

Stansfield, C. W. (2000). Translation, state assessments, and English language learners. *NABE News, 23*(8), 1, 6–7.

Stansfield, C. W. (2003). Test translation and adaptation in public education in the USA. In R. Hambleton & J. H. A. L. de Jong (Eds.), Advances in translating and adapting educational and psychological tests [Special issue]. *Language Testing, 20,* 189–207.

Stansfield, C. W., & Auchter, J. E. (2001). A process for translating achievement tests. In C. Elder, A. Brown, N. Iwashita, E. Grove, K. Hill, & T. Lumley (Eds.), *Experimenting with uncertainty: Essays in honor of Alan Davies* (pp. 73–80). Cambridge, England: Cambridge University Press.

Stansfield, C. W., & Kahl, S. R. (1998). *Lessons learned from a tryout of Spanish and English versions of a state assessment.* Paper presented at a symposium on multilingual versions of tests at the annual meeting of the American Educational Research Association, San Diego, CA. (ERIC Document Reproduction Service No. ED 423 306)

Werner, O., & Campbell, D. T. (1970). Translating, working through interpreters, and the problem of decentering. In R. Naroll & R. Cohen (Eds.), *A handbook of cultural anthropology* (pp. 398–419). New York: American Museum of Natural History.

APPENDIX 2-A

INTERVIEW PROTOCOL

A National Review of State Assessment Policies and Test Translation Practices for English Language Learners During School Year 2000–2001

Telephone Interview Protocol

State _____ Title VII___Assessment office____Date _____

I. Background Questions

1. Most states don't translate tests, but yours does. Why does your state translate its tests?
2. What has been the overall reaction to the translated version of tests by students, teachers, and parents? Have there been any problems either in the translation process or in test administration in any of the languages?
3. Are commercially available native language instruments used by the state? Name and publisher.
4. How did the state determine or decide which tests would be translated? When did the state first translate tests?
5. How many students in the state take native language versions of the test? Cite figures by language.
6. Which tests does the state translate?
7. If the state assessment system tests are translated, how many forms are translated?

    a. One
    b. Two
    c. All

II. The Translation Process

8. Who manages the translation process?

    a. The state? Which unit of the SEA?
    b. The test development contractor
    c. A translation company

9. Which of the following methods are used to translate the tests?

    a. Forward translation (with or without review and revision)____
    b. Back-translation ____
    c. Single translator (with or without reviews)____
    d. Translation by committee ____
    e. Other _____

10. How did the state determine which methods of translation would be used? Were other approaches tried? How did the state get to the current approach?
11. Does the state review the translation submitted?

    a. If so, who reviews it?
    b. How many reviews are there?
    c. Please explain the review process.

12. What criteria does the state or the contractor use to identify and select translators?
13. How much time (in weeks) is allotted for the translation?
14. Who does the page layout in languages other than English? (If the answer varies by language, indicate the languages that apply for each option.)

    a. The state____
    b. Translation contractor____
    c. A publications firm____

15. What desktop publishing programs (e.g., Quark, PageMaker, InDesign) are used to do page layout in languages other than English? (If they vary, indicate by language.)

16. What platform (Mac or PC) is used to produce the non-English version of the test? (If platform varies, indicate by language.)

17. Does the state field-test the translated versions? If yes, how does the state use the results of field-testing involving non-English versions?

III. Other Forms of Communication in the Non-English Language

18. Which of the following ancillary materials are available in translated forms?
    Check all that apply and indicate languages

    a. Administration manual____
    b. If yes, entire manual or read-aloud portions only?
    c. Answer booklet____
    d. Scoring guides____
    e. Toolkits for examinees____
    f. Score reports____
    g. Parent guide to test results____
    h. Teacher guide to test results____
    i. Other _____

19. What types of information are being translated for parents? In which languages?

IV. Technology

20. Does the state use the World Wide Web to provide information to parents in non-English languages?

21. If so, in which languages?

22. Do you have any data on the number of hits or downloads by language?

23. Have there been any problems getting these publications on the Web site for specific languages?

V. Research

24. What procedures does the state use to examine the psychometric qualities of translated tests?

25. Does the state do a separate equating or linking of the translated tests? If yes, why?

26. Explain in detail how linking is done.

27. Has the state produced any reports or evaluations concerning the translated tests?

28. Has the state or the test development contractor done any psychometric analysis of the translated tests?

VI. District Translation

29. Does the state allow districts to translate tests? If so, which tests?
30. If yes, who does the district typically contact to carry out the translation?
31. Who scores the district-translated tests?
32. If yes, how does the state treat the scores from district-translated tests?
33. What is the state's policy toward sight (oral) translation of tests by district personnel?
34. What do you know about how much sight translation is being done in districts and how well it is being done?

VII. The Future

35. What plans, if any, does the state have for expanding or curtailing the test translation program?
36. What changes would you like to see in the test translation program?

APPENDIX 2-B

POLICY DOCUMENTS SUBMITTED BY STATES

Arizona	Guidelines	2001
	LEP Guidelines: Arizona Student Achievement Program Accountability for All Students	
Colorado	Manual	March 1997
	Colorado Department of Education: Handbook on Planning for Limited English Proficient (LEP) Student Success	
Connecticut	Guidelines	2000
	Assessment Guidelines for Administering the Connecticut Mastery Test, Connecticut Academic Performance Test and Connecticut Alternate Assessment	
Delaware	Guidelines	December 31, 2000 (revision)
	Delaware Student Testing Program: Guidelines for the Inclusion of Students With Disabilities and Students With Limited English Proficiency	
	Guidelines	April 14, 2001
	(revision)	
	Delaware Student Testing Program: Guidelines for the Inclusion of Students With Disabilities and Students With Limited English Proficiency	

Kansas	Policy	November 2000
	(version 4)	
	Inclusion of English Language Learners (ELL) in the Kansas State Assessment Program	
Massachusetts	Guidelines	Spring 2000
	Requirements for the Participation of Students With Limited English Proficiency: A Guide for Educators and Parents	
Maine	Policy	March 2001
	Maine Educational Assessment: Policies and Procedures for Accommodations for the Maine Educational Assessment	
Minnesota	Guidelines	March 2001
	Basic Standards Test: Guidelines for Students With Limited English	Proficiency
Nebraska	Guide	Spring 2001
	ELL Learners in STARS Assessment	
New Jersey	Statewide Assessment	January 6, 1999
	LEP Students Receiving Alternative Assessments	
New York	Manual	2001
	School Administrator's Manual for Regents Examinations, Regents Competency Tests, and Proficiency Examinations.	
	Manual	January 2001
	A System of Accountability for Student Success: An Implementation Manual for Schools With Elementary and Middle Level Grades	
Ohio	Rules Book	November 28, 2000
Oklahoma	Manual	Spring 2001
	Oklahoma School Testing Program: Spring 2001 Test Preparation Manual—Iowa Tests of Basic Skills, Form A Level 9, Grade 3, Core Battery	
Oregon	Manual	2001

	Oregon Statewide Knowledge and Skills Assessments Administration Manual 2001: Benchmarks 1, 2, 3, and CIM for Mathematics, Reading/Literature and Benchmarks 3 and CIM for Science	
Rhode Island	Guidelines	2001
	Rhode Island State Assessment Program Requirements for Student Participation and Assessment Accommodations	
	Guidelines for Inclusion of All Students in the 1997 Rhode Island State Performance Assessments	
Texas	Manual	2001
	District and Campus Coordinator Manual 2001: Texas Student Assessment Program	
	Policy	2000–2001
	Texas Student Assessment Division: Testing Limited English Proficient Students (LEP) 2000–2001.	
	Letter	April 11, 2001
	State Testing Requirements for Limited English Proficient (LEP) Student in Grades 3–8	
Utah	Guidelines	May 11, 2001
	Guidelines for Participation of Students With Special Needs in the Utah Performance Assessment System for Students (U-PASS)	
Wisconsin	Examples	September 2001
	Examples of Test Accommodations for Students With Limited English Proficiency (LEP) for the Wisconsin Knowledge and Concepts Examinations	
Wyoming	Policy	January 2000
	Policies for the Participation of All Students in District and Statewide Assessment and Accountability Systems	

Study 3

State Practices for Reporting Participation and Performance of English Language Learners in State Assessments

Martha L. Thurlow, Debra Albus, Kristin K. Liu, and Charlene Rivera

Much of the concern regarding the participation of ELLs in state assessment has focused on how to increase participation of ELLs on tests through the use of accommodations such as test translation or through alternate assessments. However, as states develop, implement, and finalize standards-based assessment systems, it is also critical to consider issues related to reporting the scores of ELLs. As the National Research Council's Committee on Title I Testing and Assessment has observed, "In many ways, reporting the results of tests is one of the most significant aspects of testing and assessment.... It is the information, and the inferences drawn from the information that make a difference in the lives of students, parents, teachers, and administrators" (National Research Council, 1999, p. 66). Accurate and comprehensive reporting of test scores for all students, including ELLs, is therefore essential to accountability efforts.

Although score reporting is crucial to the inclusion of ELLs in state assessment systems, to date, there has been no comprehensive national picture of state practices regarding the reporting of ELLs' scores on state assessments. The goal of this study is to fill this research gap by documenting the extent to which public state assessment reports for the 1999–2000 school year collected from the education agencies of 50 states and the District of Columbia included information on the participation and performance of ELLs. This school year was selected because, although states' policies were available for the 2000–2001 school year, complete state assessment reports were not.

It is important to keep in mind that the state reports examined were prepared prior to the enactment of the 2002 NCLB, when states' policies and practices were governed by the 1994 IASA. However, as NCLB has set new targets for SEAs, intensifying the requirements of the previous law, it is important to see states' policies and practices from the perspective of the requirements of both laws. This study, therefore, offers an important "then" and "now" perspective: By examining where states' reporting efforts were under IASA, it is possible to gauge the extent to which states are adequately positioned to comply with the more stringent accountability requirements of NCLB.

The study is divided into nine parts. The first part offers a brief overview of three studies that illustrates states' past practice in reporting state assessment data for ELLs and students with disabilities. The second part provides an overview of the methods used to perform the study. The next six parts cover a variety of topics pertaining to state assessment reports for school year 1999–2000, including data availability, timeliness, and comprehensiveness; state reporting practice regarding participation data for ELLs; state reporting practice for states with large and small ELL populations; participation and performance of ELLs by content area; tests designed specifically for ELLs and alternate assessments; and examples of effective reporting. Finally, the last part offers conclusions and recommendations.

REVIEW OF RESEARCH ON STATE ASSESSMENT REPORTS

Little research has been conducted that addresses states' reporting practices for ELLs in a comprehensive way. The research team identified three studies that illustrate states' past practices in reporting state assessment data for ELLs and students with disabilities.

Findings from the 2001 Council of Chief State School Officers (CCSSO) annual survey of state assessment directors provide important details about how states approached state assessments in 1999–2000, the same year for which state reports were analyzed for this study (Olson, Jones, & Bond, 2001). Although the CCSSO annual survey of state assessment directors did not obtain data from states on the number or percentage of ELLs who took state assessments, it did elicit information about the practice of exempting ELLs from state tests. The report provided the following information about the school year 1999–2000 state practices on exempting ELLs from state tests:

- In 31 states, ELLs were eligible to receive an exemption from all state assessments, a reduction of 5 states from the prior year (i.e., from 36 states in the 1998–1999 school year to 31 states in the 1999–2000 school year).
- Another 15 states allowed exemptions from some assessments, up 4 states from the prior year (i.e., from 11 states in the 1998–1999 school year to 15 states in the 1999–2000 school year).

Twenty-three states reported including aggregated and disaggregated data in state summary reports, and another 10 states reported disseminating disaggregated data only. Fourteen states reported providing no public reports. Olson et al. (2001) concluded in the CCSSO summary report that although much attention is being focused on the inclusion of students with disabilities and ELLs in statewide assessments, "there still is much to learn about the implementation of inclusion criteria, the effects of using accommodations, and the policies and practices of states and localities" (p. 36).

NCEO sponsored a study conducted by Liu, Albus, and Thurlow (2000) examining public education reports for data on ELLs for school years 1995–1996 and 1997–1998. Only six states—Delaware, Georgia, New Hampshire, North Carolina, Rhode Island, and Virginia—reported data on test performance, and only five states—Alaska, Maryland, New Jersey, Texas, and Washington—reported on the number of ELLs who participated in testing. Of the six states that reported on test performance, all reported on writing, only five states reported on reading/ELA or mathematics, and only three states reported the performance of ELLs in social studies or science.

Finally, another study sponsored by NCEO in the same year, this one conducted by Thurlow, Nelson, Teelucksingh, and Ysseldyke (2000), found two prevailing conditions in the reporting of state assessment data. First, not all states reported data. Second, reports were not current. The study considered data reported in 2000, which were from three different school years. Specifically, Thurlow et al. found that 17 states provided data on students with disabilities. The oldest data reported in 2000 were from a 1996–1997 assessment (one state) and the most recent data reported were from a 1998–1999 assessment (one state); data from 1997–1998 were reported by 15 states.

An important reason for examining state assessment reports is to create a more accurate picture of the academic progress of all students, including ELLs (Abedi, 2001). The findings suggest that state practice for collecting data and reporting on ELL performance in state assessments varies greatly across states. Although the three studies illustrate only isolated aspects of states' reporting practices, the findings suggest a need for a methodical look at state assessment reporting practices for ELLs for the most recent school year for which state assessment reports were available.

PURPOSE AND METHODOLOGY

Purpose

This study is based on two premises. First, public reporting of ELL participation and performance on state assessments is essential to confirm that these students are achieving state academic performance standards like other students. Although some state assessments might not be deemed appropriate for ELLs at the early stages of learning English, ELLs' exemption from all assessments due to nascent English language proficiency should not be allowed to "create systemic ignorance about their educational progress" (Rivera & Stansfield, 1998, p. 67). Second, public reporting on the participation and performance of ELLs is necessary for purposes of state, district, and school accountability.

The study documents the extent to which public state assessment reports for the 1999–2000 school year included information on the participation and performance of ELLs. The study was guided by the following research questions:

1. To what extent was ELLs' participation in and performance on state assessments publicly reported?
2. To what extent were ELL test data provided in state reports disaggregated for accommodated and alternate assessments, and were both participation rates and performance data reported?
3. What characteristics of public reports constitute best practice for presenting both useful and comprehensive data on ELLs?

The findings will be of interest to a number of constituents in the education community. The study can do the following:

• Help state assessment directors identify specific areas of reporting that need to be developed or improved.
• Inform state and federal policymakers who interpret federal statutes and guide states in providing state reports to the Secretary of Education as required by NCLB.

- Help state administrators, district administrators, educators, researchers, and others make decisions about improvements in instruction.

Methodology

Data Collection

The research team collected publicly available state assessment reports between August 2000 and March 2001. Two strategies were used to collect the data. First, the research team contacted the assessment or accountability offices in each of the 50 states and the District of Columbia and requested state assessment reports.[1] Next, the research team searched for online assessment reports. The CCSSO's online listing of state education Web sites (www.ccsso.org/seamenu) provided a direct link to every state Web site. The research team used the site to link to each state's home page and to search for or identify links to state assessment data. It should be noted that a majority of the state sites did not provide direct links to ELL participation and performance data. Researchers defined useful descriptors for online data searches to include achievement, accountability, and ELLs. All assessment data found on Web sites were considered public data. Both print and Web reports were analyzed for this study.

Although state reports were sought from 50 states and the District of Columbia, reports from only 46 states were included in the study: Two states had no statewide test, and the reports of 3 states included data that preceded 1999–2000 and were therefore outside the scope of the study.

Data Verification

To verify data, letters were sent to the assessment directors for each state department of education (DOE). Included with the letters were the list of public documents used for the analyses of both print reports and Web sources. The research team tracked whether the state had reported disaggregated enrollment, assessment participation, and assessment performance data for ELLs. The letters requested that the directors verify the information and provide any corrections or additional publicly available reports.

---

[1]Specific sources of all data used in analyses of participation and performance of ELLs are identified in the appendices.

Criteria for Considering a Document Public

The criteria for a print document to be considered public were the following: (a) the document provided a clear indication that it was developed for a public audience; or (b) the document provided a table of contents, title, and page numbers. A cover letter (e.g., to the citizens of the state) was accepted as a clear indication that the document was developed for a public audience. Furthermore, an accompanying table of contents was considered to be an indication that the document was not simply a "data run" that was not intended for the public.

Except for Web sites that required passwords, all Web sites were considered public sites. Thus, any data reported on a site (e.g., press releases with preliminary scores) were considered to be public reports. However, it is important to note that the Web sites accessed for the study were not uniformly available on an ongoing basis. In the process of returning to sites to check information obtained previously, researchers occasionally found that access to the data was no longer permitted.

Procedures for Including Maximum Amounts of Data

The research design was deliberately planned to be as inclusive as possible of states' publicly reported assessment data. For example, a press release that contained test information prior to the release of a complete or formal disaggregated score report was counted as publicly available data. A state that did not disaggregate ELL data in its print report but later issued a press release that included ELL data was considered to have disaggregated data, even though the larger and more formal report did not include the same data.

Defining the ELL Population

In examining state assessment reports the research team encountered many terms to describe ELLs. Some examples are students with LEP, non-English proficient (NEP) students, and potentially English proficient (PEP) students. Study protocol allowed the acceptance of all meaningful terms for both print and Web-based state assessment reports. Also accepted as disaggregated ELL data were data on subgroups of ELLs.[2] However, it is important to recognize that because there is no common op-

---

[2]Data reported for various ethnic and linguistic groups (e.g., Asian, African, Hispanic, Chinese, Spanish) included in state documents were not included as ELL data unless the subgroup was designated LEP.

erational definition for LEP across states, it is possible that the pool of students accounted for in ELL data could differ from state to state (Abedi, 2001; August & Hakuta, 1997). The lack of a common operational definition across states not only affects nomenclature in state assessment reports, but also impacts comparability of ELL state assessment reports. For example, where one state might report on ELLs based on language proficiency scores, another might not consider language proficiency and might report performance on state assessments according to the specific services provided to the students. Table 3.1 provides a list of some of the terms that state documents used to refer to ELLs.

Of the 51 contacted state DOEs, 15 offered a correction or provided additional data, but only 13 of the 15 states cited publicly available report infor-

TABLE 3.1

Labels Identifying ELLs and Former ELLs
in State Assessment Reports

ELL Labels	Former ELL Labels
ELL: English language learner	Bilingual English fluent (students)
LEP: Language enriched pupils	FEP: Fluent (or fully) English proficient (students)
LEP: Limited English proficient (students)	FES: Spanish language background fluent English speaking (students)
LES: Limited-English speaking (students)	Language fluent LEP (students)
NEP: Non-English-proficient (students)	Non-English home language (students)
NES: Non-English speaking (students)	Non-English background students
Non- or limited English fluent (students)	Other FES: Non-Spanish language background fluent English-speaking (students)
Other LES: Non-Spanish language background limited English-speaking (students)	R-FE: Redesignated fluent English (students)
Other: NES: Non-Spanish-language background non-English-speaking (students)	
Transitional bilingual (students)	

Note.   Some of these terms (e.g., *non-English home language* and *non-English background students*) can be used to describe students who might or might not have limited English proficiency.

mation; that is, only 13 of the 15 states offered supplemental information able to be used given the report criterion to examine and include only publicly available reports.

Criteria for Counting Participation and Performance Data

Despite the fact that paper documents and Web-based reports often contained pertinent data, not all of the data gave specific details about the participation and performance of ELLs. When it was possible to calculate, it was often difficult to determine the percentage of the total number of ELLs enrolled in a grade that actually took the state tests. Some state reports gave the number of ELLs tested at each grade level yet did not list the total number of students enrolled in that grade. Some states had a column in a participation table marked "Percent," but did not indicate whether the number represented the percentage of ELLs who were tested or the percentage of students tested who were ELLs.

The study design established criteria for determining whether print reports and Web-based reports gave a clear indication of the number of ELLs who participated in the test and how those students had performed. Participation of ELLs in state testing was considered to have been reported by a state if the number of ELLs tested was documented in either a performance chart or elsewhere in a report. Also, participation was considered to have been reported if the number of students tested was not presented directly but could be calculated easily from other information provided in the report (i.e., the document provided both the number of students enrolled and the number exempted). Reports that provided percentages of students at specific performance levels (e.g., below basic, basic, intermediate, advanced) but not total numbers of students tested were not counted as having participation data. These criteria were the basis for all data reported in all tables and figures.

In this analysis, performance was viewed as having been reported if the assessment results were disaggregated for ELLs, regardless of whether participation data were reported. Performance data could be presented in a report in a variety of ways (e.g., specific scores, percentages of students at different proficiency levels, etc.) and still be considered as having been reported.

Accuracy Checks

To ensure accuracy of the data presented in this study, an independent reviewer checked the reporting information for every fifth state (20%) that had been found by the primary reviewer to have disaggregated ELL data. The second reviewer independently recorded reporting information and compared it to that recorded by the original reviewer. The study defined agreement as the number of agreements divided by the number of agreements plus disagreements. There were no disagreements, so the agreement rate was 100%.

STATE PRACTICES: AVAILABILITY AND COMPREHENSIVENESS OF ELL DATA IN STATE ASSESSMENT REPORTS

States report on assessment results for a variety of purposes and release score reports at various times during the school year. These reports vary a great deal in the degrees to which they offer comprehensive depictions of student performance. Reports are prepared by test companies hired by the states to administer and score state assessments. Commonly, several months elapse between test administrations, which generally occur in the spring of each year, and the public release of score reports, generally available in late summer or fall of the following school year. Once state data become available, it is common for the media to report student assessment results in local newspapers. Although assessment reports commonly provide data aggregated by schools, and, in some cases, disaggregated by ethnicity, publicly released state assessment reports for school year 1999–2000 often do not include disaggregated data for ELLs.

State assessment reports are examined in terms of availability and comprehensiveness. First, the extent to which state assessment reports were publicly available is documented. Because participation data (i.e., the number of ELLs tested) offer an important context in which to view and interpret results, the extent to which state assessment reports documented the participation of ELLs in state assessments is also addressed. Next, data on the comprehensiveness of state assessment reports that included ELL data are examined within five rubrics: (a) inclusion of participation and performance data, (b) variation in reporting for all regular assessment, (c) school levels for which data were reported, (d) types of tests (norm- or criterion-referenced) for which data were reported, and (e) content areas for which data were reported.

It should be noted that states across the United States tend to vary widely in terms of the number and type of required state assessments. In school year 1999–2000, the number of required state assessment components ranged from a low of 2 in the District of Columbia to a high of 38 in New York. The content areas addressed by the state assessments ranged from basic core content areas to more specialized content areas. Examples of content areas tested at the state level include ELA and mathematics; health, science, and social studies; and occupational education proficiency exams (Olson et al., 2001, pp. 48, 58–59).

Availability of State Reports

As discussed earlier, from August 2000 to March 2001 the research team collected and examined the most current publicly available state reports from the 50 states and the District of Columbia. The research team requested the most current state assessment reports from the 50 states and the District of Columbia and searched state Web sites to identify documents available publicly.

Table 3.2 provides summary information about the state reports collected and examined by the research team. All collected print or Web-based reports were examined for ELL data. In Table 3.2, a check mark indicates that a report was provided or found on the Internet. For five states—Iowa, Kansas, North Dakota, Nebraska, and Nevada—state report data met one of two conditions: either there was no state assessment in school year 1999–2000 (Iowa and Nebraska) or only data from the previous school year were available (Kansas, North Dakota, and Nevada).[3] As a result, the analysis of state practices for reporting on ELL assessments spans 45 states and the District of Columbia. As shown in Table 3.2, for the general student population, 26 states provided paper reports, whereas Web-based reports were found for 44 states, making this report format more common and more widely available. Twenty-four states provided both print and Web-based reports. Table 3.2 indicates that only 13 states provided paper reports showing ELL data and 16 states provided Web reports. Ten states provided both types of reports.

Comprehensiveness of Reporting on ELLs

Because IASA required the collection and disaggregation of state assessment data, the research team anticipated that a majority of state reports would provide data on ELL student performance. It was hypothesized that because the Title I reporting requirements were the same for both student groups, states' reporting practices for ELLs would reflect those for students with disabilities. However, this hypothesis was not borne out. For

---

[3]Because one of the purposes of the study was to examine only the most recent available reports, the study team examined but did not include in the general analysis data submitted for review for school year 1998–1999. The research team also is aware that some states generated assessment reports for the 1999–2000 school year after the March 23, 2001 cutoff date established for the data collection portion of the study; data released after the established cutoff date were not included in the study.

TABLE 3.2

Sources of State Assessment Reports

State	Report(s) Available	Report Format					
		General Student Population			ELLs		
		Paper	Web	Both	Paper	Web	Both
AK	✓	✓	✓	✓			
AL	✓		✓				
AR	✓		✓				
AZ	✓		✓				
CA	✓		✓			✓	
CO	✓	✓	✓	✓	✓	✓	✓
CT	✓	✓	✓	✓			
DC	✓		✓				
DE	✓	✓	✓	✓	✓	✓	✓
FL	✓		✓			✓	
GA	✓		✓				
HI	✓		✓				
IA[a]							
ID	✓	✓	✓	✓	✓	✓	✓
IL	✓	✓	✓	✓	✓	✓	✓
IN	✓		✓			✓	
KS[b]							
KY	✓	✓	✓	✓	✓	✓	✓
LA	✓	✓	✓	✓	✓		
MA	✓		✓			✓	
MD	✓		✓				
ME	✓		✓			✓	
MI	✓	✓	✓	✓			
MN	✓		✓				
MO	✓		✓				

(continued)

TABLE 3.2 (continued)

| State | Report(s) Available | General Student Population | | | ELLs | | |
		Paper	Web	Both	Paper	Web	Both
MS	✓		✓				
MT	✓	✓					
NC	✓	✓	✓	✓	✓	✓	✓
ND[b]							
NE[a]							
NH	✓	✓			✓		
NJ	✓	✓	✓	✓	✓		
NM	✓	✓	✓	✓		✓	
NV[b]							
NY	✓	✓	✓	✓			
OH	✓		✓				
OK	✓	✓	✓	✓			
OR	✓		✓				
PA	✓	✓	✓	✓			
RI	✓	✓	✓	✓	✓	✓	✓
SC	✓	✓	✓	✓			
SD	✓	✓	✓	✓			
TN	✓		✓				
TX	✓	✓	✓	✓	✓	✓	✓
UT	✓	✓	✓	✓			
VA	✓	✓	✓	✓	✓	✓	✓
VT	✓		✓				
WA	✓		✓				
WI	✓	✓	✓	✓	✓	✓	✓
WV	✓	✓	✓	✓			
WY	✓	✓	✓	✓			
Total	46	26	44	24	13	16	10

[a]No state assessment in school year 1999–2000. [b]No school year 1999–2000 data; data from an earlier year were available but were not analyzed as part of this study.

the 1999–2000 school year, 35 states reported disaggregated performance data for students with disabilities (Bielinski, Thurlow, Callender, & Bolt, 2001), up from just 13 states in school year 1998–1999 (Thurlow et al., 2000). Fewer states provided disaggregated data for ELLs and the comprehensiveness of these data was inconsistent.

Reporting on the Participation and Performance of ELLs

The research team considered two components of state assessment reports critical in determining whether or not a state report was to be considered inclusive of ELLs: (a) the extent to which a state documented the number tested and had participation rates of ELLs, and (b) the extent to which a state provided disaggregated student performance data.

Participation refers to data in a report that directly indicate the number of ELLs tested or to data from which this could be calculated. Participation rates are the percentages of ELLs tested or the reporting of sufficient data to make it possible to calculate easily the percentage of ELLs tested for a particular state assessment.

The second critical component of a state assessment report is whether ELL performance or academic achievement data were documented for one or more state assessments. Both participation rates and performance data are important components that are required to allow meaningful interpretations of data and the possibility of cross-checking the data reported.

The map in Fig. 3.1 shows that 32 states did not report on the participation or performance of ELLs for any state assessment. As illustrated in Fig. 3.1, of the 19 states that reported ELL performance, 16 states provided both participation and performance data for ELLs on at least one state assessment. Three states—New Hampshire, New Mexico, and Rhode Island—reported performance for ELLs for at least one state assessment, but did not document participation. Of these states, one (New Hampshire) reported ELL performance for all state assessments.

Table 3.3 lists the 19 states that reported participation or performance data for ELLs. Table 3.3 shows that 8 of 19 states' reports—California, Colorado, Delaware, Indiana, Kentucky, Massachusetts, Texas, and Wisconsin—provided both participation and performance data for ELLs for every regular state assessment that was administered and reported. It should be noted that 3 of the 7 states—California, Colorado, and Texas—are among the 10 states with the highest ELL student enrollment as reported by the National Clearinghouse for English Language Acquisition (NCELA, 2002). Three states—New Hampshire, New Mexico, and Rhode Island—provided no ELL participation data for any assessment.

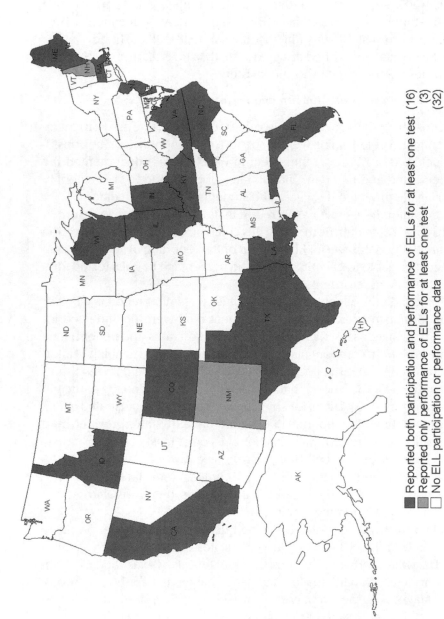

FIG. 3.1. States reporting ELL participation and performance data in school year 1999–2000.

Reported both participation and performance of ELLs for at least one test (16)
Reported only performance of ELLs for at least one test (3)
No ELL participation or performance data (32)

TABLE 3.3

States Including ELL Participation Data, Performance Data, or Both in State Assessment Reports

State	ELL Participation		ELL Performance	
	All Tests	Some Tests	All Tests	Some Tests
CA	✓		✓	
CO	✓		✓	
DE	✓		✓	
FL		✓		✓
ID		✓		✓
IL		✓[a]	✓[a]	
IN	✓		✓	
KY	✓		✓	
LA		✓		✓
ME		✓		✓
MA	✓		✓	
NH	—	—	✓[a]	
NJ	✓			✓
NM	—	—		✓
NC		✓		✓
RI	—	—	✓[a]	
TX	✓		✓	
VA		✓		✓
WI	✓		✓	
Total	9	7	11	8

[a]State report provided disaggregated data for some, not all, grade levels tested.

Note.—=No data reported.

Figure 3.2 illustrates that only about 58% ($n = 11$) of the 19 states that re-ported performance data for ELLs provided these data on every regular as-sessment administered by the state. Eight states (42% of the 19 states, or 16% of all 50 states and the District of Columbia) reported performance data for ELLs for at least one test.

Variations in Reporting on All Regular Assessments

The research team found that some states that did not report data for ELLs for any state test had, in prior years, reported disaggregated ELL performance data for one or more tests. For example, Florida reported ELL performance data for its 1999 High School Competency Test but not for its 2000 High School Competency Test. Minnesota reported ELL performance data in its report for school year 1998–1999 assessments, but at the time of the study did not report ELL data for the school year 1999–2000 assessments. North Carolina, which reported disaggregated participation and performance data by testing condi-tion for ELLs on its 1997–1998 Computer Skills Test did not report data for ELLs for the 1999–2000 school year; however, assessment reports that in-cluded ELLs were later posted for the 2000–2001 school year.

Reporting ELL Data for School Levels Tested

Even when states reported data for every test that was administered, states might not have reported data for all grades in which the assessment had been administered. Table 3.4 profiles the comprehensiveness of state data by documenting state reporting practices for reading and mathematics performance of ELLs at the elementary, middle, and high school levels. Of the 19 states that reported ELL performance data for reading and math, over three quarters ($n = 16$, or 84%) did so across all school levels. The 16 states that reported ELL performance across all school levels tested were Califor-nia, Colorado,[4] Delaware, Florida, Idaho, Illinois,[5] Indiana, Kentucky, Louisi-ana, Maine, Massachusetts, North Carolina, Rhode Island, Texas, Virginia, and Wisconsin.

---

[4]Colorado did not report ELL student performance at the elementary level for mathemat-ics; however, Colorado also did not report these performance data for non-ELLs. On this ba-sis, Colorado is counted as having reported data for all grades tested and reported based on reporting practices for the general student population.

[5]The students reported for the Illinois Standards Achievement Test (ISAT) were not ELLs receiving services, but were transitioned students (former ELL students who received ser-vices). No information is provided on the ISAT for students who had not been transitioned. Other ELL results were reported for the Illinois Measure of Annual Growth in English (IMAGE) for reading and language arts. (Illinois State Board of Education, n.d.).

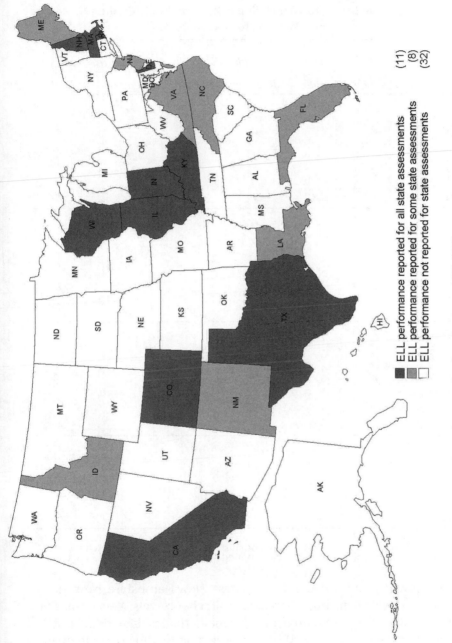

FIG. 3.2.   Comprehensiveness of ELL performance reporting for school year 1999–2000.

ELL performance reported for all state assessments   (11)
ELL performance reported for some state assessments   (8)
ELL performance not reported for state assessments   (32)

TABLE 3.4
Grade Levels for Which States Reported ELL Reading and Math Performance Data

State	Elementary		Middle School		High School	
	Reading	Math	Reading	Math	Reading	Math
CA	✓	✓	✓	✓	✓	✓
CO	✓		✓	✓	—	—
DE	✓	✓	✓	✓	✓	✓
FL	✓	✓	✓	✓	✓	✓
ID	✓	✓	✓	✓	✓	✓
IL	✓	✓	✓	✓	✓	✓
IN	✓	✓	✓	✓	✓	✓
KY	✓	✓	✓	✓	✓	✓
LA	✓	✓	✓	✓	✓	✓
ME	✓	✓	✓	✓	✓	✓
MA	✓	✓	✓	✓	✓	✓
NH	✓	✓	✓	✓		
NJ	✓	✓	✓	✓		
NM					✓	✓
NC	✓	✓	✓	✓	✓	✓
RI	✓	✓	✓	✓	✓	✓
TX	✓	✓	✓	✓	✓	✓
VA	✓	✓	✓	✓	—	—
WI	✓	✓	✓	✓	✓	✓

Note. Colorado and Virginia did not administer state tests at the high school level. The table includes only those states that reported some 1999–2000 state test data.

As shown in Table 3.4, only three states—New Hampshire, New Jersey, and New Mexico—did not report data at all school levels. New Hampshire and New Jersey reported no reading or mathematics data for ELLs at the high school level, and New Mexico reported no reading or mathematics performance data for ELLs at either the elementary or middle school levels.

Table 3.5 lists the three states reporting ELL performance data at some grade levels, but not at others, for the same test in school year 1999–2000. The state reports provided no explanation as to why data were available at certain grade levels for the general population but not for ELLs.

Reporting ELL Data for Criterion-Referenced and Norm-Referenced Tests

Criterion-referenced tests (CRTs) are tests designed to give information on how a student performs in specific areas of knowledge or skills as measured by attainment of a standard rather than in relation to a reference group. Norm-referenced tests (NRTs) are tests, often produced commercially, that give information on how well students perform in comparison to an external reference group. To examine whether differences existed in the way states reported ELL data for CRTs versus NRTs, the research team examined the tests for states that had inconsistent reporting practices across tests to assess whether or not the inconsistency in reporting was attributable to type of test. The categorization of tests as CRTs or NRTs followed state classifications.

There is reason to think that there would be fewer ELLs participating in NRTs because of the strict standardization procedures that are generally used for these tests. In contrast, more ELLs might be expected to take CRTs because these tests generally allow for greater use of accommodations, making this type of test more inclusive for students of varying language proficiency.

TABLE 3.5

States That Reported Data for Specific Tests for the General Population and ELLs for Some Grades but Not Others

State	Test and Grade Level Reported for ELLs and General Population	Test and Grade Level Not Reported for ELLs
Illinois	Illinois Standards Achievement Test (3, 4, 7, 8)	Illinois Standards Achievement Test (5)
New Hampshire	New Hampshire Educational Improvement and Assessment Program (3, 6)	New Hampshire Educational Improvement and Assessment Program (10)
Rhode Island	RI Writing Assessment (7)	RI Writing Assessment (3, 10)
	RI Health Assessment (9)	RI Health Assessment (5)

Table 3.6 profiles the types of tests in the eight states that reported on ELL performance data for some, but not for all, state assessments. Table 3.6 lists the names of the tests for which data were and were not reported for ELLs. Although Table 3.6 shows that slightly more states reported data for ELLs on CRTs, no pattern emerged to suggest a contrast in how states reported data for ELLs on NRTs versus CRTs.

Reporting ELL Data for Tested Content Areas

Few states provided data on ELLs' performance on content assessments, despite the importance of such data. Table 3.7 presents the content areas tested on state assessments and identifies states that provided participation and performance data for ELLs on state reports. As highlighted in Table 3.7, 46 states reported a state-mandated test in reading and mathematics for all students. Of these 46 states, 19 (41%) assessed and reported test scores for ELLs.

Thirty-nine of 46 states (84%) assessed writing, 34 of 46 states (74%) assessed science, and 37 of 46 states (80%) assessed social studies. For ELLs, 13 of 39 states (33% of all states that assessed by content) reported writing, 13 of the 34 states (38% of all states that assessed by content) reported science, and 11 of the 37 states (30% of all states that assessed by content) reported social studies. Assessments in the "Other" category ranged in content from spelling and health to practical living.[6] Also included in this category were end-of-course tests in a variety of content areas that included spelling, economics, and health. Assessments classified as "Other" were administered and reported on by 32 states (70% of the 46). Of these 32 states, 5 (16%)—California, Idaho, Kentucky, North Carolina, and Rhode Island—reported on ELLs in "other" tests, with Rhode Island reporting only ELL student performance (not participation).

Summary of Findings

Availability of ELL data is very limited. Only 19 states reported any kind of ELL data for their state assessments. The finding that most of the ELL data

---

[6]California's "other" test covered spelling. Kentucky's "other" test covered arts and humanities, practical living, and vocational. Massachusetts tested science along with technology and social science with history. North Carolina's science assessment included individual end-of-course tests in biology, chemistry, physical science, and physics; and social studies includes an end-of-course test in history. The state also had an end-of-course math test. The "other" test is an end-of-course test in economics. Rhode Island's "other" test covered health. Texas's science assessment included end-of-course tests in general science, specifically in biology, and social studies included end-of-course tests in general social studies, specifically in U.S. history.

TABLE 3.6

State Assessment Performance Data Reported With and Without Disaggregated ELL Data

State	ELL Data Reported	NRT	CRT	ELL Data Not Reported	NRT	CRT
FL	Florida Comprehensive Assessment Test	✓	✓	High School Competency Test		✓
ID	Iowa Test of Basic Skills (Reading, Math, Language)	✓		Iowa Test of Basic Skills (Social Studies, Science, Sources of Information)	✓	
	ID Reading Indicator		✓			
	ID Math Indicator		✓	Iowa Test of Basic Skills	✓	
LA	Graduation Exit Exam for the 21st Century		✓			
	Louisiana Educational Assessment Program for the 21st Century		✓			
ME	Maine Educational Assessment, Math, Reading & Writing		✓	Maine Educational Assessment, Health, Science & Technology, Social Studies, and Visual & Performing Arts		✓
NJ	Grade Eight Proficiency Assessment Elementary School Proficiency Assessment		✓	Grade 11 High School Proficiency Test		✓
NM	New Mexico High School Competency Examination		✓	Terra Nova Survey Plus and Custom Supplement Writing Assessment	✓	✓
NC	North Carolina Pretest		✓	Iowa Test of Basic Skills	✓	✓
	End-of-course		✓			
	High school comprehensive		✓	North Carolina Computer Skills		✓
	End-of-grade		✓			
	North Carolina Writing					
	Open Ended		✓			
VA	Virginia State Assessment Program			Standards of Learning	✓	
	Stanford Achievement Test-9th Ed.	✓		Literacy Testing Program		✓

Note. NRT = Norm-referenced test; CRT = Criterion-referenced test.

TABLE 3.7

States Reporting ELL Participation and Performance by Content Area Tested

State	Reading/ Language Arts	Math	Writing	Science	Social Studies	Other
AL	NR	NR	NR	NR	NR	
AK	NR	NR		NR		
AZ	NR	NR				
AR	NR	NR		NR	NR	
CA	Y	Y	Y	Y	Y	Y
CO	Y	Y	Y	Y	NR	
CT	NR	NR	NR	NR		NR
DC	NR	NR				
DE	Y	Y	Y			
FL	Y	Y	Y			NR
GA	NR	NR	NR	NR	NR	NR
HI	NR	NR	NR	NR	NR	NR
ID	Y	Y	Y	Y	Y	Y
IL	Y	Y	Y	Y	Y	
IN	Y	Y	Y			
IA	—	—	—	—	—	—
KS	—	—	—	—	—	—
KY	Y	Y	Y	Y	Y	Y
LA	Y	Y	Y	Y	Y	
ME	Y	Y	Y	NR	NR	NR
MD	NR	NR	NR	NR	NR	NR
MA	Y	Y	Y	Y	Y	
MI	NR	NR	NR	NR	NR	
MN	NR	NR	NR			
MS	NR	NR	NR			
MO	NR	NR	NR	NR	NR	NR
MT	NR	NR		NR	NR	NR

State						
NE	—	—	—	—	—	—
NV	—	—	—	—	—	—
NH	Y[1]	Y[1]		Y[1]	Y[1]	NR
NJ	Y	Y	NR	Y	NR	NR
NM	Y[1]	Y[1]	NR	Y[1]	Y[1]	NR
NY	NR	NR	NR	NR	NR	NR
NC	Y	Y	Y	Y	Y	Y
ND	—	—	—	—	—	—
OH	NR	NR	NR	NR	NR	NR
OK	NR	NR	NR	NR	NR	NR
OR	NR	NR	NR	NR	NR	NR
PA	NR	NR	NR		NR	NR
RI	Y[1]	Y[1]	NR		NR	Y[1]
SC	NR	NR	NR		NR	NR
SD	NR	NR	NR	NR	NR	NR
TN	NR	NR	NR	NR	NR	NR
TX	Y	Y	Y	Y	Y	NR
UT	NR	NR	NR	NR	NR	NR
VT	NR	NR	NR	NR	NR	NR
VA	Y	Y	NR	NR	NR	NR
WA	NR	NR	NR		NR	NR
WV	NR	NR	NR	NR	NR	NR
WI	Y	Y	NR	Y	Y	NR
WY	NR	NR			NR	NR
Test content for all students	46 (100%) ($N = 46$)	46 (100%) ($N = 46$)	39 (84%) ($N = 46$)	34 (74%) ($N = 46$)	37 (80%) ($N = 46$)	32 (70%) ($N = 46$)
Report on ELLs tested	19 (41%) ($N = 46$)	19 (41%) ($N = 46$)	13 (33%) ($N = 39$)	13 (38 %) ($N = 34$)	11 (30%) ($N = 37$)	5 (16%) ($N = 32$)

Note. NR = State tested but did not report participation and/or performance data for ELLs; Y = State reported participation and performance data for ELLs; Y[1] = State reported performance only; — = No data for 1999–2000 or no state test; blank space indicates no test in the content area.

on regular assessments that are presented in state reports are recent data (school year 1999–2000) is not surprising given what is known from previous investigations of state data reports for students with disabilities (Thurlow et al., 2000). The comprehensiveness of the data is still quite inconsistent. Only 11 states (21%) reported performance data for all state tests administered. Of those states that reported ELL performance data only for some state tests, no discernible rationale as to why this was the case could be uncovered. An analysis of the tests for which states did not report data suggested that there was no link between type of test and whether ELL data were reported. However, of those states that did report ELL reading and math performance ($n = 19$), 83% ($n = 16$) did so across elementary, middle, and high school levels. Regardless of the content area, three states reported ELL data at some grade levels but not others for the same test. For these states, the assessment reports did not provide an explanation as to why certain grade-level data were available only for the general population and not for ELLs.

ELL assessment information across content areas also varied. Nineteen of 46 states that tested reading or ELA and mathematics content reported performance, or 41%; 13 of 39 states that reported on writing, or 33%; 13 of 34 states that reported on science, or 38%; 11 of 37 states that reported on social studies, or 30%; and 5 of 32 states reported in other areas, or 16%. These data indicate clearly a need for improvement in both the quantity and quality of information on how ELLs are achieving in the basic subject areas.

REPORTING PARTICIPATION AND PERFORMANCE

To study the extent to which state reports accounted for ELLs, the research team used two levels of definition for participation information—participation data and participation rates. *Participation data* refers to the number of ELLs tested; *participation rates* refers to "the number of English language learners … being assessed, expressed as a proportion or percentage of the total enrollment of ELLs" (Vincent & Schenck, 2001, p. 10). Specifically, the study team examined state reports for the following data to determine whether or not each state had accounted for all ELLs, tested or untested, or only for ELL performance data.

1. Total number of ELLs enrolled in grade assessed.
2. Total number of ELLs tested in grade assessed.
3. Total number of ELLs not tested in grade assessed.

4. Total number of ELLs tested and included in score reporting. (This number is needed because some students tested with accommodations who were considered nonstandard might not have been included in reporting.)

In cases where states reported these data comprehensively, it is possible to determine percentages of students tested, not tested, and included in score reporting. This is a step toward the transparency needed in states' accountability systems.

Accounting for All ELLs

This section addresses the extent to which the 19 states that reported performance data for ELLs accounted for all ELLs, whether these students were assessed or not. The data in Table 3.8 are based on an analysis of the number of ELLs tested, the number of ELLs excluded or exempted, and the total number of ELLs enrolled by grade for each state and test. In some states, ELLs take tests that are intended exclusively for ELLs as well as regular state tests. For example, in Texas, students take the Reading Proficiency Test in English (RPTE) and the Texas Assessment of Academic Skills (TAAS).

Given the total number of ELLs enrolled in the grade assessed and the total number of ELLs tested in the grade assessed, it is possible to calculate participation rates. However, because not all examinees' scores are included in performance reports, it also is important to examine the number and percentage of ELL scores included in reports of standard and nonstandard administrations as well as the number not tested.

When a state fails to report the total number of ELLs in a grade, the meaning of the number of students not tested is unclear. Of the 19 states that reported performance data, only a few reported information for ELLs for all state tests: 2 states, Massachusetts and Wisconsin, reported the number enrolled; 13 states—California, Colorado, Delaware, Idaho, Illinois, Indiana, Kentucky, Louisiana, Maine, Massachusetts, New Jersey, Texas, and Wisconsin—reported the number tested; and 5 states—Colorado, Kentucky, Massachusetts, Texas, and Wisconsin—reported the number not tested. Only 4 states—Massachusetts, North Carolina, Texas, and Wisconsin—appeared to account for all ELLs by reporting the total number of ELLs enrolled and tested. Two of these states—North Carolina and Texas—reported all three criteria for at least some state tests: (a) total ELLs by grade, but not necessarily defined by eligibility; (b) total not tested, and (c) total tested. Massachusetts and Wisconsin met these same three criteria for all of their state tests.

TABLE 3.8

States Reporting by Total in Grade and Total Tested or Not Tested

State	Reported Total ELLs Enrolled in Grade		Reported Total ELLs Tested		Reported Total ELLs Not Tested		Reported as Enrolled and Tested	
	On Some Tests	On All Tests	On Some Tests	On All Tests	On Some Tests	On All Tests	On Some Tests	On All Tests
CA	✓			✓				
CO				✓		✓		
DE				✓				
FL			✓					
ID				✓				
IL				✓	✓			
IN				✓				
KY				✓		✓		
LA				✓				
ME				✓				
MA		✓		✓		✓		✓
NH					✓			
NJ				✓				
NC	✓		✓		✓		✓	
NM								
RI								
TX	✓			✓		✓	✓	
VA			✓		✓			
WI		✓		✓		✓		✓
Total	3	2	3	13	4	5	2	2

The reasons students were reported as exempt were sometimes unclear in the state reports. Reasons included lack of time (in years) in the United States, low language proficiency, or inadequate language proficiency for taking a state test. If a report did not specify total numbers of ELLs by grade, it did not account for all students, and the data reported were considered incomplete. Whether all scores were included in reporting also is important, because some states did not count students who took tests with nonstandard testing accommodations.

Two states had notations in their reports regarding the inclusion and exclusion of certain students' scores. California reported that all data excluded special accommodation students except the data for the special education population. Wisconsin noted that some ELLs were excluded from taking the third-grade reading test, the Wisconsin Reading Comprehension Test, because of issues of language proficiency.

Some states came close to meeting the criteria of accounting for all students by reporting the number of students tested with detailed exemption data for both the regular test and an accommodated test responsive to the linguistic and cultural needs of ELLs (e.g., native language test). However, some uncertainty still remains. Although states that reported on the total number of students not tested or exempted provided some data on the number of students who did not take a test, these states did not necessarily clearly present the actual number of ELLs in a grade that possibly could have taken the test. For example, in some states, ELLs were not included in a not-tested category because the students were not considered eligible to take the test.

Many states did not provide explanatory notes on the inclusion of all scores in their reports. Most often reports that included notes addressed the fact that some scores were excluded because of special circumstances such as special education status or accommodated testing.

The study team found that of the 19 states that reported performance data, 16 explicitly reported participation data. For Colorado and Illinois, the study team was able to calculate participation data by combining data within a state report.

For Colorado, the research team calculated the total ELLs for Spanish and other languages tested by combining data from two language proficiency categories—non-English speaker and limited-English speaker—reported by the state. Colorado's results were reported by students' language proficiency as follows: (a) Spanish, non-English speaker; (b) Spanish, limited-English speaker; (c) Other (language), non-English speaker; (d) Other, limited English speaker; (e) Spanish, fluent-English speaker; (f) Other, fluent English speaker; and (g) students for whom native language background was unknown. For Illinois, the research team totaled the number of ELLs tested by taking grade-level test results reported for "downstate" and "Chicago" and combining these to calculate a state total.

Participation Reporting Categories

Categories used in reporting participation included proficiency in a language other than English, time spent in the district or school, program services such as ESL or bilingual, special education services, former ELL status, gender, race, and socioeconomic status (SES). As shown in Table 3.9, 16 of the 19 states reported the number of ELLs participating in state assessment. Six of the 19 states—California, Colorado, Delaware, Florida, Illinois, and Texas—reported participation data of ELLs tested for a number of additional categories.

Of the six states that reported participation by additional conditions, two states, Texas and Colorado, reported results by language background/fluency. For Texas, a report provided data on ELLs by language background, grouping students by Spanish and other languages for participation and performance. Colorado reported ELL data according to the following categories: Spanish, non-English speaker; Spanish, limited-English speaker; Spanish, fluent English speaker; Other (language), non-English speaker; Other, limited-English speaker; Other, fluent English speaker; and language data invalid or not provided.

Four states—California, Colorado, Florida, and Texas—reported state assessment data by time factors (e.g., time in district). Colorado reported the results for ELLs by time in district and time in school for both the native language state test intended for ELLs and for the general English language state assessment(s).

Three states—Colorado, Delaware, and Texas—reported ELL test results by the type of program. Texas reported participation data by ESL or bilingual program services; and Colorado and Delaware reported ELL participation in state assessment reports by special education programming status. Reports from three states—California, Florida, and Illinois—provided data that designated students as former LEP, transitioned students, and exited ESL student. One state (Delaware) reported ELL data by race, gender, and SES.

Reporting on Exempted Students

To understand the degree to which state reports accounted for all ELLs enrolled for the grade level(s) tested, the research team examined the extent to which reports accounted for ELLs not tested and those exempted. The analysis identified only eight states that reported on ELLs not tested or exempted. Although all eight states—Colorado, Kentucky, Massachusetts, New Hampshire, North Carolina, Texas, Virginia, and Wisconsin—categorized exempted students according to language proficiency level, the states varied in the reasons for exempting ELLs. Table 3.10 presents the categories that account for only those ELLs not tested or exempt.

The manner in which states reported data sometimes made it difficult to discern the reason for exemption. For example, some states reported

TABLE 3.9

Report Categories Indicating Participation of ELLs in State Assessments

| State | Total ELLs Tested | Other Categories Used to Report ELL Participation Data | | | | |
		Language/ Fluency	Time	Type of Program	Former ELL Status	Gender/ Race/SES
CA	✓		✓		✓	
CO	✓	✓	✓	✓		
DE	✓			✓		✓
FL	✓		✓		✓	
ID	✓					
IL	✓				✓	
IN	✓					
KY	✓					
LA	✓					
MA	✓					
ME	✓					
NC	✓					
NH						
NJ	✓					
NM						
RI						
TX	✓	✓	✓	✓		
VA	✓					
WI	✓					
Total	16	2	4	3	3	1

an "ELL exempt" category but did not specify whether ELL status was the reason for exemption or whether this was a more general category that included all ELLs exempted for various reasons (e.g., absence, parent refusal). Only four states—Colorado, North Carolina, Texas, and Wisconsin—stated specific reasons for the exemption of ELLs in state assessment reports.

TABLE 3.10

Report Categories for Exempted ELLs

	Exempt by ELL Status		Exempt for Other Reasons Not Distinguished by ELL Status				
State	Not Tested/ Excluded	Other Language[a]	Parent Refusal	Absence	Special Education Designation	Test Invalid/ Not Completed	Other Reasons
CO	✓	✓	✓		✓	✓	
KY	✓						✓
MA	✓						✓
NC	✓			✓	✓		✓
NH	✓						
TX	✓	✓		✓	✓		✓
VA	✓						✓
WI	✓		✓				
Total	8	2	2	2	3	1	5

[a]Exempt due to lack of proficiency in a language other than English for a native language test.

Some state reports demonstrated peculiarities. Kentucky reported ELL exemptions for other reasons but did not define "other." Massachusetts listed its other reasons for ELLs not being tested in the ITBS reading assessment across several reporting categories including absence, not meeting test participation criteria (even with accommodations), and not being recommended for regular education the following school year. North Carolina reported the number of ELL special education students excluded by disability, as did Texas under the special education category of admission, review, and dismissal exempt. Texas, in addition to reporting ELL exempt, reported another "not tested" category that the report did not define. Virginia reported a more general category that grouped together refusals, disruptive behavior, and an undefined "other" category.

Types of Scores Reported

States are required by Title I to report assessment scores relative to state standards. In the 2001 reauthorization, it was clarified that states had to set at least three levels of proficiency (basic, proficient, and advanced), and report on performance within these levels. In examining the types of scores reported for ELLs, two questions of interest were explored by the research team: (a) whether reports that included ELLs reported the same score data as for monolingual students, and (b) whether partial score data from ELL test takers (i.e., examinees who took some but not all parts of an assessment) were included in calculating aggregated and disaggregated scores.

As shown in Table 3.11, of the 19 states reporting ELL data for the 1999–2000 school year, 17 reported performance levels. Eleven reported

TABLE 3.11

Score Reporting Categories

States	Performance Level 3 or more	Performance Level Fewer than 3	Indexes on Average Performance Mean, % Correct, Mean Scaled Score, Average, NCE, or NPR
CA			✓
CO	✓		
DE	✓		✓
FL		✓	
ID	✓		✓
IL	✓		
IN		✓	✓
KY	✓		✓
LA	✓	✓	✓
MA	✓		✓
ME	✓		✓
NC	✓	✓	✓
NH		✓	
NJ		✓	✓
NM		✓	
RI		✓	
TX	✓	✓	✓
VA			✓
WI	✓		
Total	11	9	12

Note. NCE=normal curve equivalent; NPR=national percentile rank.

three or more performance levels; 9 reported fewer than three performance levels. Twelve states used a variety of indexes, including mean, scaled scores, averages, normal curve equivalents (NCEs), or national percentile rank (NPR) to report average student performance. Because states supported several different kinds of assessments, in some cases, performance data were reported in more than one category.

One state (Florida) reported ELL data by the percentage of students at Level 3 and above on the Florida Comprehensive Assessment Test, even though it has five levels of performance. Four states—Kentucky, New Hampshire, New Jersey, and Virginia—provided specific information about whether the reports included only students who took all parts of the state assessment. Whereas Kentucky and New Hampshire only reported performance data for those students who took the entire state tests, New Jersey and Virginia reported performance results for students who took portions or subjects within tests and the total battery. The analysis also revealed that states took a variety of approaches to reporting on accommodated tests.

Accommodated Tests

Providing accommodated tests is a typical strategy used by states to include ELLs. Accommodations are intended to allow ELLs access to the content of state assessments without providing them with an unfair advantage over their monolingual peers. Only a handful of specific accommodations have been developed to address the unique cultural and linguistic needs of ELLs. Rivera, Stansfield, Scialdone, and Sharkey (2000) pointed out in their school year 1998–1999 study of state practices that linguistic accommodations that use the native language of the student are a type of accommodation that might allow certain ELLs direct access to the test by removing language barriers that interfere with ELLs' ability to access test content. Other forms of linguistic accommodations that might be appropriate for ELLs include use of English language glossaries, explanation of directions in English or the native language, or clarification of words on the test in English.

Because of the long-standing state practice of allowing accommodations designed for students with disabilities, the 1994 legislative impetus to include ELLs in state assessments for purposes of accountability prompted many states simply to borrow accommodations from those typically used for students with disabilities and apply them to ELL testing. This practice fails to acknowledge and accommodate the unique linguistic and cultural needs of ELLs.

The research team examined state reports to assess the extent to which the data reported separated accommodations for ELLs from accommodations for students with disabilities. Of particular interest to the research team was the extent to which disaggregated ELL performance data were reported for those tested under accommodated conditions.

As shown in Table 3.12, there were some inconsistencies in the reporting of accommodations for ELLs with and without disabilities. California noted on its SABE report that all assessment data excluded students using special accommodations except for the report for special education students. California is included in Table 3.12 because the SABE is a Spanish test and those included in the special education report are ELLs with disabilities who might have received accommodations. The state,

TABLE 3.12

ELLs' Participation and Performance Under Accommodated Test Conditions

| | | Accommodated Conditions | | | | |
| | | On State Assessment(s) | | On Native Language Test(s) | | Other Information on Test Conditions Included |
State	Test(s)	Participation	Performance	Participation	Performance	
CA	SABE Special Education Report					✓
CO	CSAP Lectura and Escritura			✓	✓	
IN[a]	ISTEP English and Math	✓	✓			
MA	MCAS					✓
NCa,[b]	Computer Skills, End-of-Course Tests, Grade 3 Pretest	✓				✓
VA[a]	VSAP SAT-9					✓
Total		2	1	1	1	4

[a]No native language test. [b]ELL-specific data only reported for Computer Skills Test.

however, did not indicate that it included the scores of ELLs tested in accommodated conditions who were not in special education.

Colorado not only reported by accommodated condition, but by specific accommodations used for both its English and Spanish versions. However, like California, it did not report on ELLs with accommodations in its English version of the CSAP. For the Spanish versions of its test, only the scores of those ELLs with special education accommodations were reported.

Indiana was the only state that reported disaggregated performance data for accommodated and nonaccommodated ELLs. North Carolina only reported aggregated accommodation data for ELLs and ELLs who received special education services. Virginia clearly noted that all non standard accommodations had been removed from its reporting summary, including its disaggregated ELL data on the SAT-9, so the reader was made aware that the ELL performance report did not necessarily include all ELLs tested.

Only two states, Colorado and North Carolina, reported performance data by the type of accommodation used. Although Colorado reported by accommodated condition used for the English CSAP, the Colorado report aggregated data for ELLs and ELLs with disabilities. North Carolina also reported by test accommodations but did not disaggregate data by ELL status on all tests with accommodated conditions reported (i.e., end-of-course tests and the Grade 3 pretest).

As described next, two states, Colorado and North Carolina, reported performance for accommodated assessments. The first state, Colorado, reported these accommodations for ELLs on a Spanish version test, suggesting that it also disaggregated ELLs with disabilities in its ELL report.

Colorado: Braille version, large-print version, teacher-read directions, scribe, signing, assistive communication device, extended/modified timing. (For the Grade 3 Lectura, oral presentation is also allowed as an accommodation).

On the other hand, North Carolina reported accommodations for its regular test with special education accommodations and one that sounded appropriate for ELLs with the mention of a native language dictionary.

North Carolina: Braille edition, large-print version, assistive technology, Braille writer, Cranmer abacus, dictation to scribe, interpreter signs test, magnification devices, student marks in test book, test administrator reads test aloud, use of typewriter or word processor, hospital/home testing, multiple test sessions, scheduled extended time, testing in a separate room, English/native language dictionary/electronic translator (end-of-course tests and Grade 3 pretest).

In the actual report it is not possible to separate performance with a native language dictionary because it is grouped with English dictionary and electronic translator.

It is important on the one hand to recognize that some ELLs have disabilities, so accommodations fitting special education and ELL populations are both expected and appropriate in reporting accommodations for those students. In fact, very few states reported performance by accommodations used for this smaller subset of students, so this is to be encouraged because it provides further information about ELLs with disabilities. However, for performance reported on tests that do not clarify the test-taking population, the decision to group accommodations for ELLs with those of students with disabilities is not appropriate and potentially perpetuates a perception that a student's lack of proficiency in a language is itself a kind of disability. Accommodations offered to ELLs as well as ELLs with disabilities should be those that appropriately address their individual needs; these should be reported in a manner that respects those differences.

Native Language Tests

A challenge for the research team was to identify clearly native language tests. Because reports did not always designate the test name, it was not always clear which tests were native language versions of standard state tests.

Although four states—California, Colorado, Massachusetts and Texas—publicly reported information on state native language assessments, the type of translated assessments offered as well as the content areas and grade levels tested varied across the four states. Table 3.13 provides descriptions of the translated tests supported in the four states.

ELL Participation and Performance in Native Language Tests

Table 3.14 provides the native language content tested for states that reported participation and performance data. Those content areas included reading, mathematics, language, spelling, writing, science and technology, history, and social science. Massachusetts aggregated performance data for ELLs across the native language and the English language tests. In contrast, three states—California, Colorado, and Texas—disaggregated performance data for ELLs by subject area.

Table 3.15 illustrates the extent to which states reported participation of ELLs on native language tests. Table 3.15 shows that for each test com-

TABLE 3.13

Native Language Assessments Offered in School Year 1999–2000

State	*Description of Native Language Assessment—State Practices for Reporting on ELL Assessments*

CA — The Spanish Assessment of Basic Education, Second Edition (SABE/2) is a native language achievement test required for Spanish speakers who have been in California public schools less than 12 months.

The SABE/2 STAR is a multiple-choice test that allows comparisons to a national sample of Spanish-speaking students.... The only exemptions allowed were for special education students whose Individual Education Plans (IEPs) explicitly exempted them from such testing and ... for students whose parent or guardian submitted a written request for exemption. Students were tested using SABE/2 STAR in Reading, Language, Mathematics, and Spelling (grades 2–8 only).... Scores associated with Immersion students as well as the optional grades and subtests/subject areas were not reported for countrywide and statewide aggregations, and will not appear on this website (California Department of Education, 2000).

SABE/2 norms include Hispanic reference-group norms for Grades 1–12, spring and fall, and national norms for all grades and times of year for reading and mathematics. SABE/2 norms are based on a national sample of students taking an English language achievement test. These national norms facilitate situations in which comparable scores are needed regardless of language (CTB/McGraw-Hill, 2001).

CO — Colorado Student Assessment Program (CSAP) Lectura and Escritura. Colorado's Spanish native language tests in reading and writing for Grades 3 and 4 are based on the English CSAP reading and writing tests for the grades. The English CSAP is described as follows:

CSAP ... is a test designed to measure student achievement in relationship to the Colorado Model Content Standards. These standards are expectations specifying what students should know at particular points in their education. As a result, CSAP provides a series of snapshots of student achievement in reading, writing, math, and science as they move through grades 3–10 (Colorado Department of Education, n.d.).

MA — The Massachusetts Comprehensive Assessment System (MCAS) is available in Spanish translation for math, science, and history/arts tests.

English-version tests: LEP students in the tested grades must take the MCAS tests in English in all content areas if the student is recommended for regular education for the following school year or has been enrolled in school in the United States for more than 3 years.

Spanish/English Tests: Spanish-speaking LEP students enrolled in schools in the continental United States for 3 or fewer years must participate in the Spanish/English mathematics, science and technology/engineering, and history and social science MCAS tests if the student continues to receive either instruction in a transitional bilingual education program or English as a second language support in the 2001–2002 school year and the student can read and write at or near grade level in Spanish. If students do not satisfy these criteria to take either the English-version or Spanish/English MCAS, they are not required to take MCAS tests, but can participate at their discretion (Massachusetts Department of Education, n.d.).

TX   Texas Assessment of Academic Skills (TAAS). This is the Spanish translated test for Texas:

TAAS measures the statewide curriculum in reading and mathematics at grades 3 through 8 and the exit level; in writing at grades 4, 8, and the exit level; and in science and social studies at grade 8. Spanish-language version TAAS tests are administered at grades 3 through 6. Satisfactory performance on the TAAS exit-level tests is prerequisite to a high school diploma. (Texas Education Agency, 2001).

TABLE 3.14

Participation and Performance of ELLs in Native Language Tests by Content and Grades Tested

State	CA	CO		MA			TX		
Test	SABE/2	CSAP		MCAS, Spanish Version			TAAS, Spanish Version		
Content	Reading, Math, Lang, Spelling	Lectura Reading	Escritura Writing	Math	Science & Tech	History & Social Science	Reading	Math	Writing
Grade	2–11	3–4	4	4, 8, 10	4, 8, 10	8	3–6	3–6	4
Participation	Yes	Yes	Yes	Yes[a]			Yes		
Performance	Yes	Yes	Yes	No[a]			Yes		

[a]Reported with English version.

Note: Only the MCAS—Native Language Version and the Spanish version of the TAAS were clearly noted in state documents as being direct translations of state tests. This does not mean that the CSAP Lectura and Escritura tests are not direct translations, but that this was not confirmed in assessment documents

TABLE 3.15

States' Reporting ELL Participation and Performance for Native Language Tests

State	California		Colorado		Texas			Massachusetts		
Test	SABE		CSAP		TAAS			MCAS Translated		
	Reading	Math	Lectura	Escritura	Lectura	Math	Escritura	Math	Science	History /Arts
ELLs enrolled	No	No	No	No	No	No	No	Yes	Yes	Yes
ELLs tested	Yes	Yes	Yes	Yes	Yes	Yes	Yes	No	No	No
ELL performance reported	Yes[a]	Yes[a]	Yes	Yes	Yes	Yes	Yes	—	—	—

Note. ELL performance data for Massachusetts are not disaggregated.

[a]California reported the percentage of students who scored above the 75th national percentile rank.

ponent, three of the four states that reported performance also reported on the number of students tested. However, none of these states had both enrollment data and the number tested for each grade, information that is necessary to arrive at participation rates for these tests. Massachusetts provided enrollment data for all test components but did not identify the number of ELLs tested because the state aggregated the scores of native language test takers with those of students who took the English MCAS.

Summary of Findings

Overall, taking into account participation reporting criteria, only a small number of states (eight) reported totals for ELLs tested or not tested for all or some state tests—Colorado, Kentucky, Massachusetts, North Carolina, New Hampshire, Texas, Virginia, and Wisconsin. In four of the eight states—Massachusetts, North Carolina, Texas, and Wisconsin—ELLs were accounted for on all or some tests by reporting: (a) total ELLs enrolled by grade, (a) total ELLs tested, and (c) total ELLs not tested. Only two states, Massachusetts and Wisconsin, appeared to have done this for all state tests.

Although only a few states reported full participation information, states did report data by a variety of factors including ELL status, type of program, proficiency in a language other than English, time factors, former ELL status, and other categories. Some states did not report totals for ELLs tested, but rather reported information across several proficiency categories or by geographic areas (e.g., downstate or major city area), a circumstance that required the research team to calculate state totals.

Two states, Texas and Colorado, reported Spanish language test results, but grouped all other ELL language groups into one category. These and other states (e.g., California, Delaware, and Florida) integrated other factors into disaggregated ELL performance reports, including type of language service, time factors, former ELL status, race, gender, and SES.

States also used various methods to report data on students who were exempted or not tested. Some states reported information by ELL status, and several of these gave specific reasons why ELLs were not tested (e.g., parent decision, absence, special education categories). For states that administered tests for ELLs in languages other than English, exemption information also was reported for students who did not take the native language test because of lack of proficiency in the native language (e.g., the number of ELLs not tested on Colorado's Lectura because of a lack of proficiency in Spanish). Still, when some states reported the number of ELLs not tested, it was not always clear whether the reason for not being tested was because of ELL status, language proficiency in the native language, absence, or some other reason.

States often reported scores by the three Title I mandated levels of proficiency, although some reported by fewer than three levels or simply reported the percentage of tested students who met the standard. NRT score data tended to be reported by scaled scores, NCEs, NPR, and so on, although a few states also reported NRT score data by performance levels. Some states reported partial test taker information.

States often did not report specifics such as participation rates, performance, or types of accommodations used for students who were tested in accommodated conditions. Two states that did report on accommodations used did not clarify which students were included in the category. For example, Colorado reported a combined category of all students who used accommodations on the CSAP, and on the CSAP Lectura and Escritura reported performance that did not differentiate between ELLs and ELLs with disabilities. Three states reported participation and performance data for native language tests.

REPORTING BY STATES WITH LARGE AND SMALL ELL STUDENT POPULATIONS

Sizes and percentages of ELL populations vary greatly from state to state. It is therefore reasonable to conjecture that there is a relationship between the size of a state's ELL population and the extent to which the state reports ELL assessment data separately from those of mainstream students. This part addresses whether differential reporting occurs based on the size of states' ELL student population.

Although large concentrations of ELLs often reside in more populous cities, Fleischman and Hopstock (1993) found that approximately 24% of the school districts in the United States served nine or fewer ELLs. Only 8% of the school districts served 1,000 or more ELLs. It is therefore important to examine the extent to which states with high and low ELL student enrollment report disaggregated ELL data on state reports.

States With Large ELL Populations[7]

The ten states with the largest K–12 ELL population, by numbers of ELLs, were California, Texas, Florida, New York, Illinois, Arizona, New Mexico, Colorado, Washington, and New Jersey. Among these states, as shown in Table 3.16, three states—Arizona, New York, and Washington—provided no performance assessment data for ELLs. Three states—Florida, New Mexico, and New Jersey—provided disaggregated ELL performance data for some assessments. Four states—California, Colorado, Illinois, and Texas—provided disaggregated data for all state tests.

As shown in Table 3.16, 5 of the 10 states with the highest percentages of ELLs—Alaska, Arizona, New York, Oregon, and Utah—reported no state level performance data for ELLs. Two states, Florida and New Mexico, reported disaggregated data for some but not for all state tests. Three states—California, Colorado, and Texas—reported disaggregated data for all state tests. In sum, the states with high percentages of ELLs reported fewer disaggregated state tests overall compared to the 10 states with the largest ELL populations.

---

[7]Data are from the annual survey of state education agencies, which ranked states by ELL student enrollment for the 1999–2000 school year. This document is maintained by the NCELA (2002).

TABLE 3.16

**Reporting of ELL Data in States With the Largest Numbers
and Percentages of ELLs**

State	Rank	No. ELLs	% ELLs	% Rank	No Tests Disaggregated	Some Tests Disaggregated	All Tests Disaggregated
AK	14	19,721	14.8	3	✓		
AZ	6	125,311	14.7	4	✓		
CA	1	1,480,527	24.9	1			✓
CO	8	60,031	8.5	9			✓
FL	3	235,181	9.9	7		✓	
IL	5	143,855	7.1				✓
NJ	10	49,847	3.9			✓	
NM	7	76,661	23.6	2		✓	
NV[a]	13	40,469	12.4	6	—	—	—
NY	4	228,730	8.0	10[b]	✓		
OR	11	43,845	8.0	10[b]	✓		
TX	2	554,949	13.9	5			✓
UT	12	41,306	8.6	8	✓		
WA	9	55,709	5.6		✓		
Total states reporting ELL test data					6	3	4

Note. Fourteen states are listed in the table because the 10 states with the largest ELL population did not correspond perfectly with the 10 states with the largest percentages of ELLs.

[a]Nevada had no data available for 1999–2000.

[b]Denotes a tie in rank.

States With Small ELL Populations

Reporting practices of the 10 states with the smallest number of ELLs enrolled were examined. These states, in rank order, were Vermont, West Virginia, Mississippi, Wyoming, Delaware, New Hampshire, Maine, Montana, Kentucky, and District of Columbia. As shown in Table 3.17, these states either reported data for ELLs on all or no state tests. Four states—Delaware, New Hampshire, Maine, and Kentucky—reported ELL

TABLE 3.17

**Reporting of ELL Data by States With the Smallest
Numbers and Percentages of ELLs**

State	Rank	No. ELLs	% ELLs	Rank	No Tests Disaggregated	Some Tests Disaggregated	All Tests Disaggregated
AL	14	7,260	1.0	8	✓		
DC	10	5,177	6.7	16	✓		
DE	5	2,284	2.0	13			✓
KY	9	4,847	.7	3			✓
LA	11	6,906	.9	4[a]			✓
ME	7	2,748	1.3	12			✓
MO	15	10,238	1.1	9	✓		
MS	3	1,799	.4	1[a]	✓		
MT	8	4,016	2.6	15	✓		
NH	6	2,471	1.2	10[a]			✓
OH	12	16,841	.9	4[a]	✓		
SC	13	5,577	.9	4[a]	✓		
TN	16	11,039	1.2	10[a]	✓		
VT	1	936	.9	4[a]	✓		
WV	2	1,039	.4	1[a]	✓		
WY	4	2,253	2.4	14	✓		
Total states reporting ELL test data					11	0	5

Note. Sixteen states are listed in the table because the 10 states with the smallest ELL population did not correspond perfectly with the 10 states with the smallest percentages of ELLs.

[a]Denotes a tie in rank.

data for all tests. The remaining states among the lowest 10 ranked by number reported no ELL data—District of Columbia, Mississippi, Montana, Vermont, West Virginia, and Wyoming.

States with the smallest percentages of K–12 ELLs were Mississippi, West Virginia, Kentucky, Louisiana, Ohio, South Carolina, Vermont, Alabama, Missouri, New Hampshire, and Tennessee. With the exception of Louisiana, New Hampshire, and Kentucky, which reported performance data for all tests, the remaining eight states with the smallest percentages of ELLs provided no data for ELLs.

Summary of Findings on Reporting and ELL Student Population Size

States with the largest ELL student populations, whether measured by numbers or percentages, were more likely to report and disaggregate test score data than were states with the smallest ELL student populations. Nevertheless, some states with large ELL student populations (e.g., New York, Arizona, Washington, and Oregon) reported no ELL assessment data, and several states with small ELL student populations (e.g., Delaware, New Hampshire, Maine, Kentucky, and Louisiana) reported ELL performance data for all tests. Overall, however, the percentages of states that reported ELL assessment data were relatively low in both sets of states. Specifically, in the 14 states with the largest populations or percentages of ELLs, 50% reported no ELL test data; this percentage counts Nevada as not reporting data because it did not have data for the 1999–2000 school year at the time that this study was conducted. In the 16 states with the lowest numbers or percentages of ELLs, 62% reported no test data.

States with fewer ELLs are in greater need than are states with larger ELL populations of improving reporting practices for ELL assessment data. States with smaller numbers of K–12 ELLs face different challenges than those faced by states with larger populations of K–12 ELLs. Although states with smaller ELL populations have fewer students for whom to track progress, these states might have an inclination to think that because ELLs account for such a small portion of the overall school age population, it might not be worth the effort to disaggregate their performance. These states also differ in their need to maintain the privacy of students in reporting data if their numbers are few. States with larger ELL student populations have most likely realized the importance of tracking ELLs' progress and are more likely to have organized state databases to identify those students who are ELLs. Still, the large numbers of students might make the logistics of tracking and entering data more difficult.

CONTENT AREA ASSESSMENT: PARTICIPATION AND PERFORMANCE OF ELLS

IASA required states to include ELLs in state assessments and to report disaggregated student data. NCLB has further strengthened the legislative requirements related to ELLs by requiring states to report disaggregated ELL assessment results as part of state accountability systems. According to NCLB, states must include and report disaggregated performance data for ELLs in the areas of reading and ELA and mathematics. By the 2005–2006 school year, states will be required to develop, implement, and report science assessment results for all students, including ELLs.

This section examines the extent to which states publicly reported participation and performance data for ELLs who took standard state assessments in reading, mathematics, and science in school year 1999–2000. As noted previously, participation data refers to the number of ELLs tested; participation rates refers to "the number of English language learners ... being assessed, expressed as a proportion or percentage of the total enrollment of ELLs" (Vincent & Schenck, 2001, p. 10). Performance data refers to data related to how well or poorly students performed on the assessment.

Participation Reported for Content Areas

The research team examined state assessment reports for reading, mathematics, and science to determine the extent to which states reported on the participation of ELLs for specific content areas. ELL participation data include the total number of ELLs tested, the total number of ELLs per grade level, and the total number of ELLs excluded or exempted from the tests for reading, mathematics, and science.

As shown in Table 3.18, 16 of the 19 states that provided ELL performance data also reported ELL participation rates for state reading and mathematics assessments. When participation rates were not provided explicitly in state reports, at times other data were provided that permitted the percentage of ELLs tested at each grade level to be calculated.

Four states—Maine, Massachusetts, North Carolina, and Wisconsin—reported the number of students enrolled at each grade level tested. However, these state reports provided different levels of clarity with regard to ELL data. The Massachusetts report was the most direct in providing ELL participation data; it reported the number and percentage of ELLs scoring at different levels by grade with enrollment by grade. The Maine, North Carolina, and Wisconsin state reports either did not report data by subject area or presented the data in such a way that the research team had to combine data within a content area to determine participation data.

For Maine, the percentage of ELLs tested was calculated by adding the number of ELL students tested to the number of ELL students excluded.

TABLE 3.18

States That Reported ELL Participation in Content Assessments

State	Reading Assessment — No. ELLs Enrolled by Grade	No. ELLs Tested	% ELLs Tested	Mathematics Assessment — No. ELLs Enrolled by Grade	No. ELLs Tested	% ELLs Tested	Science Assessment — No. ELLs Enrolled by Grade	No. ELLs Tested	% ELLs Tested
CA		✓			✓			✓	
CO		✓			✓			✓	
DE[a]		✓			✓				
FL[a]		✓			✓				
ID		✓			✓			✓	
IL		✓			✓			✓	
IN[a]		✓			✓				
KY		✓			✓			✓	
LA		✓			✓			✓	
ME[a]	✓	✓	✓	✓	✓	✓			
MA	✓	✓	✓	✓	✓	✓	✓	✓	✓
NH	—	—	—	—	—	—	—	—	—
NJ		✓			✓			✓	
NM	—	—	—	—	—	—	—	—	—
NC	✓	✓	✓	✓	✓	✓	✓	✓	✓
RI[a]	—	—	—	—	—	—			
TX		✓			✓			✓	
VA[a]		✓			✓				
WI	✓	✓	✓	✓	✓	✓	✓	✓	✓
Totals	4	16	4	4	16	4	3	11	3

Note.   Cells with dashes indicate that the state had a test but no data.

[a]State did not have science assessments.

The North Carolina report combined reading and mathematics data, so it was not possible to calculate the exact number of students who took the reading test versus the mathematics test. The Wisconsin report provided information regarding the number of ELLs enrolled, the percentage of ELLs enrolled who were tested, and the percentage of eligible ELLs tested. However, the number of ELLs performing at each proficiency level was not reported.

Performance data indicate actual participation, yet performance data in isolation do not allow for data cross-checks and are difficult to interpret. Three states—New Hampshire, New Mexico, and Rhode Island—reported performance data but did not report participation data. These three states are shown in Table 3.18 as having unreported ELL participation data in reading, mathematics, and science assessments.

The research team also examined state reports to determine the extent to which participation data for ELLs were provided for state assessments in science. Table 3.18 shows that 11 of the 19 states reported ELL participation data in science by grade level; yet only 3 of the 11 states reported the number of students enrolled as well as the percentage of ELLs tested.

Content Area Assessment Performance

Sixteen states reported on the reading and mathematics performance of ELLs for one or more state assessments. However, the manner in which states reported performance varied in terminology and in the way scores were reported. States defined as few as two and up to as many as five proficiency levels to indicate student achievement relative to the standard. States used terms such as *passed/did not pass*, or *met/did not meet a defined standard*, *basic/proficient/advanced* or *well below the standard/below the standard/meets the standard/exceeds the standard/distinguished*. States also used other methods to report performance. Some states used standard scale scores (e.g., mean scale score, NCE, NPR), whereas others simply reported the percentage or average number correct. The variability in how states reported student performance made it difficult to compare reading and mathematics performance of ELLs across the states reporting data.

Despite the variations in the terms applied to performance levels, it was possible to identify a "proficient" level in the reports of each of the 16 states that reported on reading and mathematics performance. Some states used the term *passing* and others used the term *meeting standard*.

States that reported proficiency levels across content areas sometimes reported by grade and sometimes by level (e.g., elementary). In addition, the specific tests used measured different aspects of learning; that is, some were general achievement tests in reading, and others reflected the reading or ELA component of a graduation exam. With the variability and the fact that participation rates were either unknown or variable as well, few conclusions could be drawn.

In states where both performance data and participation rates were provided or could be calculated for specific content areas, it was possible to examine the relationships between participation and performance. Tables 3.19, 3.20, and 3.21 reveal that only one of the four states with both participation and performance data (North Carolina) did not report participation and performance for all state tests across all content areas. The tables indicate whether the state data included the percentage of ELLs tested and percentage who met standards and for what

TABLE 3.19

Reading: State Reporting on Participation Rates and Performance

State/Assessment	Grades Tested	% ELLs Tested	% ELLs Meeting Standard
Maine			
Reading	4, 8, 11	✓	✓
Massachusetts			
MCAS	4, 8, 10	✓	✓
North Carolina			
Pretest	3	✓	✓
End-of-grade[a]	3–8	✓	✓
End-of-course	High school	✓	✓
HSCT	High school	—	✓
Wisconsin			
WKCE	4, 8, 10	✓	✓
Reading Indicator	3	✓	✓

Note. Cells with dashes represent data not reported.

[a]The percentage tested for end-of-grade test was calculated by subtracting the percentage excluded from 100%.

TABLE 3.20

Math: State Reporting on Participation Rates and Performance

State/Assessment	Grades Tested	% ELLs Tested	% ELLs Meeting Standard
Maine			
Math	4, 8, 11	✓	✓
Massachusetts			
MCAS	4, 8, 10	✓	✓
North Carolina			
Pretest	3	✓	✓
End-of-grade[a]	3–8	✓	✓
End-of -course Alg I	High school	—	✓
End-of-course Alg II	High school	—	✓
HSCT	High School	—	✓
Wisconsin			
WKCE	4, 8, 10	✓	✓

Note. Cells with dashes represent data not reported.

[a]The percentage tested for the end-of-grade test was calculated by subtracting the percentage excluded from 100%. Reading and math are combined and reported as one score.

grades the data were reported for reading, math, and science, respectively.

National Percentile Rank Reporting

Five states reporting reading and math performance reported normative scores from NRTs. As Table 3.22 shows, national percentile rank was used by five states, making it the type of normative score used most frequently. Two states, California and Idaho, also reported normative scores for science assessments.

Summary of Findings

Despite the importance of reporting the progress of ELLs in reading and math, states reported relatively little data for the study period. Only four

TABLE 3.21

Science: State Reporting on Participation Rates and Performance

State/Assessment	Grades Tested	% ELLs Tested	% ELLs Meeting Standard
Massachusetts			
MCAS	4, 8, 10	✓	✓
North Carolina			
End-of-course			
Biology	High school	✓	✓
Chemistry	High school	✓	✓
Geometry	High school	✓	✓
Physical Science	High school	✓	✓
Physics	High school	✓	✓
Wisconsin			
WKCE	4, 8, 10	✓	✓

TABLE 3.22

Type of Normative Score Used by States That Reported Norm-Referenced Test Scores

State[a]	Test	Type of Score
CA	SAT-9	NPR of student score
DE	DSTP	NPR of scale score
ID	ITBS	NPR of average scale score
KY	CTBS	NPR of NCE
VA	SAT-9	NPR

Note. Table includes only those states that reported normative scores. Massachusetts is not included because MCAS is reported as performance levels. NPR = national percentile rank; NCE = normal curve equivalent.

[a]$n = 5$.

states—Maine, Massachusetts, North Carolina, and Wisconsin—provided sufficient information to determine the percentage of students who took the state tests. Although 16 states reported performance for at least one test, only 4 states reported adequate participation information to allow for full analysis of performance data. For science, of 11 states that reported performance levels, 3 reported both the percentage tested and performance of the students. These 3 states—Massachusetts, North Carolina, and Wisconsin—were among the 4 that provided the same information for reading and math.

STATEWIDE ALTERNATE ASSESSMENTS FOR ELLS AND ASSESSMENTS DESIGNED FOR ELLS

Alternate assessments are "assessments designed to measure the performance of students who are unable to participate in general large-scale assessments used by districts and states" (NCEO, 2001). These assessments were first legislated for students with disabilities in the 1997 reauthorization of the Individuals With Disabilities Education Act (IDEA). Prior to IDEA,[8] but perhaps accelerated by its enactment, state policy documents began to allow districts the option of using alternate assessment for ELLs.

Based on the requirements of IASA and reinforced by the NCLB, the rationale for states to use alternate test formats or structures for ELLs is to allow them access to standards-based assessments that are available to their monolingual peers.

Other assessments designed for ELLs might not be designated as alternates to regular state tests. These tests often focus on tracking growth in English language proficiency or emerging skills in academic content. Regardless of whether the test is an alternate or other test, with regard to score reporting, IASA and subsequent laws indicate that scores are to be disaggregated for ELLs. This part examines the extent to which states were responsive to IASA in reporting disaggregated assessment data for ELLs on alternate assessments for the 1999–2000 school year.

Findings

In a review of state assessment policies for the 1998–1999 school year, Rivera et al. (2000) reported that 15 states had a policy allowing the use of

---

[8]For example, in1988, the New Jersey Department of Education published *Special Review Assessment in the Native Language* designed for use by ELLs with limited English proficiency to attain a state-endorsed diploma.

alternate assessments. Six states' policies stipulated that ELLs who were exempted from regular state tests must be provided an alternate assessment. Olson et al. (2001) reported in the data report of the CCSSO survey of state assessment directors for the 1999–2000 school year that additional states intended to or were in the process of developing alternate assessments. NCEO (2001) also reported that some states were in the process of developing alternate assessments for ELLs.

The actual number of states that reported on alternate assessments for the 1999–2000 school year was one (Wisconsin), and the actual number of states that reported on other ELL-specific assessments was two (Illinois and Texas).

Wisconsin's state report referred to the Alternate Performance Indicators (APIs), which were used to assess some ELLs by means of an Alternate Portfolio. The state's policy regarding the use of APIs for ELLs is as follows:

> Students who are limited-English proficient (LEP) and at early levels of English proficiency are, by administrative rule, excluded from the Wisconsin Knowledge and Concepts Exam (WKCE) and the High School Graduation Test (HSGT). In addition, some LEP students at higher levels may be excluded, as individually and locally determined.

> While excluded students are learning English, it is especially important for them to make progress across all the content areas. *Alternate Performance Indicators* (APIs) were developed to provide these students, their parents, and their schools with information about student achievement in the content areas covered by the Wisconsin State Assessment System (WSAS). The APIs are aligned with the model academic standards in the WSAS content areas: English/language arts, mathematics, science, and social studies. For each performance standard in each standard of the four content areas, there are sample alternate performance indicators and sample performance activities and tasks for ELLs. The activities and tasks were designed for ongoing, informal classroom assessment. (Wisconsin Department of Education, n.d.)

Illinois used the Illinois Measure of Annual Growth in English (IMAGE) to measure the progress of ELLs in attaining the English-language reading and writing skills needed to achieve the Illinois Learning Standards. The IMAGE is administered annually to ELLs participating in their first, second, or third year of a state-approved bilingual education program (transitional bilingual education or transitional program of instruction). At the time of initial data collection, there was a 3-year time period when ELLs did not take the Illinois Standards Achievement Test (ISAT), a state assessment in reading, mathematics, and writing administered in Grades 3, 5, and 8 and

Grades 4 and 7 in social science and science, or the Prairie State Achievement Exam (PSAE), the state standard assessment in reading, mathematics, writing, science, and social science administered in Grade 11.

In addition, ELLs who enrolled in a district on October 1 or later of the school year could have been excused from state testing if their lack of English language proficiency prevented them from understanding the test (Illinois State Board of Education, 2001).

Texas's assessment reports included data for the Texas Reading Proficiency Tests in English (RPTE), a reading test designed for ELLs and first implemented in spring of 2000. According to the Texas Education Agency, ELLs were to take the RPTE regardless of whether they took the English or Spanish version of the regular state test, the Texas Assessment of Academic Skills (TAAS). Once a student achieved advanced level status on the RPTE, he or she no longer took the RPTE. As noted at that time by the Texas Education Agency,

> These tests are designed to measure annual growth in the English reading proficiency of second language learners, and are used along with English and Spanish TAAS to provide a comprehensive assessment system for limited English proficient (LEP) students. LEP students in Grades 3–12 are required to take the RPTE until they achieve a rating of advanced. (Texas Education Agency, 2001)

Based on the descriptions provided by the states, all three assessments have similar characteristics: (a) the assessments were developed for ELLs, and (b) each of the assessments referenced or suggested a standards base. However, only Wisconsin reported using standards-based alternate assessments in specific content areas. As practice has changed over time within the context of policy, the nature of these tests is changing. Some states continue to use tests as English language proficiency tests whereas others are shaping tests to function as standards-based alternates.

Data Reported for Alternate and ELL-Specific Assessments

States generally did not report participation rates of enrolled ELLs when reporting data. Table 3.23 presents ELL participation and performance data found in the state reports from Wisconsin (Alternate Portfolio), Illinois (IMAGE), and Texas (RPTE). As shown in Table 3.23, Wisconsin reported the number and percentage tested of ELLs enrolled and eligible to

TABLE 3.23

ELL Participation and Performance Data on Assessments Designed for ELLs

	Participation Data Reported			Performance Data Reported	
Grade	Enrolled	No. Tested	% Tested	Reading	Writing
Wisconsin: Alternate Portfolio					
(Reading, Math, Science, Social Studies)					
4, 8, 10	Yes	Yes	Yes	No data	
Illinois: IMAGE Reading & Writing[a]					
3	Yes	No	No		
4	Yes	No	No	Yes (Grades 3–5 together)	Yes (Grades 3–5 together)
5	Yes	No	No		
6	Yes	No	No	Yes (grades 6–8 together)	Yes (grades 6–8 together)
7	Yes	No	No		
8	Yes	No	No		
9–11	Yes	No	No	Yes (grades 9–11 together)	Yes (grades 9–11 together)
Texas: RPTE Reading[b]					
3–12	No	Yes	No	Yes	na

[a]*Expanding* and *transitioning* are terms utilized by the state that indicated proficient and above performance. [b]*Intermediate* and *advanced* are terms utilized by the state that indicated proficient and above performance. Texas numbers and percentages were calculated by adding ELL students reported across five time categories for each grade for the total for each grade (not counting students with no data) and then calculating percentage at grade level using the number of ELLs tested (i.e., not number of ELLs enrolled).

be tested. Illinois reported enrollment only, and did not report number or percentage tested. Texas reported number tested, but did not report enrollment nor percentage tested.

Wisconsin's Alternate Portfolio participation data were nearly complete. The state met almost all standards set forth for this study by reporting enrollment by grade, and the percentage of total enrolled that were tested by grade. It technically only needed to include the number tested at each proficiency level in its performance data.

For Illinois, the available data were not easy to interpret. For example, although Illinois reported enrollment figures by grade level, it reported performance by grade ranges. As a result, the number and percentage of students tested by grade are not provided and cannot be calculated from the available data. Illinois identified four levels of proficiency: beginning, strengthening, expanding, and transitioning. The highest two levels were classified as proficient or above.

The data presented for Texas in Table 3.23 are just some of the data that the state provided for the RPTE. The state also reported data that were disaggregated by the number of years students had been enrolled in U.S. schools.

Summary of Findings on ELL-Specific Assessments

In sum, only three states reported data for other assessments designed specifically for ELLs. Reported participation data generally were inadequate. The literature on reporting recommends that if a state reports the total number of eligible students, the state also should report on the number of students ineligible to take the test and include an explanation of which students were included in the state's participation index (Bielinski et al., 2001). The impact of such critical omissions is to make unclear many important factors, such as the difference between the total population of ELLs enrolled versus the percentage of the ELL population actually tested; how ELLs are progressing within the subgroup, as compared to other ELLs; and how and in what ways ELL participation and performance data compare with participation and performance data of their monolingual peers.

Each of the three states—Wisconsin, Illinois, and Texas—reported performance and participation data differently. Wisconsin, which had the only self-described standards-based alternate assessment, offered the most complete reporting, but could have reported the actual numbers of students tested rather than just the percentage of students at each proficiency level. Illinois, which had another type of ELL-specific alternate assessment, reported performance by grade range at four levels (beginning, strengthening, expanding, and transitioning). Texas reported both participation and performance data by grade and time in U.S. schools.

EFFECTIVE STATE REPORTING PRACTICES

IASA and NCLB underscore the importance of accurate and comprehensive public reporting of assessment data for all students, including ELLs.

Accurate, clear, complete, and comprehensive reporting of ELL achievement data require that state reporting include participation data (i.e., number and percentage of ELLs tested) and performance data (i.e., academic achievement data).

An examination of online and print-based state assessment reports offered insight into the extent to which states reported publicly ELL participation and performance data for the 1999–2000 school year. Although no single report offered an example of perfect reporting, aspects of these reports provide relevant examples for public reporting of the achievement of ELLs. Because more research has been generated around score reporting in the special education community, an examination of participation and performance reports for students with disabilities was used to provide insights into useful state reporting practices for ELLs (Bielinski et al., 2001; NCREL, 2000; Thompson, Thurlow, & Lazarus, 2001; Thurlow, Quenemoen, Thompson, & Lehr, 2001; Ysseldyke & Nelson, 1998).

This part of the study provides examples of effective state reports from print and Web-based reports collected for school years 1999–2000 and 1998–1999. Where applicable, limited aspects of the state reporting practices also are discussed. The examples are not intended to be representative of every state with a similar reporting practice but are presented to illustrate approaches to reporting ELL achievement data taken by the states examined in this study.

Print Reporting

Reporting Participation Data

Participation data—both number and percentage of students enrolled and students tested—are a key component in understanding the extent to which state assessment reports are inclusive of ELLs. States that present participation data that are disaggregated by subgroups within the ELL category provide further useful information for interpreting performance data.

The first example of a state report that provided ELL participation data is the TAAS. Table 3.24 shows Texas's report of the participation of ELLs of non-Spanish language background in the TAAS for spring of 2000. This particular report is taken from a special study report, *Study of Possible Expansion of the Assessment System for Limited English Proficient Students*. This is not a report produced annually, but was needed for the state's decision-making process regarding expanding the assessments for ELLs by,

TABLE 3.24

Sample Disaggregated Participation Data

TAAS Participation of LEP Students in Bilingual or ESL Programs Whose Primary Language Is Other Than Spanish Tested in English, LEP-Exempt, ARD-Exempt, Absent, Other Spring 2000 (Percentages Are Based on Total Number of Answer Documents Submitted)

Non-Hispanic LEP Students in Bilingual or ESL Programs	Total Answer Documents Bilingual/ESL	Not Tested in All Tests								Total Tested English	Tested/Total AD
		Absent	Absent/Total AD	ARD-Exempt	ARD-Exempt/Total AD	LEP Exempt	LEP Exempt/Total AD	Other Not Tested	Other Not Tested/Total AD		
Grade 3	3,160	11	0.3%	158	5.0%	834	26.4%	8	0.3%	2,149	68.0%
Grade 4	2,517	2	0.1%	105	4.2%	652	25.9%	165	6.6%	1,593	63.3%
Grade 5	2,192	8	0.4%	182	8.3%	693	31.6%	2	0.1%	1,307	59.6%
Grade 6	1,745	7	0.4%	123	7.0%	621	35.6%	2	0.1%	992	56.8%
Grade 7	1,317	2	0.2%	65	4.9%	595	45.2%	4	0.3%	651	49.4%
Grade 8[a]	1,331	1	0.1%	40	3.0%	520	39.1%	89	6.7%	681	51.2%
Grades 3–8	12,262	31	0.3%	673	5.5%	3,915	31.9%	270	2.2%	7,373	60.1%

Note.   Students included are those whom districts identified as having an ethnicity other than Hispanic and participating in a bilingual or ESL program. Students not identified as participating in one of these programs are not included. Percentages are based on total number of answered documents submitted.

ARD = admission, review, and dismissal: Special education term for committee that makes educational decisions; AD = answer documents. Total documents returned are used for the total number of students tested. Source: Texas Education Agency (2000a), *Study of Possible Expansion of the Assessment System for Limited English Proficient Students.*

[a]Grade 8 includes science and social studies data.

for example, adding Spanish language tests at more grade levels. The information presented on non-Spanish-speaking ELLs paralleled a table for Spanish-speaking ELLs. As shown, this report also included data on non-Hispanic students who did not participate in the English TAAS. The table specifies three reasons for nonparticipation: (a) absence, (b) ARD, and (c) Answer Documents (AD). ARD is a special education term for the committee that is assembled to make decisions about a student's special education progress, including participating in testing. The term AD is used for the total number of answer documents returned for a testing session and used as a substitute for total students tested.

Of note in this example is that the "not tested" categories of students are labeled clearly and the number and percentage of exempt students are provided. Weaknesses of the report include not providing the total number of all ELLs in the state, including Hispanic students, enrolled at each grade level tested. This information can be estimated by combining totals of students tested. However, because students can take both Spanish and English versions, duplication can occur that affects the accuracy of the totals. Another weakness was not providing the number of students who took only part of a test. In this case, it is not clear whether the cause was absence or other reasons (e.g., not taking the test because they had not received instruction in the content area).

The second example presented in Table 3.24 was selected because it illustrates how states can report aggregated ELL participation data for different content areas; this example is from a Massachusetts report for the 1999–2000 school year. As shown in Table 3.24, student populations were identified clearly and total numbers of students enrolled at each grade level and in each content area tested were provided.

A weakness of the report is that it does not specify the number of ELLs who took the Spanish version of the Massachusetts Comprehensive Assessment System (MCAS). Although the translated MCAS is aligned to measure the same content as the regular state assessment, it is important to be able to distinguish clearly between ELLs who took the English and translated versions of the test in relation to other student subgroups. This information is important on at least two levels: (a) the performance of ELLs taking the Spanish versus the English tests can be compared, and (b) clarity of the overall participation rates of the test allows the reader to discern patterns regarding the grades in which students are taking these tests over time.

Although it might not be practical or necessary to include all test use information in one table, for purposes of reporting it is nonetheless important on a report to note the number of ELLs who took a translated, accommodated, or alternate version of a test.

Whereas Table 3.25 shows aggregated participation data for Massachusetts's students at Grades 4, 8, and 10, Table 3.26 shows disaggregated ELL data for the same students. The strengths of Table 3.26 are (a) presentation of the number of students enrolled by grade for each content area tested

TABLE 3.25

Aggregated Participation Data for MCAS, Spring 2000

Grade Level	Number of Students Enrolled	Tested in English/ Language Arts	Tested in Mathematics	Tested in Science/ Technology	Tested in History/Social Science
Grade 4	80,633	94.4%	96.1%	96.0%	
Grade 8	75,333	92.3%	93.6%	93.4%	93.1%
Grade 10	66,080	90.7%	91.6%	90.9%	
Total	222,046	92.7%	93.9%	93.6%	

Note. Students tested include regular education students, students with disabilities, and LEP students. Enrollment figures presented here are based on the number of MCAS Student Identification Forms returned from each school. From Massachusetts Department of Education (2000). *The Massachusetts Comprehensive Assessment System, Spring 2000 MCAS Tests: Report of State Results.*

TABLE 3.26

Disaggregated ELL Participation Data for MCAS, Spring 2000

Grade	Number of Students Enrolled	Tested in English/ Language Arts	Tested in Mathematics	Tested in Science/ Technology	Tested in History/Social Science
Grade 4	3,415	56.8%	72.7%	72.6%	
Grade 8	1,940	32.8%	54.1%	53.0%	52.6%
Grade 10	2,067	21.8%	41.2%	40.7%	
Total	7,422	40.8%	59.0%	58.6%	

Note. Students tested include regular education students, students with disabilities, and LEP students. Enrollment figures presented here are based on the number of MCAS Student Identification Forms returned from each school. From Massachusetts Department of Education (2000). *Massachusetts Comprehensive Assessment System, Spring 2000 MCAS Tests: Report of State Results.*

and percentage tested by content area, and (b) naming of the source documentation (i.e., MCAS Student Identification Forms) from which the data are derived. In addition, the Massachusetts report provided supporting text explaining that the participation rate for some of the content area tests increased because the state offered English/Spanish versions of those tests. Although the state report indicated that offering the translated versions of the state tests had increased participation rates, it did not specify the number of students who took the translated MCAS.

Reporting Performance Data

Performance data refer to academic achievement data documented and reported publicly for one or more state assessments. Table 3.27, which presents Massachusetts's performance data, is a companion table to Tables 3.25 and 3.26, which presented aggregated and disaggregated ELL participation data, respectively. The discussion of strengths and limitations of Table 3.27 considers this table alone and in combination with the two preceding tables.

Table 3.27 represents scores clearly by showing the average scaled score (a raw score on a test converted to another scale [e.g., percentile rank or standard score]) for each group by content area by performance level. This specificity aids in interpreting the meaning of the scores. Table 3.27 also allows for a comparison across groups and across all students tested. For the purpose of computing school, district, and state results, those students who were absent on the day an MCAS test in a particular subject area was administered and lacked a medically documented excuse were assigned the minimum scaled score of 200 and a performance level of failing for the subject area. Although Table 3.27 gives the reader the percentage of students at each performance level, it does not give the number of students at each performance level. Decision makers who use such data likely would prefer to have the actual number of students tested appear in the same table as performance data to estimate more easily and cross-check more readily the number and percentage of students at each performance level.

Reporting Participation and Performance Data

A detailed report from Wisconsin presents participation and performance data for ELLs. Table 3.28 includes participation of ELLs by total enrolled, number of ELLs excluded or excused, and number of ELLs par-

TABLE 3.27

Disaggregated Performance Level Results for MCAS, Spring 2000, by Student Status: Grade 4 (Average Scaled Score and Percentage of Students at Each Performance Level)

Subject Area and Student Status Category	Scaled Score	Advanced	Proficient	Needs Improvement	Failing (Tested)	Failing (Absent)
Performance Level						
English language arts						
All Students	231	1	19	67	13	0
Regular	234	1	23	70	7	0
Students with disabilities	222	0	3	58	39	1
Limited English proficient	221	0	3	53	43	1
Mathematics						
All students	235	12	28	42	18	0
Regular	238	14	32	42	12	0
Students with disabilities	224	3	13	45	39	0
Limited English proficient	220	2	8	35	54	0
Science/ technology						
All students	241	11	51	30	8	0
Regular	244	13	56	27	5	0
Students with disabilities	233	3	34	45	18	0
Limited English proficient	223	1	13	45	41	0

Note. Percentages may not total 100 due to rounding. For the purpose of computing school, district, and state results, students who were absent without a medically documented excuse from any subject area MCAS test were assigned the minimum scaled score of 200 and a performance level of failing for that subject area. From Massachusetts Department of Education (2000). *The Massachusetts Comprehensive Assessment System, Spring 2000 MCAS Tests: Report of State Results.*

ticipating in an alternate assessment. It also reports performance categories for the percentage of ELLs enrolled and percentage eligible to be tested. However, Table 3.28 refers the reader to the district level to obtain performance data for students who took the alternate assessment. Under NCLB, this approach needs to be rethought. Alternate assessment results must be included as part of—not separate from—the reporting of participation and performance data for the WKCE state assessment.

Reports in Languages Other Than English

Table 3.29 provides performance results for the Spanish version of the 1999–2000 Texas TAAS. It is only the Spanish portion of a one-page report that included other data in English in another column. Because of space considerations, the other column is not reproduced here. As seen in Table 3.28, only certain aspects of the test results were reported in Spanish. Other subgroups were reported in English in a separate column (e.g., results by LEP, Bilingual, Title I).

Nationally, the extent to which score reports are provided in languages other than English is unknown; however, evidence from a few states suggested that these types of reports would become available soon after the time of this study, although not for all regular state tests. For example, Oregon currently has school report cards available online in Spanish for regular state tests. The Illinois report card Web site for regular state tests also has an option for school, district, and state report cards in Spanish for 2001 and 2002. In Minnesota, an online presentation about the Test of Emerging Academic English (TEAE) stated that plans were being made to translate the TEAE score explanation text into 12 languages.

Table 3.30 presents an example of a report from Kansas for school year 1998–1999 in which data were presented clearly for three student subgroups by grade tested. Although this example comes from a report that was not included in our analysis of ELL data because it was for the 1998–1999 school year, the report was the most recent one available at that time. The strengths of the report are that it provides assessment results disaggregated by number and percentage of students across four different performance levels. Similarly, within the same report document, ELL performance data were provided for each test by additional student characteristics, including SES, gender, and ethnicity. When data are disaggregated using multiple student characteristics, student achievement gaps between and among student subgroups can be detected more readily. The report is limited by its omission of information on overall en-

TABLE 3.28

Participation and Performance Data for ELLs Reported in the Same Table

Grade 4 Reading

Wisconsin State Proficiency Summary 1999–2000 Knowledge and Concepts Examinations
Advanced: Distinguished achievement. In-depth understanding of academic knowledge and skills tested. Proficient: Competent in the important academic knowledge and skills tested. Basic: Somewhat competent in the academic knowledge and skills tested. Minimal Performance: Limited achievement in the academic knowledge and skills tested.

| | Number Enrolled in Grade | | | | No WKCE, No Alternate Assessment | | Alternate Assessment Pre-Req Skill/Eng (Excluded WKCE[v]) | WKCE Proficiency Levels | | | | | | | |
| | | | | | | | | Minimal Perform | | Basic | | Proficient | | Advanced | |
	Total Enrolled	Excluded WKCE[v]	Excused by Parent[a]	Eligible[a] to Be Tested WKCE	% of Total Enrolled	% of Eligible[a] WKCE	% of Total Enrolled	% of Total Enrolled	% of Eligible[a] WKCE	% of Total Enrolled	% of Eligible[a] WKCE	% of Total Enrolled	% of Eligible[a] WKCE	% of Total Enrolled	% of Eligible[a] WKCE
Students in nationwide sample[b]	n/a	n/a	n/a	n/a	n/a	n/a	n/a	20	20	17	17	50	50	13	13
Students in Wisconsin public schools	64,802	2,491	91	62,220	2	2	4	5	5	12	12	63	65	15	15
Students not in district full academic year	5,593	350	16	5,227	3	3	6	7	7	14	15	59	63	12	12
Students in district full academic year	59,209	2,141	75	56,993	2	2	4	5	5	12	12	63	65	15	16
In single school	55,217	1,941	65	53,211	2	2	4	4	4	11	12	64	66	16	16

Not in single school	3,983	193	10	3,780	4	4	5	11	12	20	21	53	56	7	7
With disabilities attending another district	9	7	0	2	0	0	78	0	0	11	50	11	50	0	0
Results by demographic group (Wisconsin public schools)															
Students in Wisconsin public schools	64,802	2,491	91	62,220	2	2	4	5	5	12	12	63	65	15	15
Limited English proficient	2,273	890	2	1,381	5	9	39	6	9	17	28	32	53	1	1
English proficient	62,529	1,601	89	60,839	2	2	3	5	5	12	12	64	65	15	16
Migrant	27	9	0	18	7	11	33	0	0	7	11	44	67	7	11
Nonmigrant	64,775	2,482	91	62,202	2	2	4	5	5	12	12	63	65	15	15
Students with disabilities	8,594	1,701	44	6,849	7	8	20	16	20	20	25	34	43	3	3
Nondisabled	56,208	790	47	55,371	1	1	1	3	3	11	11	67	68	17	17
Economically disadvantaged	17,665	1,047	12	16,606	3	3	6	11	11	20	22	55	58	6	6
Not economically disadvantaged	47,137	1,444	79	45,614	1	1	3	3	3	9	9	66	68	18	19

[a]All students are eligible to participate in WKCE testing except students who are formally excluded from WKCE tests or who are excused by their parents. Excluded students are either a) students with disabilities who are not able to demonstrate some of the knowledge and skills on the WKCE assessment with appropriate accommodations (prerequisite skill), or b) students whose first language is not English and who are at early levels of English proficiency (prerequisite English). Excluded students are required to take local alternate assessment. An alternate assessment report on the achievement of students excluded from WKCE testing might be available. Contact your district assessment coordinator. [b]Percentages for the nationwide sample (February 1996) are based on the number of students tested rather than "Total Enrolled" or "Eligible." [c]Percentage "Not Tested" is unavailable for this group.

Note. This table omits some of the reporting categories (e.g., gender, race, etc.) in the original chart because of space considerations. From Wisconsin Department of Public Instruction (2000). *Complete Disaggregated State Proficiency Summary Reports at Grade 4* (1999–2000).

TABLE 3.29

Performance Results Reported in Spanish

Texas Assessment of Academic Skills
Summary Report
All Students

STATEWIDE	REPORT DATE: July 2000
GRADE: 03-Spanish	*DATE OF TESTING: Spring 2000*

Test Performance

LECTURA (READING)	Mastering	
Comprension de lectura	Number	Percent
1. Significado de palabras	15,825	83
2. Ideas complementarias	13,285	69
3. Resumenes	9,281	48
4. Relaciones y resultados	14,606	76
5. Inferencias y generalizaciones	12,748	67
6. Punto de vista, propaganda, hechos y opinions	8,450	44
Number Tested: 19,161 Met Minimum Expectations	14,411	75
Average Scale Score: 1,577 Mastered All Objectives	4,731	25
MATEMATICAS (MATHEMATICS)		
Conceptos		
1. Conceptos numbericos	14,884	78
2. Relaciones y funciones matematicas/algebraicas	14,768	78
3. Propiedades y relaciones geometricas	15,497	82
4. Conceptos de medida	13,015	68
5. Probabilidad y estadistica	14,398	76
Operaciones		
6. Uso de la suma para resolver problemas	15,782	83
7. Uso del la resta para resolver problemas	12,937	68
8/9. Uso de la multiplicacion/division para resolver problemas	14,474	76
Resoluncion de problemas		
10/13. Resolucion de problemas usando estimaciones/evalucion	8,052	42
11. Uso de estrategias para solucionar problemas	8,099	43
12. Resolucion de problemas usando representaciones matematicas	11,757	62
Number Tested: 19,003 Met Minimum Expectations	14,161	75
Average Scale Score: 1,573 Mastered All Objectives	2,993	16

Note.   This is the Spanish portion of test results published in *Texas Assessment of Academic Skills Summary Report All Students* (Spring, 2000). Texas Education Agency (2000b).

378

TABLE 3.30

Disaggregated Data by Student Subgroup and Performance Levels in Kansas Writing Assessment for School Year 1998–1999

Proficiency Levels by Grade	Numbers of Students			Percentages of Students		
	General Ed/Gifted	Students with Disabilities	Limited English Proficiency	General Ed/Gifted	Students With Disabilities	Limited English Proficiency
Grade 5						
Excellent (4.40)	2,602	68	7	7.9	2.1	1.2
Proficient (3.30)	13,671	818	113	41.6	21.8	19.9
Basic (2.21)	14,524	1,801	332	44.2	54.9	58.5
Unsatisfactory (< 2.21)	2,086	696	116	6.3	21.2	20.4
Grade 8						
Excellent (4.40)	3,575	36	19	10.7	1.2	5.5
Proficient (3.30)	15,279	566	100	45.8	18.2	28.8
Basic (2.21)	13,161	1,733	170	39.4	56.0	49.0
Unsatisfactory (< 2.21)	1,355	762	58	4.1	24.6	16.7
Grade 10						
Excellent (4.40)	3,507	33	15	11.1	1.6	4.1
Proficient (3.30)	15,568	453	116	49.4	21.4	31.9
Basic (2.21)	11,448	1,195	198	36.3	56.4	54.4
Unsatisfactory (< 2.21)	975	437	35	3.1	20.6	9.6

Note. Individual student performance levels are in parentheses. From Kansas State Board of Education (1999). *Accountability Report 1998–1999 Mathematics, Reading, Writing.*

rollment or number of students eligible to be tested. Although it is helpful to disaggregate by number and student subgroup in the reporting of data, it also would be helpful to provide a column to indicate participation rates so that readers can discern the extent of participation for fuller accountability. Although Table 3.30 provides percentages of students scoring at the various levels, it does not clarify the percentage of those enrolled who were tested.

Reporting Scores on Accommodated Assessments

Comprehensive reporting allows for fuller examination of student performance. If ELLs take an accommodated test that maintains standard testing conditions, data should be aggregated with scores of all students and disaggregated by student subgroups. Aggregated data should be further indexed to report (a) students who were accommodated, and (b) students who were not accommodated.

Table 3.31 presents a report from Indiana that provides performance data for all students. The strengths of this table are that it provides disaggregated data by subgroup and reports on accommodated performance across student subgroups. State reporting across students subgroups is limited. Reported data for accommodated testing should be expanded to address questions regarding such issues as the types of accommodations allowed and whether one or several accommodations were used. Tables reporting content area performance for ELLs also should index the performance of ELLs by language proficiency level. Table 3.31, for example, would be clearer and more comprehensive if accommodated test scores were disaggregated by student cohorts with different language proficiency levels.

Web Reporting

It was found that assessment reports on state department of education Web sites either (a) posted electronic replicas of the print version of a state assessment report as a Microsoft Word or a PDF file, or (b) created customized state assessment reports that could be manipulated to examine different student groups and various aspects of the data. This section provides descriptions and reproduced samples of documents posted on Web sites. Although the same points made about print document reporting apply to Web reporting, there are additional issues that need to be addressed specific to reporting on the Internet.

For example, the Web site for the state of Delaware allowed users to access student assessment results in different ways. Among these were access to the state's regular paper reports and the option of generating user-customizable reports in spreadsheet form. The custom report generator allowed users to sort data by student characteristics or to combine data in other ways. For example, users could disaggregate data by any of the following characteristics: grade and test, race, gender, LEP status, program (e.g., regular, special education), income, and Title I status. The custom report generator also allowed the user to create multiple combinations of data (e.g., LEP status by gender and race) and to disaggregate

TABLE 3.31

Reporting Accommodated Scores

English/ Language Arts	Total # Students	Above Standard		Below Standard		Undeter- mined		M/Mdn Scale Score[a]	Low/High Scale Score Obtained[b]	SD
		N	%	N	%	N	%			
All students	71,889	48,950	68	20,728	29	2,211	3	494.2/498.9	300/830	63.4
General education										
With Accommodations	225	79	35	126	56	20	9	442.8/446.0	300/605	60.8
Without Accommodations	63,150	47,376	75	14,414	23	1,360	2	504.5/506.3	300/830	56.0
Limited English proficiency										
With Accommodations	804	102	13	582	72	120	15	406.0/405.7	300/578	55.5
Without Accommodations	590	244	41	306	52	40	7	454.5/454.9	300/619	62.3

Note. Some categories of scores omitted in reproduced chart (e.g., special education with and without accommodations). From Indiana Department of Education (2000). *ISTEP Indiana Statewide Testing for Educational Progress.*

[a]The Indiana Academic Standard for English/Language Arts is 466. [b]The lowest/highest scale score possible for English/Language Arts is 300/830.

student data by one or more selected characteristics (e.g., only low income, not low income, or both). Table 3.32 shows the basic layout of one such report, in this case, by ELL status and by income reported by performance levels. (The same layout could be customized to show student performance by actual scores or performance levels.)

A strength of Delaware's Web report facility was that all reports that were generated automatically displayed the total number of students tested in the state. This allowed readers to view disaggregated student data in a broader context. Ideas for improvement echo the previous points about locating participation information close to the performance data, even if it is a customized report. Also, in Table 3.32, although the *N* appears to be number tested, it would be helpful to confirm this interpretation.

Issues specific to Internet documents involve accessibility or the process of locating assessment data on a state Web site, labeling, or indicat-

TABLE 3.32

Web-Based Customized Disaggregated Data Report

| | | | | Performance Levels | | | | |
Location/Group	Grade	Year	N	5	4	3	2	1
State of Delaware/LEP, low income	8	2000	23	0.00%	0.00%	13.04%	26.09%	60.87%
State of Delaware/LEP, not low income	8	2000	16	0.00%	12.50%	31.25%	18.75%	37.50%
State of Delaware/LEP	8	2000	39	0.00%	5.13%	20.51%	23.08%	51.28%
State of Delaware/all students	8	2000	8,088	1.99%	6.95%	58.48%	16.39%	16.18%

Note.   From Delaware Department of Education (2000). *Delaware Student Testing Program Online Reports.*

ing the status (i.e., final, preliminary, date posted) of the data presented. The researchers generally found that the location of assessment data on the site was logically placed, with most states providing "assessment" as a menu option on the home page. Advanced state education Web sites provided a search function, which is helpful as a last resort if an assessment link is not available on the main page. On some state sites, the site's organization is not apparent, so the search facility is of particular importance. Other sites require skilled use of search terms to narrow data by the test, year, report, and other characteristics.

Characteristics of Web sites that limited their utility included (a) the use of specialized terms (e.g., continuous improvement) to describe or link assessment results; (b) the placement of assessment information in separate sections of a site (e.g., LEP student scores on a separate ESL or bilingual program page); (c) the posting of assessment data on a generic publications page within a listing of other non-assessment-related documents; and (d) the inability to determine the preparation, release, and final version dates of the data presented. Some sites simply posted the most recent published state report in a downloadable format (e.g., in a PDF file), whereas others had a combination of downloadable versions of the bound versions and data posted as press releases, test result reports from a testing company, or preliminary data.

Few of the state Web sites included text that explained inclusion in accountability reporting in the public state assessment reports. Some states, for example, included language indicating that only standard conditions were reported, but little description was devoted to the nature of those conditions or to how the scores of students tested under nonstandard conditions were reported.

An examination of state assessment policies during the 1998–1999 school year found that of the 17 states with score reporting policies for ELLs, over 50%, or 9 of the 17 states, did not have policies that required the state to report accommodated test scores for ELLs (Rivera et al., 2000). Clear reporting of participation and performance data for ELLs, both with and without accommodated conditions, is the only method to ensure that states are accountable for the achievement of all students including ELLs.

Reporting of ELL data on state assessments must include both participation and performance data to be understood clearly and interpreted appropriately. The most useful reports provide the reader with a clear view of a broad range of factors. Performance data disaggregated by content areas and performance levels cannot tell the whole story without complete data on exclusions and exemptions, as well as accommodated test conditions.

The shift toward delivery of state reports online has introduced new areas of concern. Rapid access to data and the ability to generate customized reports to support readers' interests in specific student characteristics are offset somewhat by the difficulty of locating data and of discerning whether the data are the most current available. The transition to the new technology requires continuing diligence on the part of the state education agencies to ensure that data presented are accurate, accessible, timely, and complete.

CONCLUSION

This study offers an important "then" and "now" perspective: By examining where states' reporting efforts were under IASA, it is possible to gauge the extent to which states are adequately positioned to comply with the more stringent accountability requirements of the NCLB. NCLB requires states to (a) use inclusive assessments, (b) develop a single accountability system, and (c) publicly report state assessment data for all students, including ELLs. Fulfillment of these mandates will require states to improve public access to state assessment data by presenting results in ways that are clear, concise, and readily available.

Data collected for the study included the most recently available print and Web-based state assessment reports from the 46 states that were able to provide assessment reports for the 1999–2000 school year. The 46 states' reports were analyzed (a) to assess the extent to which these were inclusive of ELL data, and (b) to document the extent to which states were comprehensive in reporting ELL data. As previously established, comprehensive reports are classified as those that include both student participation data and student performance data for all students, including ELLs. Thus, state reports were analyzed to assess how and to what extent ELL student data were reported.

Findings from the study indicate that during the study period, publicly accessible state assessment reports for ELLs did not always report complete testing information in a centralized and easily locatable manner. In general, the research team found that few state reports included information on the number of enrolled ELLs (i.e., the number of ELLs in the grade in which the test was given regardless of their participation in the test) and the actual number of ELLs taking individual state assessments. Even fewer states reported both participation and performance data. Reporting only participation data, only performance data, or partial combinations thereof does not allow a critical reader to discern how ELLs are achieving within the subgroup and in comparison to other student subgroups.

Of the 46 states' reports reviewed by the research team, 19 reported ELL student data. Of these, only 8—those of California, Colorado, Delaware, Indiana, Kentucky, Massachusetts, Texas, and Wisconsin—provided ELL participation and performance data for all regular state-required tests. Prior to reporting requirements initiated under IASA there was a significant lack of reporting on ELL-specific assessment data and in cases in which data were reported, states did not report on ELLs as a disaggregated group.

Highlights of the Findings

The following nine observations from the findings have important implications for improving the quality and comprehensiveness of state assessment reports for all students, including ELLs.

Highlight I

States reported data in a variety of ways, both in terms of the information reported and how it was reported. Some states did not report the total numbers of ELLs tested, exempted, accommodated, and so on. By contrast, others not only reported this type of information, but did so by specific characteristics or categories (e.g., type of program, proficiency in native language, time factors, former ELL status, race, gender, SES, reasons for exemption, accommodations received).

Highlight 2

States used a variety of terms to describe ELLs on state assessment reports. The lack of a common operational definition across states not only affects nomenclature within state assessment reports, but also affects comparability of ELL reports across states.

Highlight 3

Few states reported full participation (i.e., total eligible to test, number and percentage of ELLs tested, and number and percentage of scores included in reporting for each grade) information for all state tests. The reporting of participation information contributes to the interpretation of performance data for all content areas and types of tests.

Highlight 4

Most state reports included three levels of proficiency, consistent with Title I requirements. Some states, however, reported fewer than three proficiency levels or simply reported the percentage of students meeting the standard. NRT scores were, as expected, usually reported as scaled scores (i.e., as NCEs or NPRs). A few states also reported NRT data by performance levels. Scores for students who tested under accommodated conditions were rarely reported.

Highlight 5

Few states reported performance data in specific content areas (reading, math, and science) for ELLs. Only 4 states consistently provided sufficient information to calculate the percentage of students who took the tests. Thus, for reading and math, even though 19 states reported performance data on at least one state assessment, only the data from these 4 states with participation information were complete enough to be studied. Providing both participation and performance data for ELLs for the individual content area assessments informs readers about the performance data reported. For example, if some states report lower percentages of their total ELLs than other states, the interpretation of performance will be different.

Highlight 6

Some states reported proficiency levels for some content areas (usually reading and math), but not for others, such as social studies and science. It should be acknowledged that this discrepancy in reporting might reflect the priorities of NCLB. Nonetheless, this practice makes it difficult to assess ELL performance across the curriculum.

Highlight 7

Reports generally did not explain score inclusion for accountability. Some states, for example, included language about only standard conditions being reported, but there was little description of those conditions. There also was a lack of information regarding the scores of students who were tested under nonstandard conditions.

Highlight 8

Reports on tests designed specifically for ELLs were rare, with only 4 states reporting on tests in native languages or to show English proficiency. Of the 19 states that report ELL data on their regular state assessments, 3 reported on a native language version of the regular state assessment and 2 reported data on an English test for ELLs. No states reported ELL data for a state alternate assessment, although 1 state reported participation data for ELLs on an alternate assessment.

Highlight 9

The reporting practices of states seem to be influenced by the importance that states place on public reporting of disaggregated data, rather than by the size of the ELL population in the state's schools. Four states with the largest numbers of ELLs enrolled and six states with the largest percentages of ELL enrollments did not report disaggregated data. By contrast, four of the states with the smallest numbers of ELLs enrolled and one of the states with the smallest percentages of ELLs enrolled reported disaggregated ELL data.

Recommendations

Accountability provisions stated under IASA remain largely unchanged under NCLB in terms of intent. As a result, although based on an IASA data set, these recommendations are relevant to states' efforts under NCLB to demonstrate increased accountability by improving the quality, transparency, and public accessibility of participation and performance data offered in state assessment reports. The recommendations are organized into three categories: (a) reporting participation and performance in print reports, (b) terminology, and (c) print and Web reporting.

Reporting Participation and Performance in Print Reports

In reporting data, it is important to account for all students and to understand the performance data being presented for each grade on all tests within a statewide system. Reports should be as detailed as possible and include specific characteristics of the ELL population, student background information, current status in the school system, and performance and participation on the assessment. This includes the reporting of ELLs exempted from testing or not tested due to absence or other reasons.

Reporting participation data together with performance data is also important so decision makers can determine the size of the group tested (or not tested) and the ways data for mainstream students connect to data disaggregated by ELL status. In addition, it is important for states to provide enough information with the data for readers to be able to interpret the information in a report, including the extent of accommodated participation. This includes allowing readers to be able to evaluate how students performed on native language tests in relation to their peers. Overall, to make longitudinal analyses possible, it is important to establish a consistent way of reporting data across content areas and across years. State reports should do the following:

- Calculate and clearly present participation rate and performance data for every student in every grade for every state test in such a way as to eliminate manual calculations.
- Report participation and performance data at every grade assessed by content area (e.g., mathematics, reading and language arts, etc.) tested, aggregated and disaggregated by student subgroup for each state test.
- Report disaggregated data including (a) the number of ELLs in the system, and (b) the number and percentage of ELLs who participated in the assessment.
- Present participation and performance data together.
- Report data in aggregate regardless of whether data are reported by student subcategories.
- Report accommodated test results separately and in the aggregate to facilitate future study of the use of accommodations in state assessments.
- Report participation and performance on alternate, native language, and English proficiency assessments.
- States with both large and small populations of K–12 ELLs should recognize and address the unique logistical and confidentiality issues they face in reporting ELL assessment data.

- Include or explain in the report any state policy or practice required to interpret data accurately as part of the monitoring or preparation of future state test reports.

Terminology

Clear terminology helps readers make informed interpretations of the data presented. States should provide definitions of terms used in reports and not assume that readers understand their meanings (e.g., transitioned, bilingual English proficient). In some assessment reports, it was difficult to discern whether a state was using LEP or ELL as the reason for exempting students from a test or whether the student was ELL but was not tested for reasons other than language proficiency (e.g., absence).

Test names should be clear to allow interpretation of scores. For example, if ELLs take a different test that is designed to be equivalent to the standard state assessment, this relationship should be evident in the name of the assessment. To clarify further the interpretation of scores, tests that have a corresponding relationship to the regular state test (e.g., translated version) should be named in a way that shows that relationship. Similarly, care should be taken in selecting terms used to report performance to avoid confusion regarding receiving a proficient score on an ELL test and a nonproficient score on a regular state test.

State reports should do the following:

- Provide clear definitions and explanations of terms in data tables and accompanying text.
- Ensure that proficiency-level information (e.g., basic, proficient, advanced) is reported in the same manner for ELLs as it is reported for mainstream students.

Print and Web Reporting

Even if assessment data are presented following the recommendations under print reports, the process of collecting public data online can be challenging. Improvements are needed in the organization of the data on state Web sites and in the clarity of posted data.

Clear organization of data on a state Web site is important. The ease of locating assessment data is greatly improved if the SEA Web sites have a visible and recognizable link from the home page to the assessment data. Further, it is most efficient to have all assessment data available from that linked page. In some states, the practice is to separate assessment data for ELLs and students with disabilities and to isolate these from data on the general student population. This practice is confusing, and viewers might find it difficult to determine whether they have located all of the data.

Web documents that might be updated frequently, in contrast to PDF versions of paper-based reports, should be clearly marked with posting dates and also indicate whether the material is a final or interim report. Sites should indicate the approximate time when final data are expected to become public.

Web-based state reports should do the following:

- Establish a clear link from the Web home page to state assessment data to create a "one-stop" source for state assessment data from the state Web site, and eliminate the need for multiple and time-intensive searches.
- Make all assessment data available from the linked page.
- Indicate whether publicly reported data are preliminary or final on each assessment document, whether print or Web-based.
- Indicate when new copies of data reports will be made available publicly and which reports are the most current.
- Archive state Web-based reports for at least a 5-year period.

REFERENCES

Abedi, J. (2001). *Assessment and accommodations for English language learners: Issues and recommendations* (Policy Brief 4). Los Angeles: University of California, National Center for Research on Evaluation, Standards, and Student Testing.

August, D., & Hakuta, K. (Eds.). (1997). *Improving schooling for language minority children: A research agenda.* Washington, DC: National Academy Press.

Bielinski, J., Thurlow, M., Callender, S., & Bolt, S. (2001). *On the road to accountability: Reporting outcomes for students with disabilities.* Minneapolis: University of Minnesota, National Center on Educational Outcomes.

California Department of Education. (2000). About the *SABE/2 STAR* program. Retrieved January 22, 2001, from http://www.ctb.com/SABE2STAR/e_aboutsabe.html

Colorado Department of Education. (n. d.). *A guide for parents.* Retrieved June 11, 2001, from http://www.cde.state.co.us/cdeassess/as_parentguide.htm

CTB/McGraw-Hill. (2001). *Spanish Assessment of Basic Education, second edition SABE/2.* Retrieved November 14, 2002, from http://www.ctb.com/products

Delaware Department of Education. (2000). *Delaware student testing program online reports.* Retrieved February 14, 2001 from http://delsis.doe.state.de.us/DSTPPublic/

Fleischman, H. L., & Hopstock, P. J. (1993). *Descriptive study of services to limited English proficient students: Vol. 1. Summary of findings and conclusions* [Electronic version]. Arlington, VA: Development Associates.

Indiana Department of Education. (2000). *ISTEP Indiana Statewide Testing for Educational Progress.* Retrieved January 22, 2001, from http://doe.state.in.us/istep/oo-info/pdf/dsr_rt_gr8.pdf

Illinois State Board of Education. (n. d.). *Illinois State Assessments.* Retrieved June 7, 2001, from http://www.isbe.state.il.us/isat/

Kansas State Board of Education. (1999). *Accountability Report 1998–1999 Mathematics, Reading, Writing*. Topeka, KS: Author.

Liu, K., Albus, D., & Thurlow, M. (2000). *Data on LEP students in state education reports* (Minnesota Rep. No. 26). Minneapolis: University of Minnesota, National Center on Educational Outcomes.

Massachusetts Department of Education. (2000). *The Massachusetts Comprehensive Assessment System, Spring 2000 MCAS Tests: Report of state results*. Retrieved February 13, 2001, from http://www.doe.mass.edu/mcas/

Massachusetts Department of Education. (n. d.). Massachusetts Comprehensive Assessment System. Retrieved June 7, 2001, from http://www.doe.mass.edu/mcas/part_req.html

National Clearinghouse for English Language Acquisition. (2002). *Ask NCELA No. 1: How many school-aged limited English proficient students are there in the U.S.? How many in each state?* Retrieved February 25, 2002, from http://www.ncela.gwu.edu/askncela/01leps.htm

National Research Council. (1999). *Testing, teaching, and learning: A guide for states and school districts*. Washington, DC: National Academy Press.

NCEO. (2001). Special topic area: Alternate assessments for LEP students/English language learners. Retrieved December 17, 2001, from http://education.umn.edu/NCEO/LEP/altassess_lep.htm

NCREL. (2000) Critical issue: Reporting assessment results. Retrieved December 17, 2001, from http://www.ncrel.org/sdrs/areas/issues/methods/assment/as600.htm

Olson, J. F., Jones, H., & Bond, L. (2001). *Annual survey: State student assessment programs* (Data Vol. I, pp. 48, 58–59). Washington, DC: Council of Chief State School Officers.

Rivera, C., & Stansfield, C. (1998). Leveling the playing field for English language learners: Increasing participation in state and local assessments through accommodations. In R. Brandt (Ed.), *Assessing student learning: New rules, new reality* (pp. 65–92). Arlington, VA: Educational Research Service.

Rivera, C., Stansfield, C., Scialdone, L., & Sharkey, M. (2000). *An analysis of state policies for the inclusion and accommodation of English language learners in state assessment programs during 1998–1999*. Arlington, VA: The George Washington University Center for Equity and Excellence in Education.

Texas Education Agency. (2000). *Study of possible expansion of the assessment system for limited English proficient students*. Retrieved February 19, 2001, from http://www.tea.state.tx.us/student.assessment/ admin/rpte/study/index.html

Texas Education Agency. (2000b). *Texas Assessment of Academic Skills summary report: All students*. Retrieved February 19, 2001 from http://www.tea.state.tx.us/student.assessment/reporting/results/summary/sum00/index.html

Texas Education Agency. (2001). *2001 comprehensive annual report on Texas public schools*. Retrieved November 15, 2002, from http://www.tea.state.tx.us.research/pdfs

Thompson, S., Thurlow, M., & Lazarus, S. (2001). *Reporting on the state assessment performance of students with disabilities*. (EPRRI Topical Review No. 3). College Park: University of Maryland, Education Policy Reform Research Institute.

Thurlow, M. L., Nelson, J. R., Teelucksingh, E., & Ysseldyke, J. E. (2000). *Where's Waldo? A third search for students with disabilities in state accountability reports* (Technical Rep. No. 25). Minneapolis: University of Minnesota, National Center on Educational Outcomes.

Thurlow, M., Quenemoen, R., Thompson, S., & Lehr, C. (2001). *Principles and characteristics of inclusive assessment and accountability systems* (Synthesis Rep.

No. 40). Minneapolis: University of Minnesota, National Center on Educational Outcomes.

Vincent, C., & Schenck, E. (2001). *A practical discussion of inclusion issues in state-wide assessment emerging from standards-based education reform and Title I.* Washington, DC: The George Washington University Center for Equity and Excellence in Education, Region III Comprehensive Center.

Wisconsin Department of Education. (n.d.). *Alternate Performance Indicators (APIs).* Retrieved June 7, 2001, from http://www.dpi.state.wi.us/dlsea/equity/api_intr.html

Wisconsin Department of Public Instruction. (2000). *Complete disaggregated state proficiency summary reports at grade 4 (1999–00).* Retrieved February 19, 2001, from http://www.dpi.state.wi.us/spr/xls/4kce00s.xls

Ysseldyke, J., & Nelson, R. (1998). Reporting results of student performance on large-scale assessments. In G. Tindal & T. Haladyna (Eds.), *Large-scale assessment programs for all students: Validity, technical adequacy, and implementation* (pp. 467–479). Mahwah, NJ: Lawrence Erlbaum Associates.

APPENDIX 3-A

STATE ACCOUNTABILITY REPORTS

The following is a list of print and Web-based data sources that were publicly available during the document search phase (August 2000–March 2001) of this research study. Although the documents listed provided data that were used to assess the reporting practices of the states, this is not to be construed as a reference list, but rather as an assemblage of resources, many of which are not cited directly in the text of this report.

Please note that because of the fluid nature of the Internet and the intervening time spent in the analysis and report preparation phases of this study, many of the Web addresses given are no longer valid. In some cases, the site redirects viewers to other sites or to the state's education department home page, but in most cases no redirects are provided. Instead, many states simply replaced the data for the research period with current data. Other states changed the status of the data such that visitors need authorization to view the site. Some states permanently archived the 1999–2000 school year data so that these are no longer accessible on the Web. It is possible that some state education departments have archived print versions of the data, and that data are available to researchers and other interested parties on request. The purpose of this appendix is twofold: (a) to document the list of sites where print- and Web-based data were secured during the research phase of this study, and (b) to state clearly that in many cases study data are no longer accessible at the uniform resource locator (URL) searched during the document collection stage of this research project.

The research team reviewed and revisited, where possible, all of the URLs during the final phase of report preparation in spring of 2003. In total, the research team examined 293 data sources; of these, 52 (18%) were print documents, listed in the first section. The second section presents 57 (20%) Web sources in which the URL carries the same data examined during the August 2000 through March 2001 document search phase of the study. The third section presents the 184 (63%) Web sources with URLs that no longer display the data that were used in the current study.

Print Sources

Colorado

Colorado Department of Education. (2000). *CSAP performance level summary reports, test date 3/1/00*. Denver, CO: Author.
Colorado Department of Education. (2000, January 3). *Colorado Student Assessment Program: Spring 1999 testing*. Denver, CO: Author.

Connecticut

Connecticut State Board of Education. (2000, January). *Connecticut Mastery Test—Statewide Test Results School Year: 1999–2000, Grade 4*. Hartford, CT: Author.
Connecticut State Department of Education. (2000, January). *Connecticut Mastery Test—Statewide Test Results School Year: 1999–2000, Grade 6*. Hartford, CT: Author.
Connecticut State Board of Education. (2000, April). *Profiles of our schools 1998–1999*. Hartford, CT: Author.
Connecticut State Department of Education. (2000, June). *Annual report on special education in Connecticut, 1999–2000*. Hartford, CT: Author.

Delaware

State Board of Education & Delaware Department of Education. (2000, March). *Report of educational statistics 1998–99*. Dover, DE: Author.

Idaho

Idaho Department of Education. (2000). *Idaho ITBS/TAP schools norms summary 1999–2000*. Boise, ID: Author.
Idaho Department of Education. (2000, January). *Serving exceptional children: A report to the Idaho legislature*. Boise, ID: Author.
Idaho Department of Education. (2000, February). *Fall 1999 Idaho Reading Indicator state scores*. Boise, ID: Author.
Idaho Department of Education. (2000, May). *Idaho Direct Writing Assessment scores 2000*. Boise, ID: Author.
Idaho Department of Education. (2000, Summer). *Idaho State DOE News and Reports, 28*(2).

Illinois

Illinois State Board of Education. (1999). *1999 Illinois school report card: Matheny Elementary School*. Chicago: Author.

Iowa

Iowa Department of Education. (1999). *The annual condition of education report.* Des Moines, IA: Author.

Kentucky

Kentucky Department of Education. (1999, Spring). *Kentucky Core Content Test (Spring 1999) Grade 4/5.* Frankfort, KY: Author.
Kentucky Department of Education. (1999, Spring). *Kentucky Core Content Test (Spring 1999) Grade 7/8.* Frankfort, KY: Author.
Kentucky Department of Education. (1999, Spring). *Kentucky Core Content Test (Spring 1999) Grade 10/12.* Frankfort, KY: Author.

Louisiana

Louisiana Department of Education. (2000). *LEAP for the 21st century: Louisiana Educational Assessment Program for the 21st century 1999–2000, annual report: grades 4 and 8 criterion referenced tests.* Baton Rouge, LA: Author.
Louisiana Department of Education. (2000). *LEAP Graduation Exit Examination 1999–2000 annual report.* Baton Rouge, LA: Author.

Michigan

Michigan Department of Education. (2000, May). *MEAP statewide results: Winter 2000, grades 4 and 7 mathematics and reading.* Lansing, MI: Author.
Michigan Department of Education. (2000, June). *MEAP statewide results: Winter 2000, grades 5 and 8 in science, writing and social studies.* Lansing, MI: Author.

Missouri

Missouri Department of Elementary and Secondary Education. (1999). *1998–99 report of the public schools of Missouri.* Jefferson City, MO: Author.
Missouri Department of Elementary and Secondary Education. (1999). *Profiles of Missouri public schools: Financial, pupil and staff data for fiscal year 1998–99.* Jefferson City, MO: Author.

Montana

Montana Office of Public Instruction. (2000, July). *Special education annual report to the Board of Public Education.* Helena, MT: Author.

New Hampshire

New Hampshire Department of Education. (2000, October). *New Hampshire Education Improvement and Assessment Program educational assessment report, end-of-grade 3, May 2000.* Concord, NH: Author.
New Hampshire Department of Education. (2000, October). *New Hampshire Education Improvement and Assessment Program educational assessment report, end-of-grade 6, May 2000.* Concord, NH: Author.

New Hampshire Department of Education. (2000, October). *New Hampshire Education Improvement and Assessment Program educational assessment report, end-of-grade 10, May 2000.* Concord, NH: Author.

New Jersey

New Jersey State Department of Education. (1999, December). *March 1999 Grade Eight Proficiency Assessment (GEPA) state summary.* Trenton, NJ: Author.
New Jersey State Department of Education. (1999, December). *May 1999 Elementary School Proficiency Assessment (ESPA) state summary.* Trenton, NJ: Author.
New Jersey State Department of Education. (1999, December). *October 1998 grade 11 High School Proficiency Test (HSPT11) state summary.* Trenton, NJ: Author.

New Mexico

State of New Mexico Department of Education, Assessment & Evaluation Unit. (Spring, 1999). *Statewide articulated assessment system: 1998–1999 summary report.* Santa Fe, NM: Author.

New York

New York State Education Department. (1998). *Performance report of educational and vocational services and results for individuals with disabilities, 1997–1998.* Albany, NY: Author.
New York State Education Department. (1999). *1999 agenda for reforming education for students with disabilities.* Albany, NY: Author.
New York State Education Department. (1999). *Office of vocational educational services for individuals with disabilities 1999 report.* Albany, NY: Author.
New York State Education Department. (1999, February). *New York, the state of learning: Statistical profiles of public school districts, February 1999 report.* Albany, NY: Author.
New York State Education Department. (1999, April). *New York, the state of learning: Statewide profile of the education system.* Albany, NY: Author.
New York State Education Department. (2000, March). *Board of cooperative educational services 1998–99 report card.* Albany, NY: Author.
New York State Education Department. (2000, September). *2000 pocketbook of goals and results for individuals with disabilities.* Albany, NY: Author.

North Carolina

North Carolina Department of Public Instruction. (2000, August 31). *The 1990–2000 preliminary North Carolina state testing results.* Raleigh, NC: Author.

Oklahoma

Oklahoma State Department of Education. (2000, April). *Profiles 1999 district report.* Oklahoma City, OK: Author.

Pennsylvania

Pennsylvania Department of Education. (1999, March). *Pennsylvania system of school assessment academic standards school report 1999 mathematics and reading.* Harrisburg, PA: Author.

Pennsylvania Department of Education. (1999, October). *Status report on education in Pennsylvania*. Harrisburg, PA: Author.
Pennsylvania Department of Education. (1999, December). *Supplemental documentation for 1999 reading, mathematics, and writing reports*. Harrisburg, PA: Author.

South Dakota

South Dakota Department of Education and Cultural Affairs. (2000, September). *Statewide report for the South Dakota achievement and ability testing program*. Pierre, SD: Author.

Texas

Texas Education Agency. (1999). *Statewide and regional results: Student performance results 1998–99*. Austin, TX: Author.

Utah

Utah State Office of Instruction. (1999). *State summary assessment profile*. Salt Lake City, UT: Author.
Utah State Office of Instruction. (1999). *Summary of results from the Utah statewide testing program 1999*. Salt Lake City, UT: Author.

Vermont

Vermont Department of Education. (2000, August). *SASRS–99 Summary of the annual statistical report of schools*. Montpelier, VT: Author.

Virginia

Virginia Department of Education. (1999). 1999 *detail report: Virginia state assessment program*. Richmond, VA: Author.

West Virginia

West Virginia Department of Education. (2000, September). *Annual report office of educational performance audits*. Charleston, WV: Author

Wyoming

Wyoming Department of Education. (2000, May). *Statistical report series no. 2: 1999 Wyoming school districts fall report of staff and enrollment*. Cheyenne, WY: Author.

Web-Based Sources: Study Data Actively Displayed[9]

California

California Department of Education. (n. d.). California's special education statewide enrollment data. Retrieved January 22, 2001, from http://www.cde.ca.gov/spbranch/sed/

---

[9]As of June 2003.

California Department of Education. (n. d.). Language census summary statistics, 1998–99. Retrieved January 19, 2001, from http://www.cde.ca.gov/demographics/reports/

Colorado

Colorado Department of Education. (2000). Fall 1999 public school pupil membership racial/ethnicity trends. Retrieved December 8, 2000, from http://www.cde.state.co.us/cdereval/

Connecticut

Connecticut State Department of Education. (n. d.). CMT exemption rates, 1996–99. Retrieved December 14, 2000, from http://www.csde.state.ct.us/public/der/datacentral/
Connecticut State Department of Education. (n. d.). Connecticut Mastery Test, grade 4, 1999. Retrieved December 12, 2000, from http://www.csde.state.ct.us/public/der/datacentral/studentassessment/

Delaware

Delaware Department of Education. (2000). Albert H. Jones Elementary School profile information as of November 2000: 1999–2000 students and instructional staff. Retrieved December 14, 2000, from http://issm.doe.state.de.us/profiles/

Florida

Florida Department of Education. (n. d.). Grade 11 HSCT district/state reports: 2000, reading and math. Retrieved April 19, 2001, from http://www.firn.edu/doe/sas/hsct/
Florida Department of Education. (2000). Disaggregated achievement report: High schools 2000 (state totals). Retrieved January 4, 2001, from http://www.firn.edu/doe/disaggreports/

Hawaii

Hawaii Department of Education. (n. d.). Comprehensive needs assessment (CAN) system accountability. Retrieved February 21, 2001, from http://arch.k12.hi.us/
Hawaii Department of Education. (n. d.). Gender and ethnicity distribution statewide summary September 1997. Retrieved February 21, 2001, from http://www.doe.k12.hi.us/
Hawaii Department of Education. (2000, August). The superintendent's annual report on school performance and improvement in Hawaii. Retrieved February 21, 2001, from http://arch.k12.hi.us/system/

Idaho

Idaho Department of Education. (1999, July 28). ITBS: Grade 3, 4, 5, 6, 7, 8 disaggregated data. Retrieved December 19, 2000, from http://www.sde.state.id.us/instruct/SchoolAccount/PerformanceSummary/disaggregated.htm

Idaho Department of Education. (1999, July 28). Students tested. Retrieved
    December 19, 2000, from http://www.sde.state.id.us/instruct/SchoolAccount/
    PerformanceSummary/students.htm
Idaho Department of Education. (1999, July 28). TAP disaggregated results grade 9,
    10, 11. Retrieved December 19, 2000, from http://www.sde.state.id.us/instruct/
    SchoolAccount/PerformanceSummary/TAPdr.htm

Illinois

Illinois State Board of Education. (n. d.). Transitional bilingual education, transitional
    programs of instruction evaluation report fiscal year 2000. Retrieved March, 29,
    2000, from http://www.isbe.state.il.us/research/reports.htm#ReportsandData

Indiana

Indiana Department of Education. (n. d.). Annual report 1998. Retrieved January 23,
    2001, from http://ideanet.doe.state.in.us/publications/pdf_other/annualreport98.pdf

Kansas

Kansas State Board of Education. (n. d.). Kansas Assessment Program. Retrieved De-
    cember 20, 2000, from http://www.ksbe.state.ks.us/assessment/mathread99b.
    html#math

Louisiana

Louisiana Department of Education. (n. d.). Spring 2000 graduation exit exam results by
    state and district. Retrieved January 23, 2001, from http://www.lcet.doe.state.la.us/
    DOE/OSSP/ testresults/GEEsum2000.html
Louisiana Department of Education. (n. d.). Summer 2000 criterion referenced test:
    State/district achievement level summary report. Retrieved January 23, 2001, from
    http://www.doe.state.la.us/DOE/OSSP/testresults/achievement4.htm
Louisiana Department of Education. (n. d.). The Iowa Tests Spring 2000 summary of
    results. Retrieved January 23, 2001, from http://www.lcet.doe.state.la.us/DOE/
    OSSP/testresults/ITBS00.html
Louisiana Department of Education. (1999, August). DRA 1998–99 progress report:
    First, second and third grade reading ability, spring 1999. Retrieved January 23,
    2001, from http://www.doe.state.la.us/DOE/OSSP/testresults/testresults.asp
Louisiana Department of Education (2000, May). 1998–99 annual financial and statisti-
    cal report. Retrieved February 22, 2001, from http://www.doe.state.la.us/DOE/omf/
    AFSR/afsr9899.pdf
Louisiana Department of Education. (2000, October). 1999–2000 school account-
    ability report card for principals. Retrieved January 23, 2001, from http://www.
    lcet.doe.state.la.us/doe/omf/sps/spsframe.asp
Louisiana Department of Education. (2000, October). School report card for parents
    for 1999–2000. Retrieved January 23, 2001, from http://www.lcet.doe.state.la.us/
    doe/omf/sps/spsframe.asp

Maine

Maine Department of Education. (n. d.). 1999–2000 language minority student de-
    mographics in Maine schools. Retrieved February 22, 2001, from
    http://www.state.me.us/education/esl/19992000demographics.htm

Minnesota

Minnesota Department of Children, Families, and Learning. (n. d.). School district profiles: 1998–99. Retrieved February 13, 2001, from http://cfl.state.mn.us/FIN/profiles/98-99/schooldistricts.pdf

Mississippi

Mississippi Department of Education. (n. d.). Report card 1999. Retrieved February 13, 2001, from http://www.mde.k12.ms.us/account/report/
Mississippi Department of Education. (2000). 2000 annual report. Retrieved February 13, 2001, from http://www.mde.k12.ms.us/account/2000report/

Missouri

Missouri Department of Education. (n. d.). Spring 1999 MAP data disaggregated Missouri totals. Retrieved January 17, 2001 from http://Services.dese.state.mo.us
Missouri Department of Education. (1999, October 21). LEP student census. Retrieved January 17, 2001 from http://k12apps.dese.state.mo.us/webapps/lep99/LEP0200.asp
Missouri Department of Education. (2000, November 7). Missouri MAP scores. Retrieved January 17, 2001 from http://www.dese.state.mo.us/divinstr/assess/stateresults.html

New Jersey

New Jersey State Department of Education. (n. d.). New Jersey statewide assessment reports. Retrieved February 23, 2001, from http://www.state.nj.us/njded/schools/achievement/2001/index.html

New Mexico

New Mexico State Department of Education. (2000). New Mexico Statewide Articulated Assessment Program 1999–2000 summary report phase I and phase II. Retrieved April 2, 2001 from http://sde.state.nm.us/divisions/ais/assessment/
New Mexico Department of Education. (2001, January 5). Percent of student enrollment ethnic category district & school year 2000–2001. Retrieved January 16, 2001 from http://www.sde.state.nm.us/divisions/ais/datacollection/dcrfactsheets.html

North Carolina

North Carolina Department of Public Instruction. (1998, May). The 1997–98 report of student performance: North Carolina open-ended assessment grades 5 and 8. Retrieved February 14, 2001, from http://www.dpi.state.nc.us/accountability/testing/openended/openend98.pdf
North Carolina Department of Public Instruction. (2000, January). National Assessment of Educational Progress (NAEP) and Iowa Test of Basic Skills (ITBS) results for North Carolina and the nation: NAEP results 1990–98, ITBS results 1996–1999. Retrieved February 14, 2001, from http://www.dpi.state.nc.us/reportstats.html

North Dakota

North Dakota Department of Public Instruction. (n. d.). NDDPI biennial report 1999–2001. Retrieved February 14, 2001, from http://www.dpi.state.nd.us/resource/biennial.pdf

North Dakota Department of Public Instruction. (1998). 1998 North Dakota self assessment. Retrieved February 14, 2001, from http://www.dpi.state.nd.us/speced/self.pdf

Ohio

Ohio Department of Education. (2001). 2001 annual report on educational progress in Ohio. Retrieved February 14, 2001, from http://www.ode.state.oh.us/ReportCard/2001StateReportCard.pdf

Tennessee

Tennessee Department of Education. (n. d.). Longitudinal TCAP writing assessment results. Retrieved February 19, 2001, from http://www.state.tn.us/education/tswritbr4.htm

Tennessee Department of Education. (n. d.). TCAP competency test: 1998–1999 TCAP competency requirement statewide results. Retrieved February 19, 2001, from http://www.k-12.state.tn.us/pdf/testingservices/tscomptest.pdf

Texas

Texas Education Agency. (n. d.). 1999–2000 AEIS reports. Retrieved February 20, 2001, from http://www.tea.state.tx.us/perfreport/aeis/2000/index.html

Texas Education Agency. (n. d.). Annual federal data report: School year 1998–1999. Retrieved February 20, 2001, from http://www.tea.state.tx.us/special.ed/afdr/

Texas Education Agency. (2000). 2000 comprehensive biennial report on Texas public schools. Retrieved February 20, 2001, from http://www.tea.state.tx.us/research/pdfs/2kcompbi.pdf

Texas Education Agency. (2000, December). Texas self-assessment report. Retrieved February 20, 2001, from http://www.tea.state.tx.us/special.ed/cimp/selfasmt.pdf

Texas Education Agency. (2000, December 1). Study of possible expansion of the assessment system for limited English proficient students. Retrieved February 19, 2001, from http://www.tea.state.tx.us/student.assessment/admin/rpte/study/index.html

Utah

Utah State Office of Instruction. (2000). Statewide CRT results—Spring 2000. Retrieved March 1, 2001, from http://www.usoe.k12.ut.us/eval

Utah State Office of Instruction. (2000). Summary of results from the Stanford Achievement Tests 9th Edition, 2000. Retrieved March 1, 2001, from http://www.usoe.k12.ut.us/eval

Virginia

Virginia Department of Education. (2000, March 1). Report of limited English proficient (LEP) students receiving services as of September 30. Retrieved March 1, 2001, from http://www.pen.k12.va.us/VDOE/Publications/lep9299.htm

Virginia Department of Education. (2000, November 14). Report of children and youth with disabilities receiving special education. Retrieved March 1, 2001, from http://www.pen.k12.va.us/VDOE/Publications/

Washington

Washington Office of Superintendent of Public Instruction. (n. d.). Washington state educational profile for 1999–2000. Retrieved February 19, 2001, from http://www.k12.wa.us/edprofile/stateReport.asp?sReport=stateITBS1999-2000

Washington Office of Superintendent of Public Instruction. (2000, September). Study of the grade 4 mathematics assessment final report. Retrieved February 19, 2001, from http://www.k12.wa.us/publications/docs/MathStudy4.pdf

Washington Office of Superintendent of Public Instruction. (2001, February). School enrollment summary: Washington state school districts school year 2000–2001. Retrieved February 19, 2001, from http://www.k12.wa.us/dataadmin/EnrSum00.pdf

Wisconsin

Wisconsin Department of Education. (n. d.). 2000 Wisconsin reading comprehension test: An assessment of primary level reading at grade three. Retrieved February 19, 2001, from http://www.dpi.state.wi.us/dpi/spr/3wrct00.html

Wisconsin Department of Education. (2001). Wisconsin school performance report: Knowledge and concepts examination results state summary. Retrieved February 19, 2001, from http://www.dpi.state.wi.us/dpi/oea/kce_opi.html

Wyoming

Wyoming Department of Education. (2000, July 19). 2000 WyCAS state level results. Retrieved February 19, 2001, from http://www.asme.com/wycas/TestResults/StateRes2000.htm

Web-Based Sources: Study Data No Longer Displayed[10]

Alabama

Alabama Department of Education. (n. d.). 2000 SAT exam. Retrieved January 17, 2001 from http://www.alsde.edu/veri/

Alabama Department of Education. (n. d.). 2000 high school graduation exam. Retrieved January 17, 2001, from http://www.alsde.edu

Alaska

Alaska Department of Education. (n. d.). Ethnicity by school by grade as of Oct. 1, 1999. Retrieved December 18, 2000, from http://www.eed.state.ak.us/stats/

Alaska Department of Education. (n. d.). Total statewide enrollment by ethnicity and grade as of October 1, 1999. Retrieved December 18, 2000, from http://www.eed.state.ak.us/stats/

---

[10]As of June 2003.

Alaska Department of Education. (n. d.). 1999–2000 school report card. Retrieved March 28, 2001, from http://www.eed.state.ak.us/DOE_Rolodex/schools/ReportCard/
Alaska Department of Education. (2000, March). *Report card to the public: A summary of statistics from Alaska's public schools 1998–99.* Anchorage, AK: Author.

Arizona

Arizona Department of Education. (n. d.). AIMS 2000 percentage of students in each performance category by race/ethnicity. Retrieved January 17, 2001 from http://www.ade.state.az.us/standards/AIMS/
Arizona Department of Education. (n. d.). AIMS scores. Retrieved January 17, 2001, from http://www.ade.state.az.us/standards/AIMS/
Arizona Department of Education. (n. d.). Arizona enrollment figures, October 1, 1998 enrollment. Retrieved January 17, 2001, from http://www.ade.state.az.us/ResearchPolicy/
Arizona Department of Education. (n. d.). Arizona's Instrument to Measure Standards, spring 2000. Retrieved January 17, 2001, from http://www.ade.state.az.us/standards/
Arizona Department of Education. (n. d.). Stanford Achievement Test results, spring 2000. Retrieved January 17, 2001, from http://www.ade.state.az.us/standards/

Arkansas

Arkansas Department of Education. (n. d.). Educational indicators: ACTAAP testing (4th grade benchmark). Retrieved November 29, 2000, from http://www.as-is.org/indicators/
Arkansas Department of Education. (n. d.). Educational indicators: SAT-9 testing. Retrieved December 7, 2000, from http://www.as-is.org/indicators/
Arkansas Department of Education. (n. d.). General information—Enrollment data. Retrieved December 7, 2000, from http://www.as-is.org/search/
Arkansas Department of Education. (n. d.). School performance report 1999–2000. Retrieved December 8, 2000, from http://www.as-is.org/reportcard/
Arkansas Department of Education. (1999). Comparative analysis of fall 1999 to fall 1998 Stanford 9 scores. Retrieved December 8, 2000, from http://arkedu.state.ar.us/

California

California Department of Education. (n. d.). Public school summary statistics 1999–2000. Retrieved January 19, 2001, from http://www.cde.ca.gov/demographics/reports/
California Department of Education. (2000). California student trends 1998–99. Retrieved January 19, 2001, from http://www.ed-data.k12.ca.us/dev/StateReports.asp
California Department of Education. (2000). STAR state summary report for language FLU (LEP) spring 2000. Retrieved January 19, 2001, from http://207.87.22.181/star/reportyr.idc
California Department of Education. (2000). STAR state summary report for special educ and special ed service delivery. Retrieved January 19, 2001, from http://207.87.22.181.star/reportyr.idc
California Department of Education. (2000). STAR test results standards-based augmented test. Retrieved January 19, 2001, from http://www.ed-data.k12.ca.us/star/
California Department of Education. (2000). The California state summary report spring 2000 SABE/2 STAR summary report for all students—Identified as special

education. Retrieved January 22, 2001, from http://www.ctb.com.SABE2STAR/reports/00-00000-0000000-h.html

Colorado

Colorado Department of Education. (n. d.). Denver County—Student statistics. Retrieved December 8, 2000, from http://www.cde.state.co.us/cdedistrict/
Colorado Department of Education. (2000). 2000 8th grade mathematics state summary. Retrieved December 8, 2000, from http://www.cde.state.co.us/cdeassess/
(Note: Web pages similar to the preceding one are available for third, fourth, fifth, and seventh grade test summaries.)

Connecticut

Connecticut State Department of Education. (n. d.). Number of students with non-English home language 1990–98. Retrieved December 14, 2000, from http://www.csde.state.ct.us/public/der/datacentral/
Connecticut State Board of Education. (1999, November). CAPT grade 10 statewide test results, spring 1999 administration. Hartford, CT: Author.

Delaware

Delaware Department of Education. (1999, October). A study of programs and demographics for students of limited English proficiency in Delaware schools 1998–1999 school year. Retrieved December 14, 2000, from http://www.doe.state.de.us/reporting/
Delaware Department of Education. (2000, June). Delaware Student Testing Program state summary report: Reading, mathematics, writing, spring 2000 administration. Dover, DE: Author.

District of Columbia

District of Columbia. (n. d.). 1999 scores: Stanford achievement test, 9th ed. Retrieved April 10, 2001, from http://www.k12.dc.us/dcps/data_intro.html
District of Columbia. (1999, October 7). 1999–2000 citywide student enrollment. Retrieved April 10, 2001, from http://www.k12.dc.us/dcps/Lasso.acgi

Florida

Florida Department of Education. (n. d.). District FCAT writing results 1999–2000 comparison. Retrieved December 15, 2000, from http://www.firn.edu/doe/sas/
Florida Department of Education. (n. d.). Statewide FCAT Norm-referenced test (Stanford-9) results. Retrieved December 15, 2000, from http://www.firn.edu/doe/sas/
Florida Department of Education. (2000). 2000 FCAT writing results state and district summary. Retrieved December 15, 2000, from http://www.firn.edu/doe/
Florida Department of Education. (2000). FCAT reading and math 2000 district/state report. Retrieved December 15, 2000, from http://www.firn.edu/doe/

Florida Department of Education. (2000). Membership in Florida's public schools, fall 1999. Retrieved December 14, 2000, from http://www.firn.edu/doe/

Florida Department of Education. (2000, April 19). 1998/99 annual status report on the implementation of the *1990 League of United Latin American Citizens (LULAC), et al. vs. State Board of Education, et al.* consent decree state synopsis. Retrieved December 15, 2000, from http://www.firn.edu/doe/

Georgia

Georgia Department of Education. (n. d.). State report card 1999–2000. Retrieved January 22, 2001, from http://www.accountability.doe.k12.ga.us/

Georgia Department of Education. (n. d.). Superintendent Schreko releases results of the criterion-referenced competency tests (CRCT). Retrieved January 22, 2001, from http://www.doe.k12.ga.us/communications/

Hawaii

Hawaii Department of Education. (n. d.). Stanford Achievement Test results (SAT-9). Retrieved February 21, 2001, from http://arch.k12.hi.us/pdf/sat/

Hawaii Department of Education. (n. d.). Stanford Assessment Test 1994–1998 state summaries. Retrieved February 21, 2001, from http://does.k12.hi.us/reports.htm

Hawaii Department of Education. (n. d.). Statewide enrollment counts: School year 1994–95 to 1998–99. Retrieved February 21, 2001, from http://doe.k12.hi.us/reports.htm

Hawaii Department of Education. (2000). Comprehensive assessment and accountability system school year 1999–2000. Retrieved February 22, 2001, from http://arch.k12.hi.us/school/

Hawaii Department of Education. (2001, February 6). School by school results for SAT 2000. Retrieved February 21, 2001, from http://www2.k12.hi.us/COMM/

Hawaii Department of Education. (2001, February 15). Superintendent's update for the board of education & Hawaii's public schools. Retrieved February 21, 2001, from http://www2.k12.hi.us/COMM/

Idaho

Idaho Department of Education. (n. d.). IRI proficiency levels fall: 2000 state report. Retrieved December 19, 2000, from http://www.sde.state.id.us/IRI/reports/Fall2000/State.pdf

Idaho Department of Education. (n. d.). ITBS region coded summaries: Class A, Grade 3. Retrieved December 19, 2000, from http://www.sde.state.id.us/instruct/SchoolAccount/ ITBS/3_4.pdf

Idaho Department of Education. (n. d.). ITBS region coded summaries: Class A, Grade 4. Retrieved December 19, 2000, from http://www.sde.state.id.us/instruct/SchoolAccount/ITBS/4_4.pdf

(Note: The preceding report was available for each grade, 3–11).

Idaho Department of Education. (n. d.). ITBS region coded summaries: Title I. Retrieved December 19, 2000, from http://www.sde.state.id.us/instruct/SchoolAccount/ITBS/3_3.pdf

Idaho Department of Education. (n. d.). ITBS region coded summaries group. Retrieved December 19, 2000, from http://www.sde.state.id.us/instruct/SchoolAccount/ITBS/4_2.pdf

(Note: The preceding report available for each grade, 4–11).

Idaho Department of Education. (n. d.). ITBS Service 18a region coded summaries group. Retrieved December 19, 2000, from http://www.sde.state.id.us/instruct/SchoolAccount/ ITBS/3_2.pdf

Idaho Department of Education. (n. d.). Direct Writing and Math Assessments 2000. Retrieved December 19, 2000, from http://www.sde.state.id/us/instruct/SchoolAccount/

Idaho Department of Education. (1999, July 28). 1998 DWA disaggregated results Retrieved December 19, 2000, from http://www.sde.state.id.us/instruct/SchoolAccount/

Idaho Department of Education. (1999, July 28). 1998 DMA disaggregated results. Retrieved December 19, 2000, from http://www.sde.state.id.us/instruct/SchoolAccount/

Illinois

Illinois State Board of Education. (n. d.). Elementary and secondary schools. Retrieved December 19, 2000, from http://www.isbe.state.il.us/research.broch00.htm

Illinois State Board of Education. (n. d.). Illinois school report card: Benjamin Franklin Middle School. Retrieved December 19, 2000, from http://206.166.105.128/ReportCard/asps/rclist.asp?ID=788

Illinois State Board of Education. (n. d.). Transitional bilingual education, transitional programs of instruction 1999–2000 state-wide statistics. Retrieved December 19, 2000, from http://www.isbe.state.il.us/research/pdffiles/BilingualCharts00.pdf

Illinois State Board of Education. (2000). IMAGE 2000. Retrieved March 29, 2000, from http://www.isbe.state.il.us/isat/IMAGEresults00.htm

Indiana

Indiana Department of Education. (n. d.). Indiana school directory 2001. Retrieved January 23, 2001, from http://ideanet.doe.state.in.us/publications/pdf_dir2001/directory2001.pdf

Indiana Department of Education. (n. d.). Public schools disaggregation summary reports. Retrieved January 22, 2001, from http://doe.state.in.us/istep/00_info/

Indiana Department of Education. (n. d.). State achievement performance report. Retrieved January 22, 2001, from http://www.doe.state.in.us/istep/00_info/pdf/01.pdf

Indiana Department of Education. (2000, November 14). Language minority enrollment summary for school year 1999–00. Retrieved January 23, 2001, from http://ideanet.doe.state .in.us/lmmp/language.html

Iowa

Iowa Department of Education. (2000). *2000: The annual condition of education report*. Des Moines, IA: Author.

Kansas

Kansas State Board of Education. (n. d.). 2000–01 building-level reports: Building headcount enrollment by grade, race and sex, Jewell Jr. High. Retrieved December 29, 2000, from http://www.ksbe.ks.us/k12/k12.html

Kansas State Board of Education. (n. d.). LEP student count by USD for 6 years, 1992/3 to 1998/99. Retrieved December 29, 2000, from http://www.ksbe.state.ks.us/subjects. html

Kansas State Board of Education. (1999). *1998–1999 accountability report: Mathematics, reading, writing*. Topeka, KS: Author.

Kentucky

Kentucky Department of Education. (n. d.). Ethnic membership by district and grade end of year 1999–2000. Retrieved December 29, 2000, from http://www.kde.state. ky.us/odss/finance/eoy.asp

Kentucky Department of Education. (n. d.). Spring 2000 NRT performance report (CTBS/5) data disaggregation. Retrieved December 29, 2000, from http://www. kde.state.ky.us/oss/implement/nrt_2000/default.asp

Kentucky Department of Education. (2000, August). Briefing packet state and regional release 2000 CTBS/5 results for 3, 6, & 9. Retrieved January 12, 2001, from http://www.kde/state.ky.us.oaa/implement/ctbs/ctbs_2000/default.asp

Kentucky Department of Education. (2000, September). Briefing packet: Commonwealth Accountability Testing System, interim accountability cycle. Retrieved January 3, 2001, from http://www.kde.state.ky.us/oaa/implement/KCCT_ score_release_2000/kcct_2000? Accountability/Briefing_Packet_2000.pdf

Louisiana

Louisiana Department of Education. (n. d.). School year 1999–2000 enrollment by grade vs. site and ethnicity. Retrieved January 23, 2001, from http://www.doe.state.la.us/ DOE/asps/ home.asp/1=ADHOC

Louisiana Department of Education. (2000, February). Louisiana state education progress report. Retrieved January 23, 2001, from http://www.doe.state.la.us/ DOE/StRpt9899/200032DT.pdf

Louisiana Department of Education. (2000, May). 1998–99 Louisiana school and district summary report. Retrieved February 22, 2001, from http://www.doe.state.la.us/ DOE/omf/DanielsReport98099.pdf

Maine

Maine Department of Education. (n. d.). Maine Educational Assessment (MEA) scores 1999–2000 school year. Retrieved February 22, 2001, from http://janus.state.me.us/ education/mea/edmea.htm

Maine Department of Education. (1999, October 1). Statewide public school fall enrollment: Fall enrollment by grade, sex, race for school year 1999–00 public schools. Retrieved February 22, 2001, from http://janus.state.me.us/education/ enroll/fall/fall.htm

Maine Department of Education. (1999, December 1). Special education data: Race by exceptionality December 1, 1999 special education child count. Retrieved February 22, 2001, from http://www.mainecite.org/speceddata/racebyexcept.html

Maryland

Maryland State Department of Education. (n. d.). 1998 Maryland school performance report executive summary. Retrieved February 23, 2001, from http://www.msde.state.md.us/AboutMSDE/Divisions/prim2000/

Maryland State Department of Education. (n. d.). MSDE special reports: Maryland public school statistics 1999–2000. Retrieved February 12, 2001, from http://www.msde.state.md.us/ Special%20Reports%20and%20Data/index.html

Maryland State Department of Education. (n. d.). Maryland 1999–2000 state summary report. Retrieved February 12, 2001, from http://msp.msde.state.md.us/state.asp

Maryland State Department of Education. (1999, September 30). Maryland public school enrollment by race/ethnicity and gender and number of schools. Retrieved January 23, 2001, from http://www.msde.state.md.us/AboutMSDE/Divisions/prim2000/pubs1.htm

Maryland State Department of Education. (2000, August 14). Maryland special education census data. Retrieved January 23, 2001, from http://www.msde.state.md.us/AboutMSDE/Divisions/ prim2000/pubs1.htm

Maryland State Department of Education. (2000, November). 2000 MSDE report card: Maryland state data. Retrieved February 12, 2001, from http://msp.msde.state.md.us/mspap.asp?

Massachusetts

Massachusetts Department of Education. (n. d.). Grade 3 ITBS reading comprehension test results, July 1999. Retrieved February 13, 2001, from http://www.doe.mass.edu/mcas/IOWA99/

Massachusetts Department of Education. (2000, October). The performance of limited English proficient students on the 1998 and 1999 Massachusetts Comprehensive Assessment System. Retrieved February 13, 2001, from http://www.doe.mass.edu.mcas/

Massachusetts Department of Education. (2000, November). Spring 2000 MCAS tests: Report of state results. Retrieved February 13, 2001, from http://www.doe.mass.edu/mcas/

Michigan

Michigan Department of Education. (n. d.). Battle Creek Public Schools general characteristics summary. Retrieved January 12, 2001 from http://www.state.mi.us/webapp/dmb/mic/census/sddb_1990.asp

Michigan Department of Education. (1999, September). Michigan Educational Assessment Program high school tests. Retrieved January 12, 2001, from http://www.MeritAward.state.mi.us/merit/meap/results/springsummary.pdf

Minnesota

Minnesota Department of Children, Families, and Learning. (n. d.). Continuous improvement process. Retrieved February 13, 2001, from http://cfl.state.mn.us/cip/

Minnesota Department of Children, Families, and Learning. (n. d.). State profile report: State results 1999/2000. Retrieved February 13, 2001, from http://cfl.state.mn.us/GRAD/results/19992000/

Minnesota Department of Children, Families, and Learning. (n. d.). State results: Basic standards state test results. Retrieved February 13, 2001, from http://cfl.state.mn.us/GRAD/results/19992000/grad8/

Minnesota Department of Children, Families, and Learning. (2000, April 11). English language learners. Retrieved February 13, 2001, from http://cfl.state.mn.us/lep

409

Mississippi

Mississippi Department of Education. (2000, October 3). Mississippi statewide testing program. Retrieved February 13, 2001, from http://www.mde.k12.ms.us/ACAD/TD/D0000000.HTM and http://www.mde.k12.ms.us/ACAD/TD/A0000000.HTM

Mississippi Department of Education. (2000, July 31). Spring 2000 TerraNova test scores. Retrieved February 13, 2001, from http://www.mde.k12.ms.us/extrel/TerraNova.htm

Mississippi Department of Education. (2001). Selected statistics on Mississippi public education. Retrieved February 14, 2001, from http://www.mde.k12.ms.us/extrel/STAT.HTM

Missouri

Missouri Department of Education. (1999, November 24). 1999 school district report card. Retrieved October 24, 2000 from http://www.dese.state.mo.us/reportsummary/districts/039141.html

Nebraska

Nebraska Department of Education. (n. d.). 1999–2000 Nebraska state report card. Retrieved February 14, 2001, from http://www.nde.state.ne.us/2000ReportCard/ReportCard2000.html

Nevada

Nevada Department of Education. (n. d.). Nevada school districts and Nevada schools, school year 1997–1998. Retrieved February 14, 2001, from http://www.nsn.k12.nv.us/nvdoe/resources/html

Nevada Department of Education. (1998, February). Analysis of Nevada school accountability system school year 1995–1996. Retrieved February 14, 2001, from http://www.nsn.k12.nv.us/nvdoe/reports/index.html

Nevada Department of Education. (1999, April 2). Results of statewide TerraNova testing fall 1998. Retrieved February 14, 2001, from http://www.nsn.k12.nv.us/nvdoe/reports/index.html

Nevada Department of Education. (2001, February 6). District enrollment totals: Nevada school enrollments, 2000–2001 school year. Retrieved February 14, 2001, from http://www.nsn.k12.nv.us/nvdoe/resources.html

New Hampshire

New Hampshire Department of Education. (n. d.). State totals—Fall enrollments 1990–91 through 1999–00. Retrieved January 16, 2001, from http://www.ed.state.nh.us/ReportsandStatistics/reports.htm

New Hampshire Department of Education. (2000, February 23). State totals—Fall enrollments 1999–2000. Retrieved January 16, 2001, from http://www.ed.state.nh.us/ReportsandStatistics/reports.htm

New Jersey

New Jersey State Department of Education. (n. d.). 1999–2000 enrollment. Retrieved February 23, 2001, from http://www.state.nj.us/njded/data/enro00/index.html

New Jersey State Department of Education. (n. d.). Frequently asked question of the office of bilingual education and equity issues. Retrieved February 23, 2001, from http://www.state.nj.us/njded/genfo/overview/

New Jersey State Department of Education (n. d.). Vital education statistics 1999–2000. Retrieved February 23, 2001, from http://www.state.nj.us/njded/data/

New Mexico

New Mexico State Department of Education. (1999, November). The accountability report: Indicators of the condition of public education in New Mexico. Retrieved January 16, 2001, from http://www.sde.state.nm.us/divisions/ais/datacollection/ar9899.pdf

New Mexico Department of Education. (2001, January 5). Students by district and grade school year 2000–2001. Retrieved January 16, 2001 from http://www.sde.state.nm.us/divisions/ais/datacollection

New York

New York State Education Department. (n. d.). 1999 pocketbook of goals and results for individuals with disabilities. Retrieved January 19, 2001, from http://web.nysed.gov/vesid/sped/pubs/pb99/pb99_home.htm

New York State Education Department. (n. d.). Public school performance on the 1999–2000 elementary-level English language arts assessments. Retrieved January 17, 2001, from http://emsc.nysed.gov/irts/ELA4_2000/sld001.htm

New York State Education Department. (n. d.). State and city CTB reading test results, grades 3–8. Retrieved January 17, 2001, from http://www.nycenet.edu/daa/nysnyc_math/index.html

North Carolina

North Carolina Department of Public Instruction. (n. d.). Facts and figures: Students. Retrieved February 14, 2001, from http://www.ncpublicschools.org/srdc/factsfigs.htm#students

North Carolina Department of Public Instruction. (1998, September). Report of student performance on the North Carolina competency standard 1997–98. Retrieved February 14, 2001, from http://www.dpi.state.nc.us/accountability/testing/

North Carolina Department of Public Instruction. (1999, June). The report of student performance on the North Carolina tests of computer skills: 1997–1998 school year. Retrieved February 14, 2001, from http://www.dpi.state.nc.us/accountability/testing/computerskills/compskills97-98.pdf

North Carolina Department of Public Instruction. (2000). North Carolina public schools statistical profile 2000. Retrieved February 14, 2001, from http://www.dpi.state.nc.us/reportstats.html

North Carolina Department of Public Instruction. (2000, April). North Carolina exemption study: Spring 1998. Retrieved February 14, 2001, from http://www.dpi.state.nc.us/accountability/testing/reports/index.html

North Carolina Department of Public Instruction. (2000, August). Report of student performance in writing 1999–2000. Retrieved February 14, 2001, from http://www. dpi.state.nc.us/accountability/testing/writing/reports/9900.pdf

North Carolina Department of Public Instruction. (2000, August). The 1999–2000 North Carolina preliminary state testing results. Retrieved February 14, 2001, from http://www.dpi.state.nc.us/accountability/testing/reports/index.html

North Carolina Department of Public Instruction. (2000, September). Report of 1998–99 student performance North Carolina tests of computer skills. Retrieved February 14, 2001, from http://www.dpi.state.nc.us/accountability/testing/computerskills/compskills97–98.pdf

North Carolina Department of Public Instruction. (2000, September). Report of student performance on the North Carolina competency standard 1998–99. Retrieved March 2, 2001, from http://www.dpi.state.nc.us/accountability/testing/competency

North Carolina Department of Public Instruction. (2001, January). State of the state: Educational performance in North Carolina, 2000. Retrieved February 14, 2001, from http://www.dpi.state.nc.us/accountability/reporting/SOS/SOS2000/

North Dakota

North Dakota Department of Public Instruction. (n. d.). North Dakota research results for statewide CTBS/5 (TerraNova) testing NP of the MEAN NCE. Retrieved February 14, 2001, from http://www.dpi.state.nd.us/resource/assess/pg13.pdf

North Dakota Department of Public Instruction. (2000, August 15). 2000 statewide TerraNova (CTBS/5) testing program data. Retrieved February 14, 2001, from http://www.dpi.state.nd.us/resource/assess/pg42.pdf

Oklahoma

Oklahoma State Department of Education. (n. d.). Oklahoma's education statistics. Retrieved February 15, 2001, from http://www.sde.state.ok.us/pro/stats.html

Oklahoma State Department of Education. (n. d.). Statewide test scores presented to State Board of Education: New reporting levels, data categorized by ethnicity. Retrieved February 14, 2001, from http://www.sde.state.ok.us/test/StateTestsScores/default.html

Oklahoma State Department of Education. (1999, October). Oklahoma test results packet. Retrieved February 14, 2001, from http://www.sde.state.ok.us/publ/default.html

Oregon

Oregon Department of Education. (n. d.). Statewide assessment results 2000: Percent of students meeting performance standards, mathematics problem solving. Retrieved February 15, 2001, from http://www.ode.state.or.us/asmt/results/index/

Oregon Department of Education. (n. d.). Statewide assessment results 2000: Percent of students meeting performance standards reading, literature and mathematics. Retrieved February 15, 2001, from http://www.ode.state.or.us/asmt/results/2000/rdmath00.pdf

Oregon Department of Education. (n. d.). Statewide assessment results 2000: Percent of students meeting performance standards, science. Retrieved February 15, 2001, from http://www.ode.state.or.us/asmt/results/index/

Oregon Department of Education. (n. d.). Statewide assessment results 2000: Percent of students meeting performance standards, writing. Retrieved February 15, 2001, from http://www.ode.state.or.us/asmt/results/2000/writing00.pdf

Oregon Department of Education. (n. d.). Student ethnicity 1999–2000. Retrieved February 15, 2001, from http://www.dbi.ode.state.or.us/r0067Select.asp

Oregon Department of Education. (n. d.). Year ending June 30, 2000 net enrollment and ADM. Retrieved February 15, 2001, from http://www.ode.state.or.us/stats/schoolFinance/ADMCUMAVG.pdf

Oregon Department of Education. (1998, August 28). Age groupings. Retrieved February 15, 2001, from http://www.ode.state.or.us/sped/spedfund/sld001.htm

Oregon Department of Education. (2000, December 1). Actual annual 99–00 ADM by district. Retrieved February 15, 2001, from http://www.ode.state.or.us/stats/school/Finance/ActualAnn99-00ADM4.pdf

Oregon Department of Education. (2001, January 18). Oregon school and district report cards. Retrieved February 15, 2001, from http://reportcard.ode.state.or.us/reports/01/01-ReportCard-2063.pdf

Pennsylvania

Pennsylvania Department of Education. (n. d.). 1999 PSSA state summary of scaled scores. Retrieved February 16, 2001, from http://www.pde.psu.edu/pssa/99iu03.pdf

Pennsylvania Department of Education. (1999, December). Supplemental documentation for 1999 reading, mathematics, and writing assessment reports. Retrieved February 16, 2001, from http://www.pde.psu.edu/pssa/99suppl.pdf

Pennsylvania Department of Education. (2000, July). Public, private and nonpublic schools: Enrollments 1999–00. Retrieved February 16, 2001, from http://www.pde.psu.edu/esstats.html

Pennsylvania Department of Education. (2000, September). Enrollment of limited English proficient (LEP) students for districts reporting. Retrieved February 16, 2001, from http://www.pde.psu.edu/esl/lepchart.html

Pennsylvania Department of Education. (2000, October 26). Status of education in Pennsylvania: A statistical summary 2000. Retrieved February 16, 2001, from http://www.pde.psu.edu/statistics/status2000/status00.html

Rhode Island

Rhode Island Department of Elementary and Secondary Education. (n. d.). Public fall enrollment by race/ethnicity origin and gender. Retrieved February 16, 2001, from http://www.ridoe.net/ed_data/reports.htm

Rhode Island Department of Elementary and Secondary Education. (2000). *Information Works! 2000*. Providence, RI: Author.

Rhode Island Department of Elementary and Secondary Education. (2000, October 24). 2000 state assessment results released. Retrieved February 16, 2001, from http://www.ridoe.net/whatsnew/2000assess.pdf

South Carolina

South Carolina Department of Education. (n. d.). 1999 results of the cognitive skills assessment battery. Retrieved February 16, 2001, from http://www.state.sc.us/sde/reports/csab99/index.html

South Carolina Department of Education. (n. d.). High school exit exam: Results of the spring 2000 administration. Retrieved February 16, 2001, from http://www.state.sc.us/sde/reports/exit2000/index.html

South Carolina Department of Education. (n. d.). Palmetto Achievement Challenge Tests results for 2000. Retrieved February 16, 2001, from http://www.state.sc.us/sde/reports/pact00/index.html

South Carolina Department of Education. (1999). 1999 results of the Cognitive Skills Assessment Battery (CSAB). Columbia, SC: Author.

South Carolina Department of Education. (1999). 1999 South Carolina performance profiles. Columbia, SC: Author.

South Carolina Department of Education. (1999). High school exit examination results of the spring 1999 administration. Columbia, SC: Author.

South Carolina Department of Education. (1999). Palmetto Achievement Challenge Tests (PACT) results of spring 1999 administration grade 3. Columbia, SC: Author. (Note: Similar reports are available for Grades 4–8.)

South Carolina Department of Education. (1999). State profile 1998. Retrieved July 5, 2000, from http://www.state.sc.us/sde/distschs/98profil/state.htm

South Carolina Department of Education. (2000, July). Quick facts about South Carolina public schools. Retrieved February 16, 2001, from http://www.state.sc.us/sde/reports/fact00.htm

South Dakota

South Dakota Department of Education and Cultural Affairs. (n. d.). 1999–2000 education in South Dakota: A statistical profile. Retrieved February 16, 2001, from http://www.state.sd.us/deca/DATA/00digest/index.htm

South Dakota Department of Education and Cultural Affairs. (n. d.). 2000 PK–12 public enrollment by ethnicity. Retrieved February 16, 2001, from http://www.state.sd.us/deca/DATA/Enrollment/2000PublicEthnicity.pdf

South Dakota Department of Education and Cultural Affairs. (2000, February). South Dakota annual report of academic progress. Retrieved February 16, 2001, from http://www.state.sd.us/deca/data/statistix.htm

South Dakota Department of Education and Cultural Affairs. (2000, December 22). 2000 Stanford writing assessment. Retrieved February 16, 2001, from http://www.state.sd.us/deca/ta/testing_assessment/testing.htm

Tennessee

Tennessee Department of Education. (n. d.). 1999–2000 statewide results for Tennessee high school subject matter tests. Retrieved February 19, 2001, from http://www.state.tn.us/education/tstcapbr5a.htm

Tennessee Department of Education. (n. d.). 2000 TCAP achievement test statewide summary. Retrieved February 19, 2001, from http://www.state.tn.us/education/tstcap2000statesumm.htm

Tennessee Department of Education. (n. d.). State of Tennessee statewide report card 2000. Retrieved February 19, 2001, from http://www.k-12state.tn.us/rptcrd00/state.htm

Texas

Texas Education Agency. (n. d.). Student performance report executive summary 1999–2000. Retrieved February 19, 2001, from http://www.tea.state.tx.us/student.assessment/resources/studies/execsum.pdf

Texas Education Agency. (2000, July). Texas assessment of academic skills summary report: All students. Retrieved February 19, 2001, from http://www.tea.state.tx.us/student.assessment/reporting/results/summary/sum00/g6ea.00htm

Texas Education Agency. (2000, August). The Texas successful schools study: Quality education for limited English proficient students. Retrieved February 20, 2001, from http://www.tea.state.tx.us/tsss/e.pdf

Texas Education Agency. (2001, February 2). Statewide TAAS results spring 1994–spring 2000. Retrieved February 19, 2001, from http://www.tea.state.tx.us/student.assessment/researchers.html

Vermont

Vermont Department of Education. (n. d.). Vermont Department of Education school report: State of Vermont complete report. Retrieved March 1, 2001, from http://crs.uvm.edu/schrpt/

Virginia

Virginia Department of Education. (n. d.). Fall membership September 30, 2000. Retrieved March 1, 2001, from http://www.pen.k12.va.us/VDOE/Publications/rep_page.htm

Virginia Department of Education. (n. d.). Literacy Testing Program division summary, spring 1998. Retrieved March 1, 2001, from http://www.pen.k12.va.us/VDOE/Assessment/ home.shtml

Virginia Department of Education. (n. d.). Spring 2000 standards of learning test results. Retrieved March 1, 2001, from http://www.pen.k12.va.us:80/VDOE/Assessment/soltests/y2kscores.htm

Virginia Department of Education. (1999). Virginia state assessment program 1999 detailed report. Retrieved March 1, 2001, from http://www.pen.k12.va.us/VDOE/Assessment/VSAPreport/1999/s9grade499.pdf

Washington

Washington Office of Superintendent of Public Instruction. (n. d.). Iowa tests of educational development 1998–99 spring Washington State results. Retrieved February 19, 2001, from http://www.k12.wa.us/assessment.ITED.asp

Washington Office of Superintendent of Public Instruction. (n. d.). State demographic information for 1999–2000. Retrieved February 19, 2001, from http://www.k12.wa.us/edprofile/StateReport.asp?sReport=stateDemo1999-2000

Washington Office of Superintendent of Public Instruction. (n. d.). Washington state educational profile state WASL scores for 1999–2000. Retrieved February 19, 2001, from http://www.k12.wa.us/edprofile/stateReport.asp?sReport=state

Washington Office of Superintendent of Public Instruction. (1999). Washington state educational profile. Olympia, WA: Author.

Washington Office of Superintendent of Public Instruction. (1999, July 21). WebApps 2000 database information. Retrieved February 19, 2001, from http://www.k12.wa.us/title1/facts/laps/facts.asp

Washington Office of Superintendent of Public Instruction. (1999, December). Biennial performance report for part B: Washington state special education. Olympia, WA: Author.

Washington Office of Superintendent of Public Instruction. (2000, December). Eighth annual report of special education services in Washington State. Retrieved February 19, 2001, from http://www.k12.wa.us/specialed/Publications/ar8.DOC

West Virginia

West Virginia Department of Education. (n. d.). West Virginia report card 1998–99. Retrieved February 16, 2001, from http://www.wvde.state.wv.us/data/report_cards/1999/1999wvreportcards.pdf
West Virginia Department of Education. (2000). Quick facts on education in West Virginia 2000. Retrieved February 16, 2001, from http://www.state.wv.us/data/quickfacts_2000.html
West Virginia Department of Education. (2000). State assessment report 1999–2000 results. Retrieved March 29, 2001, from http://wvde.state.wv.us/

Wisconsin

Wisconsin Department of Education. (n. d.). 1998–99 school performance report statewide data. Retrieved February 19, 2001, from http://www.dpi.state.wi.us/spr.download.html
Wisconsin Department of Education. (n. d.). Knowledge and concepts examinations state level summaries 1997–1998 through 1999–2000 by student group. Retrieved February 19, 2001, from http://www.dpi.state.wi.us/oea/spr_kce.html
Wisconsin Department of Public Instruction. (n. d.). Complete disaggregated state proficiency summary reports. Retrieved February 19, 2001, from http://www.dpi.state.wi.us/spr/xls/
Wisconsin Department of Public Instruction. (n. d.). Summary results of 1999–2000 Knowledge & Concepts Examinations. Madison, WI: Author.
Wisconsin Department of Public Instruction. (2000, July 17). 2000 WRCT scores. Retrieved April 17, 2001, from http://www.dpi.state.wi.us/dpi/dltcl/eis/pdf

Wyoming

Wyoming Department of Education. (n. d.). Annual report: Wyoming advisory panel for students with disabilities July 1, 1999 to June 30, 2000. Retrieved February 19, 2001, from http://www.k12.wy.us/speced/annualreport.pdf
Wyoming Department of Education. (1999, December 30). Wyoming State Board of Education and Wyoming School Foundation Program annual reports. Retrieved February 19, 2001, from http://www.k12.wy.us/publications/9899report.html
Wyoming Department of Education. (2000, June). Background statistics. Retrieved February 19, 2001, from http://www.k12.wy.us/statistics/wybkgrnd.html#enrollment

APPENDIX 3-B

List of Acronyms for State Tests Referenced in the Study

Acronym	Test
API	Alternate Performance Indicator
CSAP	Colorado Student Assessment Program
CTBS/5	California Test of Basic Skills
DSTP	Delaware Student Testing Program
ESPA	Elementary School Proficiency Assessment (NJ)
FCAT	Florida Comprehensive Assessment Test
GEE 21	Graduation Exit Exam for 21st Century (LA)
GEPA	Grade Eight Proficiency Assessment (NJ)
HSCE	High School Competency Examination (NM)
HSCT	High School Competency Test (FL)
HSGT	High School Graduation Test (WI)
HSPT 11	Grade 11 High School Proficiency Test (NJ)
IMAGE	Illinois Measure of Annual Growth in English
ISAT	Illinois Standards Achievement Test
ISTEP	Indiana Statewide Testing for Education Progress
ITBS	Iowa Test of Basic Skills
LEAP 21	Louisiana Educational Assessment Program for the 21st Century

Acronym	Test
LTP	Literacy Testing Program (VA)
MCAS	Massachusetts Comprehensive Assessment System
MEA	Maine Educational Assessment
NC Pretest	North Carolina Pretest (end-of-Grade 3 reading, math)
NHEIAP	New Hampshire Educational Improvement and Assessment Program
NM HSCE	New Mexico High School Competency Examination
PSAE	Prairie State Achievement Examination
RPTE	Reading Proficiency Tests in English (TX)
SABE	Spanish Assessment of Basic Education (CA)
SAT-9	Stanford Achievement Test, 9th Edition
SOL	Standards of Learning (VA)
Spanish TAAS	Spanish version of TAAS
TAAS	Texas Assessment of Academic Skills
Terra Nova/ CTBS	California Test of Basic Skills, 5th Edition
VASP/SAT-9	Virginia State Assessment Program
WKCE	Wisconsin Knowledge and Concepts Examinations
WRCT	Wisconsin Reading Comprehension Test
WSAS	Wisconsin State Assessment System

APPENDIX 3-C

Description of Elements Found in State Score Reports Examined in the Study

State By Test	How Scores Were Reported	Does Participation N Match Performance N?	Reporting by LEP Category	Subgroups of Test Condition Reported
CA STAR	% scoring above 75th, 50th, 25th NPR (based on NCE) and mean scaled score	Participation Ns same as from performance Ns	By LEP, R-FE (redesignated fluent English), and FEP (fluent English proficient)	
Content Stds	Avg. no. correct/ no. possible	Yes	By LEP, R-FE, and FEP	
SABE/2 Spanish test	Reference Percentile rank for "average" student score, % above 75th RP, above 50th RP, and above 25th RP	Participation Ns same as from performance Ns	Mandated testing of students identified as "12 months or less"; nonmandated testing of students identified as "greater than 12 months"	Note that all data excludes special accommodations students, except the data for the special education population
CO CSAP	% of students at partially proficient, proficient, and advanced levels and % no scores reported	Participation Ns came from performance Ns.	By language categories[a]	Only accommodation information by Spanish version of CSAP Lectura & Escritura
DE DSTP	N and percentile rank, N, mean and standard development for standards-based score, and four performance levels[b]	Yes	LEP, and LEP by race, gender, Title I, special education, and income	

(continued)

Description of Elements Found in State Score Reports Examined in the Study (continued)

State	By Test	How Scores Were Reported	Does Participation N Match Performance N?	Reporting by LEP Category	Subgroups of Test Condition Reported
FL	FCAT	% at levels 2 and above, 3 and above, for math, reading, and writing	Yes	Current (> 2 years ESL) and former LEP	
	HSCT	Not disaggregated 2000			
ID	ID Direct Assessments	Average scores	Participation N from performance N	Limited English	
	ITBS/TAP	Percentile rank for all subjects and core total	Participation Ns are from N in core total	LEP	
	Reading Indicator	N and % of students scoring at three grade performance levels			
IL	ISAT	N and % in three levels of performance and warning category	Yes	Transitioned LEP students only (by downstate and Chicago separately)	
	IMAGE	N and % in two performance levels	Yes	LEP	
IN	ISTEP	N and % in two performance levels and undetermined, mean/median scale score, low/high scale score obtained	Yes	LEP	With and without accommodation

State	Test				
	GQE (retest info)	N and % in two performance levels, mean/median scale score, and low/high scale score obtained	Yes	LEP	With and without accommodation
KS	Math Assessment	Subscale (% correct), total power score, and N and % at four proficiency levels[c]	Yes	LEP, LEP by gender, SES, and race	See note.[d]
	KS Writing Assessment	Subscale scores and student level standard deviation. Also, N and % of LEPs in question	Yes	LEP	
	KS Reading Assessment	% correct, N, and % at four proficiency levels	Yes	LEP, LEP by gender, SES, race	See note.[e]
	KS Science Assessment	None			
	KS Social Studies Assessment	None			
KY	CTBS	NCE and NP by subject and total battery	Yes	LEP	
	KY Core Content Test 1999	% at three performance levels	Yes	LEP	

(continued)

Description of Elements Found in State Score Reports Examined in the Study (*continued*)

State	By Test	How Scores Were Reported	Does Participation N Match Performance N?	Reporting by LEP Category	Subgroups of Test Condition Reported
LA	GEE '98 (but not expected w/new test)	N and % that attained standard by subject	Yes	LEP	
	ITBS/ITED 2000	Not by LEP in public report			
		% correct for content standards, % of students at five achievement levels, and average scaled score			
	LEAP 21 1998	age scaled score	Yes	LEP	
	GEE 21 Spring 2000	Average dimension score and ELA scaled score	Yes	LEP	
	LAA	New; only have teacher guide			
MA	MCAS	Scaled score and % in four performance levels	Yes	LEP	
	ITBS	% in four performance levels	Yes	LEP	
ME	MEA	% of students at four performance levels; also by average scaled score	Yes	LEP and Bilingual/English Fluent (not an LEP category)	
NV	Terra Nova	NP ranks of the mean NCE	Not evident	LEP	

	Writing Test Graduation Exam	None		
NH	NHEIAP	% of students in two proficiency categories	No performance N to compare	Non- or LEP
NJ	HSPT 11	Not disaggregated	Only participation data disaggregated	
	GEPA	N and % at two proficiency levels and mean scale score	Yes; has participation, performance by subject total and those who attempted all three subjects	LEP
	ESPA	N and % at two proficiency levels and mean scale score	Yes	LEP
NM	CTBS/Terra Nova	None		
	NM HSCE Grade 10	% of students passing on first attempt	No participation data, only performance	LEP
	Standards-Based Assessment	None		
	Writing Assessment	None		

(continued)

Description of Elements Found in State Score Reports Examined in the Study *(continued)*

State	By Test	How Scores Were Reported	Does Participation N Match Performance N?	Reporting by LEP Category	Subgroups of Test Condition Reported
NC	ITBS	Not disaggregated			
	End-of-course	% at or above Level III and mean scale score	Yes	LEP	Yes, but not disaggregated by LEP
NC	End-of-Grade Tests	% at or above Level III and average scale scores	Yes	LEP	Yes, but not disaggregated by LEP
	HS Comprehensive Test	% at or above Level III and average scale scores	Yes	LEP	Yes, but not disaggregated by LEP
	NC Pretest	% at or above Level III and average scale scores	Yes	LEP	Yes, but not disaggregated by LEP
	NC Writing Assessment	% at or above 2.5, % of students at holistic score levels, NS and convention scores (++, +, −)	Yes	LEP	
	NC Computer Skills Test	Not disaggregated	Yes	LEP	
NC	Open-Ended Assessments	N and % tested; means by subject and mean total; for 8th-grade data N and % in four achievement levels	Yes	LEP	N modified tests but not clear how many might be LEP (includes native language dictionary in one category)

State	Test	Description	Participation	Subgroup (LEP)	Notes
ND	CTBS/5	NP of the mean NCE	Yes	LEP	Had note on exclusion due to accommodated conditions[l]
RI	New Standards Exams	% of students meeting or exceeding state performance standard	No participation data	ESOL[f]	
	RI State Writing Assessment	% of students meeting or exceeding state performance standard	Participation not reported and not all grades tested had reported performance[g]	See note.[h]	
	RI Health Education Assessment	% of students meeting or exceeding state performance standard	Participation not reported and not all grades tested had reported performance[i]	See note.[j]	
TX	TAAS	% meeting minimum experience and others have scaled score with met minimum	Yes	LEP, language program (bilingual, ESL)	
	End-of-course tests	% passing and average scale score	Yes	LEP and language program (bilingual, ESL)	
	RPTE	% of students in three proficiency levels	Yes	LEP reported in five time categories[k]	
VI	SOL	Not disaggregated for 2000			
	VASP/SAT-9, abbreviated	Statewide national percentile ranks and mean scaled scores for each section and for "partial (basic) battery"	Cannot determine	LEP	

(continued)

Description of Elements Found in State Score Reports Examined in the Study *(continued)*

State	By Test	How Scores Were Reported	Does Participation N Match Performance N?	Reporting by LEP Category	Subgroups of Test Condition Reported
	LTP	Not disaggregated			Alternate assessment has no reported performance
WI	WKCE	% of total enrolled and % of total eligible at four performance levels	Needed to calculate	LEP	
			Yes % (with % not tested) adds up to 100% based on students enrolled		
	WRCT	% at four levels of performance		LEP	

aSpanish non-English speaker, Spanish limited-English speaker, Spanish fluent English speaker, other (other language) non-English speaker, other limited-English speaker, and other fluent English Speaker, and data invalid or not provided. bLevels are percentage students in well below, below, meets, exceeds, and distinguished categories. cThe power score is an equally weighted average of the three subscale area percentages. dReport has note for tables by ethnic group and SES, which indicates that means are based on the number of students at each grade level to include all LEP students who took the standard administration of the assessment. eDivided into groups. Included in averages = Students tested without any accommodations or with either of the following test administration accommodations: individual or small-group administration, test administered by ESL teacher or individual providing language services. Not included in averages = Students tested with any of the following test administration accommodations: extended time, repeated directions, or provision of English/native language word-to-word dictionary (no definitions). fUnclear labeling whether all LEP students tested under routine conditions. Gives four groups reported, regular and special education routine conditions, this same group by whether they were in district since first grade, special needs, tested nonroutine, and LEP. gESL. Note: Reported are students who recently exited ESL or bilingual services (monitor status) or who are near to exiting special instruction (TESOL advanced status). hHealth performance was only reported for Grade 7 in one report, not Grade 3 and 10. iWriting performance was only reported for Grade 9 in one report, not Grade 5. jOne report used the following categories: LEP and by program (bilingual and ESL), migrant. Another report gave data by language background (Spanish and "other" = all other languages grouped together). kLEP was reported in five categories: by one semester or less, 1 year, 2 years, 3 years, and 4 or more years. Also there was a "no information provided" group. lReport noted that test results of students who tested in nonstandard accommodations were excluded from all summary data and that the number tested did not necessarily include all LEP students.

Conclusion

Charlene Rivera and Eric Collum

The use of large-scale testing as a tool to ensure ELLs are given access to the same high-quality education as their native English-speaking peers is not without controversy. As discussed in the introduction to this volume, some educators have objected to testing content knowledge because linguistic and cultural barriers can inhibit the accurate measurement of ELLs' academic knowledge and because the common practice has been to provide ELLs with curricula different from that offered to native English speakers.

It can be argued, however, that to exclude these students from testing is to continue to ignore the academic needs and achievements of a significant and growing part of the U.S. student population. Testing ELLs along with other students in large-scale assessments and reporting these scores publicly is currently the best way we have to ensure that the educational needs of ELLs are, at the very least, recognized. When ELLs are tested appropriately, large-scale assessment can be used as a tool to call attention to the unique linguistic needs of these students and to provide important data that can inform instruction. Furthermore, with the recent reauthorizations of ESEA, NCLB in particular, accounting for the academic progress of ELLs through large-scale assessment has been set as a high priority for educators, and there is every indication that the trend toward increased accountability will continue.

Because much of the burden for including and accounting for ELLs has fallen on states, it is crucial to document how states are attempting to meet the assessment needs of ELLs and to fulfill the mandates of ESEA. As defined by ESEA, states' responsibilities with regard to the assessment of ELLs are to ensure that ELLs participate appropriately in content assessments so that test scores meaningfully reflect the academic progress of these students. ELL test data must be reported publicly so that the progress of student groups can be tracked at the school and district levels, parents can be apprised of their children's progress, and student achievement data can be used by educators in schools and districts to inform instruction. To meet these challenges, states must continue to refine strategies to identify students as ELLs, ensure that these students are routed into proper testing conditions—using accommodated assessments or alternate assessments where appropriate—and provide student assessment data that can be readily understood and analyzed according to student group (e.g., ELL).

The three studies presented in this volume are designed to describe and analyze some of the strategies states have developed for meeting these challenges: (a) the use of accommodations for ELLs, (b) the development and use of test translations, and (c) the dissemination of student assessment data related to ELLs through state reports.

Although necessarily partial, the picture that emerges from these studies' findings strongly suggests that, with regard to the use of assessment as a tool for accountability, there continues to be a lack of focus on the linguistic needs of ELLs at the levels of policy and practice. The assessment of ELLs is discussed in state policies but the presentation and frameworks provided to guide districts in assessing these students appropriately are often fragmented and developed from policies created for students with disabilities rather than from a common understanding of ELLs' linguistic needs. Similarly, state score reports often lack sensitivity to the special characteristics of ELLs that must be considered when using ELL assessment data for accountability or instructional purposes.

Sharpening the focus on ELLs is crucial if SEAs are to be successful in including these students in state assessment and accounting for their academic progress. As the analyses presented in this volume suggest, clear and consistent policies and procedures are necessary to ensure that ELLs are identified accurately and routed into appropriate testing conditions. Furthermore, clear and consistent reporting is necessary to ensure that useful data are disseminated to parents and educators so that every stakeholder is able to make informed decisions regarding these students' academic needs.

This conclusion draws on lessons learned from each of the three studies in this volume to outline strategies state policymakers can use to increase the effectiveness of state assessment as a tool for improving educational opportunities for ELLs. This involves including students who have been accurately identified as ELLs effectively in state assessment by developing a process of determining the manner in which they can participate meaningfully in state assessment (e.g., with or without accommodations). It also requires accounting for ELLs' educational progress by providing achievement data that can be used to inform the decisions of parents, educators, and policymakers.

DETERMINING CONDITIONS APPROPRIATE FOR THE ASSESSMENT OF PARTICULAR ELLS

State policies generally provide guidance to identify and classify students as ELLs, such as definitions and lists of criteria and decision makers. These elements can (and should) be linked to the process of determining how an individual ELL is included in state assessment as well as to student characteristics included in state assessment reports. The more continuity there is between identification and classification of ELLs, the routing of these students into appropriate testing conditions, and the reporting of ELL assessment data, the more meaningfully ELLs can be included in state assessment and have their academic progress accounted for.

Student data collected to inform the identification and classification of ELLs can also be used to help determine the appropriate conditions under which these students can participate in state assessment. Such conditions include accommodations (e.g., reading test directions aloud, translated tests) and, where appropriate, alternate assessments. It is important that district and school personnel have a clear understanding of the assessment options open to ELLs, especially with regard to accommodations. These options should be made a part of a coherent process through which ELLs can be appropriately included in state assessment. Such a process must be carefully defined in states' policies and should include clear criteria and designate appropriate personnel to determine the conditions under which ELLs are tested.

To help districts determine which accommodations are most appropriate for use with particular students it is crucial that accommodations be organized and described clearly in states' policies. To this end, a framework should be adopted for accommodations responsive to the needs of ELLs. Currently, the taxonomy most often used in states' policies is one developed to classify accommodations for students with disabilities. This taxonomy organizes accommodations according to mode. For instance, presentation accommodations are those that affect how a test is presented to a student (e.g., in a larger typeface, with text highlighted for emphasis); response accommodations are those that affect how a student responds to a test (e.g., orally as opposed to written, in Braille as opposed to with traditional marking). Although this taxonomy provides a useful general framework for organizing accommodations, it provides no guidance to educators regarding how accommodations relate to the linguistic needs of ELLs.

State policies should use an ELL-responsive framework to organize accommodations appropriate to ELLs' needs. At minimum, the framework should recognize accommodations providing linguistic support. The framework elaborated in Study 1 of this volume acknowledges the unique linguistic needs of ELLs, categorizing accommodations as providing direct linguistic support and indirect linguistic support to the test taker. Accommodations are organized not by testing mode, but by how they address particular linguistic needs. For instance, linguistic support accommodations are those that adjust the language of a test. These accommodations include native language accommodations, which involve oral or written translation of test questions or items as well as allowing students to respond in their native language. English language accommodations are those that provide linguistically simplified English versions of test questions; repetition of parts of the test; or clarification in English of difficult words, test items, or directions. An ELL-responsive taxonomy like the one outlined in Study 1 of this volume can be used to examine the appropriateness for ELLs of existing lists of accommodations in states' policies.

Within the ELL-responsive framework, every effort should be made to identify and make available those accommodations supported by research. Although research on accommodations for ELLs is sparse and inconclusive, two kinds of accommodations appear to have potential to support ELLs' access to test content: native language and linguistic simplification. Combining specific direct linguistic support accommodations (e.g., bilingual glossaries) with specific indirect linguistic support accommodations (e.g., extra time) also appears to support ELLs' performance on assessments. (See Study 1, "Recommendations." Requirements for native language accommodation are discussed at length in Study 2, "Discussion and Recommendations.")

It should be made clear that not all ELL-responsive accommodations are equally appropriate to all ELLs or for assessments in all subject areas. Criteria and personnel should be designated to determine the appropriateness of particular accommodations (or of alternate assessment) for the needs of a particular student. Criteria should include student background variables such as level of English language proficiency, extent to which the student has been instructed in the content of the test, and language of instruction.

The effectiveness of these criteria can be compromised if appropriate personnel are not designated to apply them. Policies should explicitly recommend that a team of individuals make individual decisions about which accommodations to allow ELLs at different levels of English language proficiency and with different academic backgrounds. Decision-making teams should include school leadership, assessment personnel, and ESL or bilingual and general education teachers familiar with the overall school program and specific academic program of the ELL.

With available accommodations clearly mapped out and a transparent decision-making process in place for applying criteria to particular students' needs, it should be possible to ensure that students are tested under optimal conditions. Selection of accommodations should take into consideration two perspectives: student variables and the requirements for particular subject areas tested.

With regard to student variables, ELLs' proficiency in their native language or in English should be considered in selecting accommodations for these students. It is important to take into consideration differences in students' oral proficiency as compared to written proficiency in these languages if oral forms of accommodations (either in English or the native language) are available. However, level of English or native language proficiency cannot be the only determinant for selecting accommodations for these students. Selection of native language accommodations should take into consideration the language of instruction and amount of time the student has been in the United States. For instance, for an ELL instructed in mathematics exclusively in English over the last 3 years, it is unlikely that an assessment in the native language will be of much benefit. The student is likely to have only limited knowledge of mathematics vocabulary in the native language and might have limited native-language reading skills. On the other hand, providing a native language accommodation to a student receiving instruction in his or her native language is likely to be appropriate if the test is aligned with the content covered in class.

In addition to considering the selection of accommodations from the perspective of student variables, decision makers should also take into account requirements for maintaining the validity of tests in particular content areas. Irrespective of student characteristics, certain accommodations are not appropriate for use with assessments of particular content areas. For example, a native language test might be appropriate for a mathematics or science exam administered to a student instructed in the native language in these subjects. However, as knowledge of the English language is integral to the assessment of English language arts, accommodating ELLs with a native language version of the test seriously compromises test validity.

REPORTING ELL PERFORMANCE DATA
IN A MEANINGFUL WAY

The overall goal of reporting assessment results of ELLs is to ensure that the needs of these students will be made evident and that educators can respond more appropriately to the instructional needs of this growing population of students. If this goal is to be realized, ELL data must be disaggregated and presented in such a way as to allow ELL performance on particular tests and content areas to be compared to that of other student groups. Disaggregated data should also be presented for each assessment administered by the state.

For disaggregated data to be meaningful, a report must provide the overall number and percentage of ELLs participating in a given assessment. To provide a more detailed picture of these students' academic progress, it is important that state reports also include student characteristics such as English language proficiency level, time in U.S. schools, type of program in which the student is enrolled, special education services, former ELL status, gender, race, and SES. By including such information in state assessment reports, SEAs reinforce understanding of the type of information necessary for appropriate inclusion and accommodation of ELLs and could help educators and researchers to focus on within-group differences that can in turn inform decisions regarding the inclusion and accommodation of these students. In this respect, score reporting represents an important opportunity to make the process of inclusion of ELLs in state assessment more transparent.

Score reports should also include data regarding the assessments for which scores are reported. Each assessment should clearly indicate grade levels and content areas for which data were reported as well as the proficiency levels to which these scores correlated (as required by NCLB; see Study 3). Finally, the report should provide data on scores obtained for accommodated assessments or for alternate assessments and whether or not the use of the accommodation maintained the standard conditions of the assessment or created nonstandard test conditions. This information is important if a report is to indicate whether or not scores yielded from accommodated (or alternate) tests are comparable to those of the test given under standard conditions.

As acknowledged at the outset of this conclusion, the three studies in this volume examine only selected policies and practices related to states' efforts to provide ELLs access to the same level of education as their more English-proficient peers. More research is necessary if we are to understand how best to go about including and accounting for ELLs. Ongoing research is needed to provide periodic descriptions and analyses of state assessment policies and practices so that states' progress in addressing the needs of ELLs can be tracked and appropriate interventions made.

In addition to regularly documenting states' policies and practices regarding accommodations and score reporting, sustained effort should be given to investigation of the best means to develop and implement promising strategies for providing ELLs access to test content without invalidating test results. Study 2 of this volume provides a description and analysis of one of these strategies—test translation. However, other promising assessment strategies also deserve the attention of researchers and policymakers.

Linguistic simplification is currently used in a number of states and has the potential to provide ELLs access to test content without affecting test validity. Further study of the effectiveness of linguistic simplification as well as strategies states can use to develop and implement this accommodation would make a significant contribution to ELL assessment. Similarly, some states are currently investigating the viability of alternate assessments that are aligned to standards and that produce scores comparable to those produced by regular state assessments. Further research is necessary to examine whether or not these strategies and others are effective and, if so, how they can be developed and implemented by states attempting to address the assessment needs of ELLs.

In short, much work remains to be done to ensure that inclusion in state assessment systems is meaningful for ELLs. Although this volume offers a partial picture of states' strategies for including and accounting for ELLs, it is hoped that the findings will contribute to a body of research that can be used to inform states' efforts to include ELLs and account for these students' performance in state assessment and, ultimately, to ensure that these students have equal access to a high-quality education.

Author Index

Note: *n* indicates footnote, *t* indicates table.

Subject Index

Note: *f* indicates figure, *n* indicates footnote, *t* indicates table.